ROUTLEDGE LIBRARY EDITIONS: HISTORY OF CHINA

Volume 8

THE GOVERNMENT OF CHINA, 1644–1911

THE GOVERNMENT OF CHINA, 1644–1911

PAO CHAO HSIEH

Taylor & Francis Group
LONDON AND NEW YORK

First published in 1925 by Frank Cass and Company Limited

This edition first published in 2019
by Routledge
2 Park Square, Milton Park, Abingdon, Oxon OX14 4RN

and by Routledge
711 Third Avenue, New York, NY 10017

Routledge is an imprint of the Taylor & Francis Group, an informa business

All rights reserved. No part of this book may be reprinted or reproduced or utilised in any form or by any electronic, mechanical, or other means, now known or hereafter invented, including photocopying and recording, or in any information storage or retrieval system, without permission in writing from the publishers.

Trademark notice: Product or corporate names may be trademarks or registered trademarks, and are used only for identification and explanation without intent to infringe.

British Library Cataloguing in Publication Data
A catalogue record for this book is available from the British Library

ISBN: 978-1-138-48273-9 (Set)
ISBN: 978-0-429-45536-0 (Set) (ebk)
ISBN: 978-1-138-31668-3 (Volume 8) (hbk)
ISBN: 978-1-138-31670-6 (Volume 8) (pbk)
ISBN: 978-0-429-45550-6 (Volume 8) (ebk)

Publisher's Note
The publisher has gone to great lengths to ensure the quality of this reprint but points out that some imperfections in the original copies may be apparent.

Disclaimer
The publisher has made every effort to trace copyright holders and would welcome correspondence from those they have been unable to trace.

THE GOVERNMENT OF CHINA (1644-1911)

BY
PAO CHAO HSIEH

Routledge
Taylor & Francis Group
LONDON AND NEW YORK

First Published 1925 by
FRANK CASS AND COMPANY LIMITED

Published 2013 by Routledge
2 Park Square, Milton Park, Abingdon, Oxon OX14 4RN
711 Third Avenue, New York, NY, 10017, USA

Routledge is an imprint of the Taylor & Francis Group, an informa business

Copyright 1925 by The Johns Hopkins Press

ISBN 13: 978-0-714-61026-9 (hbk)

DEDICATION

To the Late Pao Tien Hsieh

the author's brother, friend, and counselor, this book is dedicated.

PREFACE

Of all the "Chinese puzzles," politics seems the greatest. The lack of scientific treaties on past political institutions makes a solution of this great puzzle much more laborious. It is chiefly for the purpose of presenting a clear background of the present political organization, and thus facilitating the study of the present government, (the actual working of which is largely based on the institutions of the past), that this volume is prepared.

The writer is contented with discussing principally the organization of the government, and only occasionally touching upon its operation. He regrets that he cannot further deal with the real working of the Manchu governing machinery, as the imperial archives are not accessible to him. Also for fear of making this work too lengthy for a handy volume, he has had to avoid going into too much of the detailed regulations of that administrative hierarchy. In the preparation of this volume, he is confronted with the danger of making it too technical for those who are not well acquainted with Chinese political institutions and yet at the same time not technical enough for those who are better informed.

To Dr. H. H. Chang and Dr. S. K. Hornbeck, the author feels deeply grateful for their help in reading over the manuscript and making a number of valuable suggestions. To Prof. W. W. Willoughby he is greatly indebted for constant advice, criticism and encouragement.

P. C. H.

Peking, October, 1924.

CONTENTS

I. Theoretical Basis of the Government 1
II. The Emperor 24
III. The Nobles and the Privileged Classes 45
IV. Important Organizations in the Central Government . 68
V. The Department of Civil Service and Civil Service Laws 99
VI. The Department of Rites and Civil Service Examinations 140
VII. The Department of Revenues: Finance and Taxation . 185
VIII. The Judiciary 215
IX. The Foreign Office 235
X. Other Services in the Central Government . . . 255
XI. Provincial Government 289
XII. Territorial Government 321
XIII. Changes After 1898 343
XIV. Policies of the Government: Conclusion 376
Bibliography 409

CHAPTER I

Theoretical Basis of the Government

In ethics as well as in politics, Confucian theories, to the exclusion of theories of other schools, have dominated China for the last twenty-three centuries. A discussion of Chinese political theory is, therefore, primarily one of Confucius' theories with incidental mention of the supplementary explanations made by his most famous disciple, Mencius, and by other followers of his teaching.

Being a writer on past institutions rather than one on a speculative future, and writing with the aim of stabilizing the traditional order, Confucius can hardly be accused, as many European political theorists have been, of hastening revolutions by building castles in the air. Indeed, Confucius never attempted to formulate a political panacea of his own contriving. The ancient practice of government formed the material on which he contemplated and wrote and from which he sought the betterment of the people. The existing state of things formed the basis upon which he prescribed a remedy. Practical statesman that he was, and because he had seen actual service, he clearly saw that the quickest and safest way of improving the political conditions of his period was to reinstitute the methods that flourished in the "Golden Age" of the ancient regime. He lived in the feudal age when strong feudal lords, though owing allegiance to the emperor, dominated by usurping the imperial authority. Five successful feudal lords wielded the imperial sceptor in different stages in the period of feudalism, as a result of military conquest; none of them, however, showed any willingness or intention to hand their illegitimate powers back to the legitimate possessor, nor was any of them able to put an end to the existing chaos by use of the powers he had usurped.

Danger of war was threatening. Rivalry and strife had become the order of the day. Good institutions of the past seemed tumbling under the blows of the feudal struggle. A protracted period of peace, such as had existed during past dynasties, seemed an impossibility. Confucius saw the evils of decentralization and war: he sought to substitute for them centralization and peace.

The most conspicuous point of his philosophy, then, was monarchism as the means to centralization and peace. He compared the oneness of political authority in a state to the oneness of the sun in Heaven. This, however, should not be confused with absolutism of the monarch or divine right. This he objected to as much as to lawless force and disorder. But he made the monarch the center of his philosophy. Every phase of his political discussion took place on or around the monarch. By so doing, he aimed to make the institution of a monarch the commencement of stabilization. Here his practical knowledge of human nature was fully availed of. He did not try to glorify or deify the lucky or poor man on the throne; nor did he take away the heavy responsibility from him so as to make him unable to commit a wrong. To the monarch, the philosopher first gave wide powers, though his powers were to be modified by other institutions. First a liaison between the state and the family was made. The ruler was a "king-father," the mandarins "parent-officials," and the people "children-people." The shrewd old scholar witnessed and believed in the fallibility of political institutions on the one side, and the infallibility of the family system on the other. By making this liaison he endeavored to imbue the organization of the state with some of the elements that made the family system stable, and his attempt proved a success. Thus, the patriarchal element within the Chinese monarchism checked the absolutism of the monarch. In all Confucius' works, ethics was taught side by side with political theory; in many cases these two branches of human knowledge were so intermingled that it is almost impossible to separate one from the other. The "three bonds"[1] and the "five relationships,"[2] conglomerations of political and social ethics, were always taught together: their traditional inseparability served in Confucian teaching as a solid example for the construction of the system.

His theory advocated love and respect for the ruler by the people, and, reciprocally, consideration of the people by the ruler. The mandates of the emperor, instead of being issued in a commanding tone, reasoned with the people, and expected to win by reasoning rather than by exacting the people's obedience to laws; the written regulations were to be upheld because of their reasonableness rather than executed because of the fact that they were backed by governmental authority. If one wonders why a centralized monarchy like that of China, without constitutional limitations, could keep itself within reasonable bounds of liberalism for more than two thousand years, the patriarchal element of the institution gives the answer. Indeed, this ingenious device stopped the execution of many brutal measures which otherwise would have been a favorite pastime of indiscreet monarchs.

In the handling of family affairs, hard-and-fast rules of conduct are often barred from operation by the abundance of the human element existing between the parties concerned. The close resemblance of the Confucian government to a family made the application of laws difficult. A sense of justice was considered more important than legal provisions, and Confucius found it necessary to emphasize the competency of men rather than the excellence of institutions. A government of men was advocated instead of a government of law. It would be a mistake to believe that the government of men in China was as despotic as that of other Oriental countries, though the principal factor of the

[1] Between sovereign and subject, father and son, and husband and wife.

[2] Between sovereign and subject, father and son, brothers, husband and wife, and friends.

machinery was the same; for the rulers in China were very much limited by traditions which guided them to the right acts and by popular uprisings which guarded them from a full display of their momentary or animal passions. Above the traditions, the virtues required of the princes modified to a great extent both their intentions and their overt acts.

The required virtues of the emperor, which will be dealt with more fully in the next chapter, were not purely ethical ideals incapable of measurement in terms of tangible things. This vague term was definitely defined by the three chief functions of the government; namely, the economic welfare of the people (Yang), their education (Chiao), and the proper employment of their time and energy (Ssu). This combination gave a tinge of state socialism to the system. The performance of the three functions by a particular monarch formed the basis from which the monarch's fitness to rule could be judged. A tinge of mysticism or deification could be found in this philosophy in its mythical interpretation of natural phenomena; to wit, the occurrence of a famine, flood, storm, earthquake, unseasonable rain or snowfall, or any other natural force that wrought destruction of property or created an unpleasant psychic state among the people. These would be viewed by the people as a warning of Heaven given to the emperor as a result of his lack of virtues. It was the monarch's duty to make good those unfavorable results of the natural forces. Inability to recover the loss or to put the psychic attitude of the disturbed back to normalcy would constitute a proof of the expiration of the "heavenly mandate" in the person of the reigning monarch.

The assignment of education to the state gave the government an opportunity to mould the thoughts of the people. No government, good or bad, teaches its people to think or act against itself. But centuries of state education did not create an attitude towards the government such as the former German government did; for the educational program had to follow traditional trains of thought and philosophy. Here again a soft and yet effective check on the government was established although the government had an opportunity, by means of education, to spread whatever ideas and ideals it wanted the people to have. One by-path leading the people away from their government was the incapacity of the ruler to bring able and energetic persons into the government service.

Having drawn the analogy between a state and a family, and, in fact, having treated the state like a family, Confucius set down a body of rules for the conduct of the relations between the emperor, the responsible head, the ministers, his colleagues in the management of state affairs, and the people. Loyalty to the emperor was as much an essential as filial piety to parents, and disloyalty was the great crime. But there the analogy ended. The theoretical justification of overthrowing an unworthy monarch was provided while no excuse was permitted for one to shake off the shackles of unkind or malevolent parents. In a family, whatever may be the circumstances, the members of the family have to abide by one another; even to a bad father or mother the filial piety of a child is due. A revolt against one's consanguine superior is both a legal and a social crime: the utmost a son can do is to avoid the presence of his parents by physical separation. The artificial bonds of a minister to a state, on the other hand, can be tightened or loosened as circumstances permit; in other words, simply because a man is born in a certain family, nothing can separate him from its other members, but a man is not bound to render his service to his native state. A subject serves his king only when the latter is worthy of the service. His worth is measured by the way the government is run, the degree to which he accepts advice, the respect he shows his ministers and the calibre of the men he has in his service. Refusal of public office, especially during a bad emperor's reign, not only does not constitute an act of disloyalty to the state, but often makes the declining appointee a hero devoted to principle.

Under this system, the state could degenerate with an unworthy ruler on the throne. But a remedy was provided in the form of the right of the people to rebel. Before, however, entering into the discussion of this particular right, the position of the people in this state should first be made clear. Mencius, comparing the relative importance of the different elements of the state, said: "the people first, territory next, the king last." Then he brought virtue back as the weapon with which to capture the people by winning their heart, coinciding with the theory set forth in the *Higher Learning* that "possession of virtue attracts the people, the people bring territory and territory produces wealth; therefore, virtue is the root and wealth the fruit." Force is eliminated from the political arena. Moral superiority is heralded as the best and only weapon of political conquest. After they have been won over, virtue is to be employed to keep them, for "whoever protects the people is their prince, and whoever tyrannizes over them is their enemy." The task is not performed by simply winning over the people. To protect and care for them, in an economic sense, is just as important a duty of the government. As the opinion of the people is dormant, active participation of the people in government is not practiced, and the degree of satisfaction of the governed can be measured by the presence or absence of uprisings. The signs of a rightly and well governed state are: lack of complaints, general economic sufficiency, ready and unconditional obedience to laws, and willingness of the able and the wise to serve the state. In this case not even an express consent is seen, as the duty of the state is to satisfy the constituents from both the political and economic points of view with the fulfillment of the duties taken for granted. All these represent a tacit consent passive in nature but efficient for the purpose.

A corollary of this tacit recognition is the mystical interpretation of popular sentiments. By this is meant what Confucius, his disciples, and all Chinese after them call the "heavenly mandate," which is really the mystical term of the passive acceptance of the reigning government by the people. This can be easily confused with the divine right theory of the West, at least in appearance. As the ruler is the "son of heaven," the authority with which he rules and holds the people satisfied under his scepter is the "heavenly mandate." But, these terms have been used to the rulers' advantage and misinterpreted, and hence have become misleading. At the first glance, they seem to denote a person sent to earth from a superhuman source, destined to rule and to be obeyed irrespective of merit, ability and fitness. But the *Tzu Yuan* Dictionary shows that the word "heaven" (Tien) in the case of the phrase "son of heaven" (Tien Tse) means elder, so the term "son of heaven" means the "eldest son of heaven." We find also in the *Record of the West* the statement, "My ruler is the eldest son of my parents." These little definitions, immaterial as they may seem, reduced the difference between the august sovereign and his humble subjects from one of kind to one of degree. Again, the modifying word "heaven" beside being attached to the word "emperor" is also employed to qualify the words "minister" and "people;" thus Mencius called the ministers who have no enemy in the empire, "ministers of heaven," and the people who live strictly in accordance with natural laws "people of heaven." These instances suffice to prove that in the original and uncorrupted sense, the word "heaven" denoted nothing superhuman or divine; it simply meant ideal, natural, or perfect. Further, the *History of Han* says that "people are the heaven of their prince: food is the heaven of the people." If the people can be the heaven of the prince, the divine character in the term "son of heaven" can hardly be sustained.

The old classics give us another reason to believe that the element of divinity is not involved in the employment of the word "heaven," for the emperor does not reign for heaven, but according to the decree of heaven and to natural laws. Here again, a definite statement of Mencius is very pertinent. He says: "One of the ways for the ruler to make himself illustrious is to observe and enact the express decrees of heaven." He defines the "express decrees of heaven" in the following dialogue:—

Wan Chang asked, "Is it right to say that Yao gave the empire to Shun?" "No," Mencius replied. "The emperor has no right to give the empire to anybody else." "Then who gave it to him?" "Heaven gave it to him." "Do you mean that heaven gave it to him by express decree?" "No. Heaven is silent. But the tacit decree of heaven is given to only the one who has good personal conduct and the ability to govern well." "Then what is meant by personal conduct and the ability to govern well?" "It means this: when Emperor Yao died, Shun retired to the South Bank of the South River after assisting him for twenty-eight years. Feudal princes did not pay tribute to the son of Yau, but to Shun; litigants did not bring the cases before the son of Yau, but to Shun; singers did not praise the son of Yau, but praised Shun. It was not until then that Shun mounted the throne. This is why I say that heaven gave him the empire." [3]

This is exactly the same principle as that in the "Great Declaration" which proclaims that "Heaven looks accordingly as the people look and heaven listens accordingly as the people listen." The *Book of History* bears the same evidence. In it we find this passage:—

The Emperor Yao said to Shun, "Ah, Shun, heaven turns to your person for the order of succession. Hold fast the doctrine of Golden Mean. If disaster happen in the empire, the authority delegated to you by heaven will end forever."

All these indicate that the ruler governs by virtue of a heavenly decree; that authority is given to only the one who has personal virtue and ability to govern; that the "heavenly mandate" is not a family property to be inherited from one generation to another, as was the practice, nay, not even to be possessed by one and the same person for life just because he happens once to possess it; that the "heavenly mandate" becomes exhausted as soon as one's virtue wanes; and that the virtue and the ability of the ruler are measured by the degree of satisfaction of the people under his rule.

[3] *The Works of Mencius*, Chapter on Wan Chang.

THEORETICAL BASIS OF THE GOVERNMENT

Taking a step further, we may safely infer that the "heavenly decree" is but the passive, silent consent of the people clothed in mystical form. Later writers, for fear of incurring the wrath, or with the desire of gaining the favor, of the emperor, made the terms "minister of heaven" and "people of heaven" obsolete by disuse, leaving only one of the ancient triumvirate fresh in literature, thus corrupting and making a myth of the doctrine to suit the taste of the reigning sovereign. Fortunately, corruption of the letter did not at the same time corrupt the spirit. So, in the middle of the seventeenth century, the Manchus naïvely claimed that Heaven gave its decree to the House of Nurhachi. Even in the days of the republican regime, we still find in many state papers, the mystical term "heaven" constantly employed instead of the plain simple word "public opinion." No doubt, the traditional and classical value of that still mystical word has a firm grip upon the "subtle" minds of 400,000,000 Orientals.

Coming back to the methods and processes of the change of a government upon the occasion of the exhaustion of the "heavenly mandate" delegated to a particular person, the theory provides that a new ruler comes in, dethrones the old and enthrones himself. He, and his descendents in turn, stay until they can no longer persuade the people to recognize passively their authority to rule. Then a rebellion starts, the successful chief of the rebellion takes his turn to rule, and a new rotation again works out in the course of time.

A review of Chinese history will reveal to us that this rotation continued from the Shang Dynasty to the end of Tsing, (1766 B. C. to 1911 A. D.) each dynasty displacing its predecessor and being in turn displaced by its successor. This right of rebellion was exercised when unfavorable natural phenomena brought disasters to, or a tyrannical government oppressed, the people. Besides a tyrannical monarch, an oppressive official might lead to the unwilling exercise of this right. But a strong or able emperor could easily suppress the uprising by statecraft or by force. Failure to relieve a famine which happened periodically with more or less regularity, would lead to a great decrease of the emperor's prestige, if not to a rebellion.

As we have seen in the beginning of this chapter, provision for economic sufficiency of the governed is one of the three fundamental duties of the government, and a good or able emperor could always make enough hay in the sunny days for the time when nature might become less generous to the people. This was not a matter of favor, but one of duty, failure to do which justified the overthrowing of the reigning house; for the inability of the government to meet the demands of its suffering subjects represented the inefficiency of the government. But history records more failures than successes in the rebellions. This means that preparation by the government beforehand or resistance at the time of the outbreak was sufficient to put down the unorganized mob; and only those who had greatly abused their power and position were dethroned, while, on the side of the rebels, extraordinarily good leaders were required to steer the way to the founding of a new dynasty.

In time of peace, this right of rebellion served as a warning to the emperor. It made his decrees argumentative instead of mandatory; it made him kind to the suffering, considerate to the ruled, and eager to obtain the service of the able and the wise; it made the Chinese emperor a distinctive institution totally different from all other sovereigns of the world. That the oppression of a local official might lead to a rebellion against the reigning dynasty instead of against the official himself was a strong evidence of the responsibility of the "emperor-father" to his "children-people." The emperor, after acquiring the "decree of heaven," was given the great power to administer his state affairs, subject only to forceful traditions and the sacred right of rebellion. The officials were his representatives, appointed or dismissed at his imperial pleasure. They were not responsible to the people. The people could call only the emperor to account. The sole means of impeaching the emperor was this right. Very often, during or after the rebellion, the emperor issued edicts of a self-denying tone, enumerating his own defects on the one hand and promising reforms and improvements on the other. Rarely were rebels severely punished in proportion to the gravity of their crime. This ancient right of rebellion, which may appear queer to people of the twentieth century who employ elections and recalls, initiative and referendum instead of an uprising, to terminate the term of the existing government, served the Chinese for, roughly, four thousand years as a fundamental institution to make Oriental monarchism more democratic than most of the Occidental aristocracies.

As a summary exposition of the Chinese political philosophy, nothing is more lucid, concise, expressive and to the point than the three principles explained by Meadows in his extraordinarily good book *The Chinese and their Rebellions*.[4]

1. That the nation must be governed by moral agency in preference to physical force.
2. That the service of the ablest and wisest men in the nation is indispensable to its good government.
3. That the people have the right to dispose of a sovereign who, either from active weakness or vicious indolence, gives cause to oppressive and tyrannical rule.

To these, two more may be added:—

1. That inability of the government to remedy sufferings of the people caused by unfavorable natural phenomena signifies the neglect of the sovereign in his duty of making the people economically sufficient and justifies the exercise of the right of rebellion.
2. That refusal of the able and wise to render their service to the government is a symptom of the weakness of the government and a vanguard of a rebellion.

[4] p. 401.

With the gist of the Confucian theory now presented, it is necessary to discuss why this theory dominated the Chinese Government to the exclusion of all others. First, Confucian theory embodies conservative doctrines. It aims to stabilize the political institutions. It accepts the prevailing system and tries to better it. It suggests a remedy for the corruption of the present system. The right of rebellion is the last resort, not to be exercised until all other means have been exhausted. Every reigning house has the ambition to perpetuate its own line of succession. Anything tending towards the retention of the house on the throne will undoubtedly receive its support. Loyalty to the emperor, one of the cardinal principles of the theory, places the monarch in the safety zone. The power and responsibility are all centered at the monarch, the only limitations upon whose power, besides the right of rebellion, are ethical doctrines and traditions which though not easy to follow exactly, are not such that slight violations of them endanger the position of the monarch: in other words, no hard-and-fast rules are to be followed by the emperor provided he conforms to the principles of virtue to a reasonable degree. To the government, advocation of the Confucian theory means propaganda for its own continuance. Human nature is so well understood, so closely considered, and so well imbedded in his system by the founder of this school that to follow it became a natural disposition of the government.

Secondly, the philosophy is practical. It is as much concerned with solid political institutions as with speculative ideas. It is a system in which political science and political philosophy are combined; its students thus become equipped with a theoretical background as well as with institutional knowledge. The lack of demarcation between the two makes the study doubly profitable. If a complete separation of theory and institutions had existed, practical men would not have touched the theory and students of the abstract principles would have neglected the institutions. Again, the theory was intermingled with personal ethics. The unconscious acquisition of knowledge in politics through the humble pursuit of study in personal ethics greatly helped to popularize the theory. Isolation of political teaching from the ethical would have produced the same effect as isolation of theory from institutions. Furthermore, the institutions were not of Confucius' own invention, but supposed to be records of the Golden Age: the theory is taught side by side with history. Its many-sided character certainly served to make it popular.

Thirdly, contrary to its element of stability but coordinated with its many-sided character, was its feasibility. Mencius had good reason to call his teacher "the timeous sage." Kang Yu Wei, one of the greatest living Confucian scholars, says in the *Works of the Eight Contemporary Great Authors*:—"The political theory of Confucius is like the drug of a good doctor prescribed according to the nature and the degree of the disease." From the *Academic Narratives* [5] the following extract may be called to witness this important character of the system:—

> Tse Kung asked, "When the Duke of Chi inquired about government, you said that government should be economical; at a second time, when the Duke of Lu asked about government, you said that government depended on the understanding of the ministers by the ruler; at the third time, when the Duke of Yih sought advice on government, you said that the chief duty of government was to make those around you happy and those away from you willing to migrate to your domain. All three questions being identical, why should your answers be so totally different?" "I answered them according to their circumstances," replied the philosopher, "The Duke of Chi was luxurious, his people suffered from his unnecessary waste; therefore, I told him to be economical. The Duke of Lu was deceived by his ministers, their deception wrought miseries on the people; therefore, I wanted him to understand them. While the people of Yih were ready to desert their state, because they were not satisfied with the Duke's rule; therefore, I wanted him to make them happy."

[5] *Works of Confucius*, edited by his grandson who was at the same time one of his greatest disciples.

There indeed is ground for students of his philosophy to believe that Confucius wrote for his age, and for his age alone. An attack upon the consistency of the philosophy seems quite proper, but whatever may be the opinions of students its quality of adaptability cannot be questioned. This element was constantly utilized by later monarchs as a soothing agent in cases of innovations that would likely arouse the objection of one party or another.

Fourthly, as it supported the existing governments, so the government gave it its reciprocal support. The most effective institution for this purpose was the employment of the works of Confucius as subjects of ancient historical, political, and moral essays in the competitive civil service examinations. This meant that a thorough knowledge of the Confucian classics was indispensable before a literary degree could be won, and an appointment to a higher post of the civil service could be expected. An opportunity to study other theories was not available to those who made schooling a preliminary training to officialdom which most of the students did; nor was it open to those who succeeded in the examinations and confined themselves to the administrative hierarchy. By mastering the theory and literature one won a degree and an appointment; and by winning an appointment one was brought into the company of those who were completely enslaved by it. What chances did other theories have in such an unfair competition? Only the unsuccessful, or the curious, scholars would peep into pages of the deserted schools; yet even this was not done until the Confucian theory had so moulded their thoughts that new things would either be rejected or accepted without sufficient discrimination.

This discussion would be incomplete without mentioning the fact that other political theories have been designated political heresies since Mencius, and have been, from that time on, ostracized from the common path of knowledge, to be tried only by the disappointed, the curious, or the cynical;

while the Confucian theory became more and more the political oracle as dynasties came and went. Other forms of encouragement took the shape of awarding a seat in a temple of honor to Confucian scholars whose door was closed to students of other schools. This temple was built by the government. To it, the greatest Confucian scholars were elected after death. A seat in it entitled the elected to sacrifices by the emperor or his representative. In short, so complete was the government support that reliable historical records show that since the centralization of the Chinese government, no more than two or three scholars of other schools were chosen for government service, and the violent attack of the orthodox Confucians soon drove them out.

Since the governments in the different dynasties were only chips of the old Confucian block, their weakness and strength can be easily described when we come to consider the government proper.

The peculiar conditions under which the Manchu Dynasty was founded demand a treatment of the theoretical basis, particularly as related to the Tsing Dynasty, in addition to a general discussion applicable to all dynasties alike.

Geographic isolation made it possible for the Chinese to work out the theory of government by moral forces and by the exercise of the right of rebellion as a check to virtueless rulers until 1260 when Kublai Kahn broke the isolation by successful invasion and occupied, with his successors, the Chinese throne for eighty-nine years (1279-1368, A. D.). In the middle of the fourteenth century the exercise of the same sovereign right of the people resulted in the complete expulsion of the Mongols and the establishment of a native Chinese dynasty eighteen years after the first appearance of the revolt. Nearly three hundred years later (1644) another invasion took place, this time by the Manchus from the Northeast, resulting in the complete subjugation of China by the sturdy invaders. Prior to the success of the Manchus, uprisings in the interior furnished sufficient symptoms of the exhaustion of the "heavenly mandate" in the Chu family.[6]

Unlike the Mongols who recognized the plain and simple rule of conquest by force, the crafty Manchus, before they were sure of their position in China, attempted to claim a rightful succession to the Ming Dynasty so that they could better enlist the service of the able and loyal Chinese who refused to serve the alien invaders. Their contention was that they entered China upon the invitation of General Wu San Kuei, a high military officer of the Ming Government; that they were revenging the Ming Emperor who was compelled to commit suicide by the rebels; that they had performed due sacrifices to the late Emperor Chung Tseng (Ming); that they retained most of the Ming institutions and its working force; and that the Mings had become extinct at the time Emperor Shun Chi (first Manchu Emperor) mounted the Chinese throne; and that, therefore, they were not invaders, but rightful successors to the Ming Government. The purpose of this claim can be shown by the proclamation made by the Prince Regent to the Southern provinces which were then resisting the Manchu supremacy:[7]

> We have heard that the revenge of a wrong done to one's sovereign or father admits of no compromise. We have also heard that to help a neighboring state out of troubles and to release it from misery is a friendly duty. Your Emperor Tai Tso of the Ming Dynasty drove away the barbarous Mongols, thus getting revenge for us. After him, good rulers succeeded one another; the people were pleased. During the last part of the Ming Dynasty, officials were corrupt, the people poor, and bandits abundant. But, the late Emperor, [the last one of the Ming Dynasty] broadened the action of kindness and filial piety with his own constantly practiced virtues.

[6] Family name of the Ming emperors.

[7] This proclamation does not appear in the *Tung Hua Lu*, an official court memorial of the Manchu emperors, but appears in the *Complete History of the Tsing Dynasty*. The date of its issuance is conjectured to be in 1644.

THEORETICAL BASIS OF THE GOVERNMENT 17

Now the rebellious thief, Li Tse Cheng, forgetting the imperial favor of generations, has committed treason against heaven by poisoning the country and making war on the government, burning the palaces and compelling the Emperor and Empress to commit suicide with his gang of bandits and for the sake of satisfying his owl-like ambitions. He wasted treasures and maltreated the people. The wrath of Heaven is incurred. The sun and moon darken. The Emperor of the Great Tsing, acting on the principle of rightful revenge, has punished the wrong doers and extended his sympathy to the wronged by putting brigandage to an end. They ran away as soon as our army was mobilized. The rebel chief will be captured; his followers executed in no time.

I, therefore, encamped my army in Peking, consoled the people, performed the mourning ceremonies for your late Emperor, conferred on him posthumous titles and built him a mausoleum. We rebuilt the palace precincts and the imperial gardens. We buried the members of the imperial family with proper ceremonies. We have preserved everything of the late Emperor. The imperial clansmen were taken care of. Your scholars and generals who showed their loyalty have been rewarded and honored. Tax rates were reduced. The wise and able were recruited to our service. We have done the utmost for your people.

But the Ming Dynasty had no rightful successors to the throne. Circumstances prevented it from continuing. Hence, we had to remove from Manchuria to settle down in Peking. We are now training our army for a clean sweep of the rebels, so that the myriads may once more live in peace. We have no ambition in the territories of the country. Our plan is only to save China.

If you, brave officers, loyal officials and faithful subjects of the South, want revenge for the Ming Dynasty in cooperation with us, you will be given ranks and titles in our government. If you still cherish the memories of the past dynasty and desire to maintain it in territories left of the Great River, we shall not forbid. But you must not betray our country and you must have peace with us. We shall remember the favor of our predecessor and you shall play the rôle of friendly neighbors. If you know that you are no match for us and surrender to us, we shall put you in prominent positions in our army for the invasion of the West. [Shensi, where Li's army held out.] If you subdue your neighboring places and come to our midst, we promise you participation in our happiness, glory and fame. All the surrendered territories shall be exempt from tax for two years. Other favors will be conferred by later edicts. Without a proper sovereign, the people's heart cannot be set at rest. If you show schemes of resistance by enthroning a fool or a weakling, or secretly work against us by the deception of open surrender, you will become traitors of our people and enemies of our country.

We shall subjugate the Three Chins [Shensi] first, then mobilize our army southward to put an end to your insubordination. Ah! It is easy to decide whether to follow or to resist; so try to be loyal ministers and principled subjects. There shall be no difference between the North and the South when both become blessed subjects of our heavenly empire . . . . . [8]

The first part of this proclamation lays claim to rightful succession in unmistakable terms. As no date of issuance is shown, the tone indicates that it was written before Li Tse Cheng was defeated in Shensi, and just after the Manchus' entrance into Peking. The fact that this document does not appear in any of the official publications proves that the claim was afterwards abandoned; for only shortly after this, the tone, as shown in the Prince Regent's letter to Sze Ko Fah, Minister of War in Nanking, was quite changed. Here, we find another of their claims:—

" . . . . Nowadays, rumors have it that an independent government has already been established in Nanking. But the revenge of wrongs done to one's emperor or father is uncompromising; and the *Spring and Autumn* lays down very inflexible laws against rebels and usurpers by the principle that unless the usurper has been punished, the murdered ruler could not be accorded a burial, and the new one, his coronation. Rebel Li Tze Cheng invaded the capital and murdered the Emperor. None of the Chinese officials or subjects has been heard to take up the task of revenge. Prince Wu San Kuei appealed to us for assistance. Our Government, moved by his loyalty and righteousness, recollecting the friendship between our countries for generations and disregarding the petty differences of late, drove out the rebels [meaning army of Li] with our trained army.

The day we entered Peking, posthumous titles were conferred on the late Emperor and a burial with proper ceremonies given to him; all the imperial clansmen were allowed to retain their original titles, and the ministers, their original position; farming

[8] *Complete History of the Tsing Dynasty*, v. 1, Chapter 3, p. 10.

was undisturbed and trade went on as usual. We are just planning to dispatch our army to the West in the fall, and at the same time, issue a proclamation to the South to enlist the service of the Southerners so that we can together revenge the wrongs done to your Emperor and your country as well as extend to you the blessing of our Government, without knowing that you gentlemen of the South are indulging in vain glory and temporary peace by ignoring the circumstances of the day and overlooking the harmful consequences of resistance. *Our Government conquered Peking from the hands of the rebels, not from the Ming Dynasty.* The rebels dethroned the Ming Emperor. We revenged the wrong at the expense of our own treasures and blood.

If you gentlemen are filial sons and righteous men, you ought to be grateful to us for our favor and plan for our reward. But, at the moment when the rebels had been executed and our Imperial army were at rest, you come out and occupy territories south of the Great River. Is it justifiable? Please do not entertain the false notion that our Northern army cannot cross the mighty Yangtse River. Remember, at the same time, that the rebels wrought disasters only to the Ming Dynasty, not to us; we revenge just for the sake of the principle of righteousness. If you insist on being our enemy, we will send our expedition eastward instead of westward. Please do not forget that the rebels succeeded in overthrowing your government when it was in full possession of the country. Can you expect to resist the advance of our great country with the meagre force recruitable in a strip of territory to the left of the Great River?

If you gentlemen really know the situation and the "Heavenly Mandate," are loyal to the late Emperor, and faithful to your prince, you ought to persuade him to give up the Imperial title and become our vassal. We shall receive your tributes, treat your prince as the sovereign of a dependency and give him a rank above all other nobles. Our original intention of subduing the rebels and succeeding to the extinct line of Ming Dynasty may thus further be carried out. If you gentlemen come to our service, we shall give you position, rank and territory; the case of Prince Wu San Kuei shall be your precedent: please think over it carefully . . . . ."[9]

This letter was written early in the first year of Shun Chi. There the claim to the right to the throne was one by right of conquest. "China was taken from the hand of the

[9] *Tung Hua Lu.* Shun Chi, v. 3, pp. 7-8.

rebels, not from the Ming Emperor," as it is said. Succession to the supposedly extinct line of the Ming Emperors was only an excuse. But the South was still resisting, so the claim of a rightful succession was only half abandoned. The intention of the Manchus was to invade China, not to relieve the Ming Emperors of their troubles. The edict issued by Emperor Shun Chi in the appointment of the Prince Regent as Commander-in-chief of the invading army shows no intention of friendly help. Part of this edict reads:—

My imperial grandfather founded this dynasty. My imperial father solidified it. Now that the responsibility has fallen on my person, Mongolia and Korea have been subdued. The Chinese territories and cities, though gradually being conquered are still stubbornly resisting our army. During the period of construction, invasion is an important activity. I am young, and am therefore unable to take the military command in person. I hereby appoint the Prince Regent to lead my army towards the conquest of the Middle Kingdom.[10]

Further denial of succession to the Mings by the Manchus is proved by later edicts, scores of which bear the statement, "Our Imperial Dynasty is founded by military conquest . . . . . " No more was the legal claim of succession made after the letter to Minister Sze Ko Fah in Nanking. The original claim was absolutely cast away after the South was subdued. It was, no doubt, a weapon of the Manchus to win the Chinese people's heart when they were denounced as invaders and barbarians, and when they wanted to secure the service of the wise and able Chinese by hook and crook. This explains why that claim was not continued after the conquest was completed.

This claim of legal right upon the part of the Manchus was emphatically denied by the Chinese. The reply of Sze Ko Fah to the Prince states the denial:—

" . . . . . The fact that the rebel chief is still at large brings troubles to you as well as making me ashamed. But, you are wrong in your contention that the Southerners have forgotten the

[10] *Tung Hua Lu.* Shun Chi, v. 2, p. 6.

THEORETICAL BASIS OF THE GOVERNMENT 21

wrongs done to their Emperor and are stealing comfort from the troublous situation. Our position is this: our late Emperor respected Heaven, followed the good precedents of his ancestors, loved his people and busied himself with state affairs; in short, he was as great an emperor as Yao and Shun. The incident of March the nineteenth (the suicide of the Emperor) was a result of betrayal brought about by incapable ministers. I, waiting for punishments due me on the one hand and hurrying to the relief of the Emperor on the other, heard of the tragic event while my army encamped on the banks of the Huei River. Nothing can describe my sorrows. Ah! how I have sinned! Even if I were executed in the public as a warning to the incapable, I would not be able to right the wrongs already done to the late Emperor.

At that time, people of the South felt as sorry as for the death of their parents. They struck their breasts, ground their teeth, and wanted to send all the able bodies of the East and the South to put down the murderer and enemy. But the experienced officials, on account of the downfall of the Peking Government, the suicide of the Emperor, and the importance of reorganizing the Government, decided to enthrone the reigning Emperor, who is a grandson of Emperor Shun Tsung, a nephew of Emperor Kuang Tsung and an elder brother of the late Emperor. He has the right to the throne, the Mandate of Heaven, and the backing of popular opinion.

On the first of May, when the Emperor arrived at Nanking, he was received by myriads of people who thronged the streets and their cheers reverberated far and wide. Then the ministers of state persuaded him to ascend the throne. He was overcome with grief. Only after his repeated declinations were rejected, did he promise to act as a regent. It was not until the fifteenth of the month after ministers and people had petitioned him again and again that he consented to be crowned. Prior to his coronation, phoenix gathered in the city, the river stream appeared clear, and other symptoms of peace and prosperity abounded. On the day of coronation, purple clouds surrounded the city like a fan and lumber floated out from the Great River for the reconstruction of the Palaces. Are these not signs of the "Heavenly Mandate?"

Several days later, I was ordered to review the troops stationed north of the Great River and mobilize them for invasion of the West. Suddenly news reached me that General Wu San Kuei had borrowed troops from your country, driven out the rebels, revenged our late Emperor and Empress, accorded them a proper burial, cleaned up the palace precincts, brought the people back to peace and order and abolished the mandate of compulsory shaving of hair so as to uphold the customs of the Ming Dynasty. To all these, the officials and people of Ming should not only be grateful to you and plan to reward you, as it is intimated in your letter, but should treat you with the best of our possession and courtesy. Therefore, we are going to send, in August, an ambassador to reward your troops as well as to form an alliance for the invasion of the West. This is why our Imperial army is still stationed in the South after having been dispatched. Yet you quote the principle of *Spring and Autumn* against the coronation of our Emperor without knowing that this principle applies only to the feudal lords, not the Emperor . . . . .

. . . . . The Imperial Dynasty had occupied the throne for sixteen generations, one succeeding another in the direct line of descent. It has helped the extinct to perpetuate and the downfallen to exist. It extended favors far and wide. Have you forgotten that your country used to be a vassal state of ours? Our archives can show you records of our suzerainty. . . . . . You came into China to help the Ming Dynasty. Your army was sent for the principle of righteousness. You can set a noble example of friendship and righteousness for posterity. But if you capitalize our disaster, cast away our friendship, resume hostility, and try to satisfy your territorial ambition, you will be ending a righteous cause with greedy action and making a farce of yourself. Is that what you are doing? . . . . .

The Emperor, his officers and the people are all anxious to put down the rebellion even at the sacrifice of their lives. It is time for the rebel Li Tze Cheng to perish. Our proverb says "The planning of virtue must be thorough; the abolition of evil must be exhaustive." Now the rebel is still at large. It not only means that our revenge has not been complete but your abolition of the evil is not yet exhaustive; I pray you to carry out the campaign of putting down a common foe and maintaining the principle with which you started your campaign. Let us combine our forces for an invasion of the West [Shensi] and put down the rebels. Then your noble example of justice and righteousness will shine in history forever; we will do our best to reward you and the two countries will live in permanent friendship and peace. . . . . ."[11]

This letter can be taken as a representative view of the Southeast. However unattractive the proposition of divid-

[11] *Tung Hua Lu.* Shun Chi, v. 3, pp. 8-9.

ing up China into two, giving the North to the Manchus and leaving the South to the Chinese, might have appeared to the Manchus, and however impractical it might be for execution, this was the opinion of the Southeast. The legal right of the Manchus to succeed to the Ming throne was refutable and refuted. If any right to the Chinese throne could be claimed by the Manchus, it was that of conquest, of physical force.

CHAPTER II

THE EMPEROR

The emperor in the old Chinese monarchy, popularly known as the "Son of Heaven," more popularly misconceived as an absolute monarch like those of ancient and medieval Europe or other Oriental countries, occupied a position unique enough to have no analogue in other states. As we have seen in the previous chapter, this term, "Son of Heaven," was the only survival of the old triumvirate (son of heaven, minister of heaven and people of heaven); we can safely deny any superhuman or theological tinge attached to it. Running through the old classics and other literature, one comes across the frequently quoted proverb, "The state does not belong to any individual, but the virtuous man takes charge of it." This old saying is as much quoted by private writers as by emperors in their edicts. The philosopher Kuo Pei Yun says: "The throne is not a treasure *per se*. It is so because people will be benefited when on it sits a sage: so the king does not treasure it, but the people do." Mencius says, "Emperor Yao did not give the throne to Shun, nor did Shun give it to Yu, nor did Yu give it to Chi: King Tang did not take the throne from Chieh, for none of them owned it."[1] Imperial edicts bear witness to this, the important ones always beginning with the phrase "By order of heaven, I succeed to the throne and hereby issue this edict . . . . ." In petitions and memoranda, reference is made to this theory as often as in edicts. Thus, at least from the theoretical standpoint, the non-ownership of the throne by the emperor was not disputed.

The emperor's temporary exercise of the sovereign power together with the right of rebellion made the emperor

[1] Chapter of Wan Chang.

responsible to the people, though the degree of responsibility was quite limited. The responsibility was not only very much limited, but easily shifted. A strong ruler could always suppress the unorganized rebels with his trained army. Force, though denounced as an undesirable weapon of government, could be easily resorted to as an effective weapon for the maintenance of governmental authority. A clever emperor could avoid a rebellion by statecraft. Furthermore, this right, being the last measure, of the people, was not resorted to until every other means had been exhausted. The risk of the attempt, the doubtfulness of its success, and the heavy punishment that would probably result if it failed, made the people extremely cautious in the exercise of this right. Indeed, the only opportunity for a successful rebellion was a combination of a bad emperor, weak ministers and unusually strong leaders for the rebellion. Historical facts, too, tended to check rebellions; for those who started the rebellion scarcely ever succeeded. The best they could do was to overthrow the existing government. But the overthrowing of a government is one thing, establishing a new government quite another thing. The latter requires constructive wisdom, while the former depends on destructive energy. Only a combination of wisdom and energy, a very rare combination indeed, could lead to overthrowing of the old and the founding of the new dynasty by one and the same person. Under ordinary circumstances, a successful rebel who overthrew the existing government was usually, in turn, overthrown by another. However, the emperor's responsibility to the people, although light and vague, nevertheless existed.

In spite of the success of clever monarchs and flattering ministers in creating limitations upon the exercise of the right of rebellion, the scholars succeeded in imposing moral standards to which the monarch was expected to conform. Failure to comply with these requirements on the part of the ruler bred contempt for him by the ruled. Not infrequently was this contempt the herald of a rebellion. Among these requirements, the first was that he must be a good example to all. Cheng Tse says in the *Annotation to the Canon of Nature* (Yi Cheng Cheng Chuan) "Heaven is the source of everything, the emperor is the model of everybody. If he acts in accordance with the decree of heaven, he will bring peace on earth." In the Chapter *Tai Chia of the Canon of History*, (Shu Cheng) we find the statement, "When the man on throne begins to be good, everybody will be rectified."

The first prerequisite to make him exemplary is the practice of virtue, the foundation of Chinese political philosophy. Tseng Tse again says in the *Sheng Li Ta Chuan*, "The imperial virtue is heavenly virtue . . . . . It is as high as the skies and as deep as the seas. He must be able to make people respect what he sees, believe what he says, and rejoice over what he does." With such a highly developed degree of individualism, though the family instead of the individual was the unit, even in the ancient times nothing short of subjugation by their heart could accomplish absolute conquest. Yet, whether he was good or bad, he exerted an influence on the people. The familiar phrase, "the superior acts and the inferior acts" draws a vivid picture of the Chinese society. Hsuan Tze says:—[2]

The emperor is the mould, the people its products; if the mould is right, the products will be right. He is the basin, the people the shape of the water therein; if the basin is round, the shape of the water will be also round; if square, so will its contents be . . . . . King Chuang of the state of Cho liked small waists, ladies starved in the court. The ruler is the source, the people its current: a clear source gives a current of crystals, a muddy stream flows from an impure spring . . . . .

Confucius expressed the same view in a clever and concise comparison by saying that "the ruler is wind, the ruled weeds; weeds bend to whatever direction the wind blows them." Were the Chinese emperor to become as impotent as the French president, who is said to neither govern nor reign, he would still possess the extra-legal power of in-

[2] *Works of Hsuan Tze.*

fluencing the people, a power immensely worthy of possession by the greatest and most absolute monarch.

Yet the power to influence was not inherent in the occupant of the throne: it was secured by identifying his interests with the people, namely, observance and practice of their likes and dislikes. So the *Cha Fu Yuan Kuei* says, "In order to be an influential ruler, one must think as the people think and be interested in what they are interested." This influence was supposed to be so great that whatever the people did or thought revealed the taste and activity of the ruler, and from that one could draw the conclusion as to what to do and what not to do. It is this that the *Canon of History* (Shu Cheng) means in its saying, "The emperor should not look at the water (to find out his looks), but at the people (to find out his deeds)."

Realizing the great importance of influence by pure virtue the standard of which had been raised to such unapproachable heights, Mencius compromised it by giving permission to violate some of its precepts provided the indulgence were shared by the people. After discussing what government by virtue meant with the Prince of Chi, who found it difficult of attainment and attempted politely to decline his advice, he set out the condition of compromise in the following words:—[3]

The prince said, "Excellent is your advice." "If you think it excellent," replied Mencius, "why do you not practice it?" "But, I cannot, because I love hoarding." "In the ancient times, Duke Liu loved hoarding . . . . . His subjects stored up grains; travellers within his domain were always well supplied with food. If you only love hoarding, you have no difficulty of becoming a virtuous ruler only if you can let the people share your love." "But, still I cannot do it, because I love beauty." "In the ancient times, the Grand Prince loved his princess consort . . . . . During his reign, there was neither complaining old maids nor bachelors. So, your love of beauty would not prevent you from being a virtuous king if you only let the people share it . . . . . ."

[3] Chapter of Liang Hui Wang, *Works of Mencius*.

This on the one hand permits the violation of virtue and on the other makes provision for the participation of its indulgence; and if wisely a king lets his subjects share his indulgence, this weakness would turn into a strength.

Besides the popular participation in his indulgence, the Emperor must adjust his desire to the needs of the people. The monarch, according to the Chinese theory, is created for the people, he owes his position and authority to their needs, and it is his duty to see that they are well supplied. The Chinese government is so personal in its nature that the monarch's ability to administer to the needs of the people forms the principal basis of judgement upon the efficiency of the government. His duties are well summed up in a short passage in the *Works of Kwan Tze:*—

> The monarch takes the people for his heaven. Their support makes him safe, their help makes him strong, their dislike puts him in danger and their hatred dethrones him. Therefore, as a good rider to his horse or a good archer to his bow, the care of a monarch for his people should be exceedingly well.

Here again we come back to the same point, namely, that the people are the center of the government. First the theory is built around the monarch; then the needs of the people are placed before his desires and ambition. Popular sovereignty, in a negative and unassertive way, is contained in this theory. Only the statements are so passive that no provision is made for the people to demand of their monarch what they want; it is left to the monarch to give them what he can, or desires to, give. Outside of the right of rebellion, no peaceful effective means of upholding the people's sovereignty, or even of expressing their opinion, is provided. The passiveness of the theory makes the obligation of the monarch moral rather than legal, the fulfillment of the moral obligation a favor rather than a duty, and the occasions of fulfillment an exception rather than a rule.

Other virtues required of the monarch are impartiality, profoundness of knowledge, diligence in affairs, respect in ceremonial occasions, kindness in heart and acts, following of good precedents of ancestors, wisdom to know men, and sagacity to accept advice. All these are qualities of ethics applicable to everybody in everyday life, yet the *Chinese Encyclopedia* devotes forty-six volumes exclusively to the treatment of these qualities as applied to an emperor. The responsibility of his position and his opportunity to exert influence on the people justify the space so devoted. The loftiness of the qualities and the difficulty of compliance with them made these virtues shibboleths of courtiers and classical scholars. A comparison of this theory with the actual powers and position of the emperor is shown by an extract from Huang Li Chow's [4] *Essay on The Ruler:*

In the ancient times, the state was the host, the monarch its guest; what the monarch works for during his life and tenure was the good of the state. Now the monarch has become the host and the state his guest; that the people and the state have no peace because the monarch wants the state and wants it for himself alone. Therefore, before one gets it, one poisons the mind and massacres the bodies of the people for its acquisition without realizing that he is only working for his descendents. After one has got it, one squeezes the flesh and blood of the people and separates their children from them for the sake of one's animal passions: he takes it for granted and says "This is the dividend of my investment." Then the great harm of the country is the monarch.

The deviation of the monarch from the democratic provisions of the theory may be attributed to several reasons. First, the Sha Dynasty was founded by an accident.[5] After that, the throne was made hereditary. The tendency of later emperors was to perpetuate their own line of descent. New institutions in favor of it were gradually added; old ones

[4] One of the three greatest scholars in the beginning of the Tsing Dynasty.

[5] Before the founding of the Sha Dynasty, the throne shifted from one family to another. Incidentally both King Yu and his son, Chi were good. For the first time in Chinese history, the son succeeded his father, making it a family affair.

against the ownership of the throne by a family were gradually abolished. Chu Tze [6] says:—

> The Chin institutions are mostly for the elevation of the emperor and the debasement of ministers, so the emperors of the late dynasties refused to change them. Ancient rulers were designated with the title Huang or Ti, but the First Emperor of Chin called himself Chi Huang-Ti. Since then, every emperor has used the double title.

The court ceremonies adopted at the beginning of the Han Dynasty elevated the position of the emperor at the expense of the ministers. By this means the emperor was placed so much above all the rest that the ancient theory of grading the emperor only one grade higher than a duke, as a duke was then a marquis, and a marquis was then an earl, was thrown overboard.[7]

The first emperor of the Ming Dynasty abolished the premiership and established the grand secretariat.[8] By this means, he appropriated all the traditional power and influence of the premier to himself, divided the prestige and influence of the premiership into several grand secretaries, and removed the last effective check on himself by altogether abolishing the office. Then, lastly, there were always some flattering ministers who aimed to gain imperial favor by petitioning for the elevation of either his position or power. This was a force constantly at work.

Leaving the theoretical background and the corruption of the theory, let us now examine the emperor's real work and power, particularly of the Manchu emperors with whom this treatise deals.

The Manchus retained all methods and institutions which the Chinese invented to modify the old principle and thus

---

[6] *The Complete Works of Chu Hsi.*

[7] "The 'son of heaven' forms one grade, the duke another, the marquis a third, the earl a fourth and the viscount and the baron a fifth grade, forming five grades in all." *Works of Mencius.*

[8] For details, see Chapter IV.

exalted the position of the sovereign and debased that of his associates. In addition, they modified the principles with the aim of further elevating the emperor. In a letter of Emperor Tai Tsung of the Manchus to General Yuan Chung Huan [9] he says: "The Emperor is the son of Buddha in heaven. The minister is a noble when he pleases his master and a rogue when he incurs his master's wrath." Again, in 1779, when a Councilor of State was dismissed, the decree for the punishment of the dismissed councilor contained the following words:—

Now the trial is over and the case decided. But, I recollect that Fu Chang An [the dismissed councilor] was employed by the late emperor for more than twenty years. I am now in the period of mourning. I am reluctant to discard things, even dogs and horses, to which the late emperor once showed his favor, not to say Fu Chang An, who, though a blockhead, had rendered a little service to my late imperial father and was liked and petted by him as a little pup.

Here the attitude of the Manchu emperors towards their ministers is shown. It would be intolerable under the old theory. To the Manchu emperors, the old practice of respect for the ministers became a byword. Were Mencius' statement "If the king treats his ministers like dogs and horses, they should treat him as an enemy" in full force, a withdrawal of all able officials from the service would have led to a rebellion.

But, the Manchu monarchs were wise enough to elevate their position and concentrate their power at the same time. The *Huang Chao Wen Hsien Tung Kao* bears witness to this point in a short passage:—

From the grand secretaries and ministers of the six departments down to an insignificant clerk in the remote corner of the empire, appointment or dismissal, reward or punishment, is all given directly by the emperor himself. This has never been practiced by rulers heretofore.

The elevation of position coupled with the concentration of power made the Manchu emperors more like oriental

---

[9] Ming defense commissioner of the Northern frontiers.

despots than their predecessors. These changes might have been brought about by the peculiar situation of the dynasty where the conquered Chinese, though outnumbered in the official directory and less favored for powerful and responsible positions, ran and controlled the government by virtue of their knowledge of the institutions, the people, the situation, and their greater ability as a ruling class. Unfortunately, the Manchus, who should have run the government, were incapable of doing so for lack of qualities possessed by their Chinese colleagues. Hence the emperors, if they were able, energetic, and ambitious like Kang Hsi and Chien Lung, busied themselves day and night for the simple reason that they could not find both enough confidence and enough ability in officials from their own race. An extract from Lord McCartney [10] shows how Emperor Chien Lung passed his days:—

> The emperor [Chien Lung] gets up at three o'clock in the morning. He first goes into the Imperial Buddhist Temple to do sacrifice to Buddha. Then he reads petitions and memorials addressed to him by officials who are privileged to do so by virtue of their position. He takes breakfast at seven o'clock. After that, he plays with court ladies and eunuchs for a little while in the gardens within the imperial precincts. Next, he calls in the grand secretaries and goes over with them business requiring immediate attention. The regular audience is then given. Usually he goes to theater or other kind of amusement after supper at three o'clock in the afternoon. Before going to bed, he usually reads what he likes. His bedtime is seldom later than seven o'clock.

Chien Lung lived in the golden age of the Manchu Dynasty when all wounds of the civil war had been healed and people were enjoying peace; neither rebellion, nor any other thing made an extra demand upon the monarch's time, or threatened his regular program. Yet he worked ten or twelve hours a day, a good day's work for any man.

Take another emperor, Kang Hsi, for instance. He was on the throne for sixty-one years. Almost at the end of

---

[10] This is translated from a Chinese translation of the original English—*Tsing Chao Chuan Sse*, Chapter 48, p. 15.

that period he wrote an essay in something of a diary style about what he had been doing and how he had been doing it. The sincere tone of his essay gives such a lively picture of the exclusive monarch that it cannot but inspire belief. The latter part of it reads:—

Having been on the throne for more than fifty years and almost at the age of eighty, I find that my country is peaceful and my people contented, though not exactly in an ideal condition of economic sufficiency and political satisfaction. I have worked all these long years carefully, patiently, and faithfully, as if for a day. The word "hard" is not enough to describe the nature of my work. Some emperors of the past died young: historical critics usually attribute their early death to luxuries and dissipation, even if they know the criticized monarchs were good emperors. This is academic cynicism. I want to vindicate the past emperors: in fact, they died of fatigue from state affairs.

. . . . . A minister can enter or retire from government service as he pleases, but the emperor has no end to his work . . . . . . Some hold the theory that the Emperor should attend to only very important affairs and leave the routine to the officials. I do not agree with this theory. For a tiny mistake in a little thing may give troubles to the whole country and a moment's carelessness may bring unhappiness to people of hundreds of generations. Therefore, whenever anything comes to me for decision, I always go over it very carefully. If I leave one or two things undone today, I will have that much more to be done tomorrow. So I always clear it at once. And then whether the thing is important or not, I never handle it carelessly. Even a word in a mistaken position I cause to be corrected. It is my nature to be careful, hence I do not mean intentionally to reject the advice of "leaving the unimportant affairs in the hands of the officials."

I am physically strong since childhood. I could bend a fifteen-strength bow and shoot long and heavy arrows. I am excellent in military tactics. But, I never executed a single one of my people without justifiable cause. The suppression of the "Three feudal princes" and the revolt in Northern Mongolia were results of my own tactics. The silver reserve in the treasury has never been used by me except for military campaigns and famine relief. Knowing that this money is the flesh and blood of my little people, I never wasted a single bit of the silver. Wherever I went, I never ordered special decorations or preparations for my visits.[11] Each of my palaces is run with ten or twenty thousand taels of silver, which is less than one per cent of the annual expenditure on reconstruction of dams and dykes.

All the above statements form a true picture of my hard work and an expression of my sincerity. Whenever I read a petition of an old official for the privilege of retirement, I wept. You all have an opportunity to retire, but when can I have mine? I am now seventy-five. A few white hairs have just appeared. Some advised me to have them dyed, but I declined their advice with a smile, because there have not been many emperors who could live long enough to have white hair.

If I am to have both my hair and my beard snow-white, will it not be romantic? But, alas! When I look back to my old colleagues who worked with me at the beginning of my reign, none can be found.[12]

This pathetic picture would certainly arouse more sympathy for the Emperor because of hard luck than envy for his wide power. That possibly is why old believers of incarnation in China prayed to be born outside of the family of the reigning house.

Theoretically, all the powers of the state belonged to the emperor, practically he did not exercise those he has delegated to his ministers. Generally speaking, all legislative, executive and judicial powers belonged to him and are at his disposal. It is from the discussion of powers which do not usually belong to European sovereigns and the means of limitation on powers that the Western peoples seldom employ that we can better understand the puzzling institution of a Chinese monarch. Whatever our method of approach, a brief discussion of the principal political powers of the monarch deserve our first attention.

Besides his possession of all three kinds of governmental powers and his ability to exercise them with more or less a

[11] The opposite was usually the case for other emperors. Roads were always specially paved with fine yellow dust before the imperial carriage passed.

[12] *Tsing Chao Chuan Sse*, complete History of the Tsing Dynasty, Chapter 33, p. 102ff.

free hand, he is, or at least is supposed to be, the religious, social and intellectual head of the nation. In the legislative line, he enacts, annuls, and amends laws by the simple device of edicts. Some of these are issued for permanent enforcement while others are for a limited time while still others are to be enforced only in particular cases in connection with which the edict is issued. The degree of enforcement is designated in the decree itself. Chinese laws, like French grammatical rules, have numerous exceptions. The exceptional cases become effective usually by virtue of an edict. The greatest privilege of legal enactment is that a law, even when it is enacted by the same emperor, can be amended or annuled by issuing an edict either expressly annulling it or merely setting out a new rule of conduct. The latter happened much more frequently, as express enactment of new laws in substitution for laws enacted by one's ancestors seemed a breach of filial piety and a breach of the virtue of following one's ancestors, while enactment of new laws to replace one's own enactment made an emperor seem inconsistent. So, in most cases, he would merely set out a new principle and let the old one die a natural death.

In the executive department, all the high officials of state were only advisors to the emperor. Not only had he the full power on account of lack of express limitations, but he reserved all the powers for himself in the *Ta Tsing Hui Tien* according to the rule that "important affairs are submitted to the emperor for approval; minor duties are to be performed by the department directly." This phrase is provided in all definitions of functions in the important organizations. Typical of the Chinese is this provision; for no definition of "important" or "minor" is given. Consequently the emperor can interfere with any business no matter whether it be important or otherwise. Among other executive powers, he had those of conferring titles, giving pensions, appointments, dismissal, promotion, demotion, establishment or abolition of services, treaty making, commanding the army and navy, deciding on boundary lines and all other powers commonly belonging to a powerful chief executive in the Western states.

Judicially, he was the highest court of appeal. If all other lower judicial authority had been appealed to in vain, he could be approached for justice. But an appeal was made to the emperor perhaps not once in a full generation. The appeal would hardly ever reach him unless some high official in the court saw or believed that justice had been denied the appellant. When a case like this happened, all the officials who had jurisdiction over it before would likely get punishment were the decision reversed. The pardoning power was frequently exercised by the emperor as a mark of favor. A quasi-judicial function of the monarch was to judge, at the death of a high official, whether he was worthy of a biography in the history of the dynasty. No man or woman's life sketch could appear in the dynastic history, the official history of the period, without the Emperor's edict conferring that honor.

As religious head, the Emperor appointed all other religious heads such as the Dalai Lama of the Lama Buddhists, the chief Taoist and Duke Kung, a direct descendant of Confucius.[13] He offered sacrifices to heaven, earth, Confucius, Buddha, etc. Unlike the many European sovereigns who have waged war on religious issues, the Chinese Emperor was a worshiper of all. The philosophical Chinese look at religion more from the ethical than from the mystical point of view. Other religious functions like the conferring of posthumous titles or giving scholars the privilege of a seat in the Confucian Temple were performed by him alone.

In the intellectual world, he was supposed to be the head. The provincial and metropolitan examinations were conducted by him. The palace examination was supposed to be conducted by him in person. He gave the questions, read the papers, and decided on the ranking of the successful

[13] A duke's title was conferred on one of his descendants and other privileges were given to him by the emperor.

candidates. The paper of the palace examination was written in a prescribed memorandum form directly addressed to him. Degrees were conferred by him or in his name. Examinations could be held any time or at any place at his pleasure. About fifteen special examinations were given by Kang Hsi and Chien Lung in their visits to different parts of the empire. He could examine any candidate, confer upon him a higher degree, or deprive him of the honor already gained. He sometimes called off the examination of a particular province as a punishment for a community offense. He lectured to the Academy of Letters and to high officials who periodically lectured to him.

He was the head of the imperial clans, a by-product of the mixing up of family and government. As their head, he gave titles, decided the right of succession, engaged and married the youngsters, named the newly born, conferred posthumous titles upon the dead, if worthy, and performed all other duties that the head of a common family had to do in the patriarchal Chinese society.

His possession and free exercise of all these powers naturally entitled him to the right of delegating some of it to the officials. The power of the Prince Regents (one at the beginning and one at the end of the dynasty) and that of the Empress Dowager Tsu Hsi was technically derived from an edict conferring on them the right to exercise these powers although practically these three edicts were issued by the three appointees instead of by the appointing authority. Some doubt may be raised as to the legal effects of the edicts issued by the Empress Dowager Tsu Hsi which read "By order of the Empress Dowager, the Emperor issues this edict . . . ." Legally the patriarchal character of the government permitted no woman at the helm. She got her powers from the emperor, and she had by no means the right to order him to issue any edict though she might issue some by virtue of the power already delegated to her. To other officials, full powers of various kinds were sometimes delegated. In times of emergency, for instance, the command of all forces in thirteen provinces was given to Tseng Kuo Fan during the Taiping Rebellion. The great scope of state affairs demanded that everything except the very important should be delegated; the emperor's only and yet always effective remedy was that he might at any time call back the delegated power.

One strange effect of patriarchism and ancestral worship on the government was that a dying emperor had the right to delegate the power of his successor to one or more ministers. Emperor Shun Chi made four grand ministers trustees of the state affairs. After life, an unknown quantity in Confucian philosophy, was then a considerable factor in the government, a product of that philosophy. By this, I mean that the emperor often honored or disgraced an official after the latter's death.

Such were the powers of the Chinese emperor in theory, if not in practice. If no moral principle were to serve as their guidance, nor other limitations to punish their abuse and check their wrong use, he would be the greatest of the Oriental despots, and his evil acts would do the greatest harm to the largest group of human beings in the world. The greatest check, no doubt, was the right of rebellion. Then, also, the moral qualities required of the emperor were calculated to put him on the right track if legal provisions failed. In order not to arouse the people to rebel, some of the moral qualities had to be practiced. But, his practice of them to the most limited degree would make him better than a despot.

Tradition and precedents, too, formed a strong check. Ministers could protest and petition for the annulment of a new law, or reenactment of an old one just suspended. To follow the examples of one's ancestors was one of the moral requirements which were hammered into the brain of an emperor while he was still a little prince. So conservative was that school of philosophy, that to decree anything in contradiction to the old customs would bring objection as sure as death would come to a mortal. Fortunately, in this respect, censorship of the past records usually made obscure the bad deeds of the former emperors and gave full treatment or even exaggeration to their good deeds; hence exemplary cases filled the records. Traditions limited the emperor in another way; for no monarch ever dared to satisfy his own whims at the expense of the people, since, traditionally, no monarch of that kind could keep his people in peace. Hence deviation from the regular reasonable government meant an invitation to a rebellion which usually ended in great disaster to the reigning house, particularly the reigning monarch.

Public opinion, especially that of the literati and gentry, checked the wrong deeds of an emperor.[14] Suffice it to say that the emperor, in spite of all his power, influence and equipment for formulation and suppression of opinion, was not only far from being able to control it, but was controlled by it. Some ministers, by ability, seniority, chance, flattery, or hook and crook, became powerful enough to check the emperor in many or all of his acts. Though the absence of premiership facilitated the manipulation of ministers, powerful ones appeared from time to time. Thus Emperor Kang Hsi dared not issue an edict to send grand secretary Ngau Bei to execution. He called him in for a private audience. He then hid several strong men in the court dressed as boys playing hide-and-seek in the court yard of the palace. When the powerful minister came in, he was caught by those "boys" and executed in the back yard before his execution was officially ordered. The prince regent's pardon of Yuan Shih Kai in 1908 was another case supporting the same principle. None of the emperors, no matter how able and energetic, was without some serviceable men who checked him. Stubborn ministers and brave censors were always ready to advise him to do this or that. If they failed the first time, they would come again until their requests were granted. He might not take the advice even though so urged time and

---

[14] A full discussion of this can be found in Chapter V.

again. He could dismiss him from service or execute him. Some cases did end with such results.

The family, the ever-lasting social unit, formed a check to the powers of the emperor. He could not recruit to his service a man in his period of mourning or one having aged parents to attend to. In two or three cases of emergency when a man in mourning was called to government service, apologetic edicts were issued with the object of making the people believe that the urgency of the situation, and not imperial authority, demanded this sacrifice of a man's propriety. When laws allowed a prisoner to remain home on account of the need of his presence by aged parents, instead of going into exile, no emperor dared to tear away an offender from the bosom of old parents whether they really needed him or otherwise. An act contrary to this law would have made the emperor a tyrant. These and numerous other entanglements of family and state shaped to a noticeable extent the acts of the monarch.

Finally, the size of the country and the massiveness of the state business made necessary the existence of fundamental, comprehensive and permanent laws. Making too many exceptions would reduce their force. This restricted the emperor's powers of amending laws or making exceptions to their applications.

Then too, it was usual for the emperor to refer cases to the grand secretaries, councilors of state, or ministers of the departments and courts for decision or recommendation. A unanimous opinion practically bound the emperor to acceptance of the decision by virtue of influence if not of legality. Submission of two or more varying decisions in a particular case would disarm the emperor of his veto as he had to choose one of them. Rarely were the decisions of the venerable body of officials rejected *in toto*. The sole means of getting rid of this oligarchic domination was not to refer matters to them. But the massive size of state affairs made this a physical impossibility.

In two respects the Manchus deviated from the Chinese practice. In the first place, the throne did not descend to the oldest son. The first eight of the ten emperors came from a direct descent of the male line: none of the eight was the first son, and the first five succeeded their fathers with elder brothers living. The last three had outlived their elder brothers. The last two, being adopted sons, were out of consideration. Secondly, there was no crown prince during the life of an emperor. Three attempts to inaugurate this institution were made; all ended with unsatisfactory results. Emperor Kang Hsi made the attempt twice and abandoned it twice. The Empress Dowager made the third and last attempt, but without success. The reason was this: the Manchus originally did not have this institution. When each of the first few emperors in Manchuria died, a struggle for the throne ensued with the consequence that the ablest came out victorious. The struggle did not end after they had conquered China. Emperor Shun Chi, the first in China, died at the age of twenty-four. He did not have an opportunity to test the suitability of this institution to the house of Nurachi. Emperor Kang Hsi reigned for sixty-one years, himself witnessing the quarrels of his sons and the unfortunate results of having an heir apparent. As the Manchu princes' struggle for the position did not end during Kang Hsi's time, so, when one of his sons was appointed to the envied place, he immediately was placed in the same position as the leading candidate for presidential nomination in the United States and became the center of attack, and the struggle would not end until the appointee was deprived of his position. Moreover, the position of the Manchus in China was not yet secured until the end of Kang Hsi's reign. Any disagreement among themselves would arouse the contempt and possibly the revolt of the Chinese. Emperor Yung Cheng, victor of the throne struggle in Kang Hsi's time, saw this, and therefore avoided the trouble by altogether abolishing the institution. Emperor Chien Lung was several times petitioned to adopt an heir apparent, but wisely rejected the advice. No other attempt was made after him until Empress Dowager Tsu Hsi wanted to threaten Kuang Hsu and ultimately dethrone him for the perpetuation of her own powers by giving him an heir who could succeed him any time she thought fit. But none of these aspirants had the luck of wearing the five-dragon robe. The crown prince, as an institution, never existed during the two hundred and sixty-six years of Manchu supremacy except in the three mentioned cases.

Twice in the Manchu Dynasty, once at the beginning and another time at the end, was a prince regent appointed during the minority of the reigning emperor. The dynastic house-law, or tradition rather, allowed no woman to meddle with state affairs, with the exception of the Empresses Dowager Tsu An and Tsu Hsi during the minority of Emperors Tung Chi and Kuang Hsu and a possible third exception of Empress Dowager Lung Yu who fought to get control of the state affairs. Taking the throne as a family possession, with the mother empress disqualified, and jealously guarding the powers, honors, and privileges inherent to the throne, the appointment of an uncle prince as regent seemed the most natural means to tide over a period during the minority of the reigning sovereign.

At the beginning of the dynasty, the Prince Regent was an extraordinarily able man. He easily exercised without dispute all powers of the emperor in the unsettled conditions. In fact, it was the first Prince Regent that conquered China. He refrained from making himself emperor only because he had all that an emperor could have, and he feared the break-up of the newly founded empire resulting from the loss of his support were he to have a *coup d' état*.

The second Prince Regent differed from the first in almost every respect. He was appointed by Empress Dowager Tsu Hsi when his infant son succeeded to the throne just before the Empress' death. It was the time when the people demanded a constitution. Against him, the Empress Dowager Lung Yu, niece of Tsu Hsi, struggled for supremacy.

Being inexperienced and politically ungifted, and facing such a difficult situation, he accepted whatever was given him by the Empress Dowager and the high officials. Thus his salary was fixed at 150,000 taels a year; his retinue, residence, position in audience, address and salutation stood, as it were, between that of an emperor and that of a prince. A few days after he assumed the duties of the regency, the Grand Secretariat and the departments in a joint memorial, with the approval of the empress, defined his powers as follows: [15]

1. The Prince Regent shall have the power to decide on all state policies, control military affairs, appoint, dismiss, reward, and punish officials. His decisions shall be embodied in mandates for execution. In case of very important affairs, for which the approval of the Empress Dowager is required, the Prince Regent shall consult the Empress Dowager in person; no one else can carry messages for him in such important matters.

2. The Prince Regent shall perform all the state ceremonies for the emperor. In case he appoints a delegate for the performance, previous consent of the Empress Dowager shall be secured.

3. The Prince shall exercise all the powers of military and naval command which constitutionally belong to the emperor.

4. The Mandates, to be effective, must bear the seal of the Prince Regent and the signatures of the Councilors of State.

5. The Prince Regent shall represent the emperor in Parliament.

6. The Prince Regent shall have the power to sign treaties with foreign powers, to appoint and receive diplomatic representatives.

[15] The official Gazette, v. 409, p. 9, Dec. 1908. Only important clauses are here translated.

7. When the emperor finishes his education, the ministers shall petition him to assume the governmental duties before the imperial wedding.

8. Amendments to these laws can be made only by the Prince Regent.

These powers made the Prince Regent an emperor in fact, if not in name. The only marked difference between a regent and an emperor in China was the address, salutation and other things in outward appearance.

CHAPTER III

THE NOBLES AND THE PRIVILEGED CLASSES

In the five elements of blessing enumerated in the *Canon of History*[1] (Shu Cheng) political power and noble titles are not included. Except in the feudal period when the vassal lords resembled European barons, and after the centralization when an empty title with a small pecuniary compensation was awarded to serviceable officials, nobility, as an institution, was hardly a factor in China, socially or politically. The Manchu government, following the tradition of the country, provided special privileges and financial aids for three classes of peoples, Imperial clansmen, Bannermen, and the titular nobles.

Two kinds of kinship to the emperor, the clansmen and the alternates (Tsung Shih and Chio Lo) were recognized, privileged, and supported. By clansmen was meant direct male descendants from Emperor Hsien Tso, grandfather of Emperor Shun Chi,[2] the term alternate signified direct male descendants from the grandfather of Emperor Hsien Tso. Chronologically, all the spouses of the House of Nurachi from the middle of the 16th century[3] and all those born after the Manchus learned to keep a family record, were made clansmen and alternates respectively. More than three hundred and fifty years of propagation well protected from the acute attack of economic insufficiency to which common people were subjected gave the House of Nurachi thousands of rice eaters with most of them making rice consumption

---

[1] These elements are longevity, wealth, health, love of virtue, and natural death.

[2] Shun Chi was the first Manchu emperor in China.

[3] Emperor Hsien Tso acceded to the throne in 1583.

their principal life work. The quarrelsome nature of the Manchus demanded a government separated from the common people; their kinship with the emperor made it improper to have the so-called nobles in the same courts as the commons; their high ranks made the ordinary mandarins too timid to impose punishment on them; finally, the historical foundation of the Court of Clansmen [4] made it proper for the Tsing Dynasty to follow the example of others and maintain a separate organization to look after the interests of the emperor's paternal relatives.

The Court of Imperial Clansmen, or Imperial Clan Court (Tsung Jen Fu), really not of much importance, appears in the *Ta Tsing Hui Tien* before all other offices, due probably to the extension to his kith and kin of the unrestricted respect for the emperor. All clansmen and alternates came under the jurisdiction and control of this court. This court was staffed by three Chinese secretaries of two different ranks attending to translation and records in Chinese, and ninety-seven Manchus pretty nearly all of whom were clansmen or alternates. The duties of this court were of a varied nature combining the functions of family, state and society: in short, forming a small government by itself.

Its duties consisted of recording birth, death, marriage, succession, promotion, demotion, appointment and dismissal of all members of the clan. *The Directory of Imperial Clansmen,*[5] a manuscript of four volumes giving data of every one of these fortunate few from the middle of the 16th century to the end of the 19th, records about seven hundred men of the clan with titles and position with all the titleless and positionless though pensioned excluded. It revised the complete record once every ten years.

A bureaucratic schedule of titles for the imperial clansmen shows twelve ranks with eight shades of difference dis-

[4] Practically every dynasty provided an office to take charge of the imperial clansmen.

[5] *Tsung Shih Wang Kung Chang Ching Shih Chi Cho Te Cha.*

THE NOBLES AND THE PRIVILEGED CLASSES 47

tinguishing some of the twelve for the males and seven for the females. A mixture of both Chinese and Manchurian languages was employed for both ranks and titles. Some Chinese titles were qualified by Manchu adjectives while for others Chinese or Manchu terms were adopted without change. When the Manchus occupied Peking, they retained the whole Chinese system, but incorporated some Manchu elements in it, thus making a superabundance of ranks, more numerous than any other system. These twelve ranks, as has been said, can be technically divided into twenty classes. There were six classes of princes; namely, Prince of Blood, (Chin Wang) Heir to a Princedom of Blood, (Shih Tse) Prince of a Princedom, (Chun Wang) Heir to a Prince of a Princedom, (Chang Tse) Fifth class Prince, (Bei Leh) and Sixth class Prince (Bei Tse); four classes of dukes, namely: the Cheng Kuo Duke and the Fu Kuo Duke "with the eight privileges" and the Cheng Kuo Duke and Fu Kuo Duke "without the eight privileges;"[6] ten classes of knights (Chang Chun); namely, three classes of Cheng Kuo knight, three classes of Fu Kuo knight, three classes of Feng Kuo knight and one class of Feng Un knight. For females, the daughter of the emperor and empress was Ko Lun princess; a daughter of the emperor and an imperial concubine, Ho Shih princess; daughters of princes and dukes, were called Chun Chu, Hsien Chu, Chun Chun, Hsien Chun, and Hsiang Chun, terms which, literally translated, would mean: matron of palace, matron of princedom, matron of district, lady of district, and lady of an estate respectively. The real demarcation between the high and the low nobles was the "eight privileges" which were granted to all kinds of princes and the first two classes of dukes, but not to the last two kinds of dukes and the knights. From the standpoint of service, possessors of the "eight privileges" rendered their service

[6] The "eight privileges" were: participation in conferences of state affairs; provision and support of a personal retinue by the government; to be present in the palace upon all state occasions, sacrificial ceremonies and banquets; and to be a beneficiary in all imperial largesses. All classes of princes had these privileges.

in court while those not possessing them belonged to a banner.

The records of the alternates were kept for the matrimonial purposes besides serving for the small allowances granted them by government. In this connection it should be remembered that Chinese custom forbade marriage of men and women having the same surname. The Manchus, after their conquest of the Middle Kingdom, making desperate efforts to live up to the traditional Chinese social laws, first adopted a policy of avoiding intermarriage among the descendants of Nurachi. This barrier was not broken down until the middle of the dynasty. During the last one hundred years, two or three Cho Los (Alternates) were married to emperors, of whom Empresses Dowager Tsu Hsi and Lung Yu were notable examples.

The privileges of the imperial clansmen meant far more than the possession of empty titles. To each prince a large house was given, and a good-sized retinue provided and supported with government allowances. The size of the household and the amounts of allowances for the retinue were scheduled with bureaucratic preciseness. Besides a piece of land [7] and an annual allowance in silver and rice [8] a special grant of one kind or another was made when it was desired to show the favor of the emperor to members of his own family. In cases of death, coronation, wedding, anniversary of the emperor, largesses in the form of curios, clothing, etc., were distributed to them. The allowances of the clanswomen consisted of silver, rice, and silk. Their husbands received a title or a rank.[9] The untitled clansmen or

[7] From 1,440 to 540 *mao* for a prince, 360 for a duke and 240 to 60 *mao* for a knight.

[8] 10,000 to 1,300 taels of silver for a prince, 700 to 500 for a duke, 410 to 110 for a knight; a number of *shih* of rice equal to the number of taels of silver was granted to the respective grades of clansmen.

[9] Husbands of princesses were made sixth class princes or dukes. Husbands of ladies got from first to the fifth rank according to the rank of the ladies.

THE NOBLES AND THE PRIVILEGED CLASSES 49

alternates received allowances from the government in silver and rice.[10]

With the exception of the eight "iron cap" princes whose titles were inherited in perpetuation as a recognition of their service in the conquest of China, titles of other princes were inherited in a hierarchic descendancy; the son of first class prince would become a fifth class prince, his son would be made only a duke and his grandson a knight. So, in nine generations, the direct male descend of a prince of blood would become an untitled clansman if imperial favor did not intereferer with the working of the regular schedule. The descendants of lower title holders become untitled earlier. But very often a title was made perpetual; still more often was its descending inheritance modified by imperial grace. In inheriting titles, besides the rule of primogeniture observed with as much strictness as circumstances allowed, the following rules were set down in an edict issued by Emperor Chien Lung in the 46th year of his reign [11] for the adoption of a successor by the sonless:—

1. The nearest male relative of the next generation shall be adopted.

2. A contract consenting to the adoption must be signed by the natural father of the adopted.

3. No successor can be adopted by a titular noble dying during his minority.

4. In case of the extinction of male line of the natural father, the adopted son can renounce the title and go back to the family of the natural father.

5. Government employees shall not be adopted.

6. A single son can succeed to two titles at the same time.

[10] 36 taels of silver and 45 *shih* of rice for a clansman; 24 taels of silver and 42.2 *shih* of rice for an alternate annually.

[11] *Ta Tsing Hui Tien Shih Li.*

As soon as a male succeeded to a title, even if he were a minor, he became automatically head of an independent family. Technically at least, no parental discipline could be applied to him.

Similar to the succession of the male was the marriage of the female since it brought a title or rank to the husband. Both succession and marriage were attended to by the Imperial Clan Court which kept a very strict set of rules for them. The emperor, of course, could take any case into his own hand, if he so chose. Princesses and ladies were never married to Chinese, except to the sons of the three Chinese princes at the beginning of the dynasty. Mongolian princes formed the primary source of recruitment of husbands for princesses and ladies. In fact, it was the policy of the government to encourage intermarriage between Mongols and Manchus on the one hand, and to prohibit intermarriage between the Chinese and either Manchus or Mongols on the other. A strong proof of government encouragement of Mongol-Manchu marriage were two stipulations: one providing for continuation or increase of the allowance of the princesses and ladies after marriage to a Mongol, the other for the termination of the pension after marriage to a Manchu. Indeed, by matrimonial bonds the Manchus sought to keep the Mongols as their allies and subordinates.[12] One of the functions of the Imperial Clan Court was to act as "go-between" in soliciting the intermarriage of influential Manchus and Mongols.

For the education and discipline of the clansmen, this court was responsible. Two schools, one for the clansmen and another for the alternates, were under the control of the court. A separate competitive examination for literary degrees was given to the noble candidates by the court. It also supervised their acquaintance and amusement, gave them advice, and directed them in their activities.

Back of this educational and disciplinary authority, was the court's judicial power over the delinquent classes of the

[12] See Chapter XII.

sturdy Manchus. It exercised two kinds of jurisdiction over the clansmen and alternates, one by itself, another concurrently with the Department of Revenue or War. All cases of minor misdemeanors were tried by the court alone which was empowered to impose punishment in the form of demotion of rank, fines in the form of reduction of allowance, whipping, or exile for thirty days or less. Concurrent jurisdiction was exercised with the Department of Revenue over all civil cases and with the Department of War over all criminal cases in which more serious punishments could be imposed. It shared with the Department of Civil Service in the choice and appointment of clansmen to civil posts.

At the beginning of the dynasty, the power, prestige and influence of the imperial clansmen were much greater than they later became, particularly those of the sons of the emperor. Their struggle for succession to the throne at the death of Emperor Tai Tsung and Emperor Kang Hsi evidenced their power. Gradually restrictions over them were created. Although no hard-and-fast rule can be cited against the princes' participation in state affairs, facts prove that it was distinctly the policy of the government to keep the clansmen out of politics. The first check was laid down by Emperor Yung Cheng, the victor of the struggle for the throne during Kang Hsi's reign. After his accession, some of his brothers were still scheming for his dethronement, though with only a forlorn hope. The emperor saw the danger of this kind of internal dissension to his own life as well as to the security of his house. With a masterful hand and unscrupulous methods he undertook to reduce the power and influence of his ambitious brothers by taking the command of the five lower banners out of their hands and placing it in his appointees. Then he issued a new law prohibiting communications between the princes and high provincial authorities, thus depriving them of their military power either in Peking or in the provinces. He accomplished this not without difficulty. But, by these drastic measures, he laid the foundation of his position and of the dynasty upon a firm basis; the end justified the harsh means. At the expense of the princes' influence, the danger of an internal strife was once for all removed. Emperor Chien Lung adopted a policy of secrecy for his son. He lived more than eighty years, ruled sixty, and dictated from behind the throne for several years. While he reigned, he let none of his sons know anything about state affairs though the oldest was already over forty years of age. Complete ignorance, in a way, certainly diminished their interest and influence.

In public documents, one often finds the statement that "Our dynasty allows no imperial clansmen to interfere with politics." This should be construed to mean that they were not allowed to exercise any of the emperor's powers, share his confidence, or participate in his formulation of policies; but not to mean disfranchisement from government appointments. On the contrary, a great many positions assigned to Manchus, as well as many high offices in the provinces not assigned to any race,[13] were occupied by the clansmen. They were, however, extremely carefully kept out of the Grand Secretariat: only three alternates were ever appointed to grand secretaryships in the whole dynasty,[14] and no clansman ever occupied a chair in the secretarial halls. In fact, after the reign of Emperor Shun Chi, the number of alternates became so great and the relationship so remote that the only bond between them and the emperor was a common ancestor and the drawing of a small pension. Tremendous caution was exercised to avoid appointing a clansman to the Council of State. Since the establishment of that powerful organization in 1730 down to the end of the 18th century the only appointee from the imperial clan was Prince Cheng in 1799. While the appointment took place on January the eighth, dismissal followed on December the twenty-second of the same year. The edict issued to dismiss Prince Cheng

---

[13] By law, no imperial clansmen shall be appointed to a province for a position lower than Judicial Commissioner.

[14] See *Chung Shu Tien Ko Li Chi.*

THE NOBLES AND THE PRIVILEGED CLASSES 53

from the Council shows the policy of the government up to the time of Chia Ching's reign:—

> Since the establishment of the Council of State, no prince of royal blood has been appointed to the office. Prince Cheng's appointment was meant to be only temporary owing to the great pressure of work. But, this, after all, is against the tradition and policy of our dynasty. Prince Cheng is hereby relieved of his duties in the Council.[15]

This policy was greatly altered in the latter part of the dynasty. Emperor Hsien Feng appointed Prince Kung Councilor in 1853. At the emperor's death in 1861, the same prince was appointed prince regent. During the reign of Kuang Hsu, Princes Ching and Yulang once sat together in the Council; the former being for many years ranking councilor. In Hsuan Tung's short reign, Prince Chun, the regent, tore up by its roots this splendid tradition. All key positions of the so-called cabinet [16] and the ranking seats of the Council of State were occupied not only by imperial clansmen, but by his closest family relatives, two of them being his brothers, one his uncle, and one his cousin.

All in all, the imperial clansmen's history in the dynasty was one of degeneration. They lost their old hardiness, absorbed the luxurious habits of the Chinese, failed to assimilate the better side of Chinese civilization, and became victims of the situation. An edict issued by Emperor Kuang Hsu in 1901 describes them in brief and yet accurate terms:—

> Since the beginning of the Imperial Dynasty, the number of serviceable men from the Imperial Clan has surpassed all other previous dynasties. All the Imperial Clansmen should abide by laws and add glories to the records of the clan. But, unfortunately, of late, the tendency is toward decadence. Those holding positions are affected by the bad atmosphere of officialdom. Their progressive spirit has waned. The Court of Imperial Clansmen is hereby ordered to notify all Imperial Clansmen to rid themselves of the bad influence and customs and try hard to be of

---

[15] *Shu Huan Chi Yiao.*

[16] Ministries of Finance, War and Navy among others.

service to the government. Those not holding positions often indulge themselves in loafing and are even influenced by political rebels and religious heresy and act fanatically without restraint. This is a disgrace to the Imperial Clan. The Court of Imperial Clan is hereby ordered to supervise them strictly and at all times. If there be those who voluntarily believe in political and religious heresies, heavy punishment shall be their lot."[17]

This edict, a reaction of the influence of revolutionary theory and Christian preaching, was issued to prevent their spreading. It described only very little of their clansmen's indolence and uselessness. Even very late in the dynasty, after the metropolitan police force was organized, the police found the imperial clansmen the greatest trouble-makers.

Next to the imperial clansmen, far less in rank, favor, prestige and pecuniary allowance, though far greater in merit, were the so-called nobles. The regular titles were five in number, with the Kung corresponding to the duke, the Hou corresponding to the Marquis, the Peh corresponding to the earl, the Tze corresponding to the viscount, and the Nan corresponding to the baron. Besides, there were four classes of minor nobles corresponding to the knights in England. Again, further subdivision made three grades of dukes, four grades of marquis, earl, viscount, baron and first class knight, two grades of second class knight, and one grade of third and fourth class knight, making thirty-one grades of nobles altogether. The regular nobles got for their annual allowance, from 700 taels of silver for a first grade duke to 260 for a fourth grade baron, plus a corresponding number of *shih* of rice. The knights' share varied from 235 taels of silver for first grade first class to 45 taels for fourth class with an equal number of *shih* of rice per year. Each received a piece of land varying in size with proportional advantage for the high title holders. Most of the titles were granted for merit in civil or military service; civil servants could not be given a title higher than viscount. Marriage to a princess would bring a title. One direct male descendant of Confucius and the Ming Emperor was made respec-

---

[17] *Tung Hua Lu*, Kuang Hsu, v. 165.

tively, a duke and a marquis. Each title was modified with adjectives; for instance, the loyal and brave duke, the respectful, persevering earl, etc. The right of inheriting the title varied. The fourth class knighthood was not inheritable; the third class knighthood could be inherited once, the next one twice; the next one thrice and so on. Each advance in grade entitled the holder to have it inherited one generation more until the top of the schedule, the first class duke, could have his dukedom inherited for twenty-six generations.

These nobles had no influence in society or politics. Also, not being organized as a class, they did not attract much attention. If they possessed any power or influence, it was not because of their title. A sale of this kind of title would have yielded as much to the government as the sale of office without disintegrating the civil service system. The Manchus jealously guarded against cheapening these titles. But, in spite of their effort, not much importance was ever attached to them.

A number of titular nobles could also be found in Mongolia and Tibet. These, however, were rather confirmed than given by the government, as most of them had position and prestige in their own localities, if not the actual title, before any favor of the Manchu emperor was shown them. These territorial titles, somewhat corresponding to Irish peerages in the British Empire, carried less honor, privilege and allowance. The whole policy of the government in granting these titles was to humor the recipients so that they would remain loyal to the Manchus.

A peculiar institution in the Tsing Dynasty which not only does not exist in any government outside of China, and which was unknown to the governments of the different Chinese dynasties, was the "eight Banners." These banners, starting as military units, became political subdivisions; yet, in spite of their transformation of character, their original military nature was jealously preserved. In time of peace they were political and localized units. By this is meant that a bannerman did not call himself a native of Peking or Canton, but, when inquired of as to his native place, would say "I am under such a banner." Again, in whichever city they might reside, they were quartered to themselves; in most cases, especially in Peking, men under a certain banner were quartered apart from those of other banners. In time of war, they were under obligation to render military service. Therefore the banner was a political as well as a military unit.

The banners originated when Emperor Hsien Tso divided all the soldiers under his command into four divisions distinguished from one another by the color of their banners. The first colors were yellow, white, red and blue. As the size of the army grew, expediency demanded further divisions: when they were split into eight. The new ones were bordered yellow, bordered white, bordered blue and bordered red. Red was used for the bordering color except the red which had white as bordering. The original four were bordered by white except the white which was bordered by red. These eight were divided into two groups, the bordered yellow, the yellow and the white formed the "upper three banners" and the other five formed the "lower five banners." Nominally, the emperor, but practically the commander of the Imperial bodyguards, had the command of the "upper three banners." The "lower five" which were further divided into three groups; namely, the vanguards, the city guards, and the infantry gendarmerie, were commanded by the princes of blood until Emperor Yung Cheng took it away from them and put it into the hands of imperial appointees. Princes received their military training from the "upper three banners."

The composition of the banners was a mixed one. Racially the Manchus, the Mongols and the Chinese formed the principal components. There was also a few thousand Mohammedans from Chinese Turkistan, several hundred Russians, and a number of Koreans. The Manchus formed the original component, the nuclei of the banners. Mongolian recruits came from voluntary registration, surrender after

THE NOBLES AND THE PRIVILEGED CLASSES   57

defeat, or conscription by the Manchu government after conquest. "The Chinese became bannermen in diverse ways," as Emperor Chien Lung says,[18] "Some followed our ancestors and fought through Shanhaikwan, some surrendered after the fall of Peking, some were degraded nobles, some used to be servants of princes and dukes, some were conscripted, some were taken into banner families as adopted sons while others came into the banners together with their relatives." The descendents of the royal family of the Ming dynasty were also put under the banners. The Manchus and Mongols had to continue being bannermen whether they liked it or not, while the Chinese had the right of renouncing their banners by naturalizing themselves in one of the provinces.

Although long peace, and, consequently, a lack of demand for soldiers, made the banners more political than military units, they remained military divisions to the last day of the Manchu supremacy. At the head of each banner, eight for each of the three principal races, was a general. (In Chinese, Tu Tung meaning general commander.) Under him were two colonels (in Chinese Tsan Ling meaning associate commander) in a Mongolian, and five in a Chinese or Manchurian banner. There were five to nine captains (in Chinese, Tso Ling, meaning assistant commander) in a Chinese, eleven to fifteen in a Mongolian, and fourteen to nineteen in a Manchurian regiment. The generals and colonels were appointed by the emperor and held office during his imperial pleasure. Many of the captaincies were hereditary, some were life appointments, and others had the post for three or five years. The power of dismissing or transferring even a hereditary captain was reserved to the emperor. In case of a hereditary captain's dismissal, usually a relative of the dismissed succeeded him. Life captaincies were divided into two types, those who surrendered with their followers, and those given followers on account of military valor. A captaincy consisted of 150 arms-bear-

[18] Edict of 1742 in *Pa Chi Tung Chi.*

ing adult males. When it exceeded the numerical limits, a redistribution would take place. Generally the number was smaller than required. The *Ta Tsing Hui Tien* gives the number of captaincies as follows:—

In Peking .... { a Manchus 681
b Mongols 204
c Chinese 266

Outside of Peking .... { a Garrisons 817
b Hunters 97
c Nomads 170

Total 2,235

The cardinal rule of appointing these captains was, like that of appointing other military officers, to appoint one of their own. Thus a Manchu company always had a Manchu captain, a Mongolian, a Mongol captain, etc. The only exception was that sometimes a Manchu was appointed to head a Chinese division.

The policy of the government towards the bannermen was two-folded: lavish grants of special privileges and encouragement of military service. The special privileges of the bannermen consisted of about fourteen million *mao* of land granted to 350,000 males of the original force, an average of forty *mao* each. The land came from the conquered Ming emperor, nobles, and the unclaimed land confiscated by a decree of Emperor Shun Chi in 1644. Lands for cemeteries, cattle raising and hunting were also granted. An annual pension of at least three taels per capita with cloth, rice and cotton made up the other means of subsistence. This amount looks very small, but, with land to work on, housing problem solved, regular grants of rice, cloth, and cotton, special grants on every occasion of birth, death, marriage or disaster, the government ever ready to show its kindness by extra gifts, and a very low standard of living, it was a competency. Yet the situation of the bannermen was not so enviable since the number of pensioned being more or less definite, many of the newly born had to be disfranchised

THE NOBLES AND THE PRIVILEGED CLASSES   59

or satisfied with a half portion. This pension too deprived the recipients of the right to trade or to labor. Half portion recipients, or even the disqualified, were not entitled to the rights common people had: hence, they were bound to be dependents. The pension was enough for one but not enough for the whole family. Worse than the heavy burden of supporting the unfortunate was the corruption of "squeeze" by men standing between the government and the recipients. The edict of Emperor Kuang Hsu issued in January, 1902 [19] verifies this:—

..... Nowadays, in spite of the fact that the Treasury is extraordinarily empty, the pension of the bannermen is still given in percentage. But, much to my surprise, the wicked colonels and captains usually discount the allowance of the privates or get allowance for themselves in the name of widows or orphans and practice all sorts of corruption. ......

With the price of things going up and the corruption of officers to reduce the amount, a sufficient livelihood for the bannermen became a matter of desire during the latter part of the Manchu Dynasty.

As far as the civil service went, the same code and the same bureaucratic system nominally applied to all. But the substantial difference and advantage of the bannermen came from the fact that official positions reserved for both Manchus and Chinese could be taken by the Manchurian and Chinese bannermen. Punishment for banner officers was usually lighter and reward higher than in the case of the Chinese forces. For them entrance to officialdom was easier, promotion quicker, and the number of qualified men compared to the number of positions reserved much smaller. Most important of all, in a government like that of the Manchu Dynasty, personal element counted most; those who helped the Tsing Emperors to conquer China were naturally looked upon with favor. In competitive examinations, the regular and principal way of qualifying for official positions, they were separated from the Chinese. The theory of this

[19] *Tung Hua Lu*, Kuang Hsu, v. 171, p. 23.

separation argued that the Chinese exceeded the bannermen in literary, while the bannermen exceeded the Chinese in military, accomplishments. This plausible argument so benefited the bannermen that sometimes even the formal processes of examinations were not necessary for them as they did not have enough candidates to win all degrees provided for. In taxation, a sort of half reduction was applied to the bannermen; not infrequently, even this half reduction was not collected. Finally, the Manchu and Mongolian bannermen practically monopolized the royal marriage market with princesses and princes. The restriction against intermarriage between the Manchus and the Chinese was not removed among comrades in the battlefield. Rarely did a Chinese and a Manchu bannerman become relatives by matrimonial bonds.

As the bannermen, as a class, had advantages over the Chinese, so within themselves, one group was preferred to another. The Manchus always got the best; the Mongols next, and the Chinese shared the worst. Take land for instance; almost 10,000,000 *mao* were granted to 200,000 Manchus; about 2,300,000 to 65,000 Mongols; and only a little more than 2,000,000 to 81,000 Chinese. Upon the average, a Manchu got about 50, a Mongol 35, and a Chinese 25 *mao* each. In the grant of rice, cloth, cotton or anything else, a proportional difference always existed. In pensions, a graduated scale varying from 48 taels for a Manchu to 3 taels for a Chinese private bannerman existed; the most highly paid Chinese received only three-fourths of what his Manchu comrade did.

In consideration of these grants, the bannermen were always under obligation to the government for military service. This noble obligation prohibited them from taking anything outside of government employment as their work. Trade, a low profession in Chinese society, became a forbidden vocation for the bannermen, partly because it would hurt the dignity of these privileged peoples and partly because of their abuse in the trade. Before the prohibition law, the bannermen traded in the name of the prince by whom they were commanded. They capitalized their advantageous position to a great extent by bringing their prince's influence to bear, which resulted to the great disadvantage of the common people. It was also believed that this restriction, together with many others, was introduced by Hung Cheng Chou, an able grand secretary of the Ming Dynasty who surrendered to the Manchus after being captured in war shortly before the complete fall of the Ming Dynasty. Hung, being loyal to Ming at heart, waited for an opportunity to restore the native dynasty. Knowing the strength of the Manchus and the weakness of the Chinese, he saw little hope for the immediate overthrowing of the conquerors; hence he turned to schemes for their expulsion in the course of time. This regulation was meant for the enervation of the sturdy bannermen.

Whatever the reason, prohibition of the bannermen to labor and trade certainly did a great deal to enervate them. Being constantly supplied with reliable sources of income, and forbidden to work, no wonder they became too stupid for civil, and too cowardly for military, service. The number of government positions was limited; the price of things went gradually up; the size of the banner population grew; the amount of land and money available for their livelihood remained the same; how could they continue to lead a life of economic sufficiency? The notorious squeeze of the Mandarins helped further to reduce the amount. Towards the end of the dynasty, the pension had become a kind of small Christmas gift on which not even the most frugal could live. Effort after effort to improve the situation resulted, at the best, in merely temporary effect, and for a very small portion of the populace. Emperor Chien Lung took a wise step when he allowed Chinese bannermen to naturalize themselves in the provinces, thus removing their legal disqualification to trade or labor. But the allurement of privileges and the distinction of being in a banner seemed to most too much a sacrifice to make. Long idleness had made them unfit for a vigorous and honest mode of earning a living; and the imperial decree produced no result. In the later period of the dynasty, we find nobles and soldiers converted into beggars, ricksha drivers, and servants and the aristocrats became the plebeians.

Other protective measures like the law prohibiting them to sell their lands, houses or anything,[20] the permission to continue the ownership of their land after naturalization in the provinces, and frequent redistribution of land among themselves, all failed to remedy the situation. At the end of the 19th century, Yu Lu, a grand councilor of state and a bannerman, described the incompetency of the bannermen in the government service [21] in his memorial to the emperor from which the following quotation is taken:

. . . . . The Imperial Dynasty appoints to its service both Manchus and Chinese alike. The number of appointees is about equal. Most of the Chinese are recruited from the examinations. They may not be really so serviceable, but with their theoretical foundation in the confucian classics, it is easy for them to acquire new knowledge of government. Among the Manchus, very few came from the examinations, that means very few have the foundation of the knowledge of Chinese political theory and institutions. A handful of the Manchus are appointed from the examinations for translators. They take a great deal of pride in their ability to translate and are very reactionary. Moreover, the long practiced corruption of examinations have created a situation where there is no means to discover talents though the need of it be urgent. Hence, when a vice-minister comes to the roll of the secretarial staff, he feels the lack of qualified men. The professional office-seekers take advantage of the situation. The appointive authority thinks it harmless to give him an unimportant position without knowing that some day, by virtue of seniority, accident or influence, he may be promoted to a responsible position. . . . . .[22]

[20] These things were confiscated if sold.

[21] Practically all Manchus in Government service were bannermen.

[22] *Tung Hua Lu*, Kuang Hsu, v. 142, p. 19.

THE NOBLES AND THE PRIVILEGED CLASSES 63

So great was the deteriorating effect of this enervating institution that the need for reforms was felt and a cry for it now and then widely heard. Yet no radical change was brought about until in the famous Hundred-day reform, when Emperor Kuang Hsu repealed this time-honored law, conferred on them the right of trading and laboring, put them under the jurisdiction of the local magistrate and virtually abolished the class itself.

As has been said, the eight banners were primarily military units and to them a great deal of encouragement in military service was always given. Let us now find out further about these military organizations. The first treatment of military character by the government was the population census. Originally the census of the population was taken once every ten years; its purpose being to revise the tax scale. But, with bannermen, a census was taken once every three years. In this census, every male not holding a government position was carefully examined. All over fifteen years of age or five feet and six inches in height were specially registered. In connection with this census, an examination of the captains was conducted. The increase or decrease of the number of men in military age and height formed the basis of reward or punishment for the respective captains.

The city of Peking was filled with bannermen. "When Emperor Shun Chi entered Peking, he quartered the eight banners in the metropolis to guard his own palaces; the yellow banner on the north, the white on the east, the red on the west and the blue on the south." The infantry gendarmes kept peace and order inside Peking. Numerous other military units were stationed at different quarters for the protection of the palaces and the residences of the princes. Outside of, and not far from, Peking, garrisons were maintained in nine districts, six to its south and three to its north, encircling the seat of the precious dragon throne. A strong garrison was kept in Shanhaikwan through which the Manchus made their entrance. Between Shanhaikwan and Peking, banner troops were quartered in four district cities to keep their road of retreat back to Manchuria clear in case of emergency. Peking, then, was entirely surrounded by bannermen, the only exception being a few hundred of the imperial bodyguards chosen from the successful Chinese candidates in the military examinations. They, however, did not undergo a change in number, trust, and influence with the bannermen. The only purely Chinese soldiers one could find in the Manchu Dynasty were the "Green Battalions" stationed in the provinces for local order.

Yet, side by side with the local forces, we find the banner soldiers in Chihli, Shantung, Shansi, Honan, Kiangsi, Chekiang, Fukien, Kuangtung, Hunan, Hupeh, Chekiang, Szechuan, Shensi, Kansu, and Sinkiang. The object of this was not for local protection, as the "Green Battalions" were there for that purpose; nor was it for defense against external aggressions, since most of the places were in the heart of the country and external danger was something unknown to China two hundred and fifty years ago. It was "for suppression of the local troubles" as Emperor Chien Lung declared in his edict issued in 1750. Emperor Shun Chi also says in his edict of 1646 that "recently bandits have sprung up in some parts of Chihli, Shantung, Shansi, and Kiangsu. I thereupon ordered some of the Manchu troops to be stationed in the prefectures of Shun Teh, Chi Nan, Teh Chow, Lin Ching, Kiang Pei, Chu Chow, Lo An, Ping Yang, and Pu Chow." By "bandits" and "local troubles," he meant political uprisings against the Manchus. Even the revolutionary parties that tried to overthrow the dynasty were always designated as "bandits" in public documents until the very last few decrees issued shortly before the outbreak of Wuchang in 1911. The garrisons, in fact, served as a check against the Chinese troops and the Chinese civil authorities. Although the viceroy or governor was legally the commander-in-chief of the provincial troops, the banner forces never came under his control. The quartering of garrisons usually took place after the suppression of a local uprising. In one and the same place, Manchurian and

THE NOBLES AND THE PRIVILEGED CLASSES   65

Chinese bannermen were often found stationed together seemingly to check each other.

The garrisons almost always occupied the most fertile part of a province. A section of the city was mapped out for their residence, for they brought their families with them. A big part of the cultivable land was given to them for farming while they were not needed for war. Emperor Chien Lung ordered the employment of government funds for the purchase of real estate for them.

A study of the location of these garrisons will convince one that the purpose of these garrisons, besides serving as spies on the provincial authorities, and acting as a check on the local forces, was to keep China subdued. First, they were maintained in all coastal provinces like Shantung, Kiangsu, Chekiang, Fukien, and Kuangtung. Secondly, a straight line was cut from the capital to the south by land in the interior through the provinces of Shansi, Honan and Hupeh. Thirdly, in the western part of the country, a concave leaning towards the capital formed the shape of the garrisons.[23] A map of the garrisons will show that they formed a circle in China with a diameter cutting right through the center of the circle. Strategic positions they were. Had the Chinese civilization not been so captivating, and their own regulations not so enervating, they would have been able to keep the Chinese under their surveillance as long as they were not ousted by force.

In judicial matters, the Tartar-general, not the local magistrate, tried cases involving the bannermen. The lack of jurisdiction over them by the local authority, idleness, economic insufficiency, all combined to make the presence of the garrison a public nuisance to the community wherever they were stationed. Worst of all, in a case of dispute, the banner authority was usually too lenient to punish them and thus denied the people justice.

We find here a group of people with distinctive legal privileges, but social and financial handicaps. It was too large

[23] In Shensi and Szechuan.

a group and had too little privilege to be nobles, yet it had far more rights and privileges than the commons, a peculiar class. Starting as a sturdy race of warriors, they became entirely enervated in the course of time. They were sent to the provinces for the suppression of local troubles; yet, from Emperor Yung Cheng, the third emperor in China, though numerous uprisings took place, hardly a single one of them was suppressed by the bannermen. The greatest rebellion, the Taiping, was entirely put down by the Chinese. The most fatal of them, the revolution of 1911, succeeded because the Chinese refused any longer to help the Manchus. Though become useless they kept on drawing their pensions and remained a privileged class until the dynasty itself perished.

STATISTICS OF THE EIGHT BANNERS

The city of Peking	118,783
At service of the Imperial Household	4,571
In the surroundings of Peking	74,192
In the surroundings of Peking	1,016
Imperial Tombs guards	5,252
Ma Lan Chen	926
Tai Ning Chen	2,975
Mongolian Bannermen in Jehol	57,758
Under the command of Commander of Chihli troops	532
Tsihar	12,980
Garrisons at Mie Yun	1,935
Garrison at Shanhaikwan	1,949
Garrison at Nanking	1,816
Garrison at Ching Chow	2,405
Garrison at Sui Yuan Cheng	2,765
Garrison at Sianfu	3,898
Garrison at Ning Hsa	607
Garrison at Liang Chow	794
Garrison at Ili	13,214
Garrison at Foochow	2,284
Garrison at Kingchow	6,092
Garrison at Chengtu	3,857
Garrison at Kwangchow	10,638
Total	334,251

THE NOBLES AND THE PRIVILEGED CLASSES 67

Figures taken from second census of the Department of Public Welfares (Min Cheng Pu) published in the *Official Gazette*, July 19, 1911. The "Hu" (household) is the unit.

The total population of the Chinese Empire is 62,484,265 "Hu" or households in the same census. The banner population is a little more than one-half per cent of the total.

CHAPTER IV

IMPORTANT ORGANIZATIONS IN THE CENTRAL GOVERNMENT

I. THE GRAND SECRETARIAT (NEI KO)

Aside from, and above, the six regular departments,[1] was the Grand Secretariat. Instituted by Emperor Tai Tso of the Ming Dynasty in 1382, this office had all the rank, honor and privileges of the ancient premiership though not the powers. The premiership was substituted by the Secretariat for the purpose of controlling the officials. After the succession to throne was made a family affair in the Sha Dynasty (2205-1766 B. C.), the people were given whatever emperor the reigning family happened to have. Yet the loss as made good by the preservation of the premiership which, usually occupied by a wise and able minister, matched, if not exceeded, the power and influence of the emperor himself.[2] It indeed served as an effective check on the dignity and power of the "Son of Heaven." The purpose of its abolition was to control absolutely the officials in government, so that whoever pleased the emperor remained and whoever displeased him was dismissed. "The lack of good government in the Ming Dynasty originated with the abolition of the premier."[3] This change consolidated all the powers of the premier into the hands of the emperor. The work of the abolished office was divided among five

---

[1] For Department of Civil Service, see Chapter V; Department of Revenue, see Chapter VII; Department of Rites, see Chapter VI; Department of War, see Chapter X; Department of Justice, see Chapter VIII; and the Department of Works, see Chapter X.

[2] Great respect was shown to the premier in ancient times. All officials at court had to salute him when they saw him. The emperor had to rise from his throne to receive him when he entered, and alight from his sedan chair in case the premier were met on the street. (See Essay on Premier by Huang Li Chou.)

[3] Huang Li Chou: *Essay on the Premiership.*

ORGANIZATIONS IN CENTRAL GOVERNMENT

Grand Secretaries, one for each Palace. The most important effect of this change was that the Grand Secretaries were not given the power to make their decisions final; that is, everything had to be marked by the vermilion pencil before going into effect.

The Manchus inherited this, besides almost everything else, from the Ming emperors. Prior to their entrance into China, they had the "three interior offices" each headed by a Grand Secretary. Various changes took place in organization as to the number of Grand Secretaries, assistants, rank, personnel, proportional division of offices between the Manchus and Chinese, etc., until in 1748 Emperor Chien Lung fixed the rank of the Grand Secretaries at 1a, the number of Grand Secretaries at six (four regulars and two associates), and the racial proportion three for each. "There is no difference in rank between the different Grand Secretaries, but the leader is always a Manchu."[4] A number of assistant secretaries and clerks of diverse grades attending to the routine work was provided. The organization and practice of this office differed from others as described by Heng Shih Chun in his Preface to the *History of the Grand Secretariat (Chung Shu Tien Ku Li Kao)*.[5]

In the departments and courts, officials treat one another as superiors and subordinates; but, here, no such thing happens. The Grand Secretary, the highest official in government, treats a rankless clerk as a teacher does a pupil . . . . . All other officials have seals, but the Grand Secretaries do not . . . . . The departments and courts have auxiliary officials and underclerks; but no such thing exists in the Secretariat. Officials in other services are graded by rank, for instance, right and left [6] but seniority in service is the only rank in this office . . . . .

This kind of arrangement made the service typically Chinese.

[4] Wu Ao, *Notes on the Grand Secretariat*.
[5] This book was written by Wang Shih Kung.
[6] In the Tsing government, two officials of the same rank were almost always designated, instead of with the words first and second or senior and junior, by the words left and right with the former a senior to the latter: hence a promotion was literally designated as "left transference."

The Grand Secretaries had two kinds of duties, general and specific. Under the first head they issued edicts for the emperor, assisted him in seeing that all officials properly discharged their particular functions, and that all laws were faithfully executed: in short, they helped the emperor in the general management of the state affairs. Under the second head, they had first the ceremonial functions. In the presentation of an Imperial ancestral tablet, they chose the title, supervised the engraving, and initiated the ceremonies. In state sacrifices, they drafted the eulogy, oration, or prayers and conducted the performance. In succession, coronation, wedding, funeral or anniversary celebrations of the emperor's birthday, or appointment of a plenipotentiary general for invasion, they determined the ceremonial program and acted as masters of ceremonies. In the presentation to the emperor of the new Metropolitan graduates (Chin Shih) for the maiden audience, they acted as ushers. In fact, on all ceremonies and formal occasions of state, they were the highest authority. Their second duty related to state documents. They drafted all edicts, manifestos, and declarations for the emperor. They transmitted communications from the ministers to the emperor and vice versa, had the privilege of passing remarks on the merits and defects of the memoranda, and were allowed to suggest a decision on a petitioned subject before submitting it for the final verdict unless the emperor had specified his inability or unwillingness to take suggestions on a particular petition. If the emperor gave a decision independently of the Grand Secretaries, they would keep a record of it. Thirdly, they acted as custodians of the state and imperial seals. They stamped the seals on important state documents, and carried them for the emperor when His Majesty was on a journey. Finally, they were responsible for the conferring of appropriate posthumous titles upon deceased emperors, empresses, nobles, meritorious officials and scholars. This list of varied activities seems to have made them assistant general managers of the state; yet, in the Chinese government, where paper provision was subjected to frequent change at Imperial pleasure, we find that "nominally they administered all state affairs, yet practically, they only read memoranda and reported on them."[7]

Sometimes, as we have seen, the emperor wrote the prescript on the memoranda. In this case it would be returned directly to the author for execution or abandonment without going through the hands of the Grand Secretaries. Were it given to "the six departments" or "the nine ministers"[8] for discussion, it would have to go through the Secretariat. When a document was drawn up by the Secretariat, it would go through twelve hands before making its official appearance. Wu Ao, describes the steps as follows in his Notes on the Grand Secretariat: *(Nei Ko Chi)*

> In drafting a document, a clerk reads the document and drafts the first copy, then the readers go through the details in both wording and form. One of the Grand Secretaries approves it. The clerk then puts the approved draft in the "draft book." The draft is then sent to the Manchu Record Office where a translation into the Manchurian language is made. The next day, the Manchurian clerk presents the draft copy in a "red book" to the emperor. His Majesty reads it and writes a postscript. The Manchu clerk takes it back to the Secretariat. A Chinese clerk records the Imperial postscript on the cover of the document. The draft is then sent to the Chinese Record Office. Another Chinese records it in another book and files it. Next, it is sent to the copying office. From this office the document goes directly to its final destination.

[7] Wu Ao, *Notes on the Grand Secretariat, Nei Ko Chi.*

[8] By the nine chief ministers, (Chiu Ching) it meant ministers of the six departments, the censors-general, the director of the Office of Transmission and the director of the Grand Court of Revision. The nine junior ministers (Siao Chiu Ching) consisted of the censor-general, Directors of the Office of Transmission, Grand Court of Revision, Court of Sacrificial Worships, Court of Imperial Entertainments, the Imperial Stud, Court of State Ceremonies, the Academy of Letters and the Imperial College. When an edict says "the nine ministers," it means the nine chief ministers; but when it says the "six departments and the nine ministers," the nine junior ministers are meant.

These twelve steps gave the clerks of the Secretariat much more work than was necessary. On this account the secretaries kept a twenty-four-hour service by dividing themselves into turns, "a day turn and a night turn. If the number of clerks were large, they would be divided into three turns. Clerks of the lower grades usually took the night turn." By handling documents, the Grand Secretaries had an opportunity to influence the emperor. Only officials of the the third rank or above had the privilege of directly addressing the emperor. Whenever they did so, they usually embodied their initiated measure, suggestion, or advice in a memorial and then sent it to the emperor. The paper, however, had to go through the Grand Secretariat before reaching the throne. Were it unacceptable to the white-headed dignitaries, they could pass a very unfavorable judgment on it and send both the original and their opinion to the emperor at the same time. A more drastic measure could also be applied: they could retain it at the Secretariat after it had had the fortune of reaching the emperor. One of the following results might be reached:

1. An edict could be issued for the execution of the plan.

2. It might be rejected and the memorandum "thrown back" to the author.

3. The emperor might give the memorandum to the Secretariat or the six departments "for discussion;" the recommendation of this conference was usually accepted by the emperor. In case the memorandum was sent to the Secretariat, the Grand Secretaries could recommend it "to be detained," that meant, to be thrown into a remote corner of the office and to let the petition die a natural death. It is said that this was a very common treatment of the unwelcomed petitions.

4. Sometimes, though rather seldom, a special form of edict called "The Secretarial decree" (Piao Chi) was directly issued by the Grand Secretaries from the Secretariat, on

the Secretariat's stationery, without going through the trouble of winning the mark of the vermilion pencil. This form of document "originated during the Ming Dynasty when Emperor Ying Tsung ascended the throne at the age of nine without the help of either a *de facto* or a *de jure* regent. The boy-emperor asked the advice and consent of his mother as to almost everything. Fearing that she might become absolute, being ignorant of the affairs of state, and barred by the house laws of the dynasty against a feminine regency, she gave the matters over to the Secretariat, which, after a conclusion of the matters was reached, issued edicts in imperial style but on the Secretariat's stationery.[9] This was certainly an exceptional case that might not happen, in fact, did not happen, in the Tsing Dynasty, yet the power of the Secretaries to kill measures was indeed greater than that of any official except the emperor himself.

Another source of their power came from their nearness to the throne and the frequent audiences given them by the emperor. Although none of the Secretariat offices was within the Palace precincts, yet the furthermost of them was much nearer to the crown than the nearest of any other office of importance.

Then too their advanced age, and the high position from which they were promoted to the Secretariat gave them prestige over their colleagues. The government made a position in the Secretariat the Mecca of a mandarin's political pilgrimage. Besides the viceroys, only ministers of the six departments or censors-general could be appointed Grand Secretaries. By the time one reached the position of a department minister, censor-general or viceroy, he had already climbed to the top of the service ladder with a long service record invoking the envy as well as commanding the respect of those tottering behind. Again, the strict rule was applied, to Chinese at least, that only metropolitan gradu-

[9] Sun Cheng Che, *Tsung Ming Meng Yu Lu*.

ates could be appointed Grand Secretaries.[10] The glory of literary success in the past and the pressure of political influence in the present combined to make the Imperial errand boys shining stars of the Mandarinate. Incidentally, it may be mentioned, this was the only high organization to which the evil influence of political commercialism did not penetrate.

Fourthly, their long term of service equipped them with great skill to utilize not only their legitimate powers but their cunning as a means to obtain benefits for themselves. The regular tenure of office in the Chinese government was three years though to the same office one might be re-appointed at the end of the first term thus making the term six years. However, under ordinary circumstances, nine out of ten were promoted, demoted, transferred, or dismissed, in short, would have a change. The Grand Secretaryship, as we have seen, was the highest office in the Government, so that occupants of this position had no further promotion. Also the emperor, on account of the dignity and importance of the office, would appoint only his confidential men to this office. Hence, it was not necessary for him to change them often as in them he had confidence. Whatever else might be the reason, statistics from an authoritative work on the office [11] show us the record of 117 out of 127 [12] Grand Secretaries who served between 1644 and 1773: one held the office for over thirty years; two over twenty-five years; four over

---

[10] In the *History of The Grand Secretariat (Chung Shu Tien Ku Li Kao)* by Wang Cheng Kung, we find the data of sixty-three Chinese appointed to the Secretariat from 1644-1773. Everyone of them without exception, had the metropolitan degree. The records of fourty-nine Manchus and fifteen Chinese bannermen show that five of the former and three of the latter were metropolitan graduates, three Manchus were provincial graduates, while thirty-nine Manchus and eleven Chinese bannermen had no degree at all.

[11] *Chung Shu Tien Ku Li Kao*, by Wang Cheng Kung.

[12] Data concerning the other ten were not given in that book.

twenty; and twenty-four over ten years. The average length of service of a Secretary was eight years and nine months, a surprisingly good record as far as length of service is concerned.

Finally, their power derived from the holding of concurrent positions must not be overlooked. As they were appointed only from ministers of departments, censors-general or viceroys, after their appointment to the Secretaryship, their original positions were still retained. The origin of concurrent positions for these venerable mandarins is of historical interest:—

In 1655, Grand Secretary Chan Ming Sha was appointed concurrently the Minister of Civil Service. This marked the beginning of a Grand Secretary holding concurrently a position of a ministership of a department. In 1645, Minister Hung Cheng Chou was given the title "to assist in all affairs of state:" this was the beginning of Associate Grand Secretaryship.[13] In 1689, Grand Secretary Hsu Yuan Wan was appointed concurrently Supervising Director of the Academy of Letters: this was the beginning of a Grand Secretary directing the Academy.[14]

Being almost a matter of accident, the tradition of concurrent positions for the Grand Secretaries did not survive without a struggle. A short sketch of its ups and downs may be seen from a paragraph in the *History of the Grand Secretariat:*[15]

Before the reign of Emperor Yung Cheng, most of the Grand Secretaries had the concurrent position of a ministership of a department. This practice was abolished at the beginning of the Chien Lung regime. But it was soon revived. In the second year of Chien Lung (1737), Grand Secretary Chang Ting Yu first concurrently directed the Academy of Letters, then took charge of the Departments of Civil Service and Revenue. Later Shih Wan Cheng held the concurrent position of Minister of Works;

[13] Minister Hung was also the first Grand Secretary appointed to a viceroyalty.

[14] Tsao Chia An, Short Notes on the Appointment and Dismissals of Grand Secretaries, *Tsai Fu Pai Pa Hsiao Chi.*

[15] *Chung Shu Tien Ku Li Kao*, by Wang Cheng Kung, p. 45, v. 1.

Chen Wan Chin that of Minister of Ceremonies; Lai Wan Tuan that of Minister of War; Fu Tsung Yung those of Ministers of Civil Service and Revenue. Also Ko Wan Chin and Tsiang Wan Lo became Associate Grand Secretaries from the ministerships of Justice and Revenue respectively without being relieved of their ministerial duties. At that time, all the positions of the six ministers were held concurrently by the six Grand Secretaries. Later Tsiang was promoted to full secretaryship with the same concurrent positions.

From that time on, scarcely a Grand Secretary was without a concurrent post. Civil Service laws demanded that in case a man held concurrent positions, one must be the principal and the other subordinate positions. "The Grand Secretaries, being given the first rank by Emperor Yung Ching, ... became the most dignified and highest ranking officials of the Government. If they, at the same time held the position of a minister, the ministership would be the concurrent position, hence subordinate to the secretaryship." [16] This is why in the 7th year of Yung Cheng (1729), the emperor ordered the Grand Secretaries to attend to the Secretarial duties before everything else.[17] In this case only one exception was made. "During Yung Cheng's reign, an uprising in the far away provinces necessitated the organization of the Council of State. Three Grand Secretaries were appointed Councilors. They, on account of the urgent business in the Council, could no longer go to the Secretariat. Later, the drafting of edicts and writing of rescripts on the memorials were done by a few selected members of the Secretarial staff inside the Palace precincts. The Grand Secretaries selected were excused from attending to secretarial duties, thus technically making their position in the Secretariat a subordinate one." [18] This was the only instance where a concurrent position, on account of the importance of its business, succeeded in subordinating the original duties of the Grand Secretaries. But, as we shall

[16] Wu Ao, *Notes on the Grand Secretariat, Nei Ko Chi.*
[17] See edict in *Shu Huan Chi Yiao*, v. 1, p. 12.
[18] Wu Ao, *Notes on the Grand Secretariat, Nei Ko Chi.*

ORGANIZATIONS IN CENTRAL GOVERNMENT 77

see, the Council of State was established, to a certain extent, as a substitute for the Secretariat. The powers of the Council were formerly exercised by the Grand Secretaries. The very act of appointing three Secretaries to the Council when first organized made a change of the shadow without change of substance. As the Councilors were given no rank, it is doubtful whether, with their political advantages, they were technically superiors to the old dignitaries. In later times, as well as at the beginning of the Council, Grand Secretaries always had a majority in the Council, again exercising their old powers and enjoying their privileges and favors only under a new name.

Mention must be made that a number of high posts in the Manchu Government were specially designated as concurrent posts of the Grand Secretaries to be held by them and by them alone.

The Council of State (Chun Chi Chu)

The only institution of any consequence in the Manchu Government which is not a residue of the old Chinese political organization is the Council of State. It was established in 1730 by Emperor Yung Cheng to assist him in the suppression of local uprisings of that time. The grand secretaries were too far away from the palace precincts for the constant conference demanded by the situation. The emperor established an office situated inside of his sacred precincts. As the grand secretaries had different individual offices for themselves, it was a nuisance to gather them for conference when the urgency of the business might press for immediate action. Furthermore, the geographic separation of the Grand Secretariat from the palaces made it inconvenient for the emperor to control the government absolutely. So, he organized this council to get the power he wanted; for, though this organization was meant for military purpose, to put down the uprisings, yet, after peace and order were restored, it survived the purpose for which it came into existence. The powers of the council were taken from the Grand Secretariat. As the creation of the Grand Secretariat followed the abolition of the premiership which was a device of the Ming emperors to acquire absolute control of the government, this council was established as a substitute for the secretariat. The substitution brought forth a further division of powers between the important officials and put the councilors in one and the same office right under the nose of the emperor. Indeed, it is quite reasonable to believe that no emperor of other dynasties in China ever practiced so much personal control of state affairs as the Manchu emperors did.

The establishment of this important office was a long sought-for object, and was accomplished with a pretext of emergency. Both its name and duties serve to sustain this contention. Take its name first. In 1730, when it was first established, it was named *Chun Chi Fang,* or the Military Cabinet. In 1736, Emperor Chien Lung changed it to *Chung Li Chu,* meaning Office of General Administrations. Right here we are reminded of the original purpose of its establishment and also of the historical fact that the uprisings were then already suppressed: if the purpose of its establishment were what it had been claimed, it had outlived its usefulness. But it remained. In 1739, upon the request of the "Princes and Ministers," the name *Chun Chi Chu,* literally Military Cabinet, was restored. The name continued until 1805, when censor Ho Yuan Liang petitioned for a change. "According to his petition, the Council was then performing general executive duties, hence it should not be designated as a Military Cabinet. Moreover, war being over, if the organization were maintained, its name should be changed so that the Government would not be mistaken for a Government by force." [19] In response to this petition, Emperor Chia Cheng issued an edict with a definition of its name. It says:—

> The name of the Council, however, originated during the reign of Emperor Yung Cheng. It has been in use for a long time.

[19] *Shu Huan Chi Loh.*

All duties it performs are of great importance. The term *Chun Chi*, Military Affairs, corresponds to the phrase *Chun Kuo Ta Shih*, State and Military Affairs of Significance, in previous dynasties. It by no means aims at military policy and tactics alone.[20]

Since this authoritative refutation of the definition of that name, no important change of name has been made. The latest edition of the *Ta Tsing Hui Tien* gives the official title of the Council as *Pan Li Chun Chi Chu*, meaning The Office in Charge of Military Affairs.

Having now a comprehensive background of its history and name, it well becomes us to find out its duties. It had the all-embracing duty of giving general assistance to the emperor on important military and political affairs. Specifically stated, they were to be ready for audience with the emperor at any time. This was carried so far that even when the emperor was on furlough, hunting, or a visit, the Councilors had to follow him wherever he went. Secondly, they read, transmitted, wrote rescripts and kept memorials for the emperor. Thirdly, they recorded what the emperor wanted to do. Fourthly, they were responsible for advice to their master on military roads, army equipment, expenditures and everything pertaining to the army. Fifthly, they were to submit a list of qualified candidates for appointment of officials of, or above, the 3rd rank, if so requested. Finally, they might be asked to give questions for the Palace or Metropolitan Examinations. Their general duty and the first of their specific duties seem to be noticeably in conflict with those of the Grand Secretaries. But, as far as memorials and edicts went, a paragraph from the *Shu Huan Chi Loh* settles all the doubt:—

Four kinds of mandates are issued by the emperor. First, Rescripts in the memorials of either the Metropolitan or provincials officials. Second, Orders to Generals of garrisons, Viceroys, Governors, Educational Commissioners, Commanders of Provincial forces, or Military Commissioners to urge the collection of taxes. These are drafted by the Grand Secretaries. Third, Sacrificial speeches, eulogies and orations for all ceremonial occasions.

[20] Edict of Chia Cheng, 1805.

These, though nominally written by the Grand Secretaries, are drafted by the members of the Academy of Letters. Fourth, Original Mandates issued at the initiative of the emperor before a visit to some place, a performance of sacrifice to an Imperial Mausoleum, on relief works, of appointments, dismissals, or transference of a Metropolitan official above a vice-minister or a provincial official above a prefect: these are called "Open Mandates." Then giving instruction, advice or warning, ordering an investigation or a review of a judicial decision: these are called "Mail Mandates." Both of these are drafted by the Councilors. "Open Mandates are given to the Grand Secretaries who send them forth to their ultimate recipients. The "Mail Mandates" are sent to the respective recipients directly from the Council.[21]

By this division of labor the seriousness of conflict of authority was greatly reduced. Another factor in smoothing down the friction of these two venerable offices was the concurrent position system. When both offices were held by the same group of persons, it did not make any difference to which one of their two offices one or another duty belonged: they have to do it just the same. Finally, the greatest cause of harmonious action between these conflicting organizations was the fact that the ultimate authority belonged to the emperor. Both of them, we should remember, were only to assist him: neither of them bore individual or institutional responsibility for whatever they might do. The practical result of this theoretical basis was that the one most in the emperor's favor would have the greatest gain whether to get a privilege or to get rid of a duty.

The Council had neither permanent office nor specific officials. Its first abode was outside, and to the west of, Chien Tsing Gate. Later, it was moved inside the Gate and next to the South Study of the emperor. A building on the west side of the Lung Chung Gate used to be the lodging and boarding place of the secretaries of the Council on night duty. Without a fixed number of officials, there was a tradition, the ranking member was always a Manchu. Some Manchu Councilors were allowed to read only documents in

[21] *Shu Huan Chi Loh*, v. 22, p. 4.

Manchurian language. But Emperor Tao Kuang removed this restriction and, after his time, they could read documents in both languages. The newly appointed were designated "Probationary Councilors," except when it was a Manchu whom the emperor wanted to make a ranking Councilor. In spite of the lack of provision for the number of councilors, there were usually four or five at the same time always with the Manchus in the majority. The records show that from 1730 to 1875, a period of 145 years, 115 Councilors were appointed. Among them were 59 Manchus, including three princes, 9 Mongols and 47 Chinese, giving the Manchus a plurality of twelve and a majority of three during the whole period. The division of the posts depended upon the situation, the Manchus being favored in time of peace and the Chinese in time of troubles, except in Yung Cheng's reign, when the traditional proportion of three Manchus and two Chinese was maintained. Emperor Chien Lung, who lived in a blessed period of peace and prosperity, appointed 31 Manchus, 5 Mongols and 17 Chinese to this influential office. In Emperor Chia Cheng's reign, troubles gradually developed, and the proportion changed to 9 Manchu to 1 Mongol and 7 Chinese. Emperor Tao Kuang saw uprisings afoot. He threw the traditional Manchu majority overboard by appointing 9 Chinese and 6 Manchus. During the reign of Emperors Hsien Feng and Tung Chi, when the Taipings occupied thirteen of the eighteen provinces, 12 Chinese and 9 Manchus were appointed.[22] Up to that period, the court had refrained from appointing any "prince of blood" to this heavy task. Nevertheless, there were two exceptions. Prince Cheng was Councilor for eleven months during Chia Cheng's reign, and Prince Kung sat at the Council table for a number of years during Hsien Feng, and Tung Chi's reigns. When peace was restored, the old tradition soon came back. Towards the end of the dynasty, we find it for a long while headed by Prince Ching: for sometime, two of the five Councilors

[22] The data above are given by *Shu Huan Chi Loh*.

were from the Imperial clan;[23] while upon other occasions, four of the five were Manchus.

Next to the Councilors were the thirty-two secretaries of the Council with sixteen Manchus and sixteen Chinese. They were usually recruited from secretaries of the Grand Secretariat, with occasional exceptions. Their rank ranged from the 7th to the 2nd. Their duty was considered to be of great importance. Regulations required that if they were appointed to concurrent positions, their duty in the Council should claim their primary attention. They could resign this position for a vice-ministership or for higher, but not lower, office. In fact, many vice-ministers, or even ministers, were willing to change positions with them in consideration of their actual power. They were divided into two turns for their duty, one group taking a whole day. Their principal work consisted in taking memorials from the emperor to the Councilors between five and nine o'clock every morning. After the Councilors had read over the documents, they brought them back to the emperor in person or had the secretaries do so. From this work, they got the advantage of being near to the emperor and the influential officials, and information as to all state affairs going on. Not infrequently they were asked their opinion on matters, thus having an extra-legal voice on the most important affairs of the Government. This explains why they were often called *Hsiao Chun Chi*, the "Little Councilors of State." Again when some big officials were appointed plenipotentiary commissioners, for a special mission, they generally asked to have one of the secretaries from the Council act as their assistant. This was done because they were well versed in the affairs of the states and because by having a secretary of the Council with him, the Commissioner could easily capitalize the prestige of the Council. This practice was forbidden in 1800 by Emperor Chia Cheng on account of its glaring abuse. In some cases a secretary was appointed special envoy. Indeed, so great was their

---

[23] Princes Ching and Yu Lang.

ORGANIZATIONS IN CENTRAL GOVERNMENT 83

power in proportion to their position that a special law was enacted to forbid the brother or son of a Metropolitan or provincial official of third rank or above to be appointed as secretary of the Council for fear of putting the official in a specially advantageous position. If appointment of the secretary took place before the appointment of the official, this rule did not apply. While there was no under-clerk in the Grand Secretariat for the sake of maintaining its dignity, there was no under-clerk in the Council for the reason that anybody connected with it stood a good chance of exercising some of its superabundant powers.

Aside from their power secured by virtue of their approximity to the throne and the importance of their duty such as recommendation for appointment, expression of their opinion on important state affairs and consequently getting the emperor to do what they thought best, the Councilors really formed a policy-formulating organ. The chief object of its establishment, as we have seen, was to help the emperor to suppress uprisings. In later periods they developed into a body of general policy formulators in all political matters, civil as well as military. The combination of policy formulation and execution was not all their powers; for, besides, they were often asked to review cases either with the emperor or by themselves.

Under a paternalistic monarchy like that in China before 1912, no definite power was given to any organization; even if it was given, the long arms of the emperor could reach it any time and take it back without legal remedy. But, as no human being, no matter how strong and energetic he might be, could rule such a large country with his own unaided hands and head, extra-legal ways of acquiring and exercising power were naturally substituted for constitutional provisions. All powers given by law or favor of the emperor to this body could not match the power it derived from the secrecy with which it operated. The provision of secret procedure in the Council business was enhanced by the fact that its military duties had a strategic character, while its civil affairs were of a discretionary rather than a ministerial nature: premature knowledge of the transactions and decisions might prevent execution and cost the Government a tremendous price. In 1747, Emperor Chien Lung further strengthened its secrecy by an edict which reads:—

The Council of State is an office for secret and important affairs. All memorials given to the Council for secret discussion shall not be disclosed. Hereafter, memorials to be transmitted to the respective ministers shall be filed in the archive of the Council. So shall all the secret memorials transmitted by the ministers be.[24]

The degree of secrecy employed in the business of this influential body can be best illustrated by the keeping and use of the official seal described in the *Shu Huan Chi Loh*.[25]

The Silver Seal (of the Council of State) is kept in the Imperial Safe. The ranking member of the Council carries the key. In case it is needed, the ranking secretary on duty goes to the Office of Transmission in person to ask for the credential to use the seal. He then proceeds to get the key to the safe from the ranking Councilor. He returns the seal immediately after stamping. The credential is a solid gold metal of one-half inch [26] wide, two inches long and one-tenth of an inch thick with the inscription "Chun Chi Chu." The secretary on duty, after using the seal, carries it back, and returns the metal to the ranking secretary who is responsible for its safe-keeping.

Additional regulations adding to its secrecy were made from time to time. The edict of Emperor Chia Cheng issued in 1800 is a fair example. It says:—

The Councilors shall go over all documents in the Council Office the very day they come in. No business between the departments and the Council shall be transacted in the Council Office. No noble or officials, outside of the Council, shall visit a Councilor or his secretary in the latter's office. A censor is hereby assigned to the Council Office to see that these regulations are strictly observed.[27]

[24] *Shu Huan Chi Loh*, v. 1, p. 1.

[25] V. 13, p. 1.

[26] Chinese Measurement.

[27] *Shu Huan Chi Loh*, v. 1, p. 10.

ORGANIZATIONS IN CENTRAL GOVERNMENT 85

Judging from the importance of its transactions, its secrecy was not without justification; the repeated edicts to reaffirm the necessity of its secrecy were far from being documents of formality. For, only sixteen years after the organization of the Council, the leaking out of news from the Council became a common thing. Thus Emperor Chien Lung found it necessary to prohibit the practice by an edict issued in April, 1746:—

> The Council of State is an office of important and strategic affairs. None of its business should be disclosed. But, nowadays, some provincial officials secure documents from the Council by bribing the underlings of the Council . . . . . Let them be upbraided.[28]

The secrecy can further be proved by the fact that the *Ta Ching Hui Tien Shih Li,* a massive work of 1220 volumes which contain all the edicts on the organization, procedure, and work of all Government institutions, does not contain a single word about the Council.

Incidentally, it should also be pointed out that this office had the special privilege of sending out messages by express relay teams. An edict of Emperor Chien Lung issued in 1750 gave it the right to use the 500 *li* relay teams if it so chose. When unmarked, its messages were sent by 300 *li* teams which was considerably faster than the ordinary official messages.

Strangely enough, the Council, an organ by means of which the Manchu Emperors expected to centralize all powers of government in their own hand, accumulated more power for itself than it collected for its master. The alarmed censors, who saw an opportunity to break their silence, petitioned again and again for the curtailment of the Council's power. The emperor, capitalizing the virtue of readiness to accept advice, issued one edict after another for the curtailment of its powers without any result until, in 1799, Emperor Chia Cheng found it necessary to deprive it of some of its powers by setting up new regulations in-

[28] *Ibid.,* p. 1.

stead of uttering empty words. His edict contains the following words:—

Ministers of State, high military officers, viceroys, governors, commissioners of finance or justice and all others who have the privilege of addressing me directly are hereby prohibited to send a duplicate of their memorials to the Council of State while that memorial is supposed to be sent to me. They shall not notify the Council of the affairs which they are to report to me in person. After the memorial has reached me, I shall either grant the memorialist an audience or let my decision be known to him through one of the six departments. This has nothing to do with the Council, and hence should not be known to them beforehand so that they would have an opportunity to shield one another.[29]

This was, indeed, a heavy blow to the power of the Council. It deprived the Council of its opportunity to know everything going on. In the days when memorials were sent through the Council, the Councilors had the privilege of expressing their opinion on the affairs mentioned in the memorials, and, consequently, of influencing the emperor's opinion on them. These regulations subjected the Councilors to the mercy of the emperor; that is, by cutting off their source of information, they could only participate in those affairs in which the emperor wanted them to. Loss of privilege in this respect led to loss of prestige among their colleagues. Not being messengers between the emperor and other officials, they could no longer help or stand in the way of other high officials. But the massiveness of the business of governing one-quarter of the whole human race, no matter how inactive the government was, coupled with the limitation of human energy, the expert knowledge of the Councilors on state affairs, and the individual favoritism by the emperor, soon brought them back to power. Hence, in the latter part of the dynasty, we find them once again important factors in the administration. The emperor, instead of curtailing that power appointed his own men or tried to win over the men already appointed: in other words, he attempted to manipulate the men instead of the insti-

[29] *Ibid.*, p. 9.

tution. The appointing of princes of royal blood to councilorships during the reign of the Empress Dowager Tsu Hsi proved this tendency.

The Censorate (Tu Cha Yuan)

From the Council, an organization instituted by the Tsing Dynasty with no historical equivalent in the past and purely for executive purposes, we now come to a third member of the metropolitan triumvirate bearing characteristics exactly contrary to the powerful Council of State. The Censorate has as long a history as, and a much more checkered career than, any other institution in the history of the Government of Ancient China. The Chinese term for Censor *Yu Ssu* literally translated, does not mean a man who censures: Yu means imperial; Ssu, historian; and the combination, imperial historian. The oldest record of this interesting institution is found in Chapter IX, Book VI [30] of *The Canon of Rites* (Li Chi), which says "The left censor records the emperor's speech; the right censor his action." The purpose of this recording was to give data to the Censors as to the correctness of the speeches and acts of the emperor: the principal duty of the Censors was originally to supervise and correct the words and actions of the sovereign so that he could live up to the high moral standard required of him as a model of the people. Hence they were given the right of freedom of speech in their criticism of the august ruler. In the Chou Dynasty,[31] the duty of the Censor was gradually shifted from correction of the emperor to that of the the officials. Being always near the emperor, he was an important official in spite of his low rank and irksome duty of criticizing others. The Chin emperor [32] in view of the importance of the duty of the censor, promoted him to a

[30] The Chinese name of the chapter is *Yu Tsao*, meaning a headgear decorated with jades.

[31] 1012 to 255 B. C.

[32] 255-206 B. C.

high rank, the equal of the Premier. Han [33] followed the Chin system rather closely. The censor was given a rank equal to that of "The three chief ministers." When the new Court Ceremonies were introduced, the censor was made master of ceremonies, adding a new duty to the office which later dynasties did not do away with. For three and a half centuries during which division and turmoils reigned in China, this office survived all overthrowing and founding of dynasties with different names and ranks, but precisely the same duty. The Sui [34] emperors deprived the censor of the right to correct the emperor and made it his special duty to censure officials. From that time on, he became a spy on the mandarins and "eyes and ears" of the sovereign. His original duty of recording the speech and act of the emperor was given to another office known as *Chi Chu Tsu Kwan*, meaning Office for Keeping a Diary of the Emperor's Movements. By this new office, recording was the only thing done; while the recorders were deprived of their ancient rights of supervising and petitioning for rectification. Nevertheless, in the later dynasties the ancient right of correcting the emperor's mistakes was not infrequently exercised, though sometimes under the pretense of impeaching an official and often with results of loss of favor, position or even the head of the petitioner. Thus the history of this office, to a great extent, represents the development of imperial domination and ministerial submission, giving traces of the advancement of absolutism in the Chinese Government.

The Censorate was staffed by two Censors-Generals, four Assistant Censors-General, twenty-four departmental Censors,[35] fifty-six provincial Censors, two Censors for the imperial clansmen [36] and ten Censors for the City of Peking.

[33] 206 B. C. to 221 A. D.

[34] 589-618 A. D.

[35] The departmental censors formerly belonged to their respective departments until Emperor Yung Cheng put all of them in the Censorate in 1724.

[36] Appointed among themselves.

The basis of division was both geographical and functional. Functionally, the twenty-four departmental censors were divided into the six regular departments with four for each; the censors for the Court of Imperial Clansmen is on the same line. Geographically, for the ten censors for Peking, the city was divided into five precincts, the central, the eastern, southern, western and northern precincts with two censors for each. The eighteen provinces were divided into fifteen circuits, each supervised by two to eight censors.[37] Of these ninety-eight censors, two were for imperial clansmen and the other ninety-six divided among the Chinese and the Manchus with exact numerical equality. The principle of equal distribution of offices between the Chinese and Manchus was nowhere so perfectly carried out as in this service. In the headquarters, the departments, or the circuits one Manchu always went with one Chinese with equal rank and the same duty. Another principle of distribution of duty, applied only to this service, was that by distribution. It meant that some men were specifically responsible for a circuit or a department, but it did not mean that outside of that circuit or department, their jurisdiction could not go. By virtue of a decision of the Minister's Conference in 1774, any censor could address the emperor on any subject he chose. The division was like the division of a legislature into committees, with definite assignment of duty in certain things but without a general deprivation of power over things not enumerated.

Minor organizations in the capital were assigned to the supervision of the departmental censors generally according to the nature of their work, as the Court of the Imperial Stud to the Department of War, The Court of Revision to the Department of Justice, the Office of River Construction,

[37] The circuit of Kiangnau was the only one with eight censors; the circuit of Shantung with six; those of Chihli, Honan, Chekiang, Shansi, Shensi, Hukwang, Kiangsi and Fukien with four each and those of Szechuan, Kwangtung, Kwangsi, Hunnan, and Kueichow with two each.

(Ho Tao Tsung Tu) to the Department of Public Works, etc. The only exception to this was the assignment of the Grand Secretariat to the Chihli Circuit where an institution was given to a geographic unit. The Council of State was the only organization not assigned to any censor. But the absence of special assignments by no means exempted them from the supervision or impeachment of the rectifying agents. In fact, due to the importance and massiveness of the business of the Councilors, they were more subject to errors and stood more chance of being impeached: their remedy did not so much depend on the lack of assigned supervisor as on imperial favor. In the geographic distribution, one province was generally the unit, but the Circuit of Chihli included the Metropolitan prefecture and Mukden; that of Kiangnan included the provinces of Kiangsu and Anhui; that of Shansi included Shensi, Kansu and Sinkiang; and that of Hukwang included Hunan and Hupeh. Kirin, Heilungkiang, Tibet and Mongolia were made special circuits.

The chief duties of the Censorate were to supervise both Metropolitan and provincial officials of all ranks and institutions in two respects, namely: the performance of their official duties and their personal conduct; assistance at the examinations of officials which happened once every three years; participation in the conferences of the "nine ministers." They transmitted all documents from the Grand Secretariat or the Council of State, made a copy of each (except those marked "secret"), checked them over, filed them in the Censorate for reference, and reported to the emperor in case of mistakes. They called the roll of the officials in a general audience and impeached the unexcused absentees. They supervised all the ceremonial and formal occasions and corrected all officials not showing proper propriety either with intention or through ignorance. They audited the accounts of the Department of Revenue and the provinces. They kept a sharp eye on the government properties, like the treasuries and granaries. They superintended the construction of public buildings and river dams, directed charity works, and conducted the casting of lots for the distribution of new appointees to departments or provinces.

Judicially, the Censorate, together with the Department of Justice and Grand Court of Revision, formed the highest tribunal next to the emperor. This tribunal reviewed all except civil cases rejected or injustly concluded by the lower courts. Incidental to their judicial duty, they policed all examinations. The Metropolitan Division of the Censorate supervised all municipal affairs with special emphasis on the judicial branch of the local government.

An edict issued by Emperor Tai Tsung in 1627 concerning the power of the Censorate reads:—

> The Censorate is a Court of critics of the Government. The censors are to criticize my negligence of duty, dismissal of the loyal and able, appointment of the unfit, promotion of the unserviceable and demotion of the meritorious. If the princes and ministers neglect their work, indulge in wine and woman, love pleasure, take property from the people without due compensation, show contempt in court ceremonies, or carelessness in dress or be absent from audience under the pretense of sickness, the Censorate shall investigate and report . . . . . If the six departments decide things wrongly or falsely report the decision of an undecided affair; the censors shall make them known to me. If an appeal is made to the Censorate, it shall decide whether it should be made known to me. It shall check its own members from receiving bribery . . . .[38]

Such an edict, no doubt, served the purpose of further assuring the censors of their duties and making them eager to exercise their powers. Indeed, the things they did had a very wide range. A memorial taken from *Memorials of the Tsing Dynasty*[39] by Assistant Censor-General Sung Chuan shows ten points: (1) To canonize Emperor Chung Tseng, (Ming) (2) To abolish the extra taxes imposed by emperors of the Ming Dynasty, (3) To assemble able men by offering high offices, (4) To emphasize civil administration, (5) To respect scholars and teachers, (6) To reward those who

[38] *Ta Tsing Hui Tien Shih Li*, v. 998.
[39] *Huang Tsing Tsou Yi*, v. 1, p. 1.

show loyalty to Ming, (7) To subsidize the traveling expenses of the candidates coming from the provinces to the first Metropolitan examination, (8) To reduce the administrative force, (9) To pay more attention to the complaints of the people, (10) To exempt the people from tax for a year. Such was the range of subjects that a censor spoke on: yet this was far from the most embracing memorial of a censor.

Above all these, they were obligated to communicate to the emperor what should be done and what should not, informing him of the general state of affairs, and thus exercising a kind of legislative function. Indeed, the only institution in the government which was entirely separated from the executive work was the Censorate. Its legislative power, however, was more of a passive nature as they did not have so much power to enact or execute laws as to annul or amend them. They were not provided with power to initiate law: all they could do was to suggest to the emperor. Their strongest weapon was impeachment: unfortunately impeachment ended their power. Whether a reasonable hearing was given to it or justice done to it was a matter for His Sacred Majesty to decide.

As safeguards to the faithful and unhampered execution of their duties, several traditions were built up. First, whenever an emperor was enthroned, the new ruler issued enthusiastic edicts commanding fearless petitions. A current of memorials from the censors then flooded the palace until some of the memorials were "thrown back" and their authors punished. A period of silence ensued. Another edict was again issued and the same cycle worked out. Second, the emperor kept the names of the censor unknown in case of impeachment. Edicts ordering the investigation of impeached officials generally began with the phrase "Somebody has petitioned that . . . . ." The impeaching censor is, by regulation, excused from facing the impeached before the emperor or a tribunal appointed by him. Thirdly, the emperor was supposed to respect the censors though, quite contrary to theory, censors were treated with contempt. The most common form of contemptuous treatment for a censor was to order that his petition be "thrown back" which meant that it was not accepted.

The greatest protection of the "speech officers" was freedom of speech. Theoretically, under no circumstances could a censor be punished on account of fearless performance of his official duties. Together with this right, was their fixed term of office. Unlike other officials who could be removed any time, they, according to theory at least, held their office for a term of three years irrespective of their work. In supporting this traditionally recognized right, edicts were again and again issued. The following issued by Emperor Tai Tsung of the Manchus in 1637 may serve as an example:—

> On all mistakes of the Government such as haughtiness, insubordination, unlawfulness, or any other inappropriate acts of princes and ministers, the Censors are given the responsibility of speaking without reservation. *Even if the accusation be not substantiated, no punishment shall befall the Censors.* Intentional silence on the part of the Censors shall constitute an act of treason. Promotion and rewards shall be the shares of the faithful at the end of three years.[40]

Yet, not all the imperial edicts were so favorable to the censors. Quite a few of them issued for the limitation of their rights can be cited. An edict of Emperor Kang Hsi issued in 1679 limited a memorial of a censor to one topic. Another by the same emperor in 1667 bade them be very concise in their memorials. A strict rule was set up against a censor impeaching an official on account of private enmity: severe punishment was provided for this. Furthermore, their duty was strictly limited to exposing, criticism, petitioning or impeachment, nothing more. Should they venture the suggestion of punishment or scheme for construction, or do anything other than bringing the facts to the notice of the emperor, they would share the fate of Censor Yin Teh who, on account of suggesting the name of a person

[40] *Ta Tsing Hui Tien Shih Li*, v. 998.

for the appointment of Director of Mint, was dismissed by Emperor Tao Kuang in 1835.

The most impaired right of the censors was their right to petition the emperor "what they have heard." By right, they were excused from cross examination in case the impeached denied the truth of their charges. But, later emperors repeatedly issued edicts, against tradition, to forbid the "I have heard" petitions. A further violation of this right, besides calling them for cross examination, was holding them to answer the counter charges made by the impeached. Quite a few of the censors got punishment as a result of such petitions.

It was decided in a conference of the ministers in 1761 that censors could address the emperor two kinds of memorials; one called "open memorials" in which the name of the censor would be made known if the situation demanded; another called "secret memorials" in which the name of the petitioner would under no circumstances be made public. The secrecy, as has been pointed out, enabled the censors to memorialize the emperor without the danger of incurring the displeasure of the officials criticized. This right was also violated by imposing punishment on the memorializer if a wrong judgment on the nature of the memorial was made; the right of deciding as to its nature was, as most other rights, reserved to the emperor. A further restriction on the "speech officials" was the requirement of the fulfillment of all formalities in their memorials, such as "elevation" or writing the name of an emperor in the sanctioned form, etc. Censor Wang Hui Ying was given to the six departments for a severe punishment on account of his failure to give "double elevation" to the words "Eastern Mausoleum" in 1887.[41] Censor Chiu Shao Hsiung met the same fate, though without the word "severe" for failure to "elevate" the names of Emperors Kang Hsi, Chien Lung, Chia Cheng, and Tao Kuang when he

[41] Edict of the 13th year of Kuang Hsu in *Ta Tsing Hui Tien Shih Li*.

quoted them in his memorial. Censor Fei Shiao Chang was dismissed from office by Emperor Chien Lung in 1785 on account of a phrase in the memorial [42] which cannot be called a mistake at all. Numerous other cases of the same nature could be cited. Running through the whole volume of edicts, we find the lot of the poor censors a very hard one, especially during the reign of Emperor Chien Lung who issued tens of edicts to reprimand the censors, but only two to praise them. The injustice of Chien Lung's treatment of the censors is proved by the fact that many censors reprimanded or dismissed by him were given words of consolation or reappointed to the service by his successor.

Reproval and upbraiding were not the only punishments that the poor censors received on account of the performance by them of official duties. Records of two hundred and forty-three years [43] show us fifty-two cases of punishment heavier than the regular punishments, which every official in the old Chinese monarchy had to face every now and then, given to officials who theoretically had immunity. The following figures from *Ta Tsing Hui Tien Shih Li* substantiates this contention:—

TABLE SHOWING THE PUNISHMENT OF CENSORS
1644-1887

Emperor	No. Executed	Exiled	Dismissed	Demoted	Total
Shun Chi	0	0	0	0	0
Kang Hsi	0	0	0	0	0
Yung Cheng	0	1	0	0	1
Chien Lung	0	0	3	0	3
Chia Cheng	1	0	4	1	6
Tao Kuang	1	0	4	6	11
Hsien Feng	0	0	0	0	0
Tung Chi	0	2	9	0	11
Kuang Hsu [44]	0	0	9	1	10
Total	2	3	29	8	42

[42] The phrase is "supposing Your Majesty is in the situation . . ."
[43] 1644 to 1887.
[44] Only twelve years of his reign.

From the above table, we find that the early emperors held the censorial immunity much more sacred. Of the later emperors, Emperor Hsien Feng was the only one who respected and strictly practiced this ancient indulgence of a virtuous ruler. The frequency of punishing censors, or, in other words, violating their right of freedom of speech, was much greater in the latter part of the dynasty. Presenting the figure in terms of averages, we have one case in thirteen years during Yung Cheng; one in twenty years during Chien Lung; one in four years during Chia Cheng; one in two years and ten months during Tao Kuang; one in one and one-fifth years during Tung Chi, and one in one and three-tenths years during Kuang Hsu.[45] Taking the whole period of twenty-six years of Kuang Hsu's reign and the whole number of twenty-one punished censors together, we have an average of one and one-quarter years for one censor. Emperor Tao Kuang showed more kindness as well as gave more punishment to the censors. His successors, with the honorable exception of Hsien Feng, kept up the great frequency of punishment and the exclusion of rewards, thus making the share of the "eyes and ears" officials much worse.

Every time a censor was executed, a long apologetic edict followed the order of punishment; for putting a censor to death was considered a sign of the emperor's unreasonableness, his indifference to advice, his absolutism, and, in short, his unworthiness to exercise the right of the "Heavenly decree." Emperor Chia Cheng's edict, for the execution of Censor Hsiao in 1817 shows an artful apology:—

In the Imperial Dynasty, sage succeeded sage. Criticism on the Government is always received with open arms. Whatever good in the memorials of the censors I have adopted. Even when a memorial shows bad judgment or improper language, I usually pardon the author. I not only never executed any of them, but never had them lashed as the Ming emperors wrongfully did. Today, in the Palace

[45] In the last twenty-six years, Empress Dowager Tzu Hsi was regent for the whole period. It is unjust to attribute these acts to the youngsters who did not have an opportunity to exercise their legitimate powers.

Trial two offenders from the official class, I Men Tai and Hsiao Cheng, are both found guilty. The decision is punishment by death. I Men Tai has violated laws and received bribes, and so, cannot be pardoned by our laws. But, Hsiao Cheng, who occupies the position of a censor, violated our laws on two counts, namely: sending selfishly a memorial upon the bidding of another and receiving bribes as a condition of sending his memorial. No act of treason against the Empire is greater than this. Lack of punishment would sanction the reception of bribes by a censor. If this act be not punished, what other crimes would not be committed? I hereby order the prisoner (Censor Hsiao) to be executed as a warning. The officials, both metropolitan and provincial, are to understand that the man I put to death is a violator of our laws and a seeker of selfish interests. He is not executed as a censor.[46]

Whatever may be the excuse of his ordering a censor to execution, the fact is that a bribe recipient in the Chinese Government service is quite a common creature, while the execution of bribe receiving officials is an uncommon act. Chia Cheng could have gotten rid of him by means other than death punishment.

Several characteristics of the Censorate, mostly advantageous to the organization, deserve our attention. The first of these was an advantage in personnel. Dividing all the positions in the Censorate, as it was, into two groups, the Manchu positions, like those in the Grand Secretariat, might have been and probably were, occupied by men without good education and proper qualification; but the Chinese censors, like the Chinese Grand Secretaries, were one and all appointed from successful candidates in the competitive literary examinations with a great many of them directly recruited from the Academy of Letters. Of the positions in the six services [47] which were specially reserved for men qualified by competitive examinations, those in the Censorate commanded as much respect and yielded as much honor as any other. The fact that the duty of a censor was

[46] *Ta Tsing Hui Tien Shih Li.*
[47] The Grand Secretariat, the Department of Rites, the Censorate, the Imperial College, the Academy of Letters, and the Supervisorate of Instructions for the Heir Apparent.

to criticize and impeach fascinated many a young graduate. The low rank of the office (5a) necessitated recruitment from fresh graduates, men who had an super-abundance of enthusiasm to work for the public, full intention to make a name, a long ambitious career to look forward to, and plenty of energy to back up the intention and ambition. Being fresh graduates, the processes of mandarinization had not completely penetrated them, the bad atmosphere of officialdom had not entirely replaced the good influence of books.

Public opinion always backed up a courageous censor. Public expectation of a good censor was the fearless impeachment of the powerful and yet wicked ministers or to point out the mistakes of the emperor. History was ever kind in the criticism of a censor. If, for impeaching a powerful and wicked minister or for pointing out the mistake of an emperor, a censor suffered death, he would be a hero of principles, a loyal official, to be praised for ages eternal.

With favorable circumstances for both recruitment and execution of duties, small wonder there is to find a group of the literary elite and moral giants in the Censorate. That is why even at the very end of the effete Manchu Government when official discipline subsided, administrative corruption ruled supreme and civil service degenerated into a profitable mode of earning a living, we still had censors who impeached men like Prince Chen and Yung Lu in spite of their power and influence over the ruling sovereign.

Finally, because of its power, a son or relative of an official of, or higher than, the third rank could not be appointed a censor, so that watchfulness and severity of criticism would not be reduced by blood relationship.

CHAPTER V

THE DEPARTMENT OF CIVIL SERVICE (LI PU) AND CIVIL SERVICE LAWS

Strictly speaking, there was no difference between civil service and politics in the old Chinese monarchy, at least not in the sense of a difference between political and administrative work as in the Western countries. Technically, however, a difference was made by civil service laws, in that there were different degrees of strictness in the application of civil service laws to officials of the third rank or above and to those below that rank. The advancement of a Chinese official in the administrative hierarchy was marked by the nine ranks, each having two grades, the highest being 1a and the lowest 9b. Those of, or above, the third rank were designated as *Ta Yuan* (high official). To them civil service laws, except for very few important stipulations, were only loosely applied. The demarcation of administration and politics then, instead of being drawn by the nature of work, was drawn by the altitude of the office or officeholder in the ladder of administrative hierarchy. Being a monarchy, though limited by the required qualities of virtue and tradition, but not by written laws or inflexible constitution, the emperor made much use of his powers in the suppression of party organization which, some day, might prove too powerful for his successful manipulation. The lack of party organization, hence the absence of party differences and group action, made every one in government service a part of the unalterable administrative machinery administering his official duties directly to the good of the emperor and the people instead of accomplishing these ends through the success of the party.

The theory of obligation to service, as we have seen in the first chapter, was that no one could be forced into government service without one's own consent although everyone was morally obliged to do his share. But, once one got into the service, that meant he was satisfied with the government and therefore, should do whatever he could: he should stay in the service until he became physically incapacitated or no longer desired by the government. The age of retirement set by Emperor Chien Lung in 1757 was 55; in 1768, 65; and by Emperor Kuang Hsu in 1892, 75. But, these regulations were more violated than observed. Even minor officials, not to say grand old dignitaries like grand secretaries or councilors of state or ministers of departments, in many cases held offices when they should have retired had the age regulation been enforced. Again, the lack of accurate birth census and the prevalence of reporting ages less than they actually were, particularly upon the part of these who entered the service late in life, on account of repeated failure in competitive examinations, made conscientious observation of these age requirements almost impossible. The practice of retirement on account of sickness, something interpreted as a Chinese camouflage, was only a foster child of the theory of no retirement and the loose application of the retirement regulations. Because one was under obligation, and yet had no desire, to stay, he had to put up an excuse. The most convenient excuse and one that the government could not very well help accepting was that of sickness. It was its convenience and practical effect that led to its frequent application. It was by no means always a camouflage and still less a lie.

The civil service laws, applied rather flexibly to, and often to the advantage of, high officials, were very rigidly applied to lower officials. With the exception of a few cases resulting from the benevolence of personal influence of high authorities or the benefit of imperial favoritism, its rigidity could easily claim the first place in the government where reason generally overruled law. The structure of the laws was as hierarchic as those of the Prussian army. Inability to fulfill all these requirements would lead to lack of respect from one's colleagues as well as from the people, hence difficulties in the performance of duties. Personal influence or imperial favor could only bend the laws but not the people whom the favored candidates had to face.

This network of civil service laws was enforced by the Department of Civil Service (Li Pu) which headed the list of the six principal departments. This department was staffed by two ministers, four vice-ministers, four bureaus with seven to eighteen secretaries to each. The duty of the ministers and vice-ministers were stated in *The Ta Tsing Hui Tien* [1] as:—

> To assist His Majesty in governing the people by attending to all affairs of the civil service system: in giving of ranks, recording of merits, examinations, appointment, dismissal of officials, conferring of titles, rewards, leaves, and determination of the native place, all officials of other services shall make their recommendations to this ministry. The ministers and vice-ministers, together with their staff, shall decide on the merits of the case: if they are important, they should be submitted to the emperor for approval; otherwise, executed directly . . . . . To present, by appointment, to the emperor, officials who are not in the regular list of audience attendants . . . . . To execute the casting of lots of expectant appointees when an appointment is to be made . . . . . In every three years, it shall assemble all the Provincial graduates (Chu Jen) who failed in the Metropolitan examinations, to select them for appointments.

These varied duties were divided among four bureaus with the Bureau of Appointments taking charge of ranks, the lists of qualified appointees, conducting examinations,[2] selecting officials for promotion or demotion and the regular monthly selection of appointees; the Bureau of Examinations for rewards and punishments; the Bureau of Records for the complete and up-to-date recording of all officials and the Bureau of Titles for hereditary titles, ranks, and conferring of ranks on relatives of officials, and native officials.

An appointment could be won by a candidate by one of the five following means: (1) winning a degree at a competitive

[1] V. 4.
[2] For civil servants already in government employment.

examination or purchasing an admission into the Imperial College (Kuo Tsi Chien), which virtually was equal to the holding of the first degree;[3] (2) By securing an official rank from the emperor on account of meritorious service rendered by the father or other family superiors of the conferee; (3) Through recommendation of a high authority; (4) Through promotion from the ranks of under-clerks; and (5) By purchase. The first, second, and third were called "regular qualifications." The first qualification was further subdivided into the Metropolitan graduates, the provincial graduates, and district students.[4] Metropolitan graduates were the most favored, then the provincial graduates, and so on. A number of positions in the central government were reserved for men with the Metropolitan degree (Chin Shih) and another number for men qualified in examination and hereditary rank. For provincial positions, any one of the five qualifications would fulfill the legal requirements. Even in the Central Government, the rule was much more strictly applied to Chinese than to Manchus. Many "Chinese positions" were open only to Chinese Metropolitan graduates, while the same positions for Manchus could be occupied by men who qualified themselves with other degrees less than a Metropolitan graduate, or even no degree at all. This legal provision by no means barred the unqualified candidates from appointment to an office, unless the offices were reserved for a special class of candidates; instead, it rather served as a safeguard for the qualified.

The disfranchised class in Chinese government service was indeed very small. This group consisted of hereditary servants, sons and grandsons of prostitutes, actors, private soldiers. If the disqualification was caused by the profession of a grandfather, it could be removed upon the recommendation of local officials. But, in this case, re-enfranchisement entitled one only to offices below the third rank.

[3] For further discussion of this mode of qualifications, see Chapter VI.

[4] The Chin Sheng, the Sheng Yuan, etc.

Bad personal conduct, false report of place of birth or age, feebleness, old age, and appropriation of public money without due authority by one's father or grandfather, made up another list of disqualifications. These again could be removed by passing a successful examination or rendering some satisfactory service. In fact, the only hard-and-fast rule for disqualification which neither money nor influence could remove in the loosely administered Chinese government was the misfortune of having parents who were hereditary servants, prostitutes, actors, or private soldiers. Aside from those disqualified by one of the four conditions, every subject was eligible to a minor office. Then, too, technical and religious appointments were qualified by profession; to wit: monks were appointed to government temples, physicians to the Imperial hospital. But they could not be promoted above their ranks, nor transferred to other positions.

The power of recommending men to government service was granted to officials of the third rank or above. Rarely did a recommendation meet rejection. This act, however, did not end the relation between the protector and the protegé: for the future success or failure of the latter would be shared by the former especially in punishments of offense as we shall later see.

A number of positions were specially reserved for men recommended.[5] The recommended must have the following qualifications:

1. At least one year's experience in the very service to which he was recommended. 2. He must have at least three years' experience in the civil service in general. 3. He must never have been dismissed by the Government. 4. He must not have any government accounts not yet cleared. 5. He must not have any demotion or sick leave during his years of probation. 6. In case of a Manchu, he must be

[5] The proportion was one out of every eight clerks, one out of every fifteen circuit intendents, prefects, or magistrates, and one out of every 130 "accessory" local officials.

able to read and write the Manchurian language and know archery.

This power of recommendation was indeed a necessary facilitating agent for the government in view of the large number of officials needed in its service. The delegation of this power only to officials of the third rank or above was not at all a poor way of limiting the privilege to the more prominent and responsible public servants. But the responsibility of the protector for the offense of the protegé made this act too much of a burden. This power, therefore, was seldom exercised. When it was, corruption abounded. Liu Yu Chi, in his memorial to Emperor Kuang Hsu,[6] well pointed out its abuses. "First of all," he said, "most of the recommendations, whether regular or special, open or secret, ordinary or extraordinary, for merit or contribution, were based on personal feelings, private relations or bribery; the recommended were usually for leisure as they were often appointed to offices where there was no work; new offices had to be instituted for them because of the difficulty of rejecting the recommended, and the surplus population of the mandarin world was caused by recommendation, and punishments for officials were frequently avoided by means of recommendations." There was certainly little overstatement of the abuses. As this memorial failed to stop the practice, worse uses of it were made at the end of the dynasty.

Hereditary ranks and offices were given to sons, grandsons, younger brothers, nephews, and younger cousins of distinguished officials. Only one hereditary rank or office would be given to one of the inferior family relatives of the official. The recipient must not be in government service the time the rank or office was given him. To be entitled to this privilege, an official must be of, or above, the fourth rank in the Metropolitan civil services; of, or above, the third rank in the provincial civil service; or the second rank in either the central or provincial military service. The

[6] *Tung Hua Lu Kuang Hsu*, v. 198, p. 11.

rank of the beneficiary depended on that of the benefactor, the difference between these two was generally four full ranks. Thus first rank officials had a fifth hereditary rank for the son; the second had the sixth, etc. The highest rank was the fifth, a second class secretary in a bureau, and the lowest, a scholarship in the Imperial College and receipt of an appointment to a petty office after graduation. These regulations did not apply to officials who died in military action or in service, in which cases the share of the beneficiary would be much larger.

The practical benefit of hereditary office which worked downward both in family relation and rank might be very well contrasted with the nominal benefit that worked upwards. By this, I mean that besides securing an appointment for his son or grandson, a government servant could also get a rank for his father or grandfather. The rank secured for one's family superiors could be higher, or equal, but never lower than the benefactor. An official of the seventh, sixth, fifth or fourth rank could get his parents and grandparents a second rank; one of the second or third could get his parents and grandparents a first rank. A wife would get whatever rank her husband had.

The purchase of office, popularly understood as a corrupt practice in the old Manchu Government, strangely enough had full legal sanction there. Clever employment of the artistic Chinese language designated the purchase as a "contribution for appointment to public office." Whatever terms might have been given to this detestable institution, a process of paying money or grains for the acquisition of an appointment was too evident to rid it of its commercial character. It should, nevertheless, be understood that it was a bad institution rather than a corrupt practice like others which were not backed up by legal provision. The first record of this institution was found in 115 B. C. during the reign of Emperor Wu Ti when a flood visited Kiangnan in the fall. With winter approaching and deaths from hunger and cold in sight, edicts were issued to have the name of all those who saved lives by contribution of grains reported to the emperor for appointment to office.[7] A hundred years later, during the reign of Emperor Cheng Ti, crops in Kwantung. failed. An edict was issued calling for contributions from the well-to-do. A contribution of food stuff valued at 1,000,000 cash or more would entitle the donor to a noble title, a position of a district magistrate or its equivalent; 300,000 cash or more would earn the contributor an intermediate official rank or the position of a petty official; 100,000 cash or more would exempt the donor from three years' tax; and 10,000 or more from one year.[8] From that time on, no definite records of a systematic sale of office could be found but there was the occasional practice of giving appointments as a reward for contributions to government in time of need. These historical resemblances, in fact, differed from the notorious Manchu institution in that others used it purely as a temporary measure in time of urgent need and never practiced it under normal circumstances. Then, too, whatever was received by former dynasties was devoted to the immediate need of the situation while the Tsing Government accepted money and made the receipts a part of the governmental income. Thirdly, a rank or an office given by other dynasties was a form of reward for a contribution securable only in emergency; but in the Tsing dynasty, a political office was a commodity the value of which was listed and the access to which was open at any time and to anybody who could pay the price. Fourthly, the volume of trade was never so big as in the Tsing Dynasty and the government was never so much corrupted by the mercenary officials.

Thus we may say that the sale of offices was principally a Manchu institution, for the early Manchu emperors had instituted the system before they entered China. In the first year of Emperor Chung Teh (1635), a famine occurred in Manchuria. Censor-General Tso Ko Fah petitioned the

[7] *History of Han.*
[8] *History of Han.*

reception of contribution of grains either to substitute punishment or to acquire qualification for appointment to office. This was adopted.[9] From that time on, every occasion when the government needed money formed a cause of resorting to this practice. Each time a more extensive scale and a more complete list was used, until the Taiping Rebellion perfected the system.

At first two kinds of sales were conducted by the government: sales of rank without office and sales of rank and office. The former, being a cheaper sale, of only a nominal nature, entitled the purchasers to wear the court uniforms of the rank which he bought and to fix the front entrance of their abodes with the dignity of an official, but practically did not at all affect the Government. It is to the sales of offices that we here refer.

Offices could be purchased for one's father or for one's self. The purchase might be advancement of rank, say fifth to fourth, or fifth to third. It might also be from a plain subject to the fourth rank. The highest rank for sale was 1b: this was sold only to officials of third rank. A plain subject could buy at one time up to the fourth. Not infrequently separate purchases were made, say to buy a seventh rank first, then from the seventh to the fifth, and from the fifth to the third, and so on. It might be a purchase of a turn. We shall see later that the expectant officials were divided into lists with a definite number of positions reserved for each; a purchase of a turn would mean an earlier appointment. It might be a purchase of merit where the bought merits were reserved for the cancellation of punishment. It might also be a direct cancellation of punishment. In short, all sorts of sales were conducted.

The prices of the ranks and offices varied in different periods of the dynasty. Sample prices are the following:—[10]

[9] *Pa Chi Tung Chi.*
[10] From *Chou Chi Lu* by Yang Ching Jen.

1. In the 10th year of Shun Chi (1654)

   100 *shih* of rice and 100 taels of silver for a 9th rank, if purchaser be a plain subject.

   1,000 *shih* of rice and 1,000 taels of silver for two grades.

   500 *shih* of rice and 500 taels of silver for two merits.

This table was comparatively very simple. The able Emperor Chien Lung inaugurated a much more scientific scale completed in three separate years. In 1755, an ordinary subject was entitled to an office of 8th rank by contribution equivalent to, or more than, 300 *shih* of rice or 300 taels of silver. The same contribution from a rank holder would entitle him to a corresponding promotion. In 1756, two tables were fixed, one for Cantonese and the other for Fukienese:

Purchaser	Payment	Office
Cantonese *Siu Tsai*[11]	2,000- 4,000 *shih* of rice	Secretary (Li Mu)
Cantonese *Siu Tsai*	4,000- 6,000 *shih* of rice	Registrar (Chu Pu)
Cantonese *Siu Tsai*	6,000-10,000 *shih* of rice	Assistant Magistrate (Hsien Cheng)
Cantonese Subject	2,000- 4,000 *shih* of rice	9th rank
Cantonese Subject	4,000- 6,000 *shih* of rice	8th rank
Cantonese Subject	6,000-10,000 *shih* of rice	7th rank

Purchaser	Payment	Office
Fukienese *Siu Tsai*	1,500- 2,000 *shih* of rice	Secretary (Li Mu)
Fukienese *Siu Tsai*	2,000- 4,000 *shih* of rice	Registrar (Chu Pu)
Fukienese *Siu Tsai*	4,000- 6,000 *shih* of rice	Assistant Magistrate (Hsien Chen)
Fukienese *Siu Tsai*	6,000-10,000 *shih* of rice	Asst. Dept. Magist. (Chou Pan)
Fukienese Subject	1,500- 2,000 *shih* of rice	9th rank
Fukienese Subject	2,000- 4,000 *shih* of rice	8th rank
Fukienese Subject	4,000- 6,000 *shih* of rice	7th rank
Fukienese Subject	6,000-10,000 *shih* of rice	7th a rank magist.

In 1757, Service marks and grades began to be sold at 50 taels a service mark and 200 taels a merit.

[11] Students who have passed the district examinations.

CIVIL SERVICE AND CIVIL SERVICE LAWS 109

Emperor Tao Kuang got the better of his illustrious father by further scientifically determining the market price of an office. In 1838, he made up the following price list:—

Rank of purchaser	Price	The Purchased Office
Ordinary subject	1,000 taels or more	Office of 8th rank
8th rank official	2,000 taels or more	Office of 7th rank
7th rank official	3,000 taels or more	Office of 6th rank
6th rank official	4,000 taels or more	Office of 5th rank
5th rank official	6,000 taels or more	Asst. Salt Contr., 4b
District Magistrate—7a	5,000 taels or more	Prefect, 4b
Independent Sub-Prefect	10,000 taels or more	Sub-Prefect, 5b
Prefect, 4b	15,000 taels or more	Circuit Intendent, 4a

In 1843 the same emperor set up a price list for both rank and office purchasable by common subjects:—

Rank of purchaser	Price	Rank or Office Secured
Subject (Rankless)	200 taels or more	9th rank
Subject	300 taels or more	8th rank
Subject	1,000 taels or more	8th rank & Dist. Salt Cont.
Subject	2,000 taels or more	7b rank and Asst. Magist.
Subject	3,000 taels or more	6th rank & Assistant Sub-Prefect
Subject	4,000 taels or more	6th rank & Commissary of Record in Judicial Commission, 6b
Subject	5,000 taels or more	6th rank & Commissary of Records in Finance Commission, 6b
Subject	6,000 taels or more	6th rank & Second Class Sub-Prefect, 6a
Subject	8,000 taels or more	5th rank & Inspectorship of Salt, 5b
Subject	10,000 taels or more	5th rank & First Class Sub-Prefect, 5a
Subject	15,000 taels or more	4th rank & Assistant Controller of Salt, 4b
Subject	30,000 taels or more	4th rank & Circuit Intendentship, 4a

This list was applicable to all provincial positions, while positions in the central government counted one rank higher.

For provincial graduates or holders of a minor degree, the credit of one rank was given.

From the above lists we can infer that the price of a circuit intendent, the highest office in the province purchasable, was worth 30,000 taels. The salary of a circuit intendent was 105 taels a year with two or three thousand taels of allowance for the same period. It would then take the purchaser at least ten years to gain back the capital were he to earn it legitimately and honestly. Unprofitable as it might appear, the ranks and files of the "waiting officials" who qualified by purchase suddenly increased so that the same emperor found it necessary to make up another price list for the purchase of the privilege of getting an appointment before the regular turn came.

Official	Price	Privilege
1st & 2d Sect. in Bureau Indep. Dept. Magistrate	20,000 taels or more	To be appointed first
5th rank officials	15,000 taels or more	To be appointed first
3rd class Sect. in Bureau District Magistrate	10,000 taels or more	To be appointed first
Others in 6th & 7th rank	8,000 taels or more	To be appointed first
8th to rankless	4,000 taels or more	To be appointed first

Another list for the purchase of privilege with lower figures, and consequently less enviable privilege, was made up at the same time:—

Purchasing Official	Price	Privilege
Ind. Dept. Magistrate	10,000 taels or more	Getting appt. alternatively with the regular waiting list.
Other 5th rank officials	8,000 taels or more	do
District Magistrates	6,000 taels or more	do
Other 6th and 7th rank	4,000 taels or more	do
8th rank	3,000 taels or more	do
9th and rankless	2,000 taels or more	do

Many expectant officials did not purchase the privilege of early appointment. Instead they bought merits and grades which counted something in their advancement and did not cost as much. The following list of price of grades and merits was made up by Emperor Tao Kuang in 1843:—

Rank of Officials	Price	Commodity
3rd or above	1,500 taels or more	One grade
3rd or above	300 taels or more	One merit
4th rank	1,200 taels or more	One grade
5th rank	1,000 taels or more	One grade
6th rank and Magistrate	900 taels or more	One grade
Other 7th rank	800 taels or more	One grade
8th rank	700 taels or more	One grade
9th and rankless	600 taels or more	One grade

The limit of this kind of purchase was that not more than five grades could be purchased at one time by the same person.

With all these different lists and scales, the superabundance of waiting officials brought about by payment of money and the great corruption of the mercenary public servants coming from these sales, the Government was receiving only about 4,500,000 taels from the monopoly of sales of offices. A monetary income for the Government, for which the system was introduced, was the only benefit that could be claimed for this rotten system. On the other hand, its detriments to the Government as well as to the people were serious and diverse. First of all, it commercialized public service. The Chinese had the theory that appointment to public office was a recognition by the Government of the merit and ability of the appointee. So appointment to Government offices was a great honor, the appreciation of which should be shown by rendering good service to the people and the emperor. The system of purchase made it a business transaction. The appointee who had to invest a certain amount of money before getting the office, could honestly and legitimately get less than one-tenth of the investment in a year. Besides, his fate was always hanging in the balance: he might be appointed today and dismissed tomorrow. Even if he could serve a whole term of three years, not more than twenty-five to thirty per cent of his capital could be earned back. Certainly the honor and prestige of an inferior in an administrative hierarchy like that of the Chinese, which so helplessly depended on the whims and fancy of the high ranked mandarins, was not worth so much sacrifice of treasure. With what else than a commercial purpose could a man have bought an office at that high price? If for pecuniary profits one went into the political market, with what other means than corrupt ones could he expect to earn back his investments, knowing full well the smallness of the salary? The corrupting of the civil service system was an inevitable result of the commercialization of offices.

A second evil effect was the disintegration of the intellectual aristocracy. Aside from its democratic features, the strongest point of the government was its ability to take the intellectual leader into the service. Buyers of offices were necessarily those eliminated by the examinations. It did not mean that anybody eliminated by the examinations would be unworthy of an appointment. But the worthy and yet unfortunate might be poor or proud. When the financial element entered, all other factors of qualification or disqualification would have to give way. A group of the officeholders, who, according to the theory of the government, should not be exercising governing functions, would be at the helm. The disintegration might take place in this way. The able and qualified, seeing the rich purchasers stepping into the field, would refuse to join them. Anyway, the injection of elements unsuitable for government work could not be avoided so long as the sale of offices was practiced.

Thirdly, it inspired the gift and reception of bribes. When a man had spent 30,000 taels for a rank, he still had to wait. Very likely, if he were capable of paying more, he would rather do so than wait with the rest. But the stiffness of the civil service laws could be softened by benevolent personal influence which could be best secured by money.

By legitimate purchase one became expectant: by illegitimate bribery one ended the terms of expectation. Without the system of purchasing offices, officials were promoted or demoted for merit or demerit. But the new system sanctioned the promotion or avoidance of demotion by payment, thus placing money on a par with service. During the former periods, officials refrained from bribery, or negligence of duties and other corruption because any of them could easily destroy their career. With the entrance of money in politics, one could commit all kinds of wrongs and receive all forms of bribes, for although bribery might pull one down from the climbing of the official ladder, but a small portion of the bribe would help one to get up by leaps and bounds.

No doubt, of all institutions of the Manchu dynasty, the sale of offices was the worst. During the Taiping rebellion, it became a part of the Government: after that time, the Government began to show at every turn its incapacity. Towards the end of the dynasty, when buying and selling offices was most practiced, the efficiency of the government was at its lowest ebb. Indeed, to call the sale of offices one of the principal causes of the Manchu downfall would not be too severe a verdict upon this abominable institution.

Appointments might be divided into eight classes: (1) to supervise or control an organization, (2) to take charge of the affairs with a probationary rank, (3) to an office but with a higher rank, (4) to investigate or supervise a service, (5) concurrently to administer an organization, (6) to execute a special mission, (7) to learn the regulations and the art of administration in some service, and (8) temporary or acting administration.

Racially, all positions were divided into seven groups to be occupied by only men from each group. They were: (1) positions for the Imperial clansmen, (2) those for the Manchus, (3) those for the Mongols, (4) those for the Chinese bannermen, (5) those for the hereditary stewards of the Imperial Household Bureau, (6) those for the aborigines,

Tibetans, etc., and (7) those for Chinese. This division was substantially modified by supplementary rules much to the disadvantage of the Chinese. "Imperial clansmen can occupy Manchurian and Mongolian positions above the third rank. Chinese bannermen can occupy Chinese positions equivalent to, or higher than, the Senior Secretary of a bureau except in the Department of Justice or Manchurian positions of the third rank or above. Mongols can occupy provincial positions assigned to Chinese. 'Accessory' officials in the provinces lower than the sixth rank are not assigned to Manchus and Mongols. Provincial officials lower than a commissioner of finance or justice are not appointed from the Imperial clansmen." [12] The original purpose of distribution was to satisfy the Chinese. Gradual modifications in the distribution came out; none of them provided for the occupation of other positions by the Chinese although nearly all other groups of office aspirants were given the opportunity to step into the shoes of the Chinese.

The appointees were divided into six classes, namely: (1) the immediate appointees, (Chiu Pan), (2) the expectant appointees (Pu Pan), (3) the appointees for an advancement within its own rank (Chuan Pan), (4) the appointees changed from one institution or service to another (Kai Pan), (5) the appointees to be promoted (Sheng Pan), and (6) the appointees to be transferred (Tyau Pan). The immediate appointees were either those who had won degrees in the competitive examinations or those who had won a rank by virtue of their father's service to the government, coming up for the initial appointments. The successful candidates of the examination were appointed Member of the Academy of Letters, third class secretary of a bureau, secretary of the Grand Secretarial Staff, District Magistrate, or Instructing Official of a Prefect: the order of appointment and the rank of the office were strictly in accordance with the order in the examination. The appointment of hereditary candidates took a wider range. They might be

[12] *Ta Tsing Hui Tien*, v. 7.

appointed, in the Central Government, from second class Secretary of a bureau to clerks; in the provinces, from Assistant Prefect or sub-prefect to Instructing Officials of low grades. Practically speaking, however, the successful candidates stood a much better chance than the hereditary candidates. The acquisition of a literary degree virtually insured an appointment; while a hereditary rank might be given just for the sake of generosity without either the need or the desire of securing the fortunate one to the government service. A third element of the immediate appointees composed of those who had finished a term of apprenticeship in the departments and came up for permanent appointments. In this element, graduates of the Imperial College, (Kuo Tse Chien) could also be included. Fourthly, the Provincial Graduates who failed in the Metropolitan Examinations made up a portion of this class. It was provided that provincial graduates of "near provinces" and those of "far provinces" would be entitled to an appointment after having failed in the Metropolitan Examinations with three chances and one chance respectively. These were appointed junior secretaries of the departments and courts or district magistrate and assistant sub-prefects. The order of their appointment was determined, first by the year of graduation, then by their individual rank of graduation. Either one of these would seal the fate of aspirants to office with legal preference to the first factor. In case both were the same, a graduate from a "near province" would be chosen as he could not have the privilege until he had failed three times.

The "waiting list" contained the names of ten kinds of candidates who were waiting for appointments. Briefly stated, they were (1) on account of the abolition of the office or curtailment of its force; (2) those who were relieved of their position on account of appointment of one of blood superior relative to the same locality or service; (3) those who returned from a furlough for mourning, attendance upon aged parents, for sickness, wedding, repairment of family tombs, or burial of parents; (4) those who had served a term of suspension of appointment on account of errors; (5) those who had purchased a right to be appointed; (6) those transferred from other departments or provinces; (7) those who had finished their special duties on account of which their permanent positions were vacated. These expectant officials would not get their appointments until their turn came.

The highly hierarchic character of the administrative system placed definitely one office above another. Even the same rank and title had sharply demarcated degrees of superiority or inferiority; to wit, the "left" vice-minister was higher than the "right" vice-minister, and the "left" vice-minister of the department of civil service was higher than the "left" vice-minister of the department of revenues, and so on. This sharp and conclusive distinction gave rise to a separate class of appointees called Chuan Pan, which consisted of officials who, by sheer seniority, had earned the right to a little step of promotion in the service ladder, say, from circuit censorship to a departmental, or from senior secretaryship of the second to that of the first bureau.

Within the same rank, expectant officials were divided into several groups according to the offices they waited for. Take the first rank for instance. The ministerships of the departments formed one group, the censorships-general another, the viceroyalties a third. When a candidate was in the waiting list of viceroyalties and wanted to be transferred to be a candidate of a censorship-general, he had to go through all the formal processes of having his name changed from one list to another before he could expect the appointment he desired. Military officers who wanted to change to the civil service formed a second nucleus of the list: the same rank would be given in a transference of this kind. Provincial officials seeking appointment to central service also came under this class; this transference, unfortunately for the transferred official, was always followed by a degradation of rank. Two other elements enlarged the list; those who were transferred by special edict or after an examination. These transferees usually gained rank. A demoting transference completed the list. Demerit of an expectant official during his term of expectancy would secure for him this treatment. Thus, transference was chiefly a matter of gaining or having to lose rank. But the hierarchy was so wonderfully systematic that without a special edict of the emperor, half a rank at a time was the common promotion or demotion; one full rank at a time would immediately become the gossip of the mandarin circle.

The "Sheng Pan" or nomination list consisted of the office holders who had successfully removed all obstacles and patiently climbed up to a place where they were entitled to remain. The fortune of having one's name in the nomination list might be brought forth by seniority in service, advancement in salary, special choice of the emperor or recommendation to him by influential mandarins. This list was sent in whenever the emperor asked for it. But, unless he made a special choice, the strict rule of the hierarchy had its full sway. A scale of promotion, described by eighteen full pages of the *Ta Tsing Hui Tien* laid down the principle upon which the list could be made up. The list usually contained names of officials half rank below. For the appointment of a Grand Secretary whose rank was 1a, central officials of 1b like the ministers of the departments and the censors-general would be listed; for a minister (1b), names of the vice-ministers (2a) and a few others of 2b or 3a were listed. Generally half a rank was the promotion. The most noticeable deviation from this rule was the inclusion of the name of the Assistant Supervisor of Instruction of the Crown Prince (Tso Chuan Fang Shu Tzu) in the list of choice for a vice-minister where the difference between the qualified candidate and the office was three full ranks (5a to 2a). This list exercised a great control over the emperor when he had no special person in mind. It practically amounted to making a nomination to him and having him make the appointment. A range of choice certainly existed in such a list, but those not on the list were eliminated.

The last method of making an appointment was a direct transference of an official from one service to another without any technical change of rank, seniority, salary or whatnot. A transference of this kind was not made simply for the sake of change. Where rank, honor and privilege might be the same, the amount of power might be different. So this kind of change was often a promotion without showing favoritism, or a demotion without "loss of face." Not infrequently was this a weapon of the emperor to prevent an official from becoming too expert in the management of the business of a department, or to build up a party in the organization or service where an official had worked too long.

The emperor's power of appointing every government employee from Grand Secretary down to under-clerk, was, however, found impracticable simply because of the massiveness of the business. So three kinds of government appointments were given. The first was "special appointment" made by the emperor himself. To this class belonged the appointments of Grand Secretaries, Grand Councilors, Ministers, Vice-ministers, Censors-general, Assistant Censors-general, directors and deputy directors of the five courts and other high civil officials in Peking. Very often the appointment was made to the surprise of the mandarins; but sometimes, a list of the qualified candidates was requested by the emperor. Upon this request, the Council of State would submit the list, usually with a preferred candidate called to the attention of the appointing authority. The emperor also made the appointment of Manchurian assistant directors of the Courts of Ceremonies and Banqueting, colonels and captains of the banner forces, and some minor officials of the five courts, from lists submitted by the Department of Civil Service.

Intermediate officials like the secretaries of the departments, directing officials in the minor organization in the central government and other officials from fourth rank to seventh were appointed upon the recommendation of the

Department of Civil Service. Some positions, like the Manchurian Tutorship of the Imperial College (6a) and the Chinese directorship of the Imperial Board of Astronomy (5a), were, in theory at least, recommended for merit; others like the assistant directorship of the Imperial Board of Astronomy (6a) and minor officials in the Academy of Letters and the Supervisorate of Instructions of the Heir Apparent were reserved for men of seniority; the censorships were reserved for men of the Censorate. The secretaries of the departments were often recommended by the respective departments to the department of civil service which, in turn, recommended them to the emperor who made the appointments.

The third kind of appointment was that of officials of the 7th rank or lower. These were made directly by the departments themselves by the process of selection or examination.

For provincial officials, the viceroys, governors, finance commissioners, judicial commissioners and commissioners of education were appointed like grand secretaries and ministers, directly by the emperor. The salt comptroller might be appointed by the emperor directly or upon the recommendation of the viceroy or governor. From circuit intendents to magistrates, appointments were made, theoretically, by the emperor himself, but, practically, like the intermediate officials in Peking. Some officials below a magistrate were appointed from the Department of Civil Service in Peking while others of the same category were appointed by provincial authorities.

Besides the previous two classifications, first according to method of qualification then method of appointment, the "Monthly appointment" was a regular institution in the Chinese civil service system. There were two kinds of monthly appointments, namely: the "General appointment" in the even months [13] and the "Emergency appointments" in the odd months.[14] The Initial Class (Chiu Pan) and the

[13] The 2nd, 4th, 6th, 8th, 10th and 12th months.
[14] The 1st, 3rd, 5th, 7th, 9th and 11th months.

Promoted Class (Sheng Pan) came under the general appointment; the Waiting Class (Pu Pan) received their appointment in odd months. A further difference was made within the month on a racial basis; Manchurian, Mongolian, and Chinese. Bannerman positions were to be filled on the fifth day of the month, clerks on the twentieth, and Chinese on the twenty-fifth. This time condition was required of only the intermediate and minor officials; namely, positions of, and lower than, a first class secretary in the capital and those of, and lower than, a circuit intendent in the provinces. The *Ta Tsing Hui Tien* [15] provided for the central government 359 Manchurian positions, 59 Mongolian, 4 Chinese Bannermen and 161 Chinese; and in the provincial governments 4084 positions without any racial qualification to be filled by means of the monthly appointments. After the racial qualification, the candidates would be divided into two principal groups according to the way they qualified, whether by examination or otherwise. Then all qualified applicants for the same position would be listed on a general list with their method of qualification as a determinating factor for sub-division. A proportional number of appointments was made on a please-everybody basis, so many for those qualified from examinations and so many for those qualified by other means.

A further study of this civil service hierarchy would compel us further to classify the candidates' list from the standpoint of the time when they emerged from expectancy to realization. The following lists were produced by the Department of Civil Service in the appointing days:—

1. "The list for immediate appointment" consisted of officials who had finished their leave of absence and come to report for duty, those who had been transferred from other services or organizations, and those who had completed their terms of probation: a reappointment or reaffirmation of an old appointment rather than a new one.

[15] V. 9.

2. "The regular list" consisted of expectant officials who qualified themselves in different ways including seniority, purchase, hereditary favor, graduation, demotion, etc. The positions available for this class of candidates were divided into several classes according to method of qualification, so that, even within their own list, a position open to men who qualified by means of money would not be occupiable by one who qualified himself by his own talent.

3. "The picked list" broke the monotony of this hierarchy. It consisted of men picked from a list for lower offices. The condition of being thus fortunately picked was supposedly good service, but practically good influence.

4. "The combined list" had the names of the provincial officials transferred to the central service.

5. "The substitute list" was always ready in case the regular lists were exhausted. But only expectant officials of the same rank would be picked for substitutes.

6. "The list to be put before all others." This list consisted of the new metropolitan graduates. This list, in fact, did not come under the monthly appointments, as those upon it would be appointed before all other expectant officials.

The complicated classifications and different groupings were very forcibly backed up by reference to records. As we have seen, one of the four bureaus of this department was entirely devoted to the keeping of records of the candidates as well as of occupants of offices. We will now proceed to find out their specific duties as a record-keeping institution. In the registry of this bureau, one could find seven kinds of information about civil service men: their place of birth; occupation of their fathers and grandfathers; a verdict of the department on their personality and speech so as to assure that they were not disqualified; the circumstances of their unemployment whether it was leave of absence, dismissal or transference; the length of service in a particular organization and in the Government in general; records of probation or apprenticeship; whether one had any close blood relative in the same service; and copies of their credentials all entered into the record books of the bureau. The superabundance of expectant officials made the least bit of suspicion as to the qualifications of the would-be mandarins a source of trouble for them. In addition to these facts, age, naturalization and names of the mandarins were carefully registered, particularly the names. Several kinds of names had to be avoided; identity with the name of a prince, prominent minister, or another official in the same office or locality; meaning something pertaining to the emperor, or similar to that of an Imperial Mausoleum. The Manchus and Mongolians, having no family names to start with, were not allowed to adopt any, and also forbidden to have names resembling those of the Chinese. The age of the candidates was rather loosely kept, and seldom revised. "When some of the expectant officials die, the local authorities fail to report it to the central government because their family neglected to go through the formal process of reporting it to the local officials. The lists of waiting officials are thus piled up. Some of the expectant mandarins are, according to records, over one hundred years of age. Their incapacity by death is not known until they fail to report for duty after an appointment and another man has to be appointed in his place."[16] In 1892, in reply to the above quoted memorial, Emperor Kuang Hsu issued an edict compelling the expectant officials to retire or rather causing their names to be dropped from the list when they reach the age of seventy-five.[17] In view of the wide practice of personal influence and other corruptions, it is justifiable to entertain some suspicion of the accuracy of the records. Indeed a little change in them for the purpose of skipping some of the tedious steps was quite inevitable.

By passing an examination, a Chinese candidate was entitled to receive an appointment. By passing another exam-

---

[16] Memorial of Kao Hsieh Tseng 1892, *Tung Hua Lu.*
[17] *Tung Hua Lu.*

ination at the end of his term, he was allowed to remain in office or win a promotion. Certainly the triennial examination for the officials was just as much an institution as was the triennial examination for the students. The term of office, except that of the Grand Secretaries and Councilors of State, was three years. At the end of this period, the examinations for central officials (Tsing Tsa) and provincial officials (Ta Chi) would take place. As not all the officials were appointed at the same time, the examination was given only to those who had served for one year or more.

In Peking, officials of, or above, the third rank would have their records submitted to the emperor by the Department of Civil Service. As these were not under direct supervision or control of the department, and as the emperor himself usually knew personally these officials, this examination was merely a formality; the records presented were simply biographies of the examined. Then records of officials of the fourth and fifth ranks were submitted to the emperor by the department with occasional remarks of the departmental authority attached. They might be given an audience by the emperor or just passed off for reappointment or promotion. The examination was more or less nominal. For officials below the fifth rank, their records were first made up by the vice-minister, if a department or the assistant director, if a court, with the opinions of the vice-ministers and assistant directors. They were then sent to a board of Examiners appointed by the emperor from the Grand Secretaries, ministers, or the Censor-general. The Board went over all the records or sometimes called the minor officials in for a personal examination and then submitted the records to the emperor. The recommendations of the direct superiors were usually accepted by the Board, transmitted to the Sovereign, who, in turn, seldom rejected the opinion of his delegates.

In the provinces, the records of the Commissioners of finance and justice were sent by the viceroy or governor to the Department of Civil Service for the sake of formality.

As these commissioners were appointed by the emperor, the merit or demerit of their records would not reach the final verdict until the mark of the vermilion pencil was made. The circuit intendents, prefects, and magistrates were strictly examined by the viceroy or governor who submitted the records to the Department of Civil Service which again presented it to the emperor. The recommendations of the viceroy or governor generally were sustained. "Accessory" officials not belonging to either of the two preceding classes were examined by their direct superior and then had their records sent to the viceroy or governor who would treat them as records of the second group, with, however, the recommendations of the immediate superior usually accepted.

These examinations were based on four determining elements; namely, personal conduct, executive ability, service record, and age. Relative importance of the different elements were proportional to the order. The comparatively great importance given to personal conduct was certainly typical of the Chinese government representing the influence of the virtue theory. The examined were divided into three classes: only with a first class conduct could an official entertain the fond hope of winning a first class recommendation. The other three elements averaged up either for first, second or third class recommendations. Any one of these, however, would insure the examined another appointment of equal rank if not an advancement.

The unsatisfactory were separately listed with one of the six determinating elements. These were looseness of conduct, inactivity, frivolousness, lack of talent, old age, and sickness. The first or second would bring forth absolute dismissal; the third, demotion of three grades; the fourth, demotion of two grades; and the fifth and sixth compulsory retirement. Worse than any one of these six was avariciousness or cruelty.

Placing the ethical standard of the government workers before their serviceability, the system of examination was thus open to abuses. Conduct of a human being was indeed

CIVIL SERVICE AND CIVIL SERVICE LAWS 125

a difficult thing to judge, especially when the superior and the inferiors had only occasional contact. But building the government on a foundation of personal morality and influence, it was natural for the Chinese government to give this intangible quality a greater weight than solid work. The negative character of the government, and the actual influence of an official on the people, on the other hand, rather justified this unusual arrangement. The fact is, when a state is governed by men rather than by law, moral conduct as a quality of its workers should be above everything else.

The rewards of the meritorious were of three kinds, a record of merit, an advancement of grades, or an immediate promotion. A record of merit might seem unsubstantial; but three merits equalled one grade, and one, two or three merits might be given at a time. An advancement of grades might be given as advancement in rank or advancement in salary. Three grades equalled one-half rank. The merits or grades, besides their positive force to advancement, also had their negative force of cancelling demerits unless they were recorded for private offenses. Grades were of two kinds, transferable, meaning good for any other rank or office, and non-transferable, good only for the present rank and office. Grades given on account of military service were always transferable while those given for civil service were not, unless so designated. Immediate promotion was the highest reward for an official after examination. Having such a hierarchic ladder in the system, promotions were commonly of one-half rank. The Government was jealously strict as to this rule: their favorite way of getting around it was, not to make big jumps, but to take little jumps with extremely great frequency.

Dismissal, demotion, and compulsory retirement did not complete the list of punishments for the "parents of the people." To transmit an edict to upbraid a mandarin was a peculiar yet frequently applied form of chastisement. This would cost the chastised no material loss but its moral effect might put the punished in such a position that he would prefer some solid penalty. The other tangible punishment was fine of salary, ranging from one month to two years. This was applied only to light offenses. Demotion and dismissal were further divided. It might be only in rank, but not the office. It might be both and thus cause the degraded to be transferred to an appointment of a lower rank and post. This could not go beyond two and a half ranks at a time. In case the rank of the punished were not high enough for demotion, absolute dismissal was substituted. Dismissals were of two kinds, dismissal from rank and dismissal from post. In the first, the position of the dismissed was retained by him, while in the second the dismissal was absolute. Technically, dismissal was a greater punishment; but, practically, it was better than demotion and transfer: for at the end of four years the dismissed could be reappointed to equal rank and similar post unless the phrase "Not to be appointed again" was attached to the document; while a demoted had first of all to make up his demerits by merits, and until they had accomplished this, they could not possibly get back the original rank, otherwise they would have to struggle up again from whatever steps in the bottom of the ladder to which he was doomed. Dismissal was the heaviest punishment for an official imposed by the Department of Civil Service. More severe acts could be taken by the Department of Justice or the Emperor, but the tribunals could not sentence an official to capital punishment unless his rank and position were both taken from him beforehand.

In case of a man committing two errors in one and the same act, the more serious one would be the basis of punishment. If errors were made in concurrent and yet separate positions, only the heavy one would be a basis for punishment. For titular nobles, demotion would be from the higher one whether title or post; dismissal might be one or another or both, regardless of their comparative grade. When the office and rank of the punished were not identical, the office was always the basis of punishment, whether higher or lower than the rank.

CIVIL SERVICE AND CIVIL SERVICE LAWS   127

Cases for punishment might be brought up by an Imperial edict, or by petition of the direct superior to the Department of Civil Service. A quite common practice was the petitioning to punish oneself. This was not an instance of the famous self-denial of the Chinese. In the network of the hierarchic administrative law of China, an official committing an error could scarcely expect to escape due punishment except when strong influence in the Court was available. Since it was bound to come, petitioning for it would show one's own awareness of the fault and penitence, and hence might result in a lighter punishment. Decrees directing the punishment of an official who applied for it often contained the phrase "The punishment should be heavier, but, in view of the fact that the author of the mistake had been aware of his offense and shown penitance, he should be punished only by . . . . ."

One of the three steps usually preceding a punishment was an investigation with a fair hearing given to the defendant, a conference of the Council of State, six departments or nine ministers after the impeachment by the censors or direct superiors. The degree of punishment was decided by the respective department in whose jurisdiction the error was committed; for instance, in documental form, date-limit of transmission, etc., by the Department of Civil Service; financial and other civil cases, by the Department of Revenues; ceremonies, education and examinations, by the Department of Rites; communications and defense, by the Department of War; criminal cases, by the Department of Justice; constructions, by the Department of Works, and so forth. The departments, however, did not have a free hand in the decision. In no other part of the Chinese Government was law so strictly applied as in this. The *Ta Tsing Hui Tien* provided that in case no law exactly fitted in the case, regulations and cases would be the guide of the decision; if not even these were available, the decision of the Department would be accepted and the case made a sample case with the approval of the emperor.

A strange and yet effective weapon of manipulation in the Tsing Government was to separate different members of the same family in the same service or locality. The purpose of the separation was to separate public duty from private considerations. As the Chinese society was built purely on family lines and every kind of business, governmental or otherwise, was devoid of business exactitude, this institution was devised to divert personal elements as much as possible from public activity. But, behind this, there was a deeper motive: it was to prevent the least opportunity for party organization. The institution of monarchy of the Chinese model could not have powerful parties without endangering itself. In the Chinese society, the easiest kind of a party was a family party. By avoiding frequent contact of the family members in official business and keeping them from concentrating and all becoming experts in the business of the same department or province, emperors of the diverse dynasties succeeded in preventing the organization of big political parties. It may have been due to this rule that in spite of the highly technical character of the civil service laws, no administrative bureaucracy was built up. At any rate, these laws of avoidance (for lack of a better term) were among the most faithfully executed laws of the old monarchy. Their minuteness and great length forbid a full treatment here. But a few of their general principles are absolutely necessary for an understanding of the Manchu Government. First, a family inferior should avoid working with a family superior, unless the former is a principal and the latter a subordinate official. Secondly, one should avoid the department or province where a member of one's family occupied a position higher than the one to which he is appoinnted: when equal in rank, one who entered the service later should avoid the senior. Third, avoidance of paternal relatives were much more strict than maternal ones. Fourth, a foster child should follow the foster father in avoiding relatives. Fifth, in the Departments of Revenue and Justice where the bureaus were divided according to provinces, secretaries and clerks in the bureaus must be transferred in case one of the relatives should hold a position of the third rank or higher in the province the business of which the bureau handled. Sixth, on account of the difficulty of getting qualified men for the superabundant posts provided, Manchurian, Mongolian and Chinese bannermen secretaries in the Grand Secretariat, Mongolian secretaries in the Department of Territories, secretaries in the "five departments" in Manchuria and Manchurian Ceremonial assistants were exempt from these rules.

In the provinces, this principle was much more strictly applied. None with the same family name and from the same district as the Viceroy or Governor could hold office in that province. In case of a viceroy, the province under his direct control was the limit; of a governor, Financial Commissioner, Judicial Commissioner, or others whose jurisdiction could reach the whole province, the province proper and a neighboring province (if it be governed by the same viceroy) would be the limit; of a circuit intendent, prefect, the province where that political subdivision belonged should be a territorial limit of avoidance. A position in the province of birth was forbidden; naturalization in another province disqualified a candidate in either of the two provinces. A fellow-provincial could not be employed even as an adviser. Finally, the avoidance of more remote relatives should be applied in order to show that one strictly abode by all regulations.

The law of mutual responsibility requiring one official to be answerable for the offense of another is an institution that has no equal in any other government. This law was introduced by Grand Secretary Hung Cheng Chou in 1650 and promulgated by Emperor Shun Chi in the same year.[18] It had first of all to do with the records of the candidates. As we have seen that a complete record of birth place and family history of three generations back had to be submitted

[18] See *Tsing Chien Yi Chi Lu*, or A Chronological History of the Early Tsing Emperors.

to the Department of Civil Service for reference, we also should know that these records had to be certified by the local authorities. But, in case the candidate came from a distant province, to go back for verification would be paying too much for the whistle; therefore, fellow-provincials holding office in the capital were permitted to verify his records. For any error that required mutual responsibility made by the verified, the verifiers virtually shared the punishment. A direct superior quite frequently had to share the punishment of his subordinates and a recommender that of the recommended, though the latter might have nothing to do with the former after the recommendation. The punishment of Weng Tung Ho and Chang Yin Huan because of their recommendation of Kang Yu Wei after the failure of the Reform Movement in 1898 illustrates the regular working of this law. But it was often carried much further than this, for a superior was responsible for acts of his inferior over whom he had neither supervision nor control. Take the provincial examination, for instance. The Commissioner of Education, who nominally headed the educational officers of the province, practically was only a judge in the examinations, nothing more. The Proctor of the Examination was the business manager of the examination. His duties were not at all connected with those of the commissioner. Being appointed directly by the emperor, he was not under even the superintendence, not to say control, of the Commissioner. Yet for his offense, the Commissioner, whether with or without knowledge of it, had to share the punishment.

Another extension of this law was that for offense of the present, past holders of the office might be called to answer. In the Metropolitan Examination in the 9th year of Chien Lung (1744) twenty-one competitors were found guilty of carrying reference books into the Examination Hall. As this was against law and the duty of the Examiners and other officials for the Examination was to prevent acts of this kind, it was justifiable to punish the officers of that

CIVIL SERVICE AND CIVIL SERVICE LAWS 131

particular examination. But, instead, an edict was issued [19] ordering the punishment of all examining officers from the first to the 9th year of the reign by the Department of Justice with the excuse that the present violation of law was a result of the failure of the previous examining officers, therefore the past examiners should be just as much responsible for it as the present.

In rewards as well as in punishments, this law had applications. As the recommender often got punished on account of recommending unsuitable men, he would get rewarded when his proteges rendered conspicuous service. But there was one difference in the application of this law: the responsibility to share punishments worked only upwards while the mutual share of rewards might work both ways. In other words, the subordinate officials never got punishment for offenses of their superiors though he might profit by the Government's recognition of their service.

This law was indeed the pivot of the administrative machinery. By injecting private relations into official duties, it succeeded in making the officials much more careful in their acts. The fear of bringing disgrace to one's superior or protector, thus showing one's ingratitude, kept the officials in check. Mutual correction and mutual shielding as methods of mutual protection were in extensive and faithful practice. The dread of suffering the consequence of another's offense made one very particular in the choice of one's company and virtually ostracized the one not *persona grata* to the Government. The only way of escaping the responsibility was to make the offense known to the emperor before it was found out. So, first by enacting this law, the emperor gained the control of the officials: then, by supplementing this law, he completed the control.

These advantages of this peculiar law were, however, not without a corresponding set of disadvantages. It first of all fostered the tendency to recommend mediocrities to the Government. The full set of civil service law suited the

[19] *Ta Tsing Hui Tien Shih Li.*

mediocrities much better than intellectual giants or administrative wizards. The seniority rule, the waiting lists, the official pomps, the formal ceremonies all contributed to enslave the mind and enervate the body of a young candidate. Worse than these was the law of mutual responsibility. The whole system being an imperial machinery of manipulation, men of energy and activity could easily step out of the regular path. The list of the able ministers executed by the Manchu emperors chilled a candidate at the door of government service. Men of unusual ability withdrew themselves from the administrative arena. The few exceptions were either submerged in the enervating atmosphere of officialdom or refused protection and ended their life as petty officials with bitter disappointment. The first evil effect of this law, then, was the mediocratization of the civil servants.

Then, even if some adventurous mandarins were bold enough to recommend some one who had not been tamed, they would be liable to cover the offense of their proteges rather than reveal them to the throne. Other officials, with the benevolent purpose of saving the face of a friend or reciprocating his favor, would keep silent; for only by leaving the "sage-ruler" in the mist, could ministers hope to save their face, prestige, position and even life. Thus we see that the practice of mutually shielding each other's offense often defeated the law of mutual responsibility.

A discussion of the Chinese civil service system would be incomplete without giving a brief account of an extra-administrative institution,—the under-clerk. Viewing from a structural standpoint, Chinese officials could be divided into two classes, the "principal" and the "accessory" officials, designated in Chinese as "Cheng Yin" and "Tso Erh" respectively. This distinction did not exist in the Central civil service: but in the provincial administration, all the head officials from a viceroy to a district magistrate were designated as "principal" while an "accessory" was an assistant in the different offices or services, in the administration of a political subdivision, like an assistant salt controller, assistant prefect or magistrate, etc. The stratification was not based on ranks, method of appointment, nor the amount of influence or power, nor the position of relative importance in the whole government machinery; but on the nature of the duty and the relative position in that particular office or service. Thus a magistrate of a district with the rank of 7a was a principal while an assistant prefect with rank of 5a was accessory. With this distinction in mind, we can proceed to find out the third and lowest stratum of the civil service hierarchy, the under-clerk.

The under-clerk, an office boy in theory, was, in many cases, the "boss" of the *yamen*. The first qualification for this apparently undignified yet practically remunerative position was the lack of qualification for a regular position in the Government. A knowledge of writing, arithmetic and law and regulations completed the list of requirements. The recruitment of an under-clerkship was either by appointment, special examination, or purchase. One fact to substantiate the contempt of the Government for this class of employees was the conducting of their examinations in places other than the regular examination halls, as these halls were considered too dignified for them. The successful candidates were divided into five classes and appointed to rankless positions with their lucrativeness as a basis of classification.

The tenure of office was either five years, for life, or hereditary. Examinations were given them every five years. For the first kind, a promotion to the 9b ranked office might be awarded; for the second and third, examinations were for retention or dismissal. The number of under-clerks provided were about 1,400 in the capital, and between 300 and 2,000 in each of the provinces, usually over 1,000, and quite a few provinces had more than 1,500.

Technically, they were errand boys, copying documents, carrying messages between the officials and the people, acting as attendants at a trial, urging the payment of taxes, doing all kinds of things the officials wanted done yet could not personally do. Practically they knew the laws, the forms of documents, the conditions of the people and the likes and dislikes of their direct superiors. Their expert knowledge of the technicality of the administration coupled with the officials' lack of it made them the virtual heads of the department or locality. Their lack of a career to look forward to, plus the ineffectiveness of the control by the officials, opened the way to corruption. The contempt of their superiors and the people made them search for compensation outside of honor and respect. Treated like knaves, they acted like knaves. An edict of Emperor Chien Lung issued in 1736 describes pretty well the working and corruption of these underlings:—

> The magistrates being immediate governors of the people, ought to be just, honest and undisturbing. But in cases of lawsuit and tax collection, misunderstandings have often arisen between the officials and the people and the people have often been wronged. This is all due to the wickedness and corruption of the under-clerks and the failure of the magistrates to rectify them. I have heard that in the Magistrate's office, there are extra under-clerks besides those regularly provided. These rogues gather together in the offices, come out to cheat and rob the people in the name of government service. Frequently before the decision of a legal action is reached, the fortune of both the plaintiff and the defendant is already swallowed up by them. A great portion of the tax is squeezed by them before official collection. They befriend bandits, free important prisoners, harm the innocent and commit all sorts of offense . . . . Not only harm to the magistrate's office is done but the whole government is poisoned by them. In transaction of official business, the under-clerks of a superior office demand money from those of a subordinate organization, who, in turn, squeeze the money out of the poor innocent people. If the people refuse, all kinds of difficulty would befall them. Worst of all, all official correspondence between the officials and their superior or the people first go through their hands. They always avail themselves of the opportunity. If the sender be from a subordinate office, the amount of money offered determines the speed of transmission. Hence the corruption of these yamen parasites is a systematic chain coming from above, not beginning with the magistrate.

Again, in 1799, Emperor Chia Cheng in his edict, pointed out the corruption of these minor public servants with the following words:—

The worst institution in our government is the under-clerk. Provincial officials often bribe the under-clerks in the departments for speedy communications in report, discussions in reward or punishment, promotion, transfer and whatnot. The under-clerks on the other hand, make the best of their opportunity by squeezing as much as possible by means of both deceit and threat. Tribute and tax-bearers from the provinces suffer immeasurable harm. Between the time the report is handed over and the time a receipt of the government comes to the hands of the bearer, the squeezing of the under-clerks has, by one and a thousand ways run up to thousands. This is called "Fees for the departments:" yet they pocket and distribute it among themselves publicly. The viceroys and governors fully know these corruptions but have made no attempts to stop them. The business transacted between governors, commissioners and magistrates also go through their hands: they also profit by these transactions. *In some cases the officials even form a partnership with them.*

From private writers as well as in government documents, we find the corruption of the under-clerks well known and the institution fiercely attacked. Koo Ting Lin's *Essays on Provincial Government,* says that "The corruption of the office of a prefect or magistrate lies in the under-clerks. They monopolize and inherit the jobs. The more wicked become under-clerks of an upper office by hook and crook, then exact present from those below. The men in power know it, but can do nothing with it."

With such full knowledge of their operation and such an enthusiastic desire to terminate their evils from both the throne and the public, why could they perpetuate untouched their evils throughout the whole dynasty? The reason is simple enough: the institute of under-clerkship was a residue of the civil service system. Before one entered into political life, literature was the study: after the entrance, the knowledge of law and regulation should be the requisite. Unequipped with a knowledge of law and regulations as most of the officials were, on whom could they depend for the performance of their duties if not on the professional, nay, hereditary under-clerks? The law of avoidance forbade appointment of a native to any provincial positions; the execution of official duties demanded a fair knowledge of the locality; from whom could a magistrate or prefect get the knowledge of local conditions, if not from the under-clerks? Ambitious and industrious magistrates might be able to get acquainted with the place they governed; but, before they could secure a fair idea of it, their terms would be almost gone; all would have been done for naught. Therefore, even honest and energetic magistrates were compelled to take an attitude of benevolent indifference. Wicked magistrates, on the other hand, would look at the under-clerkship as a source of increasing their own incomes. A partnership with the under-clerk would be exceptional: appointment in consideration of monetary compensation was nothing surprising.

From the standpoint of the under-clerks themselves, reasons abounded for keeping up their dishonest, illegitimate and yet profitable business. "They know the people would not be able to fight them either in law or by force, because they had the officials back of them. Not knowing how much longer they can have the opportunity, or whether others will apply the same thing to them tomorrow, they naturally do the utmost while they can. Moreover, they feel they belong to the government; they have no common interests with the people." [20] Furthermore, the corruption of an official often furnished them excuse for their own corruption; not infrequently the threat of disclosing the corruptions of their superior was the means they used. The purchased under-clerkship, like other purchased positions, had to make the bargain with the government a paying proposition. Taking all these conditions into consideration, together with their low salary, what source of revenue could they live on aside from corrupt practice?

[20] Huang Li Chou, *"Essay on the Under-clerks"* Ming I Tai Fang Lu, p. 36.

In going through this thick network of civil service laws, one cannot help being impressed by the fact that China, instead of being known as a government of no laws, was really one of a super-abundance of bad laws, loosely administered and grossly abused. Out of this impression, several characteristics of these laws will not escape our attention. Fundamentally the whole set of these laws was drawn up to make the throne safe for the "Son of Heaven," not to make the service efficient. Many of them, entirely artificial in nature, against the traditions of the country, and without enough government backing for strict enforcement, became in course of time weapons of evil doing for the under-clerks.

Counteracting the tendency of decentralization caused by the vastness of the country and the lack of means of transportation and communication, the laws made desperate attempts to centralize the machinery of governing one quarter of the human race by the "tribute-fed and eunuch-ridden" court. Before appointment, one must make a pilgrimage to Peking for examinations; the Mecca of the Mandarin could not fail to produce an impression upon the poor place-seeker; His most august Majesty's dignity, power and favor could not but inspire loyalty and suppress the illegitimate desires of the ambitious and wicked. At the end of three years, an official term in China, every official with a responsible position in the provinces had to make another political pilgrimage to the capital, to have his old impression of awe and admiration, his old inspiration of loyalty and service reshaped. For the appointment, the appointee had to send in a memorial expressing thanks to the emperor for His Majesty's favor, thus stamping on the mind of the civil servants the emperor's ownership of the positions, making the oath of allegiance a written document privately addressed to one person instead of being publicly administered in the name of the country. The constant reports to the departments by the provincial authorities retightened the bond between the capital and the provinces. The audience given by the emperor to the civil pilgrims kept the former informed of the conditions. In spite of the ineffectiveness of the government, Peking reigned by virtue of crafty regulations.

Having made sufficient provision for the safety of the throne, the government enacted further laws to play one office or person against another by a system of checks and balances. The law of avoidance prevented the concentration of members of a family in an organization or a locality. The law of mutual responsibility established a mutual surveillance, nay, mutual spying upon one another's conduct. The prohibition of party organization made joint action a crime. Individual audiences might be given for the purpose of finding out power, influence or conduct of some special official. Finally, the censors, professional spies of the mandarin world, were likely to perform their "eyes and ears" function by impeaching an official to the throne. The whole system, if divested of checks, would be nothing. So we can see that by centralization, control was acquired; by checks it was maintained.

The system of expectants was a milling process of mandarinizing the good, energetic and honest youths. Appointment from lists bound the Department of Civil Service to appoint, not men they knew or thought suitable for the position, but the men who had acquired the right to wait for the appointment and those who had waited long enough. Seniority was thus placed before everything else. Unluckily enough, in spite of their seniority, their ignorance of the working of the government was quite surprisingly complete: naturally they depended on the under-clerks to untie the knots, unconsciously giving all powers of administration to the parasitic minions. While they were acquiring this wonderful qualification, seniority, they had to go through a whole milling process of unnecessary social functions, to learn all the "tricks of the trade" with a probable opportunity of incidentally connecting themselves with a political scandal.

Specialization was checked by this system. The short term of office and the rare chance of reappointment, the frequent transference of locality and organization, the avoidance of appointing natives in a province, and the casting of lot as a means of determining the fate of the expectants as to the service or province in which he might expect an appointment all prevented the civil servants from obtaining expertness in their work.

This set of laws, we should not overlook, was not built up in a single period or by a single emperor. Like the English Constitution, it grew bit by bit through the tedious yet safe process of evolution: but, unlike the English Constitution, old laws were neglected, not displaced; new laws counteracted, but did not replace. It is well said that "the creators of laws, failing to foresee the change of circumstances in the future, neglected provisions for new interpretation and easy amendment: later executors of these laws, enslaved by their letter, dared not make any amendment; instead they created new laws to counterbalance its deteriorating influence. Hence, the more laws we have, the more corruptions and violations we see. The whole trouble lies in the lack of enforcement after enactment."[21] The growth of these laws followed the demand of more complicated regulations arising out of the increase of the expectants and the desire of the emperor to have a greater control of the Government: the tendency of its growth was towards centralizing the powers in the emperor and checking the powers of the officials.

With the possible exception of its ability to centralize the government to a certain degree, none of the features of this civil service system is worthy of praise. The Manchu downfall has been attributed to the growth of racial sentiment of the Chinese, the Government's inability to stop foreign aggression, the hunger of the starving millions and one and a hundred other reasons and causes: a study of the civil service system, however, would not fail to reveal it as one of the principal factors in the undermining and overthrowing of that government.

[21] Koo Ting Lin, "Essay on Law," *Yih Chih Lu*, v. 8, p. 22.

CHAPTER VI

THE DEPARTMENT OF RITES (LI PU) AND CIVIL SERVICE EXAMINATIONS

The Chinese word "Li" literally translated as "ceremonies" or "rites" derived this meaning from its corrupted sense: for lack of more approximate words in the English language, these terms are here adopted. Before any discussion of the department or the examinations, a brief explanation of the real meaning of the term "Li" will help us to understand the establishment of this department. By ceremony or rite, a Westerner denotes the formal conduct with which one acts towards another as a matter of etiquette or politeness. At its best, it is an expression of culture without regard to intent; a social term, not a spiritual symbol. But, this magic word means much more to a Chinese, particularly in earlier times. "It includes not only the external conduct, but involves the right principles from which all true etiquette and politeness spring."[1] It represents, then, besides the outward appearance of refinement, the very man himself. "Li" means propriety: in China where the absence of a noble class or other class distinction prevailed throughout her history, a hierarchic set of ceremonies symbolizing the status of the men, governing the formalities of occasions from wedding to funeral, from daily dress to court uniform, distinguished one group of individuals from another. By it every one should abide; violation of it would cause public disapproval or constitute a legal offense. An ordinary subject, usurping the right of conducting a funeral like an official, would bring contempt upon himself: a mandarin wearing the dress of the emperor, or even that of a higher official might cost him his head. Its practice resembles

[1] Williams, *Middle Kingdom*, v. 1, p. 645.

church-going in the West. By living up to it, public esteem is earned. Indeed, the ancient rites were not formalities *per se*; a religious tinge, we may say, entered into quite a few of the formal occasions upon which no other sign than ceremonies presented themselves. Furthermore, the word has been to a certain extent, used to mean institutions as in the book *Chou Li*, which literally translated, would mean the ceremonies of the Chou dynasty, yet it is practically a book of the political institutions of that ancient dynasty. Even down to the modern Manchu dynasty, "Li" was still looked upon, not as ethical in character, but as an effective weapon of political utility. The ceremonies, void of their old glorious meaning still served for the barbarous Manchus as a means with which to guide the myriads.

The corruption of the word was, fortunately or unfortunately, more in spirit than in form. In the beginning of the 20th century, we still could find a special department, one of the principal six, specially devoted to the minute set of ceremonies, from coronation to mutual salution of officials. The Confucian principle, "Decorum should be maintained in a hurry as well as in danger," had not entirely vanished from practice after twenty-three centuries of corruption.

By this complicated word, the department we now deal with was named. This "Li Pu" was divided into five bureaus; the Bureau of Ceremonial Systems attending to court ceremonies, ceremonies for conferring of titles, court uniforms, retinues, weddings of officials, imperial clansmen, and members of the Imperial Household, Education, and Examination; the Bureau of Sacrificial Rites, for state sacrifices,[2] funerals, conferring of posthumous favors, editing the calendar, and miscellaneous sacrifices; the Diplomatic Bureau, for entertainment of tribute-bearing agents, trade with dependencies, government gifts to officials; the Bureau of Supply for preparation of diplomatic banquets,

[2] To Heaven, Earth, Imperial ancestors, Confucius and meritorious officials, etc.

sacrificial offerings and general purchase and supplies of the whole department; and the Engraving Bureau for the manufacturing of official seals. Two ministers [3] and four vice-ministers,[4] besides supervising these five bureaus, drafted the program of ceremonies, submitted them to the emperor, and, after his approval, acted as masters of ceremonies upon all occasions. In the documentary world, this department kept records of all ceremonies the emperor attended, records of the descendants of Confucius, of Buddhist, Taoist, medical and astronomical officials in addition to those connected with education. It is reported to the emperor for rewards all cases of filial piety, righteousness or loyalty.

The Department of Music, furnishing ancient music for court dances and other ceremonials with ancient instruments, was an organization subordinate to the Department of Rites. The Manchurian minister of the Department held concurrently the ministership of Music. The number of ministers in this department was not fixed as high officials with good knowledge in music frequently secured a concurrent appointment to this ministership.

Of all its duties by far the most important was the educational. Education in old China did not simply mean schooling, but also meant the preparation and selection of men for government service. The assignment of this duty to this department was a residue of the old conception that rites formed the first of the six subjects of study. Structurally, this assignment was a step towards centralization, as it provided all government organizations with qualified men. It, however, deviated from the old system: for "in the Chou and Han dynasties, examination and appointment came from the same office. The Tang Emperors delegated the power of Examination to the Department of Rites and the selection to office to the Department of Civil Service. Since then qualification and appointment were separated." [5]

[3] One Manchu and one Chinese.
[4] Two Manchus and two Chinese.
[5] *Huang Chao Tung Chi.*

From the 7th century down, a civil servant had to go through the Department of Rites for qualification, the Department of Civil Service for one of the two departments that he had gone through. This certainly centralized the control of appointment although it worked awkwardly for other departments and the provinces. This defect of the system, nevertheless, did not seem too glaring; for as the absence of technical work in the government demanded no special appointees, the government was able to stumble along with men recruited upon the same basis of selection.

Let us recollect here that the first and most honorable, though the hardest and possibly the slowest, way of qualifying for government service was success in examinations. All positions, except those occupied by men not allowed to compete in the examinations, were open to successful candidates coming out with laurels from the literary arena. Like voting in a democratic country, this competition could be universally participated in: like qualifying to vote in a universally enfranchised nation, legal provisions regarding qualifications were rather for the exclusion of the unfortunate small minority than for entitling the lucky few to a quasi-monopoly of privilege. The permanently disfranchised were bond-servants, servants, private soldiers, undertakers, prostitutes, actors, beggars, boatmen, and the convicts. The sons and grandsons of the first eight categories inherited the disqualification unless their removal was recommended by local officials while the convicts carried their disqualification into their graves without, however, leaving it to their posterity. At the fourth generation, the disqualification automatically ended. The temporarily disqualified were (1) those living outside of their native province; (2) those caught helping other candidates in the competitive examinations; (3) mourners over the deaths of their parents or grandparents; and (4) users of pseudonyms. Racially, the examinations were given only to Chinese and members of other races willing to take their chances in the competition. This meant that peoples of other races seeking government employment did not have to go through these tedious processes. Among the excluded, practically not legally, were the aborigines, Mongols, Tibetans, members of the imperial clan, Manchu and Chinese bannermen and sons of nobles or husbands of a duke's daughters.[6] Exclusion from the examinations in no way barred them from civil service: on the other hand, the aborigines were provided with a number of positions for which aspirant appointees could qualify themselves in other ways. Mongols and Tibetans did not participate in spite of their eligibility in the Metropolitan Prefecture largely on account of intellectual incapacity. Imperial clansmen and bannermen were given special examinations with easier literary requirements. The dissipation of the bannermen incapacitated so many of them for military activity that in their examinations they usually tried to get excused from tests in archery upon the pretended ground of near-sightedness. An edict issued by Emperor Chien Lung in 1775[7] bears interesting witness to this point. It says:—

According to the records of the examiners in horsemanship and archery, there are 73 out of 125 applicants reporting near-sightedness with the aim of getting excused from examination in military arts. Twenty of the 73 have been ordered to take the examinations as usual while 53 of them who are really handicapped, may be excused from these examinations. But, horsemanship and archery are the foundation of the banner forces. They are necessary even for scholars. It cannot be true that 73 out of 125 are near-sighted. This is no doubt a false report . . . . . Simply because they do not know these sports, they offer physical handicap as an excuse . . . . The 53 applicants who could neither ride on horseback nor shoot with bow and arrows shall be disqualified from the examinations.

But most of the emperors, with the insidious idea of checking the growth of Chinese influence by taking in bannermen, indulgently excused them from these tests. Again, the dissipation of the bannermen, especially in the latter part of the dynasty, had been so complete that had these strict requirements been kept up, it is doubtful if any of the bannermen applicants could really have made a good

[6] See edicts 1605 and 1810.
[7] *Ta Tsing Hui Tien Shih Li.*

enough performance in their lost arts to satisfy the critical and searching examiners.

The number of bannermen candidates was sometimes small enough to necessitate the cancellation of the examinations. The last group of those excluded from competition arose from their special privilege. They consisted of sons of titular nobles or important officials; to them imperial favor was within reach, influence furnished a short cut; the main road of the official ladder seemed to them a long, tedious, perilous and unprofitable journey. Incidentally, some sons of important ministers, either for the sake of fair play, glory of literary conquest, or compelled by a strict father, participated in the contest together with the commons. But, for them, the keeness of competition was not so much felt either because of good preparation or strong influence. The fame of conquest, glory of an appointment, and the fond hope of an official rise appealed to the commoners most.

Popularly, four kinds of degrees were supposed to result from literary competition: technically, however, only two kinds were conferred. The much misconceived office, "compiler of the Academy of Letters" is almost always mistaken to be the highest degree, while an admission into the district or prefectural college, in fact merely an act of qualifying for provincial examination, is frequently misnamed a first degree. The entrance into a prefectural or district college (Yu Hsueh), the necessary step before coming to a provincial examination, will be taken up first.

In connection with the examinations, it should be pointed out that the schools in ancient China were under state management and control. In later dynasties, the inefficiency of the government gave rise to private schools and private tutoring. The policy of centralizing education, however, survived in the form of an Imperial college in Peking,[3] and a college in each of the prefectures, sub-prefectures, or dis-

[3] In the beginning of the Tsing Dynasty, there were two National Colleges, one in Peking and another in Nanking. The latter was abolished by Emperor Kang Hsi.

tricts. Four reasons have caused the entrance into these colleges to be mistaken for a conferring of a degree: first, only a fixed, small number of the students could, after keen competition, get in each year or every other year; second, only students of these colleges had the right to compete in the provincial examination; thirdly, the colleges were only nominally maintained and had virtually no curriculum, resembling an office rather than an educational institute; fourthly, some minor officials were appointed from students of these colleges, and finally, as soon as a student passed this examination, he became a minor gentry. The difficulty of qualifying in these colleges gave importance to the students who qualified, and the special privileges they enjoyed elevated them above the struggling commoners. In spite of all these features, a scholarship remained a scholarship, not a degree *per se*.

Along educational lines a province was governed by a Commissioner of education (Ti Hsueh Sse), appointed by the emperor from the rank and file of Metropolitan graduates holding position of, or lower than, a vice-minister. For a term of three years, he was educationally supreme in the province, independent of even the Viceroy or governor. During his tenure of office, he made two tours in the province, covering every political sub-division except those where only a few scholarships were given once in several years, in order to examine students of the private schools with a view to appointing the deserving to the district college. Being an official of the third rank, appointed directly by the emperor, he had the privilege of directly addressing memorials to the throne: this privilege brought to him the right of recommendation, and hence the duty of discovering talented students who, either discouraged by previous failures, unattracted by the lure of officialdom, or too proud to compete with the local students, refrained from the participation in the examinations. He had jurisdiction over the district students, and local magistrates could not punish the properly qualified students of their own districts without his approval and consent.

Under him were a number of educational-administrative officials in the prefectures and districts, some appointed by the emperor, others by the Department of Civil Service. Having no privilege to address the emperor directly, they had to go through the office of the Commissioner for any communication between the central Government and their respective areas. A few of them were metropolitan graduates, most of them provincial graduates, some with only an accessory degree. These prefectural or district professors took charge of the education of the students within the sub-division, whether government or private. In busy districts, they had assistants. The duty of the professors was chiefly instructional in character as the district schools had only a nominal existence, the administrative side amounting to nothing.

The whole educational system, as can easily be seen, centered in the examination: the whole examination centered in literary cleverness. Therefore the ability to write good essays was the one object to be attained at all cost by students. Nominally, both literary ability and practice of virtue formed the basis of selection. But virtue being such a vague thing, literary talent gradually came to occupy the whole field. From the entrance examination to a district college up to the Palace examination for an immediate appointment, essays determined the fate of candidates. Of all forms of literary exercise, the "eight-legged" essay occupied the predominating position. The word "leg" here meant paragraph: eight-legged meant a prescribed form of eight-paragraphed composition. It was divided into: (1) the preliminary remarks consisting of two sentences; (2) introduction, three sentences; (3) general discussion, a short paragraph; (4) specific reference to the subject, a paragraph of one to three sentences; (5) the first rhymic paragraph, a short one; (6) second rhymic paragraph, a long one; (7) the preliminary concluding paragraph; and (8) final concluding paragraph, sometimes with reference to the following sentence or paragraph of the subject. Paragraphs 5 and 6 must be written in phrases of four or six words scarcely with more than two phrases of the same number of words successive, but with sentences matching one another in poetic couplets. The whole essay must be more than 360 and less than 720 words. Subjects for the essays were taken from the *Four Books* or the *Five Canons*.

With the central feature of the examination clear in mind, let us proceed to inspect the entrance examination to a district college. Upon the arrival of the provincial Commissioner of Education, the district magistrate or prefect or what-not, assembled all the students at the prefectural or district city to test the knowledge and luck of the aspirant candidates in the district or prefectural examinations. The preliminary session consisted of two "eight-legged" essays on subjects from the *"Four Books"* and a little poem of six couplets of five characters to each line. A great number of the contestants were eliminated in the primary for the wrong use of words, violation of the rules of rhyme, poor calligraphy and a hundred other reasons that would hardly ever attract attention in ordinary reading. In the re-examination or final, the same test was given so as to ascertain that nobody got it simply by luck, in addition to writing from memory one or two hundred words of *The Annotations of the Sixteen Imperial Commendments*[9] *(Sheng Yu Kuang Hsün).*

Every year, approximately 50,000 students were taken into the district colleges by this process. They received a sort of allowance from the provincial government either in money or rice. Shun Tien Fu, the Metropolitan Prefecture,

---

[9] The sixteen commendments written by Emperor Kang Hsi are: (1) Practice filial piety and fraternity to improve human relationship; (2) Respect kindred in order to display the excellence of harmony; (3) Harmonize your neighbors in order to avoid litigation; (4) Emphasize farming and silk-culture in order to provide for economic sufficiency; (5) Practice economy in order to reduce consumption; (6) Honor the schools so that the traditions of the students will be inspired; (7) Reject heresies in order to uphold the orthodox learning; (8) Explain laws in order to warn the foolish and the wicked; (9) Be courteous and humble in order to better the customs; (10) Attend to your own business in order to stabilize

and the province of Kuangsi gave either; the province of Kuei Chou gave both; the rest of the administrative divisions gave money. Kuei Chou gave annually 4.00 *shih* of rice and one-half tael of silver to each student. The highest figure in rice was twelve *shih*; the lowest, Kuangsi, two *shih* per annum. The highest annual money allowance was given by Shantung at 9.6 taels per annum; the lowest by Kansu at .695 taels; the majority gave between two and five. In the same province, some districts gave more than others; thus in Shantung, where the highest figure is quoted, some received only 8.6 taels; while in Kansu, the least remunerative of all, some received 4.32 taels annually. Only sixteen of the twenty-two provinces had a fixed amount for every district student.[10]

The highest class of these students were called salaried students (Lin Sheng). Besides the provincial allowances, a great majority of them got subsidies from their prefecture, district, village, literary clubs or clansmen. In addition to these salaried students, about 50,000 additional students (Tseng Sheng), 80,000 extra students (Fu Sheng), and 4,650 purchased scholarships were annually given: the emperor was also ready to increase the number once in a while to show his grace to the people. Students of other categories enjoyed exactly the same honor, right and privilege as the "salaried" students except in the provincial allowance, which scarcely amounted to anything. The presence of purchased scholarships seems to show to the embryonic man-

---

society; (11) Instruct your sons and brothers so that they will not commit any wrong; (12) Stop false accusation so that good people would not be harmed; (13) Take precaution against runaways and the hidden, in order to avoid punishment on account of mutual responsibility; (14) Make prompt payment of taxes in order to avoid the press of the collectors; (15) Co-operate with your neighboring villages to defend yourself against bandits; (16) Forgive wrongs and anger to lengthen your life. There are sixteen essays written by Emperor Yung Cheng, in the form of annotation to these commendments. The essays ranged from 590 to 644 words each.

[10] *Hu Pu Chih Li.*

darins the same degree and kind of corruption as the purchase of offices: the difference of the two kinds of purchase was, however, marked. The purchase of an office was a transaction between a private citizen and the government; the purchase of scholarships, was between a political subdivision and the central administrative machinery: in other words, the payment of an office was made by one man and the office for himself; that for the district scholarship was made by the people of the whole district, and hence belonged to the whole district. The purchased office vanished with the death of the buyer; the bought scholarship was perpetual in the district. Three hundred and fifty of these purchased scholarships were given for contributions to government expenses; 4,300 for contribution to military campaigns chiefly during the Taiping Rebellion. As we have seen that only the qualified students could have the privilege of taking the provincial examinations, we can readily infer that the purchased scholarships were to enlarge the entrees of a certain district in their provincial contest, providing a greater possibility to outdo their rival districts in the race for literary honors and government representation. The total number of students qualified in each of the two tours of the Educational Commissioners in the whole country was, then, roughly estimated, about 286,500; as the Commissioners took two tours during their tenure of office of three years, so in every three years, 573,000 students were qualified for the provincial examinations.

Once qualified, the students began their milling process. The curriculum of the district colleges contained five subjects:[11] (1) the ceremonial performance at the birthday of the emperor, New Year's day, Winter Festival, birthday of Confucius, God of Literature and whatnot; (2) book knowledge of more than 200 books, all edited or written by the emperor or his appointees with his sanction: they consisted of books on classics, history, literature, poetry, government, imperial edicts, military tactics, Manchurian and

[11] *Ta Tsing Hui Tien.*

Mongolian literature; (3) a further study of the "eight-legged" essays to meet the exact requirements of the prescribed form; to wit, to make them between 360 and 720 words in length, to write the subject two spaces below the top of the line, elevate the name of Confucius, emperors, heaven, government, court, palace, etc.; (4) ethics, both personal and public, including filial piety, loyalty to the emperor, respect for teachers, and a list of diverse things combining to make a gentleman in the old Chinese sense; (5) forms and style of writing, expression and calligraphy.

The students were subject to call for an examination by the Commissioner any time. He had the power to dismiss them from the colleges, or promote or demote them from class to class. The looseness of administration of the government extended to the educational phase of its activities. For all the enumerated duties of a district student, no part of the curriculum, except the ceremonial functions, and occasional lectures by a prefectural or district professor, was rigorously carried out.

Besides the provincial allowances and district subsidies, the qualified students enjoyed the privilege of being exempt from taxes and of getting access to the educational facilities in the district, prefecture, or province. The greatest of their privileges was that as soon as they were admitted to the district college, they became members of the gentry: they were invited to share the discussion of all local affairs, did not have to prostrate before the magistrates or prefects, no corporal punishment could be given them, and sundry other rights or exemptions.

For fear of the abusive use of their advantageous position, they were forbidden to make acquaintance with powerful mandarins in the Metropolis, to befriend the local officials except the educational, to enter the office of the magistrate, to help litigation or witness a case, to criticize the government, to organize parties except for literary improvement, to print privately what they wrote, to become an underclerk or go into military service. Being under the jurisdiction of the Educational Commissioner instead of the magistrates, their violation of these prohibitions met punishment from the Commissioner. Degradation or suspension from the participation of the provincial examinations or suspension from the provincial allowances were some of the light fines for the students. Dismissal from the district college was the limit of the Commissioner's jurisdiction. Further punishment could be given them by local officials, but it could not be applied until dismissal had first taken place.

The regular steps for the district students to take was to compete at, and win a degree from, the provincial examinations which we shall deal with separately. Failing this they might become a "presented student" (Kung Sheng). Once in a while, the term varying from one-half to ten years, one of the "salaried students," who had several times failed in the provincial examinations would be given the title of "annual presented students" (Sui Kung Sheng) merely for reason of seniority; two others would be chosen "extra annual presented students." Sometimes, as a mark of imperial favor, one more "presented studentship" was given: then the regular would become the "presented student by grace," (Un Kung Sheng) the first extra would be appointed the "annual presented student." Once in every six years, the governor and Commissioner assembled the district students after the repeated failures of the latter to obtain a provincial degree, for an examination in which the successful ones would become "superior presented students" (Yu Kung Sheng). Then the selected ones were sent to Peking. There a re-examination took place which resulted in dividing them into several classes; the first and the second classes would receive appointments as district magistrates or professors; the third class as accessory educational and administrative officials in the districts. Once every twelve years, there was a general examination for the failed district students to pick out one from a district and two from a prefectural college and give them the title of "picked students" (Pi Kung Sheng). They were then sent to Peking for re-examination and classification. The first and second class would receive appointments of 7th rank official in the central government, magistracy, professorship, etc. The first and second categories of the "presented students" merely got an advancement in literary rank and the privilege of studying in the Imperial College; the third category got an appointment; the fourth could either get an appointment directly or have the privilege of competing in the Metropolitan examination without first getting a provincial degree.

These groups of students were almost always an important factor in their respective localities. Coming from the same place they knew and befriended each other before qualifying for the local college. After admittance, they clung to their place of birth waiting for the provincial examination. The management of local public affairs came into their hands because of their legally advantageous status before the law and intellectual knowledge. Magistrates respected, nay, feared them, because the former knew not when they would succeed in a future examination and secure appointments more influential than their own; while living within their administrative area the latter were outside of their jurisdiction. An offense against a student might cause a conflict with the Commissioner of Education whose right to address the emperor directly might bring trouble to the little magistrate any moment; without trouble from higher quarters, an indulgent Commissioner could easily keep the authority of a magistrate at bay by a benevolent refusal to dismiss an offending student from the district college. The union, a strong one among the students themselves, could exert influence even to endanger the position of the magistrate if he became too harsh to the scholars. The Commissioner himself was sometimes at the mercy of the organized students: by refusing to take examinations under him and boycotts of other kinds, some commissioners were punished by the government for failure to instruct the students properly. Acting collectively, they were a body without a soul. No way of punishing them existed. With this advantage, they, aside from controlling local affairs and influencing local officials, formulated public opinion.

A meeting of a literary club often turned into a caucus: in this opinions were formed, and from it circulation of opinions started.

Their privileges were not infrequently abused. Koo Ting Lin, in his *Essays on the District Students*,[12] shows the dark side of this institution. He says:—

The purpose of having the district students is to gather together the bright young men of the different districts, place them in the government schools, and train them into useful officials; thus sharing the responsibility of the emperor in the government of his people. The district students of the present age, amounting approximately to about half a million in the whole country, can by no means live up to their original expectation. What they learn nowadays is a few pieces of literary products of the past to cheat a higher degree. Yet, not one out of several decades can produce a decent essay: not one out of thousands has a respectable knowledge in classics. All others occupied themselves in instigating lawsuits. For this reason, they have been looked down upon and treated indecently by officials . . . . .

The sale of scholarships, not always by the Commissioners, frequently by swindlers, corrupted the institution to a great extent. An edict in *Ta Tsing Hui Tien Shih Li* well says that "Some cheaters follow the Commissioner in his examination tour; posing as relatives of, or advisers to, the Commissioner, call up the rich applicants and promise them a sure scholarship in consideration of a payment. In another part of the same works, seven traditional corruptions of the institute of district students are pointed out:—

(1) Getting a degree, by bribery, directly from the commissioner, without even going through the formal processes of attending the examinations.

(2) Getting applicants of one district and assign them studentships of another district.

(3) Changing a military to a literary studentship.

(4) Calling the applicants to the office instead of holding the examination in the regular halls.

(5) Giving out questions before the examination took place.

[12] *Works of Koo Ting Lin*, vol. 1, p. 9.

(6) Selecting students because of the influence of their father or relatives.

(7) Substituting one qualified student for another.

The corrupt practice of selling scholarships was due to a deeper motive than the honor and glory of the qualification. "The degree lifts one from the common flock, renders one immune from the squeeze of the under-clerks, and entitles one to interview local officials without going through the usual extraordinarily humiliating ceremonies. So the struggle for a place in the district college was not one for honor or fame alone, but for protection. At least seventy per cent, or 350,000 get it for this reason. The original purpose of these men has thus been thrown overboard. All human beings, of course, need protection. So they work day and night for it. If they fail to get it with literary talent they get it with money. Seventy to eighty per cent of them get their place by bribery. The consequences of being caught, however severe they may be, are out of consideration: circumstances have forced them to this corrupt practice." [13]

After all struggles by pen, money, or influence, on the 9th, 12th, and 15th days of the eighth month, the district students came to their second struggle for a step further up the ladder of administrative hierarchy. This provincial examination which was the first of the two processes for selection to government service that were officially and technically recognized by the government, is popularly mistaken as a second degree. Except in the Metropolitan prefecture where a number of degrees were open to men from all provinces, the provincial citizenship, if one may so call it, was the most essential qualification besides a scholarship in the district college.

This examination was presided over by a Chief Examiner, an Associate Examiner, both appointed by the emperor from a list of officials, vice-ministers or lower, and with a Metropolitan degree, for this special mission. Next to these two

[13] *Works of Koo Ting Lin*, vol. 1, p. 11.

were eight to eighteen Assistants, appointed by the viceroy or governor from the provincial officials with at least a provincial degree. The Chief and three or four Associate Examiners for the Metropolitan Prefecture were appointed by the emperor from officials with at least the position of assistant censor-general: the assistants, eighteen in number, were also appointed directly by the emperor.

The number of qualified candidates recruited from each of the examinations taking place during the last three hundred years ran up roughly to 573,000: dividing them into twenty-one provinces, a little over 26,000 candidates would be ready for competition in an average province. The total number of degrees conferred in all provinces together, was about 1,810: one out of every three hundred could get a degree.[14] But this method of counting was deceitful; unsuccessful candidates could come up again in the next examination, thus almost doubling the number of candidates and lessening by about 50 per cent the possibility of success.

Like the district scholarships, 182 out of 1,810 of the provincial degrees were purchased. Two kinds of additions to the number of degrees were made during the Taiping Rebellion; a temporary addition only for a certain examination, and the permanent addition for every examination, were not for the abolition of the system itself. The price for a temporary degree was 100,000 taels; that for a permanent degree, 1,000,000 taels. The government was virtuous enough to make ten permanent additional degrees the highest number purchasable; any excess over that amount would be credited to the temporary addition. Just as an increase in the number of district students increased the representation of the district in the province, so the additional degrees in the province gave the province a better chance of winning the laurel from Peking because its number of representatives was enlarged.

Two hundred and fifty-four degrees, besides the 1,810, were assigned to bannermen. One hundred and seven of the

[14] For number of provincial graduates, see accompanying list.

1,810 were open to candidates having qualified as "presented students." A rather large proportion of the 1,810 was assigned to sons and relatives of officials.

TABLE SHOWING THE NUMBER OF PROVINCIAL DEGREES (CHU JEN) CONFERRED IN EACH PROVINCIAL EXAMINATION [15]

Locality	No. to District Students (Sheng Yuan)	No. to Presented Students and Imperial College Students (Kung Chien)	No. to Students of the "Five Classics" (Wu Cheng I A.)	No. of Purchased Degrees (Chuan Nah A.)	No. to Bannermen (Chi A.)	Miscellaneous Degrees (Tsa A.)	No. of Accessory Degrees (Fu Boun)	Total No. for the Province
Shun Tien Fu	8		2	7	39		12	68
Fengtien Fu	8		4				3	15
Chihli	104	6	5		4		24	143
Kiangsu	69	6		18	20		23	136
Chekiang	94	6		10	12		25	145
Kiangsi	94	6		12	12		25	149
Fukien	87	6		10	12		23	138
Hüpeh	47	6		10	12		15	90
Hunan	45	6		12	12	2	16	93
Shantung	72	6		2	4		17	101
Shansi	60	6		8	12		18	104
Honan	71	6		8	10		19	124
Shensi	42	6		9	11		14	82
Kansu	30	6		10	12	2	12	72
Szechuan	60	7		20	22		22	131
Kuangtung	71	7		14	16	2	22	132
Kuangsi	45	7		8	8	1	14	83
Yunnan	54	7		10	12		17	100
Kueichou	40	7		2	12		13	74
Anhui	45			9	12		14	80
Sinkiang	1							1
Taiwan				3				
TOTAL	1,147	107	11	182	254	7	348	2,064

[15] Data from *Ta Tsing Hui Tien*.

This special proportion was made by Emperor Kang Hsi in 1700, when the sons and relatives of the officials, either by superior knowledge of essay writing or influence, took a large number of the degrees, thus barring the poor commoners in the upward climb of the mandarin world, lessening the opportunity of the mandarins to incorporate new elements into their circle to invigorate itself. The definition of an official here meant any one in Government service occupying a position of the 7th rank or higher.[16] The proportion made by Kang Hsi being found too favorable to the privileged, Emperor Yung Cheng revised the schedule making it one out of every twenty in a large province, one of fifteen in a middle-sized, and one of every ten in a small province.[17] Even so arranged, it was still found that the chances between the privileged and the commoners were eight to one. The imperial clansmen and the bannermen had examinations of their own.

The program of the provincial examination occupied three sessions. The day before the examination took place all candidates were locked up in the little cells one of which was assigned to each contestant. There they stayed until the third day. Before they were locked up for the first session pompous ceremonies took place. Among the great rites, one small phase of the ceremonial program is of interest; the Chief Examiner, presiding over the ceremonies, prayed to the spirits that if any revenge were desired by inhabitants of the underworld, it could be done within the examination halls. The examination indeed was taken as much as a test of morality as of intelligence, or skill in essay writing. After they have been locked up, the candidates had to write three essays, one on a subject from the *Academic Narratives,* (Lin Yu) one from the *Doctrine of the Mean* (Chung Yung) and a third from *The Works of Mencius* (Meng Tze), besides

---

[16] See *Ta Tsing Hui Tien Shih Li.*

[17] The provinces here are measured by the number of degrees provided, not anything else: thus provinces like Chihli, Kiangsu, Fukien, etc., were large, Kuangtung, Szechuan, etc., middle-sized, Kuangsi, Yunnan, etc., small.

a poem of eight couplets with five words in a line. Coming out on the 10th of the month, they went in for the second session on the 11th. In this session, five essays, one on each of the "Five Classics" were written by each of the competitors. Ending the second session on the 13th, the third session called them in again on the 14th, in which five essays on the government were required. The 16th day of the month found them out of the cells, some happy over the satisfactory work done, others worrying about the disgrace of defeat. Forty-five days of waiting in a large, forty days in a middle-sized, and thirty days in a small, province ended their anxiety, hope, or fear, as well as determined their career.

All the essays were supposed to be original. Quotations were allowed only from memory, hence the memorizing of passages in the old Chinese schools. Theoretically, all three sessions had equal weight in the determination of the degree. But the practice was that the essays on the *Four Books* came first, although supposed all-round general excellence was necessary for success, failure in the first essays practically eliminated a candidate: thus, unconsciously, unbalanced emphasis was given to the essays of the first day, those on the *Four Books*. Again, usually more than 10,000 contestants participated, the greatest number of assistants was eighteen; each candidate handed in thirteen essays and one poem. Each assistant had to read between 8,000 and 10,000 papers within thirty days, averaging about 300 every day. It was impossible under such circumstances for them to read over the essays carefully. The prescribed form and the requirement of general excellence in every one of the essays came in as a great help for the assistants: they generally read the first paragraph, always consisting of two sentences in the "eight-legged" essay. Hence, in the practice of corruption, the first two sentences were often used as a signal, as no candidate was allowed to write his name on the paper, a distinctive couplet could easily single out a particular essay from all the rest. Theoretically, the Chief Examiner had the sole decision. He had absolute power in both qualification and ranking. However, when he was thought to have acted unfairly, the candidates had the right to impeach him before the emperor; in this case they had to have enough evidence to satisfy the emperor, in order to avoid getting punished for a false accusation. True to the principle of checks and balances, the assistants, appointed by the provincial administrative authorities, were there to check him. The edict of Emperor Chien Lung in 1789 says "The appointment of Associate and Assistant Examiners in the provincial and central examinations is for the purpose of checking the unfairness of one another." With this object in view, all examiners were appointed from outside of the province in which the examination took place. The assistant examiners were locked up during the whole period in which they read the papers. They were divided into halls according to the subject they specialized upon: for instance, the hall of the *Canon of Rites* of the *Four Books,* etc. When they had finished reading all the papers, they met together for a final decision as to the graduation and the ranks of the graduates. The Chief Examiner, having the authority to reject papers submitted by the Assistant Examiners, had the final decision on both. But all papers came first of all through the hands of the Assistant Examiners. They had the power to recommend a paper to the Chief. This power of recommendation implied a power of throwing out a paper, for without the recommendation of an assistant examiner, no paper could reach the attention of the chief. The absolute power of the chief to reject the recommendation of his assistants again checked the possible corruption of the subordinates. These checks, one positive and the other negative, balanced and counteracted each other. Hence, unless all of them had understandings, or some one from outside made the necessary connections, nothing corrupt could go through without being checked. Upon discovery of corruption, both would be held jointly and individually responsible.

At 12.00 noon, the day of announcement, the candidates, like nominees in an election, waited with hope and anxiety. The viceroy or governor, together with the Chief Examiner,

RITES AND CIVIL SERVICE EXAMINATIONS 161

announced in the former's yamen the decision of the Examiners and conferred on behalf of the emperor, the degree to those who had satisfied the examiners. A host of professional "reporters" carried away the announcement to break it to the happy new graduates who would generously compensate them for the report. The next day, the viceroy or governor gave the new graduates a banquet in his office in the name of the emperor, thus giving a formal recognition to the new recruits of officialdom.

After the examinations were over, all the papers had to be sent to the Department of Rites in Peking for safekeeping, and, incidentally, for checking. The department could impeach the chief examiner and his associates, if in examining these papers, any trace of corruption or any mark of injustice was found. The right of printing the essays as examples for later candidates was reserved to the government; it being, as we shall later see, more a means of censorship than a measure of monetary gain.

Provincial graduation entitled the lucky few to a competition in the capital with successful candidates from other provinces in the following spring.

Insufficient means of communication necessitated an early start upon the part of the provincial graduates. Some began their journey with their brilliant success in the province still fresh in their memory, and the hope that Providence would be as generous to them in Peking as in the provincial capital. As a mark of respect for scholars, the provincial governments, out of the treasury, paid the traveling expenses of the candidates. Seventeen of the eighteen provinces paid them in silver, varying from one to twenty taels, while Yunnan paid three taels of silver and a horse.[18] Nine of the provinces paid ten or more taels and the other nine, from one to seven taels. Small the sum may be, but the low

[18] The expenses paid are Kuangtung and Anhui, twenty taels; Kiangsi and Hupeh, seventeen; Fukien, fifteen; Hunan, fourteen; Kuangsi, twelve; Chekiang and Honan, ten; Shansi, seven; Shensi, six; Kansu, five; Chihli and Szechuan, four; Shantung, one.

standard of living in the olden times allowed the spenders of these sums a comfortable, if not a luxurious, journey.

In the third month, the provincial graduates gathered from all corners of the empire, crowding into the little cells in the prison of the literati, patiently grinding through the three sessions which they had rehearsed in the provincial examination, but with a much keener competition and a harder program. The first session in the metropolitan examination consisted of writing three expository and one critical essay on historical subjects; the second, four expository essays in classics and one short poem of eight rhymes with five characters in each line; the third, a thesis on current political topics. As in the provincial examinations, the "Hall-Assistants" first read over all the essays; but, unlike the former, this process was employed simply to eliminate the authors of essays which were not written in the prescribed form. The Chief and Associate Examiners then read over all the cast-off papers, nominally in search of talent, but actually for checking the prejudice of the hall assistants. Thirty days of anxious waiting brought the candidates news of victory or defeat. The victors then hurried to prepare for the Palace Examination: those who had failed either went home or received appointments of an inferior rank.

The chances of success in the Metropolitan examination was about one in ten. Data of 93 examinations conducted from 1646 to 1886, show that only 24,174 degrees were conferred, with an average of 234 degrees for each examination and 100 for each year: yet a further investigation into a comparison between the number actually conferred and the number provided for by regulation shows almost fathomless imperial grace.[19] In these 240 years, 80 regular and 23 extra examinations were conducted; 87 of the examinations graduated more, seven graduated less, and 9 graduated the regulation number, 150. Had there been no examination given by imperial favor within that period, only 12,000 de-

[19] See appendix of the chapter.

grees would have been conferred, and the chances of provincial graduates would have been lessened by fifty per cent. Yet the ratio of ten to one drawn from a comparison between the number of provincial and metropolitan graduates is deceiving; provincial graduates who failed had the right, which they usually took, to come up again for a second trial. The ratio of ten to one, true to the first examination, would not be true again in the next; the rank of applicants would be increased by the left-overs. This is easily proved by the fact that every three years, only 2,064 provincial graduates came out, yet in metropolitan examinations seldom less than 4,000 contestants participated. The accumulative effect worked so unfavorably to the provincial graduates that only one out of every thirty or forty competitors in the metropolitan examination stood a chance of winning a degree.

These metropolitan degrees were divided into "Southern" and "Northern." By southern, is here meant the provinces of Kiangsu, Chekiang, Anhui, Kiangsi, Fukien, Hunan, Hupeh, and Kuangtung; by northern, the provinces of Shantung, Shansi, Honan, Shensi, the Metropolitan Prefecture, Mukden, Szechuan, Kuangsi, Yunnan and Kueichow. The number of applicants from each section in a particular examination determined the number of degrees allocated to each section. The cause of the division was that the southerners, by virtue of their literary skill, almost always got more than their share. A recollection of the purpose of the examinations which were conducted for selection to government service, and not for literary honor, will show that the idea of geographic representation could not fail to assert itself. A further study by provinces of the graduates in the different examinations, would clearly reveal a fair representation of all the provinces, with, however, the more literarily developed, having the advantage.

The first honor in the examination was sometimes conferred not for literary excellence, but for the sake of pleasing a province or a group of officials who belonged to the same school as the winner.

The Department of Rites made the announcement of the graduates at 12.00 noon in the departmental office, with a similar host of "reporters" ready to break the news to the "new nobles" and to receive the reward. Then the department again gave a banquet to the new graduates in the name of the emperor; and thus they were formally recognized.

The successful candidates went to the Palace Examination a little more than a month later. This examination was supposed to be conducted personally by the emperor; he was supposed to give the subject. Fourteen officials of the first rank were appointed as assistant examiners. A large board of readers first went through all the essays scrutinizing them carefully as to form before they reached the hands of the assistant examiners. The whole examination consisted of one session: the program of the session, one essay on current government problems. The form of the essay was prescribed by the *Ta Tsing Hui Tien* [20] in the following words:—

> The essay in the Palace Examination shall begin with the clause "I have heard" or "I answer." The introductory paragraph shall occupy four or eight lines of twenty-four characters each. The second paragraph shall begin with the phrase "I respectfully understand that His Majesty . . . . ." The words "I respectfully understand" shall be at the bottom of the fourth or eighth line with all the four or eight lines filled. If there be sub-questions included in the question, they shall be answered one by one. The first answer shall begin with the phrase "Studying the imperial edicts in prostration, Your Majesty's servant has found out that . . . . ." Then a quotation from an imperial edict must follow. Each of the subsequent answers shall also begin with a quotation from an imperial edict and introduced by the phrase "The imperial edicts also say . . . . ." The essay shall be ended with the words "His Majesty's servant, being shallow in knowledge and lacking experience, can scarcely avoid saying what he should not say, and hence deliberately offending your imperial dignity. Trembling incessantly, Your Majesty's servant respectfully replies." The word "deliberately" in the concluding paragraph shall be at the bottom of the line. The body of the essay shall be written two spaces from the top. The terms "emperor," "imperial edict," "imperial dignity," etc. shall be written two spaces above the regular line. No correction, addition

[20] V. 33.

or punctuation shall be allowed. The style of the essay shall not be of the alternative four and six worded sentences. The minimum length of the essay shall be 1,000 words; the maximum unlimited.

What a systematically prepared outline for the poor candidates, particularly for those who did not know how to begin their essay! But what restrictions on the freedom of opinion and style! A single violation of the minutely set down rules in the form of the paper would seal the fate of the applicants regardless of the value of the essay in other respects. What a pity for the poor students, in their time of preparation, to waste their lives in learning how to write the thing according to the prescribed form while they could profitably learn something, with that amount of time, money and energy that would be much more useful! What an enslaving of the brains of the young students by these little literary niceties, apparently so harmless!

To ensure the enforcement of this prescribed form, the readers and assistant examiners reading over the papers had either to discard them or to submit them with their signature certifying the correctness of the papers. Were any mistakes found out afterwards, the certifiers would have to face a punishment varying from a fine of three months' salary to flat dismissal, depending of course on the seriousness of the undetected mistake.

The evaluation of the essay was based on three things: literary style, subject matter and penmanship. Theoretically, the second elements counted most, then the first, the third being only of very little value; but tradition had it that only artistic penmanship with good literary style could win a candidate the first honor. Unaccompanied by both these, the highest place a candidate could be given was the second grade. The choice of the first one in the palace examination was made by the emperor himself. The assistant examiners picked out ten best papers, and presented them to the emperor, who marked a dot on the name of the best one with his vermilion pen. In this case, the emperor played the part of the Chief Examiner, the assistants that of the "hall assistants." Without a recommendation of the assistants, none could reach the attention of the emperor; without his final decision none could get the high grade. Thus, the laws he had made to check his officials, came to check himself.

The palace examination was not a separate examination in the sense of giving out higher degrees; it was really a civil service examination in the respect of dividing the qualified men into groups. The metropolitan graduates went in as equals; when they came out from the examination, they were divided into three grades, with the three highest men in the first, about twenty-five per cent of the total in the second, and the rest in the third grade. The first and second grades were all appointed to the Academy of Letters as editors or compilers, the third to either third class secretaries of the departments or magistrates. These appointments, differing from the conferring of degrees, which are conferred by his representatives were made by the emperor himself after the new civil servants had been presented to him in a special audience. In addition to the actual appointment, the final goal of all examinations, a banquet was given them by the emperor, thirty taels of silver were bestowed on each of the successful candidates, and fifty more for the three men in the first grade. The names of the successful candidates were engraved upon a tablet in the Imperial College.

While the successful ones went ahead in their climb of the official ladder, the failed graduates from the provinces might try again until their luck would take pity on their misfortune. Or, they might get an appointment as third class secretaries in the departments or as magistrates after one trial for graduates from remote provinces or three trials for graduates from near provinces. A third way for appointment was for them to try their luck in the "Grand Selection" held by imperial favor once in several years, to pick men from the provincial graduates for appointments to magistracies or prefectual professorships. Were they to fail in all the attempts, they still could receive a sum of money from the government and travel back to their home provinces.

Aside from the regular examinations held in the provinces and the capital, the "Translation Examination" was open to men who could read and write the Manchurian and Mongolian languages. Sixty district scholarships in Manchurian and nine in Mongolian were given annually. Ten per cent of these could be made provincial graduates in every year. Some of them, a small proportion of course, could further their career by making themselves metropolitan graduates at the time the other provincial graduates tried their luck. Seven applicants sufficed to hold an examination. But the palace examination was not open to them because the only kind of position they could get was as translators; that needed no further classification. Their metropolitan examination consisted of only one session: translation from Chinese to Manchurian and Mongolian languages and vice versa.

The "special examination for the learned men" was once in a while given to men who had refused to compete with others or had failed in spite of their great knowledge. The candidates had first to be known far and wide; they had to be recommended by an official of the third rank or above. Five examinations of this kind have their records in the *Ta Tsing Hui Tien Shih Li*, all of them occurring before 1751. The degrees conferred on these were those of the metropolitan graduates, and the positions appointed were those of compilers of the Academy of Letters, the highest of both degree and appointment open to regular competitors. In all the five examinations, only eighty-three degrees were conferred and the same number of appointments made. All these were conducted by the emperor himself in the Palace, and consisted of but one session. The assumption was that they had already a metropolitan graduation and had come up for appointment. Very probably they were not subject to all the formalities the regular candidates had to submit to.

During an emperor's visit to a province a special examination for the graduates and the students of the province was sometimes given. Fifteen of such examinations are recorded, all taking place before the reign of Chia Cheng. No regular degree was conferred. A prize in some commodity, say books, or an appointment to office was the reward. Not infrequently metropolitan graduates took part in such examinations. The records of Chien Lung's examinations show that for graduates, the appointment, after this test, was a secretaryship in the staff of the Grand Secretariat. The reward for the students was a provincial graduation.

Aged students and graduates were given degrees or honorary positions according to the following schedule:—

Original position	Age	Degree or position given by Grace
District student	90	Provincial graduate.
Presented student	80	Provincial graduate.
District student	80	Accessory Provincial graduate.
Student of Imperial College	80	Accessory Provincial graduate.
Provincial graduate	100	Tutor of Imperial College 6a.
Provincial graduate	95	Editor of Academy of Letters 7a
Provincial graduate	90	Corrector of Academy of Letters 7b.
Provincial graduate	80	Director of Schools 8a.

This was merely a matter of decoration; the civil service laws made seventy-five the age of retirement. Were they practical appointments, it would be quite ridiculous to appoint men to the service who were near to their grave. Yet, the honorary positions gave them considerable prestige.

The power of conferring the degrees, like every other power in the old Chinese monarchy, was absolutely reserved to the emperor. The provincial authorities and the Department of Rites gave the degrees only in his name. Being a representative of the emperor in the conferring of degrees, neither the governor, viceroy, nor the Department of Rites could deprive a graduate of his degree without the express sanction of the ultimate conferring authority, the emperor. Degrees might be secured without going through the regular tedious process, by advanced age, great knowledge with a recommendation of a high official, death of a father who was a high official, contribution of money to the government, and political influence of one's father or grandfather. The power to confer naturally implied the power to deprive. Very often men found unworthy of their degrees were deprived of them. It should be pointed out once more that the deprivation of degree was often a punishment resulting from a criminal offense, not an academic disqualification. No graduate could be corporally punished before the degree had been taken from him. Suspension of examination was also sometimes employed as a collective punishment for a province. In 1726, Emperor Yung Cheng suspended the examination of the Province of Chekiang on account of the "rebellious writings" of Cha Shu Ting; it was restored in 1728 upon the joint recommendation of Viceroy Li Hui, Governor Wang Kuo Tung and Commissioner (of Education) Wang Lan Sheng. This punishment was applied again in 1901 by virtue of the second article of the Protocol between the Chinese Government and the allies that for a period of five years in all localities where injuries had been done to foreigners by the boxers, no provincial examinations should be given. Ineffective as it may appear, as a judicial measure, nevertheless, taking the old situation, where examinations were the principal means of recruiting civil servants, their suspension practically meant preventing the people of those places from entering Government service; in other words, lack of representation in the Government.

In this, as in all other governmental institutions of monarchical China, the two wonderful laws, law of avoidance and law of mutual responsibility were strictly enforced. The Chief, associate and assistant examiners avoided appointments in their own provinces and had to reside 500 *li* away from the border of the province, if from a neighboring province. In the Metropolitan examinations, sons and relatives of the examiners and assistants had their papers read by men outside of the regular examining staff or excluded from the participation. The law of mutual responsibility started with the examination for entrance into a district college. At the examination five applicants had mutually to guarantee one another as to the validity of their places of birth. A similar method of guarantee was employed in the provincial examination; a guarantee of the local officials or officials in the metropolis to verify the province of birth of the candidate was absolutely necessary in the metropolitan examination. Severe punishment was the lot of those mutually guaranteeing one another if it were found out that the true place of birth was not reported.

The strength and weakness of the examination system can be approached from three angles, i. e., the administration of the system, whether efficient or corrupt, the relation of the system to the government, and its relation to the nation, the people and their civilization. The first consideration, being one of purely governmental function, seems to interest us more; the second, viewed as a political institution, maintains the political science interest; the third, as a social institution, though not entirely within the scope of our subject, is, nevertheless, the most important phase of this time-honored institution.

Great care, undoubtedly, was taken to guard against corrupt practices in the examination. The candidates were locked up while writing the essays, as were the assistants, during their period of reading them; guards were posted in every corner of the halls; censors were assigned to supervise the guards, and communication between men in and outside of the halls was absolutely forbidden. As a prevention against smuggling reference books into the halls, utensils brought in for use during the examination were strictly regulated. The *Ta Tsing Hui Tien Shih Li* set down the following regulations:—

1. Hat and clothing shall be without lining.
2. Soles of shoes shall be thin.
3. Cushion shall be single blanket.
4. Paper bags shall be unlined.
5. Ink stands shall be of thin stone.
6. Brush holder (made of bamboo) shall be hollow.
7. Water stands shall be porcelain.
8. Charcoal shall not exceed two inches in length.
9. Candle stand shall be of single layer zinc: its chamber shall be hollow.
10. Cakes and other eatables shall be cut into pieces.
11. All the things to be brought into the hall must be contained in a regular examination basket.

A careful search was given to every candidate before he entered the halls. The least bit of suspicion would subject the candidate to close surveillance. The possibility of a corrupt practice thus seemed meagre. The effort of the government to make this institution the purest branch of its service should have been easy of attainment. But, in spite of all these regulations and preventions, hook and crook were found as useful and dependable in the competition as brain and brawn; not a few of the degree winners got their honor by dollar or influence instead of the pen. Corrupt practices came from every corner of the system as well as from every part of the empire.

The emperor himself, the ultimate authority for the conferment of degrees, first corrupted the system by giving degrees to sons and grandsons of influential mandarins and contributors of money to government, thus putting the official and the financial classes over the commoners, and destroying the equality of opportunity in the competition. The assistant examiners, as Emperor Kang Hsi pointed out in his edict in 1721 formed another source of corruption. He says:—

> The greatest corruption in our competitive examination nowadays is well known to me. The time taken by the competitors to compose their essays is only six or seven days. The total number of papers does not exceed four thousand. But it takes more than forty days for the assistant examiners to read over and pass judg-

ment on them. This is too long; all corruption arises out of it. Other corruptions, like carrying reference books into the halls, handing in essays for another candidate, which is occasionally practiced by a few, are not so harmful since the search before the entrance into the hall is strict and the policing effective. The danger of severe punishment after discovery also serves as a check.

But when the three sessions are closed, the guards and supervisors detailed to the examinations recalled, the line of communication is established between the outside expecting world and the assistant examiners by the senders of food who pass through the nominally locked gates every day. News as to who will succeed leaks out; the official announcement is rendered useless. Worse still, the change of paper, shifting the order of the successful candidates are often done. Chief examiners, all of whom hold responsible position and high rank and have a bright career before them, are not so corruptible. But the wicked assistant examiners of low positions and with a dim career will do anything for their selfish advantage, therefore they are the sorest spot of the whole system.

The censors know it, but, for fear of revenge, they have sealed their mouths. The chief examiners may find out afterwards; but their mistake is already an accomplished fact. They do not want to lay the blame on themselves as they will have to share their punishment in case of discovery of the corruption. The upright ones inside the hall, influenced by friendly feelings, are loath to check each other. This institution of competitive examination, an extremely important one, shall not be corrupted thus. The right and left wings of the Metropolitan Gendarmerie are hereby ordered to resume their policing activity within the examination halls.

The corruption practiced by competitors was just as glaring and in many more ways. Substitution was a risky and yet common practice. By this is meant that a man went in the hall, wrote the essays, and handed them in in the name of another candidate in consideration of a sum of money. Selling essays was another favorite by-path for reaching the goal. Its process is well described by Emperor Chien Lung in an edict saying:—

I have heard that, in the recent examinations, there are professional law violators living around the examination halls in Peking. They specialize in housing writers who make their living in selling essays to contestants. The dishonest competitors bribe the guards and the supervisors smuggle the subject out by wrapping them around pieces of stone. When the essays are written up, they give signals in the form of lamp posts high above the roof, burning fire crackers or sending a well trained pigeon to fly around the halls, and then smuggle the essays in. The Censorate and the Metropolitan Prefect are hereby ordered to send out reliable persons, to search for this kind of illegitimate writers and give them severe punishment. The inhabitants around the examination halls are hereafter forbidden to post lamp on the roof, burn fire crackers, send out trained pigeons or throw stones during the examinations.[21]

Then smuggling of reference books into the examination halls was another evil practice on the part of the candidates. This practice was, indeed, a foster child of the system.

The limited sphere from which the subjects come enabled the smuggler of a few books to be in full possession of the necessary equipment. The "eight-legged" style was the most important form of essay recognized; to carry a full supply of it would not take much space. The advancement in the art of printing in early China made it possible for the publishers to issue pocket editions of the essays for the candidates who were willing to pay anything for some book handy enough to be carried into the cell without being found out. Like smugglers in the commercial world, every part of the body, cloth, or any other worldly belongings formed a safety zone for the illegitimate traffic. In 1744, a representative of Emperor Chien Lung searched the applicants before entering the halls. Twenty-one were found guilty of smuggling reference books. The result of the examination was that about 400 candidates handed in blank papers and about 2,000 refused to be further examined after the first session.[22]

Finally, the practice of taking degrees from the frontier provinces, where competition was not so keen, was an abuse of the official class. At this juncture, the readers should be reminded that the place of birth was an important element in Chinese government service, that one-half of the

[21] *Ta Tsing Hui Tien Shih Li.*

[22] See edict issued in the 9th year of Chien Lung. *Ta Tsing Hui Tien Shih Li.*

law of avoidence was devoted to prohibition of holding office in the native place; that each province was provided with a number of degrees proportional to the literary development of the place; that degree winning meant government appointment, hence, to a certain extent, representation in government. When Tso Tsung Tang was Viceroy of Kansu and Shensi, he petitioned the emperor to allow the people of other provinces to naturalize in Sinkiang and Kansu and to give the naturalized the right to take examinations there with the aim of populating these provinces. It turned out, however, that many immigrants came in for the privilege of taking the examination. Since that time, most of the provincial degrees in those provinces were won by men from other places. Thus corruption originated.

Despite all these corruptions, a fair verdict upon the administration of this branch of government activity would be a favorable one in comparison with other branches of the effete Manchu Government. Emperor after emperor spared no efforts to purify the system. The unity of interests of the candidates, to a very limited degree, checked successfully the growth of corruption. The cases of corruption were exceptions rather than the general rule. If any organization or institute of the Tsing Dynasty could claim effective management or immunity from the bad influence of official atmosphere, it was the examination system.

From the standpoint of governmental administration, this system was the principal factor in centralizing the political machinery: for that purpose it aimed at uniformity. Politically speaking, there is no doubt that uniformity was achieved, but at too costly a price, for censorship arose out of the desire for uniformity. The prospective appointees to the position of chief examiner were not allowed to express their opinions on current politics [23] so that no candidate could win a degree by studying the opinion of the chief exam-

---

[23] See edict of Emperor Chien Lung, 1754, in *Ta Tsing Hui Tien Shih Li*.

iner. This looks just; but the chief examiners were appointed from the highest officials. Who could foretell that they were going to be appointed a chief examiner. The honor, the financial compensation, and the attraction of the possibility of building a faction for one's self from the fresh graduates were too much for any one to sacrifice for the sake of expressing one's opinion that, after all, did not count for much under the monarchical regime. Thus the tongue of almost every high official was sealed, cleverly, easily and yet unconsciously.

Censorship of books served as a second means of standardization. The *Four Books,* the *Five Classics* and one hundred and ninety-eight other imperially edited or written books, all that the government wanted the students to learn, were the only ones for their study unless the students were too proud to haggle in the literary market. Even of the approved books, only an approved edition was allowed; private publications with annotations or opinions of scholars not included in the imperial editions were tabooed. The *Ta Tsing Hui Tien Shih Li* contains two interesting edicts upon this point, one of them saying:—

> For subjects of examination, the examiners shall pick out phrases from only the imperial edition. The viceroys and governors are to order their subordinates to collect and destroy all the private publication not edited by the emperors . . . . . violators of this law shall be severely punished.

The second of these edicts, issued also by Emperor Chien Lung at a later date (1793) reenforced this censorship law. Part of it says:—

> Edicts have been issued to viceroys and governors authorizing them to forbid private publications, collect and send the same to Peking to be destroyed. But I am afraid that as time passes the order is gradually forgotten. Here I want to remind them of their duty once more. The classics are edited by Confucius and should not be freely interpreted. Some unlearned scholars, who fail to purchase a government position with their shadowy knowledge, try to trade it for money. They annotate and explain only the parts of the classics that are used in the examination and make the editions handy for dishonest competitors . . . . .

It is clear that slavishness in thought was offered as a price for uniformity; and this, no doubt, was too much. The "eight-legged" style essay made it a competition in space-filling and imitation rather than writing. Nominally all essays had to be original; practically none of the subjects could be outside a beaten path of literary adventure since the same form of essay had been used for at least five hundred years,[24] written on by tens of millions of scholars on the same set of subjects. Unfortunately enough, as an edict of Emperor Yung Cheng pointed out, only a small portion of the canons and classics had ever been used. "In both provincial and metropolitan examinations, the subjects are usually phrases of praise on account of the fear of the examiners to incur my displeasure. But this will give better chance to young men without much knowledge than old learned scholars. Hereafter, the examination subjects shall not be all of that nature so that every competitor may have a chance."[25]

The censorship of books and the standardization of literary forms for the competition essays subordinated real knowledge to formal requirement, and thus, as pointed out by Censor Yang Hsin Shiu in a memorial to Emperor Kuang Hsu during the "Hundred Days Reform"[26] that the original purposes of the examinations, of encouraging learning and picking out the learned, were decidedly defeated by the results brought about by the censorship, i. e., discouragement of real study and inability to discover the very few talented ones who have not come under the bad influence of this statecraft.

It has been contended that the competitive examination brought the best and ablest of men to the government serv-

[24] The "eight-legged" essay was supposed to have originated in the middle of the Ming dynasty, about 1500, which was 800 years after the introduction of competitive examination in essay writing as a basis of civil service examination by Emperor Tai Tsung of Tang dynasty in the early part of the 7th century.
[25] *1735, Ta Tsing Hui Tien Shih Li.*
[26] *Tung Hua Lu,* Kuang Hsu, v. 144, p. 12.

ice. Certainly the system, being one on which the hope of the government rested, was, for the most occasions, honestly executed, and the best writers of "eight-legged" essays were selected. But supporters of this argument have confused the art of writing with the art of government. They may argue that most of the best civil servants were provincial or metropolitan graduates; but, in advancing that argument, they have forgotten the absence of competition. I mean that practically all high class government employees came from that class and not a fair number of men recruited by other means could be secured for comparison. Their argument is not supported by facts unless they can show that all or at least a majority of those recruited from the examinations were efficient and honest, which is far from the truth. So long as executive ability is not identified with literary genius, the contention of getting the best administrators from contests in essay writing is unsound.

Again, essay writing is different from sound knowledge. As the government aimed to get all the learned by these means, its object was not attained. Very often the rejected students were really learned; or the rejection of the government made them seek real knowledge instead of vaporous fame.[27] The learned were, in many cases, reluctant to present themselves for the competition. If the rejected were of scholarly temperament, they might have shut themselves up for knowledge, but, unfortunate would be the emperor who had ambitious rejected scholars in time of famine or drought. Hung Hsiu Chüan of the Taipings was a district student rejected at the provincial examination. But how could the examiners determine the temperament or ability of the candidate while they are there to judge the quality of their essays with the law of avoidance separating them into two worlds until the verdict was given?

[27] Koo Ting Lin, leading scholar in the beginning of the Tsing dynasty in one of his letters to his friends, says "Being rejected from the examination, I went home with earnest purpose to seek real knowledge with my doors shut."

For centralizing the government, the examination system was certainly an effective weapon. None of the students, under this system, could secure a decent appointment without a pilgrimage to Peking. After that trip, no matter how short or ineffective, the pilgrim would be awed by the dignity of the son of heaven, enervated by the luxuries of the courtiers, imbued with the spirit of officialdom, and a convert of the mandarinate. No other insidious means of transmutation could be more effective.

A peculiar by-product of the system was the "teacher-and pupil" relationship. Under the monarchical rule, party organization being an act of treason, the best method to disguise political affiliations was the academic connection. Hence, party leaders, instead of being "bosses" assumed the academic title of a "teacher;" the rank and file all enrolled themselves as humble "pupils:" "teachers" and "pupils" were the Chinese pseudonym of protectors and protégés. This relation rose primarily from the examinations where the examiners were teachers and the graduates pupils. An edict of Emperor Tao Kuang in 1839 recognized this relationship.[28] The edict says, "In the provincial and metropolitan examinations, the examiners picked the candidates on the basis of the merit of their essays. The successful candidates become grateful to them. Relationship of teacher-and-pupil developed. This is permissible." "Permissible" it was, but the abuse of it rose from the extension of this relationship to superiors and subordinates. So, in the same year, another edict was issued to forbid the practice, giving the following reason:—

Nowadays, the custom of the provincial officials is for the magistrates to become pupils of the circuit intendents or prefect and the viceroys or governors to become, in turn, teachers of the latter. Profit and influence are the bonds of the relationship. The teachers ask favor of his superiors for his pupil-subordinate, and the pupils practice corruptions in the name of the teachers. Official duties are neglected for private gain . . . . . The first rank officials are here-

[28] *Ta Tsing Hui Tien Shih Li.*

by ordered to rid themselves of this relationship so that others may be given an example.[29]

The worst feature of this academic liaison was the formation of political parties on the basis of literary inclination.

The weakest point of the system in relation to the administration of the government was the separation of recruitment and appointment. By excellence in writing essays, one got a degree which always brought him an appointment. But how many of the winners had learned anything about practical politics, or the art of governing? Yet, if one did not go through the grinding process of wasting his life in words and phrases, his hope of an appointment was only a hope. So aspirants to offices were between the devil and the deep sea, with the result that most, if not all, studied for the degree instead of for the work; when they came to the practical work, their ignorance put them at the mercy of the under-clerks as they had learned only what they did not need. The day before he got a degree, he was under the Department of Rites bending over his desk, trying to memorize passages of the ancient books on personal ethics and social etiquette; after he had won a degree he would be an expectant of some kind, waiting for the imperial favor that might bring him a lucrative post. What could he do with all these memorized passages and well expounded paragraphs when a litigation, a tax account, or something else came along? Furthermore, as Huang Li Chou well pointed out in his *Essay on the Selection of Scholars*,[30] "although the method of selection was strict, yet the appointment was too lenient. Once a man has shown his ability to write a few compositions and a poem, he is guaranteed a post: other elements that make up the quality of a public servant were not counted. Strict selection leaves out many a learned scholar, while lenient appointment puts many an unqualified one in the service."

[29] *Ta Tsing Hui Tien Shih Li.*
[30] *Ming I Tai Fan Lu,* p. 10.

Such being the working of the competitive examination, aside from helping to centralize the government and stabilize the throne, nothing good can be found in it. Considering the heavy tax the people had to pay for the attainment of these two objects, it is not too severe to call it a crafty insurance policy of the throne bought by a disproportionally heavy premium of the people's intellectual bondage and the government's administrative inefficiency.

Looking at the larger aspect of the system, its influence on the people, it did not bring about the good results which it has been credited with. S. W. Williams [31] attributed to this system the credit of making literary pursuits more preferable to the Chinese than war, and also among other things, of preventing slavery in Chinese society. Dr. Williams has failed to see that these were the result of the whole Confucian philosophy on which the examination was based rather than results of the system itself. History reveals that the system was initiated by Emperor Tai Tsung of the Tang Dynasty about 630 A. D.; it also tells that the preference of peace to war already existed, and that slavery had no existence prior to the period when the crafty emperor successfully utilized the newly invented institution as his own safeguard. Not even in the warring period was a soldier more respected than a philosopher-minister. Not even back in the dark ages of feudalism can a severe critic of the old Chinese society find a recognized status given to the abominable institution of slavery. As long as the Confucian principle of government by moral patriarchism prevailed, the insidious pen was bound to overrule the strong sword. Intelligence recognizes no caste. Thirteen centuries of the history of competitive examination has failed to show any sign that this system prevented slavery. On the other hand, we find among numerous regulations of the system, a law disqualifying the bond-servants; we find the desperate efforts of the government to respect and privilege the successful candidates for the military service examination ex-

---

[31] *Middle Kingdom*, v. 1, p. 562f.

actly to the same degree as the civil, only to be defeated by the lack of popular support. At its best, it can claim only a part of the credit of maintaining the civilized idea of preferment of the head to the fist and the humanitarian structure of the society by absence of slaves.

Again, writers, Europeans especially, have maintained that this system has united China as a nation. In saying so, they have ignored the historical facts. The first emperor of the Chin Dynasty united the whole country without the system. Since then China has been a united country except for short periods, which were not avoided after the inauguration of this system. Also they have confused the centralization of the government with the unification of the people. They point to the oneness of the written language as a result of the institution. But, let me ask, what came out first, the written Chinese language or the examination system? A step further. Was there any other written language in China besides the only one known to man before this system was made a state activity? The *Five Classics* and the *Four Books,* the foundation of the system, were just as much studied before the Tang Dynasty as after it, nay, more studied, at least from a scholarly point of view. The unity of language was there: the utmost the examination system can claim, is its maintenance. Were it to be the undisputed sole claimant of linguistic unification, and its claim justly made, it must have unified the spoken language. But, today, after more than thirteen hundred years of its unifying effects, we find roughly four different principal dialects in that Oriental country. The handful of civil service applicants who made their triennial trips to Peking did little aside from getting themselves mandarinized as far as the social influence of the system went. Not even the provincial examinations held within the borders of a strip of territory were strong enough to remove the noticeable differences in the local dialects in the diverse districts in Kaungtung, Kiangsu and Fukien. A review of both the pre-examination and post-examination conditions of the language flatly denies the unifying effect of the examination system.

Indeed, the Confucian philosophy had already firmly molded the thought of the people in the eleven hundred years, from Confucius to the inauguration of the examination system. Confucian classics were made the cornerstone of the system simply because it had been the philosophy of the people; unity in thought, in other words, was already a *fait accompli* while the system struggled for its existence in the nursing cradle of the Tang emperors. Finally, its influence in centralizing the government is still debatable. The Tang Dynasty, father of the system, fell down because of decentralization. This agency of centralization was not employed until centralization itself has been accomplished for eight hundred years. The occasional break-ups between dynasties visited China just as frequently after the system had been in force as before. So, again, the credit of centralizing the government is one to be credited to the philosophy of the ancient sages, and not to the clever methods of the gracious emperors. Here again, its greatest claim was, in part, to keep the thing intact.

The second count of the social charge against this system is that it corrupted the classics. Let history prove this contention. Before this institution, every student of classics was, if not a seeker of truth, a man eager to understand what it said: all the classics were studied without prejudice. But, after the appearance of this system, students treated it as a stepping-stone towards government employment; merely the part that, speculatively, stood a good chance of making a subject for the examination would reach the attention of the youths. Exceptional lovers of philosophy or classics might still go on the old way: they, however, were either born scholars or discouraged by repeated failures in their sale of literary talent. Government censorship of publication of the classics, an inherent activity of the unifying agent, contributed quite a share in moulding the ideas and ideals of the students, stupifying the active brains of the whole race. Dividing the 2,400 years of life of the classics edited by Confucius into two periods, 1,100 years before the examination system for the first, 1,300 years after the examination for the second, we find that the pre-examination period, a shorter one, was much more prolific in the production of both independent works and annotations to the classics of quality, than the post-examination period in spite of its greater length. Furthermore, a great majority of the valuable works, independent or annotatory, are products of men who were denied the benefits of the system, whether in honor or official appointment.

Judging the system from all its results, taken as a whole, it can claim little more than that it stabilized the throne and to a certain extent linked the provinces with the national capital. Being an offspring of the Chinese classics and philosophy, critics of the institution should have enough historical background to safeguard them from the mistake of assigning to it the accomplishment of its parents. Dispassionately, looking at the results it wrought, it is hard to refrain from giving credit to the "Old Buddha" for her courageous abolition in 1904 of the outlived institution, even though it was with a great deal of reluctance and insincerity that she issued that edict of abolition.

APPENDIX I—(Chapter VI)

TABLE SHOWING THE NUMBER OF METROPOLITAN DEGREES (CHIN SHIH) CONFERRED IN THE METROPOLITAN EXAMINATIONS

Date	No.	Date	No.	Date	No.	Date	No.	Date	No.
1647	400	1706	300	1760	191	1809	241	1853	237
1648	300	1709	300	1761	207	1811	237	1856	192
1649	400	1712	192	1763	187	1814	225	1859	192
1652	450	1713	186	1766	206	1817	249	1860	191
1655	450	1715	200	1769	143	1819	224	1862	196
1656	351	1718	174	1771	161	1820	241	1863	198
1659	350	1721	176	1772	169	1822	223	1865	252
1661	450	1723	180	1775	153	1823	240	1868	271
1664	150	1724	214	1778	158	1826	257	1871	326
1667	150	1727	210	1780	153	1829	215	1874	345
1670	300	1730	407	1781	168	1832	203	1876	339
1673	150	1733	347	1784	115	1833	222	1879	323
1676	195	1736	300	1787	137	1835	269	1880	323
1679	150	1737	313	1789	97	1836	174	1883	316
1682	200	1739	316	1790	102	1838	182	1886	316
1685	150	1742	316	1795	114	1840	183	1890	326
1688	150	1745	307	1796	148	1841	200	1892	317
1691	150	1748	259	1799	210	1844	229	1894	281
1694	150	1751	241	1801	271	1845	213	1897	
1697	150	1752	235	1802	245	1847	211	1898	348
1700	300	1754	241	1805	233	1850	207	1903	315
1703	162	1757	235	1808	259	1852	244	1904	272

Data from *Ta Tsing Hui Tien Shih Li* and *Tung Hua Lu.*

CHAPTER VII

THE DEPARTMENT OF REVENUES: FINANCE AND TAXATION

In the administrative sextet of the Peking Monarchy, the Department of Revenue was second in rank and influence, being outranked by only the Department of Civil Service. At the head of the department, above the regular ministers, there was a supervising minister, traditionally a Manchu and occasionally a Chinese. Then came the two ministers, (one Manchu and one Chinese) and four vice-ministers, (two Manchus and two Chinese). The duties of these officials, as defined by *Ta Tsing Hui Tien*, were as follows:—

> To assist His Majesty in his duty of providing for the myriads, the ministers and vice-ministers shall control the land; keep a record of the territories of the Empire and the boundaries of the provinces; and take a census of the population. In all collections of taxes and excises, payments of nobles and government employees, auditing of the accounts of the provincial and central treasuries and granaries, transportation of taxes and tributes, officials shall submit their accounts and plans to this department: its ministers and vice-ministers, together with their staff, shall decide on the cases and enact their decision except in very important cases which shall be reserved for the decision of the emperor.

Aside from these, the department was responsible, along financial lines, for currency and coinage, direction, control and custody of customs houses, granaries, and treasuries. It concurrently exercised the right of determining the standards of weights and measurements with the Department of Works, and issued commercial regulations, seafaring directions and passports to the seagoing adventurers. It presented all financial officials to the court. It initiated agricultural ceremonies, protected the forests and encouraged silk culture. Judicially, it reviewed all civil cases: it had concurrent jurisdiction with the Department of Justice if, in the trial of the case, bodily punishment was applied in the interrogation.

These important and various duties were performed by fourteen bureaus as follows:—

1. The Bureau of Kiangnan (Kiangsu and Anhui)
   a. To audit the land and poll tax accounts of the province of Kiangsu, and Anhui, and the accounts of the Government Silk Factories in Nanking and Soochow.
   b. To collect from the provinces and report to the emperor accounts concerning the amount of the balance charged of the land and poll tax in certain provinces due to the loss incurred in inaccurate weighing of the specie (always 1.25%) and the arrears of land and poll tax in all provinces.

2. The Bureau of Chekiang:
   a. To audit accounts of the land-poll tax in the province of Chekiang, and accounts of the government silk factories in Hangchow.
   b. To report to the emperor annually the population and the grain produce in the Empire.

3. The Bureau of Kiangsi:
   a. To audit the accounts of land-poll tax of the province of Kiangsi.
   b. To audit and report on the inter-provincial support of their military expenses.

4. The Bureau of Fukien:
   a. To audit the accounts of the provinces of Chihli and Fukien.
   b. To audit accounts of miscellaneous expenditures of the province of Chihli drawn from the central treasury.
   c. To audit the accounts of the customs duties collected at Tientsin.
   d. To administer all government relief work.
   e. To audit accounts of the rents received by the government from its houses for rent to bannermen.
   f. To control the orchard land of the Imperial Household Court, and the nomadic prairie of Tsihar.

5. The Bureau of Hu-Kuang (Hunan and Hupeh):
   a. To audit the accounts of the land-poll tax of the provinces of Hupeh and Hunan.
   b. To audit accounts of duties levied in the inland customs houses in the province of Hupeh.
   c. To audit the accounts of surtaxes on land, commodities, salt, and tea in the Empire.

REVENUES: FINANCE AND TAXATION   187

6. The Bureau of Shantung:
   a. To audit the accounts of the provinces of Shantung, Fengtien, Kirin, and Heilungkiang.
   b. To pay allowances to the officers of the banner forces.
   c. To control the government monopoly of salt and ginseng.

7. The Bureau of Shansi:
   a. To audit accounts of the province of Shansi.

8. The Bureau of Shensi:
   a. To audit the account of the provinces of Shensi, Kansu and Sinkiang.
   b. To control the government tea monopoly.
   c. To act as general paymaster of the government except in cases specified.

9. The Bureau of Honan:
   a. To audit the accounts of the land-poll tax of Honan province.
   b. To audit the expenses of troops stationed in Tsihar.
   c. To urge the revision of any provincial report not accepted by the Department of Revenues.
   d. To be ready to investigate any report, and report the same to the emperor upon receipt of his orders.

10. The Bureau of Szechuan:
    a. To audit the accounts of the land-poll tax of the province of Szechuan.
    b. To audit the accounts of the receipts of inland customs in Szechuan.
    c. To control the confiscated specie and commodities.
    d. To report on the condition of crops in the Empire.

11. The Bureau of Kuangtung:
    a. To audit the accounts of the land-poll tax of the province of Kuangtung.
    b. To control the succession of the bannermen.
    c. To appoint *Chinese* officials in the Department and to assign the unassigned duties to members of the Department.

12. The Bureau of Kuangsi:
    a. To audit the accounts of the land-poll tax of the province of Kuangsi.
    b. To audit accounts of the customs revenues of the province of Kuangsi.
    c. To direct and administer the Mints in Peking, and regulate coinage.
    d. To regulate mining enterprises.

13. The Bureau of Yunnan:
    a. To audit the land-poll tax accounts of the province of Yunnan.
    b. To report on the collection of mining royalties in Yunnan.
    c. To attend to the safe transportation of grain tributes from certain provinces to Peking.
14. The Bureau of Kueichow:
    a. To audit the accounts of land-poll tax of the province of Kueichow.
    b. To supervise the inland and maritime customs houses.
    c. To audit the fur tributes.

From the above list of varied duties, we can derive some general principles as to the division of the departmental duties. First, the bureaus were divided according to provinces and not services. As there were then twenty-two provinces, but only fourteen bureaus, some had to go without specially allotted bureaus, others had to attend to the business of more than one province; thus the Bureau of Shantung had the Three Eastern Provinces; the Bureau of Kiangnan had Kiangsu and Anhui; the Bureau of Fukien had Chihli and Fukien; the Bureau of Hukuang had Hupeh and Hunan; and the Bureau of Shensi had Shensi, Kansu and Sinkiang: the other nine were confined to their own respective provinces. Besides the principal duties of auditing accounts of land-poll tax, each bureau, with the exception of the Bureau of Shansi, was assigned some other duties; the duties however were very poorly divided, resulting in an overcrowding of work for some, and the lack of work, for others. Taking the duties item by item, some like the tribute of furs, or the auditing of the accounts of the silk factory at Hangchow, or the ginseng monopoly, could easily be taken care of by a few clerks; while others, like the payment of employees, the supervision of customs, the salt monopoly really required big forces of workers for their efficient administration. Not even when viewed from the standard of the old monarchical regime was this division free from criticism.

It has been pointed out in the first chapter that economic activities were one of the three principal kinds of activities

REVENUES: FINANCE AND TAXATION 189

in the government; that silent, passive recognition of the
government by the people depended largely on the government's ability to provide them with food; that an uprising, a
signal of dissatisfaction towards the government, caused by
natural forces like famine which were avoidable by preventive or remedial measures of the government, could succeed
only when the government was unable to meet the situation.
Acting on this principal, the government undertook a number of economic activities, nearly all of them under the
Department of Revenues. Twelve policies were adopted as
preventives and as remedies for the people's economic
insufficiency. Farming was encouraged by conferring a low
official rank to successful farmers, exempting them from taxation, or closing the courts to civil cases during the agricultural seasons. In the uncultivated regions, a farmer
could borrow a piece of land from the government. He paid
little or no rent in the first few years besides the extremely
light tax: at the end of ten years, if the leases were found
satisfactory, he would be given the land gratis. The cultivation of tobacco was forbidden, as this article was not a
necessity. The manufacturing of wines was prohibited because it was considered a waste of grain. Special laws were
enacted to protect the farmers from the lawless. Soldiers
were often detailed to catch and kill locusts and crop-destroying worms. Relief work in time of flood, in the form of
giving a tent if houses were destroyed, giving of funeral
funds if persons were killed, medical expenses if injured,
repairing expenses if farms were flooded, made up a third
policy. Relief work in famine, that occurs once in a while
according to its own sweet will, took shape in the distribution of grains. Every time a famine occurred, the local
officials were required to report it to the emperor within
sixty days. An investigation was then immediately conducted. Two scales of free distribution, one on a racial
basis, another on the basis of the degree of famine, were
provided.[1] Other measures of relief work like cheap sales of

[1] See Appendix I of this chapter.

food stuff, loans of food stuffs, reduction of tax rates, postponement of dates of tax collections, importation of food stuffs by government, conducting a campaign among the rich for contributions, employing the sufferers at public works entered upon for the purpose of employment, helping the sufferers to immigrate, etc., according to the provisions of *Ta Tsing Hui Tien*, were proper and regular duties of the Peking administration. Even the likin system was not applied to transportation as a means of famine relief.

The granaries of the government in different provinces contained under ordinary circumstances, eighteen and a quarter million *shih* of grains [2] ready for the distribution in case of famine. Local conditions decided the kind of grains for storage, e. g. rice for the South and wheat for the North. A fixed amount of grains besides the principal one was also required for storage. A change of the grains, from 30 to 70 per cent annually, was required of the granaries. Reports of these had to be sent by the viceroys or governors once every year. A rule of mutual responsibility also applied here, only in another sense; that is, neighboring provinces were required to help one another. Grain loans between the people were encouraged and assisted by the government. Finally, private organization of granaries was not to be interfered with by the officials. These granaries, like all other government property, were guarded by the bannermen.

Then, too, a list of other economic help from the government was provided in the same work. Among these, may be enumerated the exemption of the coming tax, cancellation of arrear taxes, revision of tax rates with a view to reduction, payment for services of the people rendered to the government,[3] organizing of charitable works, such as orphanages, poorhouses, hospitals, rewards for faithful widows, filial sons and daughters, pensions for impecunious officials, care for foreigners landing on account of shipwreck, or other uncontrollable occurrences.

[2] See Appendix II.

[3] All work of the people was supposed to be rendered gratis.

Having such an ambitious program on hand, it is interesting to find out whether, under the inefficient Manchu Government, any part or the whole of the program was ever carried out. One, indeed, finds plenty of records of tax exemption and distribution of grains and money. Every famine, drought, or any other natural phenomenon, was always followed by the government's efforts to save the people, unless that thing was not known to the government, as these happening might be taken as a sign of the misconduct of the local officials and hence, if they were reported to the emperor, might bring them demotion or dismissal. The corruption of the granaries, as Censor Chang Chao Lan well observed,[4] depended upon the sales of public stored grains by officials for their own profits without reporting to the government. Indeed, it is doubtful when the government took a measure of remedy for its suffering subjects, whether the rotten officials made it an opportunity for purse-fattening or not. Yet the efforts of the government are not to be denied, meagre though the results may have been.

The theory that all the property of the empire belonged personally to the emperor, gave him a free hand to take from, or give to, any of his subjects a piece of land. This great power, however, was very prudently exercised. The founder of a dynasty, first of all, never tried to take away from the people their possessions; ownership in the preceding dynasty held good for the new one. The one exception was, when the banner soldiers settled down, the Manchu Government did collect a lot of the people's land for a consolidated piece to give to the bannermen as a consequence of the inability of the privileged to get along with the Chinese; but this was not done without compensatory pieces of land being given to the Chinese when their original property was taken away though the new property might not have been as good as the old. The *Ta Tsing Hui Tien* records 1,047,-783,839 *mao* of land in the whole country. Roughly 70 per cent of this was owned by the people, thus called the

[4] *Tung Hua Lu*, v. 1, 41, p. 11, memorial to Emperor Kuang Hua.

"people's land;" 7.8 per cent by soldiers who farmed during the time when they were not called to drills or service; 1.9 per cent by the bannermen and imperial clansmen together; 17 per cent as frontier land which every adventurous subject could avail himself of; .058 per cent as "officials' land;" and .1 per cent as "scholarship land" to aid the poor and needy students.[5] Scarcely any other government, with its extraordinarily large host of protégés, could refrain from appropriating more for the benefit of the privileged.

For reasons more social than political, the land in China is divided into very small farms not exceeding several *mao* each, thus avoiding big farms, serfdom, absentee landlordism, and other evils in the matter of distribution of land.

Coinage in China did not assume much importance during the agricultural stages. The government, nevertheless, reserved all rights of coining money and regulating the exchange rates of copper and silver coins. Besides the central mint in Peking, there were fifteen smaller mints.[6] Copper coins could be made by the government for a seniorage of 9 per cent. The rate of exchange between silver and copper was 1,000 small copper cash for one tael of silver.

The government owned a number of monopolies. Salt, the most important one, yielded twelve and a half million taels in 1887 from 8,900 government refineries. Ginseng constituted a second kind of monopoly. Each year the government conducted a ginseng expedition into the mountains in Manchuria. Five-sixths of the precious herb would be sold at five taels of silver for one tael of ginseng. One-sixth of it was kept by the government. A heavy tax of four taels of silver for one tael of ginseng was levied at Shanhaikwan on any of the privately transported herbs. The tea produced at Shensi and the mining at Kuangsi were also monopolized by the government which sometimes collected a tax, and

---

[5] See Appendices III and IV.

[6] They were located in the provinces of Chihli, Shansi, Kiangsu, Kiangsi, Fukien, Chekiang, Hunan, Hupeh, Shensi, Szechuan, Kuangtung, Kuangsi, Yunnan, Kuiechow and Tibet.

sometimes sold it to the former, while on the latter, a ten per cent tax was levied.

Taxes, the principal source of income of the Chinese Government, can be roughly divided into two kinds, namely, land-poll taxes and commodity taxes. At the beginning of the Tsing Dynasty, land and poll taxes were two distinct and separate things. The poll tax was then levied according to the last census. But Emperor Kang Hsi found that the census quota was too much below the real figure on account of the desire of both the people and the local officials to escape the burden of collecting and paying the tax. Therefore he ordered that the census taken in his 52nd year (1713) should supply the standard figures for poll taxes in order that he might get an accurate census in the future. Down to 1887, this census was still quoted as a standard figure for the poll tax in spite of the great increase of the population. Gradually, this was combined with the land tax; so, in 1857, with the exception of eleven prefectures, twenty-two sub-prefectures, and fifty-four districts, land and poll taxes were a combination called "Ti-ting," literally, land-poll tax. With the exception of the "hunting land" in Manchuria, and 356,700 *mao* of sacrificial land, Government buildings, barracks and canals, no land was exempted from taxation, except as a special privilege. In addition to the poll tax, the land tax was a combination of the "general service money," levied as a substitute of forced labor; the "post-station money" levied as a substitute for the work of the subject for the relay communications, partly a military duty; and the surtax. The last was originally an illegal charge of the magistrates on the tax payers to make up the silver lost in weighing or through the use of an unsatisfactory balance. Much abuse arose from this charge, and edicts were repeatedly issued to abolish it; to wit, the decree of 1644 and the laws of 1665 and 1678. But squarely meeting the real situation created by a lack of provision for local administrative expenses and the low salaries of the magistrates, Emperor Kang Hsi sanctioned it again in 1709, thus perpetuating this practice to the end of the dynasty.

The decree of Emperor Kang Hsi said, "It is impossible for the magistrate to support his family and to pay his secretaries without any extra charge in taxes. A magistrate charging ten per cent extra may be regarded as a good official. If he were not excused from impeachment, it seems to me it would be irksome for one to impose the same penalty on so many of one's subordinates."[7] The regular surtax was ten per cent of the regular tax; but untrustworthy magistrates almost invariably made it higher; some causing it to reach even fifty per cent of the original.

The collector of tax was the magistrate. Bearing in mind the fact that tax-collecting was one of the most regular as well as efficiently performed functions of the government, the magistrates formed the link between the emperor and the people. Tax collection being the chief work of the local magistrates, the civil service laws were frank enough to judge the service of the magistrates by their ability in fulfilling this obligation. There were two taxing seasons in the year, from 2nd to 4th month in the Spring, and 8th to 11th month in the Fall: the viceroy or governor was left with the power to make the time to suit local conditions in case of needed change. Fifty per cent of the annual tax came in at the end of the first period. Provincial and local officials had the right to recommend partial or complete exemption of the year's tax on account of bad crops; recommendations of this kind scarcely met disapprovals when the amount of tax paid by the district was low and refusal on the part of the emperor would make him look like a tyrant, pitiless for the sufferings of his poor people. The magistrate divided the people into small groups of five or ten households, each recorded on a separate sheet. He called the first one to pay, then the second, the third, and so on until the whole list had been called on and taxed. Records of the tax were made in three folded sheets, one given to the payer, the second kept

[7] This was in reply to the memorial of Loo-yu, Governor of Honan. See S. K. Chen, *The System of Taxation in China in the Tsing Dynasty*, 1644-1911, p. 54, Columbia University Studies, vol. IX, 1914.

in the magistracy and the third sent to Peking after the payer had brought his tax to a box in the magistrate's office and had it weighed by a standard balance and accepted by the magistrate. Absentee land owners paid taxes to the district where his land was situated, not where he lived.

The rates varied not only from province to province, but also from piece to piece in the same province. The highest was 2.974 taels in Hupeh and the lowest .0002 tael in Kansu for an annual payment on one *mao* of land. The 1,047,783,-839 *mao* of land in 1887 yielded the government 31,184,042 taels of silver, averaging approximately .031 tael for each *mao*—a very low rate.[8]

Before the different kinds of new taxes were introduced, the land tax formed the chief source of government income; from way back in the Shia Dynasty, down to the eve of the Taiping Rebellion, this was at least one-half of the Government receipts. From the standpoint of administration, this "farmer of revenue" system, as Montesquieu called it, had one advantage, the low cost and easy collection. The function of collecting being entirely given to the chief administrative officials of the districts, not a single special man had to be employed for this purpose. When time came, the payer brought in the tax. The long period of time provided for collection lessened the pressure on the payers. But when the people failed to do their share the position of the magistrates was in danger, and professional tax collectors were employed by the magistrates out of their scanty salaries to insure collection. The surtax system, too, was open to glaring abuses. Being sanctioned by the Emperor Kang Hsi, and no attempt being made by later emperors to abolish it, it is only a veiled increase of the tax. But an open increase would not have yielded so much corruption. As the regular ten per cent was in some cases raised to fifty, it may here be pointed out that possibly none of the magistrates kept up the ten per cent rate. The worst feature of collection came from the exchange. In many of the remote

[8] For figures, see Appendix V.

corners of the country copper cash was the common medium of exchange. The tax was collected in terms of taels of silver. An exchange rate of 1,000 copper cash for one tael of silver was established by the Government. But local officials frequently raised the rate to two, three, or four thousand copper cash for a tael. A legalized speculation really took form in these cases. As a result, an impecunious magistrate was invariably a good parent-official of his children-subjects.

Of the commodity taxes, the sale monopoly and the likin were the most productive. The first, nominally a government monopoly, was practically a tax. The origin of this monopoly, as described by Dr. S. K. Chen [9] is interesting:—

Kuan Tsi, a prime minister of the State of Tsi, in the Eastern Chou Dynasty, 770-249 B. C. thought that the natural resources of a country should be owned by the state, and created the government monopolies of salt, iron, timber and other minerals as the only source of public revenues because he disapproved taxation as a means of raising public revenue on the following grounds: (A) because the productive capital of the country would be lessened by taxation; (B) because any kind of private properties subject to taxation would be depreciated in value; and (C) because taxation cannot be disguised.

As these monopolies yielded adequate revenues the State of Tsi became the richest and most powerful of all rival states. Consequently, the Salt monopoly became one of the most important sources of public revenue.

Since the time of Kuan Tsi no effort was made to bring it back to a private basis. Little was done by the government regarding improvement of its production and distribution. Down to the end of the Manchu Dynasty, the salt areas were divided according to supply, not to demand, with the result that some districts were over-supplied and others under-supplied. This was due to the territorial division of the administration. Administratively, the viceroy or governor was the head of the salt business in the provinces. Under them there were five Salt Controllers,[10] thirteen Salt Inten-

[9] *The System of Taxation in China in The Tsing Dynasty*, p. 79.
[10] Chihli, Shantung, Kiangsu, Chekiang, Kuangtung.

dents,[11] and 157 assistants of various rank. It would have been a wonder if this handful of effete officials had been able to handle all the production and distribution of salt, a universally consumed commodity, in a way to satisfy the demand of one-quarter of the human race without an organization of distributing agents. Three types of distributors existed, though not at the same place: 1. The Government monopoly of distribution where all transportation and occasionally even the retail was done by the government; 2. The private monopoly.[12] 3. The competitive trade was applied to places where no application for the monopoly was received.

The following table [13] shows the method of distribution in the provinces:—

Salt producing provinces	Method of distribution
Fengtien	Private Monopoly, public monopoly
Chihli	Private monopoly
Shantung	Private monopoly, Competitive trade
Shansi	Public monopoly, Competitive trade
Kiangsu	Private monopoly, Competitive trade
Chekiang	Private monopoly
Fukien	Public monopoly, Competitve trade
Kuangtung	Private monopoly
Szechuan	Public monopoly, Competitve trade
Yunnan	Competitive trade

The above table shows that only four of the ten producing provinces had a public monopoly as a distributing agent; every one of these four was accompanied by other methods; three by competitive trade, and one by private monopoly. Three of the six provinces where private monopoly was the distributing agent, took up the distribution by itself: every

[11] Shansi, Fukien, Yunnan Szechuan, Anhui, Kiangsi, Hupeh, Hunen, Shensi, Kuangsi, and Honan one each, Kansu, two.

[12] These agents purchased the right to manufacture and sell salt from the government in a certain territory in consideration of a sum of money paid to it by the private dealers.

[13] From *The System of Taxation in the Tsing Dynasty*, p. 79.

one of these three, (Chihli, Kuangtung and Chekiang) was an important one.

The total volume of production of salt in 1911 shown by the report of the Department of Finance in 1911 was 2,686,793,600 catties. The average rate of tax on a catty was .018 tael or $.027 silver. According to this figure, salt would have yielded 48,000,000 taels to the Government in that year. But, taking a more conservative estimate, the one given by the *Ta Tsing Hui Tien* for the year 1887, we find the receipts from salt monopoly amounting to 12,557,552 taels, about 35 per cent of the land tax and 70 per cent of the likin.

The obnoxious likin system, introduced during the Taiping Rebellion to finance the imperial troops in the struggle, the most productive of revenue outside of the land-poll tax in the second half of the 19th century, has now become a by-word of corruption. Unlike the salt monopoly in which the government put taxation under the veil of commerce and industry, this was a simple charge. It yielded 16,548,199 taels in 1887, equalling one-half of the income from the land-poll tax.[14]

Retreating a step back to the history of taxation in China, we find that the very early taxes were levied in terms of commodities. The next step was a change from commodities to copper cash, the third step was from copper cash to silver, and the fourth from a given weight of silver to silver dollars. Down to the time when all materials were collected for the last edition of the *Ta Tsing Hui Tien* in 1887, the ancient standard of taxation was still, to a very limited degree, employed. The mentioned work gives the quota of 3,624,532 *shih* of rice, 52,441,600 catties of hay, 123,600 thousand of copper cash as derived from the provinces, besides a tribute of hard wood, pearls, ginseng, and numerous other native products to be sent to Peking by the provincial officials.

Miscellaneous taxes were like those on weeds, transportation of tea, minerals of private miners, contracts of sales,

[14] See Appendix V.

travelling sales, landing tax (on cattle transported from one place to another at the destination). The general characteristic of these taxes was their abuse by the collecting officials. The amount yielded to the government was not worth mentioning in the *Ta Tsing Hui Tien,* yet the people may have paid considerable sums to satisfy the collectors.

The political history of China reveals an undue negligence, amounting almost to indifference, on the part of the government in its finance. Owing to the remarkable lack of activities of the government, receipts from land-poll tax and monopolies always yield sufficient expenditures for a normal government; the sole occasion of bankruptcy was when an indolent ruler led a life of unnecessary waste of the state treasures. The treasuries might be empty, the minister of revenues might cry for need, but bankruptcy was never a principal cause of the fall of a dynasty; the crisis, if it ever existed, was forgotten as soon as its termination arrived. Dynastic histories show little records of the financial state of the different periods except in connection with taxation. Prior to the intercourse with the West, a financial history, in the modern sense of the term, was an unknown entity in the billions of Chinese books. Indeed, a wasteful ruler was cursed more because this wastefulness was deemed unethical than because it was regarded as a political abuse.

With an empty treasury, the Manchus mounted the Chinese throne. As a debt-ridden state, China was left after two and a half centuries of Manchu rule. Despite the lack of changes, a review of the financial history in the Tsing Dynasty will help us to understand much better its financial conditions and policies on the verge of reforms.[15] Lack of changes in the Tsing Dynasty, however, should not blind us to the fact that the Manchus improved the original Chinese financial records by showing greater details in the balance sheets of the Government. Emperor Shun Chi char-

---

[15] For further details, see *Financial History of the Chinese Republic, Chung Hua Min Kuo Tsai Cheng Shih,* by Chia Shih Yi, chapter 1, vol. 1.

acterized his administration of finance by three features: the frequent exemption of taxes, the curtailment of administrative expenses, and the clearing of tax arrears. During his reign the total receipts of the Peking treasuries amounted to only 28,381,039 taels. His son, Emperor Kang Hsi, centralized his efforts upon the systematization of financial reports from the provinces, reduction of government expenses in general, and reduction of the expenses in the Imperial Household in particular. The Rebellion of "the three feudal princes" made the collection of taxes an impossibility for thirteen years during his reign. This fortunately resulted in a curtailment of expenses in the imperial palaces. According to the emperor himself, the expenses of all palaces together were less than one of the late Ming palaces; the sum total of thirty-six years of expenditures was less than one year's under the emperor of the Ming Dynasty. Let a few items of palace expenditures serve as illustrations:—[16]

Item of expenditure	Amount in Ming	Amount in Kang Hsi's Reign
Flowers and decoration	960,000 taels	Nothing
Receipts from The Court of Banquets	240,000 taels	30,000 taels
Wood	27,860,000 catties	600,000 catties
Hard coal	12,000,000 catties	1,000,000 catties
Bedchamber and Paranquin decorations	28,000 taels	Nothing
Court of Banquets	1,000,000 taels	100,000 taels

This gives a fairly good idea of the curtailments made by Kang Hsi, The Rebellion of the "three feudal princes," the campaign against the Rakchas, and the Dzumgars, dam constructions, and exemptions of tax after military operations either lightened the treasuries or led to smaller receipts. The policy of the government was to enrich the people by inaugurating constructive financial measures. Decentralization of finance began in this period as a consequence of assigning the income from the land-poll tax and salt mo-

[16] Figures from Complete History of the Tsing Dynasty.

noply to the provincial governments. In spite of all these handicaps, his sixty years' reign left in the imperial treasury a balance of 8,000,000 taels; the annual receipts of the government was increased to 35,000,000 taels.

Emperor Yung Cheng adopted an active policy for the increase of revenues rather than for the curtailment of expenditures. His financial administration was marked by three main features: an attempt to increase the receipts from customs duties by encouragement of commercial transportation, strictness and promptitude in the collection of tax, and the recall of all loans made by his father to provincial officials. In his period, too, military campaigns in Kokonor (Chinese Turkistan) and against the Dzumgars; increase of the administrative force, and enlargement of the size of the army ate up more and more of the government's stored treasure: this was saved merely by improved methods of accounting. Thus a sharp turning point, from a liberal policy of enriching the people to a strict policy of providing a sufficiency for the government, was made. Meanwhile, the annual revenues of the government increased to 40,000,000 taels; and Yung Cheng handed his son a balance of 24,000,000 taels in 1735.

A period of extravagance and liberalism dawned in the reign of Emperor Chien Lung. With a big sum left over from his father, living in a stage of general tranquility and satisfaction, and with a pompous and extravagant disposition, he embarked on a new policy. The repeated exemption of taxes, relief work in times of famine, reconstruction of river dams and canals, suppression of the rebellions of Tsinchow and the Dzumgars, all required tremendous sums. Heavy deficits would have resulted except for the inauguration of several new sources of revenue. They were contributions from the people, loaning of money to the provinces, and increase of salt prices. A further improvement of the balance sheet was made by exhibiting the expenditures as well as the receipts of the government. The upward trend in receipts was not checked; the figure running up to 43,000,000 of income as against 31,000,000 of expenditures with a net balance of 70,000,000 taels in the treasury when he retired.

His son continued this free spending policy in spite of the great increase of expenditures caused by the reconstruction of river dams and canals, suppression of the Mohammedan Rebellion in Hupeh and Szechuan, the Miao Tze Rebellion in Kueichow, the Rebellion of the Boatmen, the Honan Rebellion, the export of bullion as a result of unfavorable balance of trade caused by importation of opium and what-not. While the expenditures increased from 31,000,000 to 35,000,-000, the receipts shrank by 2,000,000. The bankruptcy of the dynasty was deferred only by his partial success in curing the traditional corruption in financial administration, the inauguration of new taxes on miscellaneous commodities, increase of salt prices and contributions from the officials out of their allowances.

Up to this time, the government was able to maintain a balance of some sort. The deficit began during Emperor Tao Kuang's reign as a result of the heavy military expenses for the suppression of the Mohammedan Rebellion. Amidst the old items of expenditures like the reconstruction of dams and canals, new ones like payment of principals and interests on indemnities, provincial appropriation for new services, increase of the army, in addition to expenditures on foreign wars began to claim a regular place in the balance sheet. The finances of the government hung upon the verge of bankruptcy notwithstanding an increase of revenue from the clearing of provincial debts to the central government, cultivation of frontier lands in Sinkiang, prohibition of private coinage and contributions from the provincial treasury.

The Taiping Rebellion and foreign wars caused a loss of income from taxes and the salt monopoly of thirteen provinces, and the latter led to an increase in indemnity, while the great expense of the "Imperial hunting trip" more than counterbalanced the fruit of the remedial measures specially designed to meet its needs, such as the notorious likin system, the sale of offices and degrees, issuance of new coins and paper money, and the conversion of taxes in commodities into money. The financial ebb during Hsien Feng's reign ran so low that no data are available.

The unfortunate Tung Chi succeeded his father amidst political and financial chaos. In his early years, the unsuppressed and the newly suppressed provinces did not pay, or were excused from, taxes. Some of the miscellaneous taxes, specially those levied to tide over the emergency, were abolished; the illegal extra charge was done away with, naval expenses increased, and thus a favorable balance sheet became a thing of the past. Against all these marine customs duty was the only new income, yet its infancy and the limited amount of trade at that period yielded even in good years, only 12,000,000 taels. An average deficit of 10,000,000 taels a year was recorded.

The last thirty-five years of financial history in the Tsing Government under Emperors Kuang Hsu and Hsuan Tung can be divided into four periods. In the first period, 1875 to 1884, foreign wars, the Mohammedan Rebellion, relief work, river dams and canals repairing, naval defense, and indemnity still claimed a great portion of the expenditures and threatened the government with a deficit. But the downfall of the Taipings brought back to the Manchus thirteen taxpaying provinces; while the increased volume of trade in the sale of offices, increase of tax and duties, cultivation of frontiers lands, establishment of new customs houses, and the improvement of the salt administration yielded the government not only enough for its expenditures, but also a balance of three to ten million taels per year.

In the second period, which ran from the Franco-Chinese War to the Boxer uprising, Chinese Government finance was dominated by foreign wars and their consequent indemnities. Old activities, like the repairing of the river dams and canals or relief work, proved far less expensive than the payments of interest upon debts and indemnities. A program including a reduction of administrative expenses, increase of salt price and other taxes, introduction of new taxes, encouragement of contributions (sale of offices), purification of the likin system, and the inauguration of a wine and tobacco monopoly, was mapped out. But the actual increase of incomes was brought about by contributions of salaries by officials, foreign loans, internal loans, taxes on raising poppy, percentage discounts of soldiers' pay, surtaxes, and confiscations. The modern expenditures, however proved too much for the ancient receipts; a deficit of about 10,000,000 taels per year existed throughout the whole period.

The third Kuang Hsu period was marked by increase of taxes, contributions of officials, introduction of new taxes, and increased profits of government monopoly on the one side, and the increase of indemnity and new administrative offices on the other side of the balance sheet. A deficit of 20,000,000 taels was annually recorded. The Hsuan Tung period was dominated by an increase of thirty per cent in the receipts, making it 260,000,000 taels annually. Despite the new increase, the balance sheet was still unbalanced and a deficit lingered in the budget, defying all efforts of financial reconstruction.

In the course of two hundred and sixty-five years, the total annual receipts of the government increased from 28,-381,039 taels in the beginning to 263,610,000 taels at the end of the dynasty, an increase of nearly 1,000 per cent. Expenditures, on the other hand, increased more rapidly. The stored fats of the early emperors were easily eaten up. The traditional financial outlook of appropriating money according to receipts was not broken until the third period of Emperor Kuang Hsu, when the pressure of the expenditures admitted no curtailment and the income was insufficient for the purpose. This change of the traditional outlook led to a change in the matter of taxation. Increase of taxation, traditionally regarded as a tyrannical measure, practiced usually in a roundabout way if ever practiced, avoided by all emperors whenever possible, was, because of its help in increasing the revenues, openly proclaimed in the latter part of the dynasty. One thing, the confusion of government funds and the private property of the emperor, remained throughout the whole dynasty whether the government treasury was full or empty. The attempt to draw up a civil list proved merely a camouflage.

The *Ta Tsing Hui Tien* classifies the government expenditures into fifteen classes, the total sum of each is reproduced as follows:—[17]

1.	The Imperial Mausolea	106,861
2.	Through the Department of Revenues	180,000
3.	Sacrificial	206,604
4.	Ceremonials	24,134
5.	Salaries of Officials	1,908.084
6.	Civil Service Examinations	190,979
7.	Army maintenance	14,913,215
8.	Relay Communications	2,077,561
9.	Scholarships	152,309
10.	Rewards and Charities	225,125
11.	Reconstructions and Repairs of Dams and Canals—Not fixed.	
12.	Purchases	91,703
13.	The Government Silk Factories	307,833
14.	Allowances for Officials	4,724,305
15.	Miscellaneous	415,959
	Total—taels	25,524,677

Grouping these fifteen items, we find them classifiable under seven headings, occupying widely varying portions of the total expenditures of the Government:—

	Item	Amount in Taels	Percentage in Total Expenditures
a.	Ceremonials and Sacrificials	337,609	1.32
b.	Education and Examinations	330.760	1.29
c.	Civil Officials	4,845,453	19.—
d.	Military	18,718,474	73.33
e.	Charity and Rewards	225,125	.88
f.	Purchase and Manufactures	579,641	2.27
g.	Miscellaneous	415,959	1.63

[17] The figures are for the 13th year of Kuang Hsu, 1887, minutely itemized. These are only the totals.

In the second table, *a* includes 1, 3, and 4; *b* includes 6, 7, and a part of 14; *c* includes 5 and 10; *d* includes 7, 8, and most of 14; *e* includes 10; *f* includes 2, 12, and 13; *g* includes 15. These show merely the expenditures paid by the Department of Revenues. A great amount of money spent by the central government and paid by the provincial treasuries is not included. The Central government in Peking, not having had a centralized system in finance, used to appropriate money for different offices or services from the provincial treasuries directly to the recipients without going through the National Treasury. Taking the itemized expenditures as they were, military expenses took up almost three-quarters of the total expenditures of the Government, a surprisingly big percentage for the inefficient army that could not even protect the people from bandits. Of these eighteen and three-quarters million taels of silver, the "Green Battalions," (Chinese local forces) took up two-thirds, and the Manchu forces (Bannermen) the rest.[18] These figures will produce a misconception if the fact is forgotten that the Manchus, having conquered China by military force, concentrated the military administration and command and left all other activities, except the civil service salaries, to the local and provincial authorities, and that, therefore, a great part of the expenses for scholarships, reconstructions and repairs of dams and canals, allowances for officials, etc., were paid out of the provincial funds. The expenses for reconstruction of dams and canals, being out of the government's control, varied from nothing to four or five million taels a year. The central government usually appropriated a small sum for these purposes. In case of further need, provincial governments were privileged to borrow money from the central government. Of other items, the next most undeterminable item was rewards and charities. Besides expenditures in money, supplies like rice, beans, grains, horses, clothing were given out by the government. Conversion of these into money would considerably swell the figures.

[18] For detailed figures, see Appendix VI.

Silver being the standard metal for money, a proportional exchange rate between it and another kind of metal, copper, was maintained. At the beginning of the dynasty, one tael of silver was worth about from 700 to 800 copper cash. During the reign of Hsien Feng and Tung Chi, the price of silver almost doubled. The receipts of the government consisted of both copper and silver while the expenditures were all in silver, thus bringing considerable disadvantage to the Government.

The Government funds were deposited in five ways:—

1. The "sealed deposits" were kept for the central government in the provincial or prefectural treasuries under the custody of the viceroy, or governor and the commissioner of finance. The custodians were responsible to the Department of Revenues.

2. The "separate deposits" made by the provincial treasuries in the district or subprefectural treasuries for local needs. The custodians were responsible to the depositors.

3. The "district reserves," left over in the district or subprefectural treasuries by the commissioner of finance as a result of exemption from remittance to the commissioners.

4. The "provincial reserves," kept by the commissioner of finance made up of money remitted to him from local officials.

5. The "remitted deposits," remitted to the commissioner of finance, or a circuit intendent from the central government for special purposes, as, for example, the reconstruction of river dams or relief work of a famine, etc.

In the provincial governments three kinds of funds were kept: expenses for provincial administration, funds to be remitted to Peking, and funds for the help of other provinces in case of need.

About fifty per cent of the expenses of the central government was from contributions from the provinces, as all receipts of the government, with the exception of customs, tariff and likin, were collected by the local authorities for the central government. Consequently, no province remitted any money to Peking until all its own expenses were paid. Funds for different localities or organizations were assigned, the payee receiving the payment directly from the payer often without the knowledge of the central government. When a new item of expenditure came up, the government, though having large sums of money to its credit, had no money at its disposal, and had to look around and find out some items of expenses which could be cut or that would yield a balance for the new item.

Contributions of the provinces to the central government were made in separate sums for different services or purposes, to wit: for the Court of Imperial Household, the Department of War, the Department of Revenues, defrayment of central executive expenses, indemnity payments, and foreign debt charges. In all these transactions, the power and influence of the minister, viceroy, or governor, was more important than regulations. Mr. Chow Tang well observed in *The Essentials of Chinese Finance*:—[19]

> The minister of revenues, having no higher rank than, and exercising only concurrent jurisdiction over the provincial finance with, the viceroy or governor, has no right to issue orders to the latter. Were a measure or proposal to come up from either of them, they had to submit it to the emperor. A strong viceroy can do what he pleases by thwarting all the measures of the ministers, a weak one will yield to the ministers even in affairs of the provincial finance. But, finance being a delicate question, the greedy is loath to give it to others, the energetic takes it as a help for the execution of his plans; so the Department of Revenues, nominally the central organ for finance, becomes only a decoration in Peking . . . . .

Between the provinces, a system of mutual help prevailed. Nature being more generous to some, the government tried to make up for this partiality by a very poor method. Of the twenty-two provinces, twelve received aids from other provinces, five both received and gave aids, and five gave aids without compensation.[20] These inter-provincial aids were

---

[19] *Chung Kuo Tsai Cheng Ta Chang*, p. 7, 1892.

[20] Chuan Shih Li, *The Relation Between Central and Local Finance in China*, p. 54, in Columbia University Studies, vol. XCIX.

assigned by Peking; but the assignment was all that the central government did; for, after the assignment, the remittances took place without going through the formality of letting the central government in as a middleman. Some unfortunate provinces might be able to get help from the central government financially. This, though a more centralized process, was done by means of remittances from the more fortunate provinces.

The lack of separation of the finances of the different grades of government or "communism of revenues" encouraged the deficient provincial governments eagerly to request the support of the Board of Revenues which, in turn, was compelled to depend entirely upon the aid furnished by the richer provinces. Secondly, it encouraged the concealment of revenues by the richer provinces, owing to the reluctance of these provinces to share their revenues with the poorer ones.[21] Not only were the governors unwilling to show surplus revenues, but the receiving of support from other provinces was so tempting that inefficiency in provincial finance was encouraged.

APPENDIX I—SCALE OF FAMINE RELIEF
Gift of Government to Each Adult Subject in Famine in Pecks (tou) of Grains

Kind of Farmer	Percentage of Famine					
	100	90	80	70	60	50
I. MANCHUS						
A. Bannermen's land	12.5	12.5	10.0	10.0	7.5	7.5
B. Official land	12.5	12.5	12.5	10.0	10.0	7.5
C. Military Settlers land	22.5	22.5	22.5	22.5	15.0	15.0
II. CHINESE						
A. Very poor	7.5	6.0	4.5	4.5	3.0	...
B. Poor	6.0	4.5	3.0	3.0	...	...

Figures are taken from *Ta Tsing Hui Tien*, v. 19.
To start with, 1.5 pecks for Chinese and 2.5 pecks for Manchus with half portions for children.

[21] *Ibid*, p. 58.

APPENDIX II—REQUIRED GOVERNMENT GRAIN RESERVES
DEPOSITED IN PROVINCES FOR FAMINE RELIEF

(*Shih* is the unit)

Province	Regular Reserve (Chang Chang)	Extra Reserve (Yu Pe Chang)	Reserve for Manchus (Chi Chang)	Total
Fengtien	390,708		38,893	429,601
Kirin	35,374		127,172	162,546
Heilungkiang			115,370	115,370
Chihli	100,650			100,650
Shangtung	2,945,300			2,945,300
Shansi	1,893,319			1,893,319
Honan	417,861	220,919		638,780
Kiangsu	395,980			395,980
Anhui		a154,140		154,140
Kiangsi	105,697			105,697
Fukien	2,962,559			2,962,559
Chekiang	30,614			30,614
Hupeh	1,947,819			1,947,819
Hunan	1,561,255			1,561,255
Szechuan	626,880	8,400		645,280
Kuangtung	2,860,730			2,860,730
Kuangsi	1,274,378			1,274,378
TOTAL	17,559,124	383,459	281,435	18,224,108

Note:—(a) represents beans instead of grains.

Date of the Provinces of Shensi, Kansu, Yunna and Kueichow are not securable.

Private or local organization reserves are not included.

The Province of Kiangsu had in reserve 1,040,570 thousands of copper cash besides the grains.

Figures from *Ta Tsing Hui Tien*, v. 19.

APPENDIX III—TABLE SHOWING DISTRIBUTION OF CULTIVABLE LAND IN *MAO* BY PROVINCES

Province	People's Land	Military Settlers' Land	Bannermen's Land	Frontiers Land	Officials' Land	Scholars Land
Fengtien	6,806,763	1,294,674	16,060,709	101,518,709	265,124	
Kirin	1,429,214				54,000	
Heilungkiang					81,600	
Chihli	a68,334,925		969,898			
Shantung	123,600,758	2,238,905				41,742
Shansi	48,068,899	8,380,706				27,798
Honan	64,474,442	6,000,839				199,904
Kiangsu	71,860,438	39,764,932				
Anhui	36,924,352	4,170,289				18,387
Kiangsi	46,752,382	582,464				6,735
Fukien	12,604,473	786,513				9,070
Chekiang	46,457,307	224,130			89,078	
Hupeh	c59,220,195			58,102,760		
Hunan	31,628,134	3,238,741				7,380
Shensi	b26,598,068	3,993,244				
Kansu	31,256,832	6,272,956			77,886	783,186
Szechuan	a46,415,890					
Kuangtung	34,193,764	521,944				15,117
Kuangsi d	c9,696,283					
Yunnan f	8,395,572	914,398			9,081	9,215
Kuiechou g	2,685,272	63,156			12,136	4,442
Sinkiang				11,480,191		
At large			c2,077,737			
TOTAL	777,315,963	78,497,891	19,108,534	171,101,660	588,805	1,072,976

Note:—Figures are from *Ta Tsing Hui Tien*, v. 17.

APPENDIX IV—EXPLANATORY NOTES OF THE TABLE SHOWING DISTRIBUTION OF CULTIVABLE LAND IN *MAO* BY PROVINCES

1. This is a reclassification from the figures given by *Ta Tsing Hui Tien*.

2. Sometimes two or three classes of land are quoted in one figure; so in the tables the following signs are used for combination:—

    a including Military Settlers' land
    b including Scholars' land
    c including Officials' land
    d including land for sacrifices cultivated by 339 households
    e including 743,792 *mao* of Bannermen's land and 1,333,945 *mao* of land owned by imperial clansmen
    f signifies figures from report of 1853 (Other figures are from report of 1885)
    g signifies figures from report of 1812.

3. Some figures are from *Hu Pu Chi Li*, 1874 edition.

4. 341,663 *mao* of land which were exempt from tax, are also included.

5. People's land includes all lands designated in the source books by the names of Min Tien, Sha Tan Ti, Yuan Ti, Keng Ming Ti, Lu Tien, Tui Chuan Ti, Chi Ti, A Wei Ti, and Yi Tien.

6. Military Settlers' land includes all land known as Mu Chuang Ti, Tsin Chun Ti, and Tuan Tien in the source books.

7. Frontiers' land includes what are called Kai Ken Ti and Fang Ti.

8. Officials' land includes all land known as Kuan Tien, Kuan Chuan Ti, Yang Lien Ti and Chen Ti.

9. Scholars' land includes what the source books call Hsueh Tien, Yi Hsueh Tien and Chien Ti.

APPENDIX V—TABLE SHOWING GOVERNMENT RECEIPTS
FROM TAX AND LIKIN

Province	Likin in Taels	Tax in Taels	Tax in shihs of Grain
Fengtien	408,638	375,823	132,319
Kirin		284,002	23,197
Heilungkiang		17,880	8,283
Chihli	303,056	2,604,482	94,438
Shantung	105,172	3,514,634	435,915
Shansi	195,495	3,003,886	117,060
Honan	78,526	3,499,655	28,015
Kiangsu	2,281,181	3,525,817	306,933
Anhui	475,432	1,848,950	104,589
Kiangsi	1,323,712	1,943,777	137,813
Fukien	1,760,565	1,235,140	125,832
Chekiang	2,076,347	2,856,869	292,629
Hupeh	1,314,557	1,049,633	168,084
Hunan	1,181,979	1,175,130	139,865
Shensi	386,547	1,623,856	198,387
Kansu	413,388	315,926	507,651
Szechuan	1,601,789	675,291	17,209
Kuangtung	1,685,931	1,094,931	604,194
Kuangsi	670,879	478,768	130,166
Yunnan	333,442	a375,179	a129,649
Kueichou	150,563	b147,323	b135,288
Sinkiang		59,145	279,806
At large		3,774	
TOTAL	16,548,199	31,709,871	4,117,322

Note:—Figures are from *Ta Tsing Hui Tien*, v. 17, taken in 1885. *a* signifies figures from 1853. *b* signifies figures from 1812. Besides these, 123,603 thousand copper cash and 35,742,594 catties of hay were collected in 1885 as tax.

APPENDIX VI—TABLE SHOWING EXPENDITURES
ON LAND FORCES IN 1885

Province	Banner Forces	Green Battalions	Total
Chihli		1,321,953	1,321,953
Fengtien	641,991		641,991
Kirin	432,173		432,173
Heilungkiang	331,127		331,127
Shantung	110,262	361,348	471,610
Shansi	273,484	389,740	663,224
Honan	119,188	289,223	408,411
Kiangsu	317,250	578,664	895,914
Anhui		197,198	197,198
Kiangsi		225,166	225,166
Fukien	125,564	851,470	1,007,034
Chekiang	153,904	692,125	846,029
Hupeh	319,023	286,000	605,023
Hunan		425,047	425,047
Shensi	357,856	208,259	566,115
Kansu	206,584	351,597	558,180
Sinkiang	449,203	1,568,039	2,017,242
Szechuan		952,329	952,329
Kuangtung	168,702	1,115,777	1,284,479
Kuangsi		205,768	205,768
Yunnan		355,664	355,664
Kueichou		491,537	491,537
TOTAL	4,006,411	10,866,904	14,913,215

CHAPTER VIII

THE JUDICIARY

Prior to the discussion of the administration of justice, a few words about the theory, development, and special features of the Chinese laws will greatly help in the understanding of the system. In a country where ethics was the principal regulator of human conduct, virtue the chief requirement of the rulers, arbitration the common means of settling disputes, compromise the general consequence of disagreement, law took only a secondary place in the encouragement of good, and the discouragement of evil doings. The philosophy of the people regarded disputes as evidence of an absence of virtue; an appeal to law as an acknowledgment of this lack of moral quality; an appearance in court, for women especially, was a tremendous blow to one's social prestige, if not a disgrace. The government, on the other hand, made repeated attempts to discourage appeals to law by making the punishments so severe that, on account of their severity, people would not dare try the courts unless driven to them as a last resort. Indeed, the discouragement by the government of appeals to law reduced litigations to an incredibly small number, although discouragement also came from the inefficiency of judicial administration, as well as the severity of law. Thus the corruption of the bench, difficulty of securing, and ease of purchasing, justice, the risk of undue, severe punishment, the abundant means of settling disputes outside the Magistrate's court, the ethical prejudice against settlement of disputes by law, all combined to make law a curse instead of a blessing to the people. Then, too, the laws in China were not things to which people had been educated. Except the professional writers of writs, people were guided by conscience, rather than by statute, looking at things to find out whether they were right or wrong, rather than whether they were legally legitimate or otherwise. Finally, the application of law as a means of rectification was held theoretically justifiable only after persuasion and ethical appeals had been made in vain. Such being the background of law, little wonder is there to find in China a code of laws and a system of administering that code totally different from the Occidental.

The law making power, we should here recollect, was an imperial power, possessed and exercised by the emperor, and by him alone. Not infrequently, however, was a law proposed by a minister and sanctioned by his imperial master; in fact, the great majority of the laws were initiated by ministers, and a fairly good law proposed by a minister stood a very good chance of being adopted, though the final deciding power belonged unconditionally to the monarch. Whenever a new law was enacted, explanatory edicts as to the reason and necessity of its enactment prefaced the announcement of the law. In most cases, it was first put into trial, then given a prohibitionary term, and perpetuated only after successful experiments. Scarcely ever was a law contrary to the wishes of the people given permanent operation. The absolute power of the emperor in repealing or annulling laws came in very handily to remove laws objected to by his "children-people."

The whole code was of 436 divisions under seven classes; divided according to the six departments. There were 46 divisions of the penal, 28 of the administrative, 82 of the civil, 26 of the ritual and ceremonial, 71 of the military, 170 of the criminal and 13 of the constructional. The 46 divisions of the penal and 170 divisions of the criminal can certainly be put into one class, both being punitive in nature. They had as many divisions as all others put together. There were more than 3,900 crimes punishable by capital punishment. This undue proportion produced two impressions on the penal code, that is, it was complete,[1] and it was

---

[1] Prof. H. A. Giles says that it has received "unqualified admiration from eminent Western lawyers."

the only code China has ever had. Contrary to the second impression, more public laws than private law can be found in China. *The Historical Evolution of Chinese Codes,*[2] a study of the history of different codes in China by a Japanese scholar, translated into Chinese by Chen Tsung Min, well observes:—

Of the several hundred codes edited in the different periods of the 4,000 years of Chinese history, none is strictly and purely on private laws. Laws of marriage, succession, property, mortgage, debt, etc., are stated only in broad principles embodied in codes of public laws. Why? Because the sense of private property is weak among the Chinese, and tradition is against the development of that sense.

In the Chinese history, there has never been any nobility or caste except those of the imperial clan. The high officials resemble nobles; but they are not hereditary. Hence, a struggle between the patricians and plebeians as in ancient Rome was impossible of occurrence in China, the opportunity for advocating, and fighting, for private rights as a result of class struggle never presented itself. Moreover, the government was started a republic. The Sha Emperors made it a hereditary monarchy merely by accident. But, in the Chou Dynasty, the Confucian philosophy which regulated the acts of the government with ethical ideas, sprang up. The emperors at least pretended to treat their people as their sons. The tyranny of nobles like that of medieval Europe had no place in the history of the people; its reaction, a struggle for liberty, was unknown. Again, the Confucian school emphasized the natural order, pointing to the theory that men are naturally unequal, therefore, they ought to make the best of their respective situation, and no more. On the other hand, the Romans thought that inequality of protection was a hindrance to development, so they sought equality of protection from law. They fought against the nobles. Their civil law developed. The Chinese have left them to the grace and kindness of the rulers. How can one expect laws for protection of private rights under the circumstances?

Whether public or private, all laws were made for the preservation of the then existing order, and nearly every one for the safety of the throne occupant, and to a limited degree for the preservation of the almost negligible difference between the nobles and the commoners.

[2] *Chung Kus Fa Tien Pien Chuan Yuan Ka Shih.*

The "Ten Crimes"[3] which occupy a position in Chinese law as important as that of the ten commandments in Christian religion, show clearly the policy of the government in enacting laws. With the exception of the third and the fifth, none of these crimes was called a crime because it was wrongly done by one person to another, but it was a crime because done by an inferior to a superior. Were these wrongs done to equals, they would not have been wrongs to such punishable degree. Some acts, beating, scolding, crimes when done to superiors by inferiors, would become an assertion of rights when done to an inferior by a superior. Even the killing of a son by a father, homicide pure and simple, would not make the father a criminal in the eyes of the law, though a brute in public opinion.

The seventh item shows a confusion of ethics and law. Under the Chinese system, it was certainly a moral obligation for the son to take care of his father. But this provision, lack of filial piety, legitimatized the father's claim to his son's support, making a failure of moral obligation at home a crime against the state. This shows another characteristic of the Chinese law, namely, lack of enforcement of some of the laws. As pointed out in the *Historical Evolution of Chinese Codes*, some of the clauses were put there because they sounded well for a code, others were put in for reference, still others were embodied because they had been handed down from the ancestors and therefore not to

---

[3] 1. Treason, rebellion against the reigning dynasty. 2. Destruction or impairment of imperial property, particularly sacrificial property. 3. Betraying the country to a foreign country. 4. Beating parents, grandparents or other senior relatives, plotting against, or killing, them. 5. Homicide. 6. Stealing, or imitating, things of imperial style. 7. Lack of filial piety, scolding parents, not supporting or entertaining them full-heartedly, not wearing mourning clothes for the full period, etc. 8. Cruelly killing, beating, or bringing lawsuit against a family superior. 9. Unrighteousness—a subject killing an official, a private soldier killing an officer, an inferior official killing a superior, a pupil killing a teacher, not mourning over the death of a husband. 10. Illegitimate sexuality with a family superior.

be changed. If any law in China deserved the bitter and yet veritable criticism of the Japanese author, the seventh of the "ten crimes," the filial piety clause should have the full share, for it was just as impossible for the magistrates to enforce this law by finding out and punishing every unfilial son as for every son to be filial no matter how efficient the police or how high the ethics and how strong the social compulsion.

Foreign students of Chinese laws very often have the erroneous impression that the criminal code was the only code there was in China. This comes from the fact that, with very few exceptions in the administrative code, "the five punishments"[4] were applied to offenders against all classes of laws. But these penal consequences did not alter the civil or administrative nature of the provisions.

The patriarchalism of the social, and the paternalism of the political, institutions, the inadequate conception of law, the inefficiency of judicial administration, the easy access to non-legal means of satisfactory settlement of disputes, together with perfect isolation, and, hence, lack of contact with other nations having legal systems worthy of study, combined to make Chinese laws what they were up to the beginning of this century.

The judicial ladder was no less hierarchic or multi-graded than the civil service. Geographically speaking, the lowest court in a province was the magistrate or sub-prefectural court. Either a district magistrate, a first class sub-prefect, a second class sub-prefect, tried cases of the first instance. This, the lowest court, had jurisdiction over all kinds of cases within the territory and was empowered to impose all degrees of punishment. The magistrate or the sub-pre-

[4] 1. Whipping with small bamboo stick. 2. Whipping with large bamboo sticks. 3. Exile to less than 500 *li* from home for one to three years. 4. Permanent exile from home for two or three thousand *li*. 5. Death punishment.

fect himself was the only person in the whole territory who could try a case; for the *Ta Tsing Huie Tien* provided that only "principal officials" could receive complaints or written accusations from a subject, and without a written accusation, no action could be taken by the judicial authority. After a decision was reached, all the records were sent to the prefect (in case of an independent sub-prefecture, this process was eliminated) who had the power to review the case, if one of the parties was not satisfied with the decision. Then they were sent sometimes to a circuit intendent, sometimes directly to the Commissioner of Justice, either of whom had the right to review the case. The Commissioner of Justice (appointed directly by the emperor) was the highest judicial authority in a province, whose decision could be reviewed by the governor or the viceroy, the almighty official of the provinces. The Commissioner collected all documents from the lower courts and sent them to the Department of Law in Peking. The province, then, had, in addition to the governor or viceroy, four grades of courts, each reviewing the decisions of the lower ones; none but the district or sub-prefectural courts received cases of the first instance.

In Peking, the scale was quite different. The Metropolitan Prefect consists of two magistracies.[5] A case of the first instance could be tried by the representative magistrate, reviewed by the Governor or the Metropolitan Prefect and then go up to the Supreme Bench; or it could go to the Court of the Gendarmerie which had jurisdiction to decide cases with punishment less than exile.[6] Or a case might be submitted to a censor in Peking: the city being supervised by five censors each taking one precinct, it had to

[5] Districts of Ta Shing and Yuan Ping.

[6] The court of Gendarmerie was presided over by a minister or a vice-minister of a department specially assigned for the purpose unless the commander-in-chief had been a civilian official with ministerial rank. In that case the commander-in-chief himself tried the case.

be submitted to the one who had the territorial jurisdiction over the case.

After failing to get justice from all the provincial courts, the case could be brought up to the "Three Supreme Tribunals" in Peking. But, no case would be tried until it has gone through all the provincial courts. Nor was a question about the degree of punishment tried. The composition of the "Three Supreme Tribunals" was the Department of Law, (Hsing Pu)[7] the Censorate, and the Grand Court of Revision. A brief sketch of each of the three organizations, except the Censorate which has been dealt with at length in Chapter IV, is necessary for a better understanding of their jurisdiction and work.

The Department of Law was one of the six regular departments of the government. It was run by two ministers and four vice-ministers (three Manchus and three Chinese). Their duties were "to assist His Majesty in the rectification of his myriads by directing affairs and issuing orders of law and punishments. In the decision of degree of punishments, the justice of the decision, pardons, and confiscations, officials shall report to this department: the ministers and vice-ministers, together with the members of the department, shall decide on the merit of the case. A report shall be made to His Majesty in important cases; the department exercises final jurisdiction over cases that can be decided by law."[8] This department, like others, was divided into bureaus.

[7] This is usually translated as the Board of Punishments. The word "punishments" is, however, only a literal translation of the Chinese word "Hsing." Hsing is defined as law in Giles' Chinese-English Dictionary, the Tsi Yuan and the Kang Hsi Dictionary. Hence, the term "Department of Law" instead of Board of Punishments is used here.

[8] *Ta Tsing Huei Tien*, v. 53.

THE GOVERNMENT OF CHINA

	Bureau	Jurisdiction	Receives cases from
1.	Chihli	Chihli, Peking, Metropolitan Prefect	Left Wing of Tsihar, Bordered Yellow, Plain White, Bordered White, Plain Blue, East Half of Plain Yellow banners.
2.	Fengtien	Fengtien, Kirin, Heilunkiang	Court of Imperial Clan, Department of Territories
3.	Kiangsu	Kiangsu	Censorial Circuit of Kiangnan, Tartar General of Nanking, Tartar Lieutenant-general of Chingchow, Viceroys of Canals and Rivers *Pardons, Atonements*
4.	Anhui	Anhui	Bordered Red, Hsuan Wu Mon Precinct of Peking
5.	Kiangsi	Kiangsi	Censorial Circuit of Kiangsi, Central Precinct of Metropolitan Censor, Plain Yellow, Shi Chi Mon Precinct of Peking
6.	Fukien	Fukien	Department of Revenue and its Departmental censor, Offices of Granaries, Bordered Blue, Fu Ching Mon Precinct of Peking, Tartar General of Foochow
7.	Chekiang	Chekiang	The Censorate, Censorial Department of Law, Censorial Circuit of Chekiang, Censorial Precinct (South), Lieutenant Garrison General in Chia-pu
8.	Hukuang	Hupeh, Hunan	Censorial Circuit of Hukuang, Tartar General in Chingchow
9.	Honan	Honan	Department of Rites, Censorial Circuit of Honan, Court of Ceremonials, Court of Banquet, Metropolitan College, Court of Worship, The Imperial Astronomical Observatory, The Imperial Hospital, The Eastern Censorial Precinct in Peking, Plain Red, Teh Shing Mon Precinct of Peking

THE JUDICIARY

	Bureau	Jurisdiction	Receives cases from
10.	Shantung	Shantung	The Department of War, Censorial Department of War, Censorial Circuit of Shantung, The Imperial Stud, Tartar Lieutenant-general of Chingchow, Viceroy of Ho-tung *Check the cases of the Gendarm Office*
11.	Shansi	Shansi	Right Wing of Tsihar, and cities to the North, Half of Plain Yellow in Tsihar, Plain Red, Bordered Red, Bordered Blue, Tartar General of Suiyuancheng, Tartar Lieutenant-general in Kueihuacheng, Senior Tartar Lieutenant-general in Tingpin, Governor of Kobdo, Imperial Resident of Urga *Examine the Annual Reports (Judicial) from the Provinces*
12.	Shensi	Shensi, Kansu	Grand Court of Revision, Censorial Circuit of Shensi, Western Censorial Precinct of Peking, Tartar General of Sianfu, Tartar General of Ninghsa, Tartar Lieutenant-general of Liangchow, Tartar General of Eli *Prisoners' Food Distribution*
13.	Szechuan	Szechuan	Department of Works, Censorial Circuit of Szechuan, Tartar General of Chengtu *New Laws, Cases to be reviewed after the decision of the nine Ministers, implements of Punishment*
14.	Kuangtung	Kuangtung	Headquarters of the Imperial Guards, Plain White, An Ting Mon Precinct of Peking, Censorial Circuit of Kuangtung, Tartar General of Kuangchow
15.	Kuangsi	Kuangsi	Court of Transmission, Censorial Circuit of Kuangsi *Records of Court Trials, Prisoners' Wearing Apparels*

	Bureau	Jurisdiction	Receives cases from
16.	Yunnan	Yunnan	Bordered Yellow, Tung Chi Mon Precinct of Peking, Censorial Circuit of Yunnan *Seals of the Department*
17.	Kueichow	Kueichow	Department of Civil Service, Censorial Department of Civil Service, Censorial Circuit of Kueichow, Plain Blue, Chao Yang Mon Precinct of Peking *Appointment and promotion of members of the Department of Law, examination of Underclerks of the Department*

These bureaus, as we see, were divided territorially with the province as a unit; fourteen of them had one province each, two of them had three each, one had one province besides the city of Peking and the Metropolitan Prefecture. Functionally, every one of them was given documents for keeping and checking the provinces. Eight of the seventeen had administrative duties within the department itself besides the documents sent in by their territories. The distribution of duties was rather inequal.

Every member of the Censorate had judicial duties of some kind. The Censor-General, besides being one of the highest judicial triumvirate, received individually cases to which a trial had been denied or unjustly concluded by the provincial authorities. But, if the complainant had failed to appeal to any of the lower courts, his case would not be tried until the decision of that Court had failed to satisfy him.[9] Nor would they try civil cases.[10] They had the right to call for all records of the case from all the courts to which that case had been tried before the annual report to the Department of Law was made by the provincial authorities.[11]

[9] Decision of the Ministers' Conference, 1657.
[10] *Ibid.*, 1661.
[11] *Ibid.*, 1658.

The Grand Court of Revision was staffed with two directors (one Manchu and one Chinese) and four assistant directors (two Manchus and two Chinese). The directors, aside from acting as supreme judges in the high tribunal, participated in the conference of the "nine ministers." It had under it two subordinate courts, The Left Court and the Right Court, with three justices and one associate justice each. Judges of these courts, with departmental or circuit censors and secretaries of the bureaus in the departments, formed a "Little Three Supreme Tribunal," the findings and decisions of which were submitted to the directors of the court. They gave the final decision concurrently with the censor-general and the ministers of the department to which that particular case belonged. Individually, the jurisdiction of the Left Court reached cases sent for review through the Department of Law or the Censorate from ten of the provinces,[12] and the Right Court those from eleven provinces,[13] while those from Chihli and the Metropolitan Prefecture were tried alternately.

The Office of Transmission acted, in a way, as prosecutor for the state, in cases tried by the "Three Supreme Tribunals." In front of this court, there was a drum which the complainant would beat to gain first a hearing of this court. If, in the opinion of the director of the office, the complaint was justified, a memorial would be sent to the emperor who issued an edict ordering a trial of the case.

The "Three Supreme Tribunals" decided all appellate cases. In criminal courts, all cases punishable by death had to be decided by these tribunals. A unanimous opinion was required for the final decision of any case; if there was a dissenting opinion, both the majority and the dissenting opinions were submitted to the emperor who gave the final verdict.

[12] Fengtien, Kirin, Heilungkiang, Kiangsu, Anhui, Chekiang, Shantung, Szechuan, Kuangtung, Kueichow.
[13] Kiangsi, Fukien, Hunan, Hupeh, Honan, Shensi, Kansu, Sinkiang, Kuangsi, and Yunnan.

Above this venerable body, the emperor himself formed theoretically at least, the highest court of appeal. He held two trials a year, "the Autumn trial," and the "Palace trial:" the former came in the first ten days of the 8th month, and the latter took place ten days before the Winter Festival. "In either of these trials, the Nine Ministers, the Supervisor of Instructions and the departmental and circuit censors shall assemble outside of Tien An Mon, present to the emperor, in a Yellow Book, cases which they have already tried: the emperor then gives his decisions which shall be made public."[14] This became more a ceremonial than a judicial function. In practice, not infrequently, the emperor, instead of trying cases personally, appointed some Grand Secretary or Councilor of State to preside over the bench, thus depriving the "Three Supreme Tribunals" of their regular duty.

One kind of case, an offense against the "Eight Criticisms," meaning any criticism against one of the eight classes of people whom the emperor has put above reproach,[15] was tried by the emperor himself. Neither the local officials nor the metropolitan authorities had jurisdiction over cases of this kind. But a trial seldom took place as the decision would be given by the emperor after the case was reported to him, the poor offender thus having practically no chance of a hearing. The sole check on the abuse of this typically absolute, monarchical law and its despotic administration was the effect on the criticized official; for an accusation of the violation of this law would lead to an investigation of the criticism which would certainly lessen the imperial favor

[14] *Ta Tsing Huei Tien*, v. 53.

[15] 1. Imperial clansmen, relatives of the Empress Dowager or Empress. 2. Old faithful officials of the government who see the emperor often. 3. Those who have rendered service to the government in battlefield, by surrendering with their followers or settling in the frontiers. 4. Great learned scholars. 5. The very able employees of the government, civil or military. 6. The diligent and dutiful employees of the government. 7. Any official, both civil and military, of, or above, the third rank. 8. Guests of the State.

for, and confidence in, the criticized one, if it did not directly cause his downfall.

The time taken for the trial of a case was limited. In the provinces, if the decision of a case involved only whipping or lashing, ten days; if exile, twenty days; if heavier than exile, thirty days after all parties had made their first appearance.[16] For the "Three Supreme Tribunals," six months was the time limit for a case of death punishment, four months for other kinds of case with the privilege of extending the limit if necessary. For the benefit of the farmers, courts were closed during the crop season, running from the first of the fourth, to the thirtieth of the seventh month, except for the trial of very important cases like treason or rebellion.

Contrary to the centralization of the executive was the decentralization of the judiciary. Absence of separation of powers probably caused the confusion of powers in the Chinese government. But in no other organization or service was the authority so disintegrated as in this: not even in the old Chinese system could one find another branch of the government work so hopelessly divided among different persons and offices. Out of a democratic society, the government created artificial legal barriers separating one group of persons from another. The imperial clansmen formed one class which was under the jurisdiction of no other court than the judicial section of the Court of Imperial Clansmen, an administrative organization; the nobles and officials formed another class whose members were not amenable to the decrees of the common courts until they were deprived of their titles or dismissed from their offices; the banner forces, Manchus in general, were tried and punished by their captains; even the long-stretching arms of the powerful viceroys could not reach them without the consent and assistance of their respective commanders; the scholars, from the day they gained a district scholarship, were exempted from the jurisdiction of the magistrate, and came under

[16] Edict of Tao Kuang, 1830, *Ta Tsing Hui Tien Shih Li*, v. 1007.

the benevolent protection of the Commissioner of Education, so that no tribunal could touch him without the consent of the commissioner which was expressed by depriving the student of his scholarship. The common or "stupid" people as they were sometimes called, were the only objects on which the laws operated normally; this, to be exact, was only under normal conditions. The disfranchised, deprived of the opportunity to become one of the privileged, nevertheless, received the same protection as the commoners, except in the case of bond-servants committing offenses against their masters.

In addition to the different operation of the same laws upon different groups of people, different codes of law were made for different peoples. What was commonly known as the "Chinese Penal Code" was really Chinese, in that it had Chinese origin, was built out of Chinese customs and traditions, was written for the Chinese, and was applied to the Chinese alone. A separate code was written for the Mongols, and one for the Tibetans. The same code, the one for the Chinese, provided a punishment for Manchus different from that applied to the Chinese for the same offense.

The nature of the facts of the case determined who should be the judge. The Department of Revenue formed a court of appeals for cases concerning taxes or property or other things distinctly civil in character. The Department of Works was asked to assign men to judge a case concerning an offense against public property. Concurrent jurisdictions occurred in some kinds of cases. If an imperial clansman was involved in a civil case, both the Court of Imperial Clansmen and the Department of Revenue would have jurisdiction. If the other party to the case was a Mongol, the Department of Territories would step in making it a three-handed game; furthermore, were the Mongol a soldier, the Department of War would also be involved in the scramble for jurisdiction. The result of this confusion of jurisdiction was that "everybody's business made it nobody's business," or every one took up the case and a dispute arose out of, and among, the judges. Fortunately, in none of the services in the Chinese government was there specialization, the professional or service line being imperceptible. The danger of favoritism was greater in the case of agnate relations of different services than in the case of colleagues of the same service. The hierarchic construction of the administration and the importance of personal influence weighed heavily in a jurisdictional dispute, with the result that when a dispute arose out of concurrent jurisdiction, it was customary for the weak to yield to the strong, the impotent to yield to the influential, the low to yield to the high, unless the law was plainly against the strong, the high or the influential. Above all, the fact that the emperor was the highest judge, eliminated all serious disputes that could come between the different parties. His unlimited power enabled him to take cases into his own hands at any time, and place it in the hands of any service or official. Hence no serious disputes ever arose in spite of the jurisdictional diffusion and confusion.

No less than the degree of diffusion and confusion was the degree of substitution. The Chinese court, first of all, was a passive agent which took no initiative in the settlement of disputes; it took up a case, even one of murder, only when it was presented to it. In very few cases did the state act as prosecutor. Indeed, upon many occasions, instead of justice provided by government was substituted arbitration by family elders, by local organizations or by guilds. The reason for this substitution was, besides social prejudice against court adjustments, the delay and expenses of seeking justice from the magistrate. An average magistrate had jurisdiction over one-quarter of a million people and about 1,160 square miles of territory.[17] It was a matter of

[17] There were altogether 41 independent first class sub-prefectures, 72 first class sub-prefectures, 81 second class independent sub-prefectures, 145 second class sub-prefectures, 1,303 districts, making 1,642 political subdivisions in the eighteen provinces and Manchuria. The area of these places was 1,535,000 English square miles for China proper and 365,000 English square miles for Manchuria.

physical impossibility for one person to attend to the disputes of all the people under his jurisdiction. The handful of body guards and constables under the command of the magistrate or sub-prefect could by no means cover all the territory in the detection of crimes. Inevitably decisions were hastily or wrongly given on account of ignorance of facts. The Patriarchal system under which arbitrary powers were invested in the male head, left little for the judicial department of the government to do. Disputes between members of different families were usually settled by heads of the families. The self-governing organizations established by, and for the protection of, a number of villages, easily arbitrated more satisfactorily to the people than the magistrates could. Members of the guilds had a similar status in the guild as members of the family had in that time-honored institution; guilds though fraternal in appearance, were not uncommonly paternally managed. Disputes of members of the guild were likely to meet more speedy and satisfactory settlement by arbitration. Disputes between members of different guilds were similar to those between members of different families, and were arbitrated by heads of the divers organizations. In some of the villages in Canton, settlement of disputes took the form of village feuds, when arbitration failed. This illustrated how unwillingly the people were to place their cases before the courts.

The pardoning power belonged exclusively to the emperor. He alone could pardon a criminal; not infrequently, however, this was done upon the recommendation of the Grand Secretaries and "Three Supreme Tribunals." The fundamental difference in the use of this power lay in the fact that, in Western countries, a pardon is given on the merits of the case, while the Chinese emperor gave it in celebration of his birthday, coronation, wedding, or because of his serious illness: in other words, he pardoned a man not because justice demanded, but because he was pleased or grieved; it was a result of favor or fear, not justice. One kind of criminal, however, could not be pardoned under any circumstances, namely, those guilty of one of the "Ten crimes." Pardon could also be purchased by certain classes of offenders on certain conditions.[18]

Comparing this judicial system with a modern Western one, it is found that the provisions for "due process of law," jury trial, advice of counsel in a trial are missing; that the judiciary is not independent from the executive; that the tenure of a judge—who, in the Chinese system, is only one in the civil service, and whose judicial duties are only part of his official work—is not secure against removal; and that, in short, the judiciary is only a part of the executive. Another factor adding to the difficulty of getting justice from the Chinese courts is that the accusation is made in a written complaint, and, in the trial, no questions except those mentioned in the complaint can be asked, thus making the writing of good accusative or defensive answers an art which yields big profits to its possessors. This might produce an impression that in the face of law, justice was of no consequence. Contrary to this impression, however, we find cases of officials exiled, dismissed, or demoted because of wrong decisions.[19] The laws themselves provided enough

[18] 1. Private soldiers, subjects for minor offense. 2. The aged, minors, the disabled, students of astronomy, women for minor offenses. 3. Wives of officials, commitment of an offense without intention, etc.

[19] An imperial edict issued in 1822 says:—Yen Si Hu, a subject in the district of Yu Tze of the province of Shansi, raped one Miss Chao No. 2. The magistrate, in the trial of that case, compelled Miss Chao to admit the act as a compromise so that the prisoner could be freed. Miss Chao afterwards committed suicide on account of the violation of her honor and the injustice done her. Chao Tien Chung appealed to the Metropolitan court on behalf of Miss Chao. Chiu Hsu Tang (Governor of Shansi) was ordered to review the case in person and make his decision strictly according to the merits of the case. The said governor affirmed the verdict of the magistrate. Censor Liang Chung Tsing impeached the governor and requested that the case be turned over to the Department of Law, and recommended thorough investigation of the charges of bribery and corruption in the case. In this case, Yen Si Hu, who indirectly committed homicide as a result of his rape, shall be imprisoned and wait for execution in the fall. Miss Chao No. 2 who sacrificed her

protection for the people under those circumstances; the difficulty lay in the difficulty of access to, and the passive character of, the courts.

Finally, it must be mentioned that the personal element entered heavily into the administration of justice. Nepotism, corruption, and purchase of decisions, certainly prevailed. These, being extra-legal, were eradicable, if, by chance, an upright and honest magistrate was sent. But the law itself provided an unequal treatment of different peoples, to wit, relatives were not allowed to testify against one another. Offenders of law with parents or grandparents of seventy years of age or above, were not punishable by exile, life exile, or death, nor were sons of a widow who had not remarried for twenty-five years or more, amenable by them unless:—

1. There was another adult male in the family.

life on account of the violation of her honor, shall be rewarded by the Department of Rites according to regulation. The dismissed magistrate of Yu Tze district, Liu Si Ling, who tried this case in the first instance, and who dared to utilize laws for his personal interest with the result of the cost of a life, shall be sentenced to hard labor in Eli. The retired prefect of Tai Yuan, Shun Tsung, who let his subordinate receive bribery, without being able to detect the corruption, and in turn, shielded the fault of his subordinate by forging a confession in order to cover up the crime of abusing an interrogation by punishment, shall be exiled to Urumtsi. The retired sub-prefect of Chi-chou, Ching Shun, and the sub-prefect of Ping-ting-chou, Chia Liang Chai, who failed to get to the bottom of the case with the purpose of flattering their superiors, shall be dismissed and exiled to the frontier military posts in Sinkiang. The retired Magistrate of the district of Tai-yuan, Chiang Chung Tsung, who has shown his inability by carelessly examining the corpse of the deceased and erroneously recording the confession, is hereby dismissed. The Commissioner of Justice, Lu Yuan Wei, who committed grievous injustice by a wrong decision of the case, is hereby dismissed. Governor Chiu Shu Tang, who failed to try the case which is specially assigned to him, let his subordinates deceive him, and made a wrong report, should be dismissed; but to show my favor, he is demoted to the rank of Commissioner of Justice . . . . . *Ta Tsing Huei Tien Shih Li*, v. 1007.

2. In case of homicide, the victim had no other adult male in his family.

3. A son could be adopted from the close relatives of the parents of the prisoner.

4. When the prisoner had committed acts against the principle of filial piety.

5. In very serious cases.

In all these cases, the pardon was made by the emperor upon the recommendation of high officials. False recommendations or failures to recommend made the respective officials answerable and punishable.

The inequality in treatment was provided as follows:—

1. In blood relations, offense of an inferior against superior of a family, punishment was one degree heavier than among equals; for offense of family superior against inferior, punishment was one degree lighter than usual.

2. Socially, offense of the franchised people against a bond-servant was punishable one degree lighter; offense of a bond-servant against a franchised, was punishable one degree heavier than usual.

3. Geographically, laws for the frontiersmen were more severe.

4. Officials could not be tried until they had been dismissed from office. No punishment could be applied in interrogation if the prisoner had been a holder of an office of the third rank or above. Bannermen and astronomical students could avoid bodily punishment by a monetary contribution.

5. Women, except in cases of sexual affairs, homicide, or robbery, did not have to appear in court if able to find a substitute. Except for the mentioned crimes, punishments could be avoided by a monetary contribution.

6. The aged and the disabled could also commute punishment by money contributions.

Thus inequality in legal protection came from all sides. Justice might be obtained; but the means to that end, law, was all at sixes and sevens, open to the abuse of the influential, an instrumentality of the clever and the wicked, and a constant source of grievances to the good, honest, and yet stupid people.

CHAPTER IX

THE FOREIGN OFFICE

Prior to the commencement of commercial relations with the West, China had no foreign relations in the sense of diplomatic negotiations between two sovereign states dealing with each other on equal footing. Hence, up to 1840, during three quarters of the life of the Manchu Dynasty, the rôle of China was to conquer, impose conditions, exact tribute, civilize, then neglect, reconquer, re-civilize and finally re-exact the same tributes again and again. History tells of the conquest, the rebellion, the imposition of tributes, etc., but once the tributes were sent, the duties of the dependencies were performed. The payments of tributes by the dependencies were exactly like the payments of taxes by the provinces, the only bond between them and Peking, the sole standard of measurement of the loyalty of the subordinate to the central government. Without a description of the reception of tributes, the kind of foreign relations China conducted for almost two hundred years during the Manchu Regime, a treatment of the Tsing diplomatic relations is not complete. This very short sketch of China's relations with outside countries in the pre-communication period, however, should not impress foreign readers as part and parcel of China's diplomatic history, although in this chapter it is dealt with.

The list of vassal states consisted of Korea, Liu Kiu Islands, Burmah, Indo-China, Siam, Sumatra, etc. All these were conquered by China either by arms or otherwise. The regulations of tribute—payments, as to the amount of tribute, the number and rank of the bearers [1] and the roads

---

[1] Strangely enough, by process of voluntary imitation, most of the vassal states had about the same system of government as the Manchu Government, or, at least, they learned enough of the Tsing system to make it believed, in the tribute payments, that the Tsing system had been adopted.

over which the bearers should travel in their Peking-ward journey were all definitely set out. Violation of these regulations sometimes led to the rejection of the tributes, a sign of disapproval by the Peking court, to be made good by additional tributes or humiliating apologies. The tributes were received by the Bureau of Outside Affairs in the Department of Rites. Negligence in the making of tribute payment implied insubordination and invited a military expedition from China to exact payment.

Another sign of the Chinese authority was the appointment of the King or prince in the vassal state. All the rulers of tribute states were either directly appointed by, or enthroned with the consent of, the Chinese emperor. In all cases a native received the appointment. Rebellion by the people against the appointed or approved prince entitled the vassal government to help and protection by China. If the rebels succeeded in dethroning the Chinese appointed ruler, and if their success did not lead to discontinuance of tribute payments, the rebels were entitled to the same protection. Indeed, many of the native rulers were appointed upon the request of the people; some were made rulers after having petitioned Peking and promised the continuation of tributes. After this appointment, and as long as the tributes were paid, the vassal states were left to do whatever they pleased.

The tributes were usually of small value. Military campaigns to enforce their payments often ran up to tens of millions of taels. Financially speaking, sovereignty over the surrounding states was a losing business for China. Both presentation of tribute and the submission to the ruler appointed by China simply represented the recognition of Chinese supremacy which served as a stimulant to tickle the vanity of the emperor during the period of isolation and as a bulwark against European and Japanese aggression in later date.

While desperate efforts and expensive campaigns would be conducted to enforce the payment of tributes, no attempt was ever made to "chinafy" any of the vassal states with an aim of making it part of China or even part of the Chinese Empire. A queer combination of desires, to dominate on the one hand and then to neglect on the other, was the policy of the Chinese Government towards all its vassal states. Such being the policy, the act of negotiating required neither consultation, nor tact, nor consent of the vassals: all China had to do was to impose a set of conditions and require the others to meet them. The words of the Chinese Emperor were laws; the resident, if any, appointed from Peking was the regent; the relation between the tribute-paying and the tribute-receiving state was similar to the one between the king and the feudal barons of the Middle Ages. The fine art of diplomacy had no occasion for relations of this sort. The situation was saved by the practice of the rule of golden mean; the conditions were never too harsh for compliance.

From this state of affairs, China was led to dealings with the West, spoiled by the easy conquest and ready submission of her little neighbors, deceived by her ignorance of her antagonists, thus making a prey of herself by the false notion of absolute, universal supremacy. Gradually, as the aggressive Europeans and Japanese advanced the scope of diplomacy on the basis of an equal footing enlarged by defeats in battlefield or in conference, China's vassal states, one by one, dropped from her domination or protection, to be replaced by independent states which imposed terms on China, whose protests were regarded as but the blowing of the wind.

But between the first and the second stages, negotiations between China and Russia, conducted on a more or less equal footing, were carried on for China, for 132 years (1727-1858), by the Department of Territories. The practice was not abolished until in 1858 by the Treaty of Tientsin.[2] For Russia, all the treaties made in this period, were signed by the Privy Council. By this arrangement, the much argued point of equality was successfully laid aside, the practical

[2] Article II, Peace Treaty between China and Russia signed at Tientsin, 1858.

results of the treaties showing this expediency to be nothing short of wisdom.

The first generally recognized regular organization for handling foreign affairs was the Tsung-Li Yamen. This office, however, had a forerunner, the Soothing Office (Fu Chu), which was scarcely known to the world.[3] This office was established by Emperor Hsien Feng in 1860 when he was "on his hunting trip" in Jehol, as a result of the siege, and after the capture of Peking and the burning of the Summer Palace (Yuan Ming Yuan) by the allied armies of England and France. Undoubtedly the purpose of its establishment was to make treaties after that unprecedented defeat.

The office was situated in the Chia Shing Temple outside of Ti-An Men. Prince Kung headed the office, with the assistance of Heng Chi and Chung Shao. After the exchange of the peace treaty, the establishment of the Tsung-Li Yamen followed; and the "Soothing Office," having completed its Mission, died a natural death after about three months of existence.

On the 11th day of the 12th month, the 10th year of Hsien Feng (1860) the Court at Peking, by the establishment of the Tsung-Li Yamen, or Foreign Office, seemed to have fully realized the impossibility of further resisting the recognition of the European Powers on equal terms in diplomatic dealings.[4] This organization was headed by a number of princes,

[3] The name "Soothing Office" implies something of contempt upon the part of the Chinese Government. In dealing with bandits, two words were used in official documents, Fu, meaning soothing, or governing by intolerance and the word Chio meaning persecution. It was certainly improper for the Chinese Government to use this word Fu in inaugurating a new office for foreign affairs.

[4] The full name of this organization is Tsung Li Kuo Kuok Tung Shang Shih Wu Yamen meaning the Office for Commercial Relations of Diverse Countries. A close study of the full name cannot but impress one with the belief that the recognition of equality was not sincere and that the opening of regular diplomatic relations was a fake; for the name of the office says that is for Tung Shang, Commercial Dealings, not foreign affairs in general. Later, the two words "Tung Shang" were dropped from the title.

councilors of state, ministers and vice-ministers of the Six Departments. No definite number of members to be appointed from each of the classes was fixed, nor was the total number of these officials, technically known as supervising ministers, the same at all times. The number varied from three to seven. All of these were "specially appointed" by the emperor from the Departments or other services and held this new appointment as a concurrent position. The office was then managed by something like a board, always with a Manchu prince at the head, dominating his colleagues within and evading the responsibility and demands from without. "The titles of the 'Supervising ministers' differed among themselves. The adjectives 'controlling,' 'directing,' 'keeper of the key,' 'assist in directing,' 'managing,' 'junior' and 'probationary junior' and whatnot, have been used to designate the 'Supervising ministers.' The word 'controlling' represents the highest rank; 'keeper of the key' was usually only an additional adjective phrase for ministers with the first or second word, 'managing,' 'junior' and 'probationary junior' represented three distinct ranks of ministers in the office in their order as stated. At the establishment of the office, three 'supervising ministers' were appointed, then two additional ones with the title of 'assistants in directing.' Later, the two additional ones were not appointed . . . . . In official documents, all these were addressed as 'Grand Ministers' because they were specially appointed and had special duties. In theory, they were always appointed by the emperor; but exceptions did occur, as in 1861, when Emperor Hsien Feng was requested to appoint an assistant supervising minister; in 1885, Emperor Kuang Hsu was requested to appoint a minister to manage the affairs of the Yamen. The post was usually a concurrent position. One exception occurred in 1861 when Prince Kung was relieved of all other duties to devote his whole attention to this office, and another happened in 1885 when Chang Yin Huan was relieved of his duties of circuit intendent to become a 'Probationary Junior Supervising Minister' of the office. The only man ever appointed Grand Minister of the

Yamen from a rank lower than that of a vice-minister was Cheng Lin who was promoted from a senior secretaryship of the service.[5] All of these resided in Peking unless the emperor was 'on a hunting trip' as in case of Emperor Kuang Hsu in Sian-fu during the Boxer Rebellion . . . . ."

Officially stated,[6] the duties of the Yamen were to conclude treaties, regulate tariff rates, regulate commercial transactions, send and receive diplomatic agents, settle boundary disputes between China and other states, and disputes between the people and the missionaries. It is certainly a lamentable fact that documents relating to foreign affairs are not printed in the *Ta Tsing Hui Tien Shih Li* like documents of other departments of the Government. But it is safe to say that, China being a weak power, most of the energy of the Yamen officials was spent in evading the demands of the European and Japanese diplomats and in shifting the duties to one another among themselves. It was not uncommon for foreign representatives to call on the Yamen again and again meeting different ministers at different times, securing the ministers' seeming approval, one by one, with no definite results; for, though organized as a board, the ministers never sat together as a board, and yet, individually, none had the power to handle the affairs by himself, far less was any one willing to accept the responsibility. Yet something had to be done, some one had to do it. The prince who headed the list of ministers was the one to act; other ministers, the "junior" and "probationary junior" especially, were practically powerless.

Next to the "supervising ministers" were the forty-eight secretaries.[7] This secretariat underwent three stages of development. In the first period, the Yamen was not yet one of the regular departments of the government; the division of the work of the Yamen was then made according to the nature of the work along the old line of division.

---

[5] *The History of the Ministry of Foreign Affairs.*

[6] See *Ta Tsing Hui Tien*, v. 99.

[7] 22 Manchus and 26 Chinese.

First, a small number of secretaries [8] were taken from the Cabinet, the Council of State, the Department of Territories, and the six regular departments. The work on tariff was handled by the secretaries from the Department of Revenue; means of communication by those from the Department of War; ceremonial documents by those from the Department of Rites; Russian affairs by those from the Department of Territories; important and delicate matters by those from the Council of State. It was then a convenient division of labor: the only work of organization was to put the different parts together. This arrangement left out the Departments of Civil Service, Works and Law; the secretaries taken from the regular departments were not necessarily competent men for this new line of work; the division prevented a unity of work; so, finally, a new organization took shape.

Time was the determining factor in the division of labor in the new organization. Affairs of different natures were then put together. The secretaries were divided into classes each of which would take a day, business of all kinds coming in upon the day of their turn. This change did give a sort of crude unity to the office, but its lack of specialization led to further organization.

The third and final step of organization of this office was a mixture of divisions by territory and by function; the first for linguistic reasons, and the second for efficiency. To the first group belonged the Bureaus of Russia (including Japan), England (including Austria-Hungary), France (including Holland, Spain, and Brazil), and the United States (including Germany, Peru, Italy, Sweden, Norway, Belgium, Denmark, and Portugal). To the second, belonged the Bureaus of General Business, Assistant General Business, Archives, Library, and Communications, and the Treasury of the Yamen.

Long after the centralization of diplomatic relations that followed the natural death of the viceregal diplomacy, two provincial authorities still enjoyed the power of more or less

---

[8] The number varied from department to department.

independent diplomatic negotiations with foreign powers, not as residues of the old regime, but with newly delegated authority: these were the Superintendent of Trade for the Southern Ports, and the Superintendent of Trade for the Northern Ports. The former, as stated in *Ta Tsing Hui Tien,* was to control the foreign affairs south of Yang Tse Kiang by either assigning them to local authorities, attending to them himself, referring them to the Tsung-Li Yamen, or reporting them to the emperor, besides auditing the accounts of the customs duties; the latter attended to all diplomatic negotiations along commercial and military lines, supervised all diplomatic dealings in the Northern Ports and reported all negotiations to the Tsung-Li Yamen. All other provincial authorities, like the viceroys, governors, and Tartar-generals had the responsibility of attending to commercial relations between China and other powers.

Out of the numerous demands made upon China by European countries and by Japan for a better mode of international communication or negotiations there was only one that gave benefit to the demanders; that is, the change of the Tsung-Li Yamen into the Department of Foreign Affairs (Wei Wu Pu). Article XII of the Peking Protocol signed on 7th of September, 1901 says: "An Imperial Edict of the 24th of July, 1901 (Annex No. 18), reformed the Office of foreign affairs (Tsungli Yamen), on the line indicated by the Powers, that is to say, transformed it into a Ministry of foreign affairs (Wai-wu Pu), which takes precedence over the other six Ministries of State . . . . . ."[9] The fact that the Edict for the establishment of the department and the appointment of officials thereof antedated the treaty, does not at all argue against the belief that this office was a result of the 1901 Protocol; for understandings had already been reached before the edict was issued, and the Chinese Government organized it beforehand only to save its own face.

[9] J. V. M. McMurray, *Treaties and Agreements with and concerning China,* v. 1, p. 284.

With the old Tsung-Li Yamen as a basis, the new organ for diplomatic relations made the following changes: The institution of supervising ministers remained; but the number of supervising ministers, formerly varying from time to time, was made definitely three. Next to these officials with high-sounding terms, a body of responsible executives consisting of one minister and two vice-ministers was provided. In between the executives and the purely civil service, was a class of quasi-executives, called councilors, whose duty it was, on the one hand, to assist the minister and vice-ministers in the execution of the policy, if any; and, on the other hand, to supervise the civil service men.

In the department itself, the organization of bureaus was changed and placed upon a functional basis. Four bureaus were established:—

1. Bureau of Peace, for ceremonial occasions, decoration of foreign representatives, appointment of diplomatic agents, civil service men in the department, and training of diplomatic officials at home.

2. Bureau of Investigation, for travelling, education abroad, study of industries and mechanics, and employment of foreign technical experts.

3. Bureau of Accounting, for customs duties, foreign trade, navigation, loans, currency, postal affairs, and expenses of the department and of the legations and consulates.

4. Bureau of General Affairs, for boundaries, defense, missionaries, travelling (of foreigners in China), police, and protection.

The old system of regional division was nominally retained; the old regional bureaus, however, had no other duty than translating documents.

The introduction of the so-called cabinet system in 1911 merely did away with the three supervising ministers, and one vice-minister; the rest of the organization and personnel remained practically unaltered. Even in the days of the

Republican regime, with all its new terms and new addresses, the substance of this organization is still intact.

Thus were the foreign affairs of the Manchu Dynasty managed.

Efforts were made to improve the service; signs of improvement in the organization were not lacking; yet the general efficiency of the service was not increased in spite of its reputation as the least corrupt of all departments. But, as a foreign department deals with foreign countries, its success or failure is measured by diplomatic victory or defeat. Its administrative efficiency could easily be outweighed by the formulation of a good or poor policy and the degree to which the execution of the policy, whether good or bad, would satisfy the people. Viewing it as a part of the government, looking at it from the executive rather than the administrative viewpoint, it is essential to interpret it from its larger field, to find out how the foreign policy was formulated, by whom, and why. Instead of the administration of the department, we shall now consider the control of foreign affairs.

For a long time, before the establishment of the Tsung-Li Yamen, diplomatic relations of China were in the hands of the provincial officials. Students of China's foreign relations often take the Opium War and the peace treaty thereafter as the beginning of Chinese foreign relations; but the viceregal management of foreign relations dated much further back. In fact, this was a residue of the ancient practice according to which the frontiers generals and civil officials directly negotiated with vassal states bordering China. Even down to the end of the Ming Dynasty, when the Manchus were claiming an equal footing with the Celestial Empire, the conduct of affairs between the Mings and the Manchus was directed by the frontier generals. In China's dealings with the West, prior to the treaty after the Opium War, viceregal management of foreign affairs was carried on for at least a hundred years. Thus, in 1762 (twenty-seventh year of Chien Lung), Russian negotiations were handled by the Chinese Imperial Residents at Urga [10] until the end of Emperor Tao Kuang. But the power of the provincial authorities in the matter of foreign relations was not definitely conferred, the viceroys and governors taking it as a matter of tradition, and the central government looking at it as extra-legal activities of its representatives in the provinces. An incident in 1857, shortly before the end of this regime, gave to it Imperial sanction. Before the Treaty of Tientsin was concluded, the envoys of England, France, Russia and the United States sent a joint communication to Grand Secretary Yu Cheng requesting the appointment of a plenipotentiary to a conference at Shanghai. The note first reached Viceroy Ho Kuei Ching of Liangkiang with a request that it be forwarded to the ultimate recipient. But Viceroy Ho reported the case to the emperor. A Court Conference met. The decisions were:—(1) Grand Secretaries should attend only to internal affairs; (2) Relations between China and England, France, or United States should be handled by the Viceroy of Liang-Kuang; (3) Relations between China and Russia should be handled by the Imperial Resident in Heilungkiang. Thus, almost at the end of the period, the legality of the practice was confirmed.

This power was exercised not alone by the chief provincial authorities. As in the case of other duties, it was often re-delegated. In 1860, a treaty was signed by the sub-prefect of Ting Hai for China, and Commander Kollington for England [11]—a very extreme case of local management of foreign affairs by a civil authority. Another incident tends to show that not only provincial civil officials, but also military officers of the provinces, had a hand in the game. In 1868, during the Mohammedan Rebellion in Yunnan, Lieutenant-General Ma Ju Lung of the provincial forces signed a treaty with a French officer for mutual help in the matter of food supply.[12] In no other government can one find so

[10] There were two Residents, one sent from Peking, another appointed from the natives, but both directly appointed by the emperor.
[11] Liu Yin, *Modern Diplomatic History of China*, p. 48.
[12] *Ibid*, p. 123.

complete a decentralization of the management of foreign affairs.

But the provincial authorities, after all, were merely cat's paws; for every step in a negotiation had to be made known to the throne. Documents of this nature came from the provinces, went through the Department of Rites to the throne, and then came out through the Council of State. While using the governors as instruments, the central government did the directing work. The appointment of Commissioner Lin with full power to deal with the situation did not give him such full power as his titles designated. Hence, when he was executing his well planned policy with a considerable measure of success, though much to the disappointment of the English, his lack of support in the Court of Peking prevented the completion of his plans, brought him a humiliating dismissal, and threatened his life. The frequent change of viceroys, and the gross ignorance of nearly all of them of foreign conditions made the formulation of an intelligent foreign policy, not to mention its execution, a day dream.

Most of the negotiations during this period, were, in fact, more or less commercial. Whenever something more than a commercial matter came up, a special envoy, designated as a viceroy, was appointed. Seldom did the provincial authority in time of peace sign an important treaty during this whole long period. The bulk of negotiations handled by provincial authorities was commercial in nature. The appointment of the Superintendent of Southern Trades and the Superintendent of the Northern Seas, after the organizations of the Tsung-Li Yamen, marked the continuation of management of foreign affairs by provincial officials. Even down to 1898, one could find an edict making the viceroys, governors and Tartar-generals in the provinces, members of the Tsung-Li Yamen, so that they might have a freer hand in dealing with commercial questions of the locality. As to the politico-diplomatic side of the question, the close supervision of the central government, the control of the central government over the viceroys and the absolute power of removal, made the representatives in the provinces nothing more than errand boys. The real reason for having them conduct foreign affairs was that the court at Peking still had the false notion that China was the Celestial Empire, and that all other nations were her vassal states, and, therefore, that the Court would not deal directly with them. The tremendous powers wielded by viceroys and governors in the Tsing Dynasty did not assume any noticeable aspect until after the supression of the Taiping Rebellion; the fact that before the suppression of that rebellion they were merely instruments, not brains, in diplomacy was explicable by the viceregal impotence in the pre-rebellion days.

The Tsung-Li Yamen succeeded the viceroys in the management of foreign affairs when the Court at Peking found out that dodging was no longer a feasible device to uphold and prolong the falsely assumed and self-satisfying notion of superiority over foreign states. In forty years of its life, three princes of blood, nineteen Manchus and thirty Chinese were appointed Supervising Ministers of the office. Twelve of them (eight Chinese and four Manchus) were appointed more than once. Three of them (two Chinese and one Manchu) were once dismissed. The numerical difference in favor of the Chinese does not necessarily mean that the latter had a majority in the office. There was no tenure of office; the date of their retirement was not recorded, except the three cases of dismissal. It can be contended that in spite of the numerical handicap, the Manchus had the control of the Tsung-Li Yamen. The available data, giving the number of ministers appointed, by no means conclusively prove that the Chinese had control of the organ by which foreign policies were initiated. An absence of tenure of office naturally would remind us of the data about the Grand Secretaries, of whom an equal number was provided for Chinese and Manchus, but because the Manchus held their office longer, more Chinese appointments were made, and it appears as though the principle of equal representation was violated in favor of the Chinese. The case of the Councilors of State can serve as another example. Always a Manchu majority was in the Council, very often it consisted of four Manchus and one Chinese, but the number of appointments for Manchus barely exceeded those for Chinese. The long tenures of the Manchus can be best illustrated by the first three appointees of the foreign office, all Manchus. One of them, Kuei Liang, died two years after his appointment; the other two, Prince Kung and Wen Hsiang, held that office continuously for fifteen years. The reason for a longer tenure of the Manchus is simple enough: the emperor had more confidence in them; there were fewer qualified men among them. Until the very end of the dynasty, when Yuan Shih Kai organized the first and last short-lived cabinet in 1911 in which the portfolio of foreign affairs was given to Liang Tun Yen, no Chinese ever headed the foreign office. Always a prince of blood was at the helm; and for fifty years, only three princes, Princes Kung, Ching and Tsai Chi, were appointed.

Chronologically, from 1861 to 1876, all supervising ministers were Manchus, from 1876 to 1877, three Manchus and one Chinese; in 1884, three out of five appointed at the same time were Manchus; in 1899, when the troubles of the boxers were brewing, four Manchus were appointed to the foreign office. In the first twenty years, six Manchus and six Chinese, in the last twenty years, sixteen Manchus and twenty-four Chinese, were appointed. The proportion of Chinese members gradually increased except during the period immediately before the Boxer Uprising. The change of personnel, from Manchus to Chinese, was due to the following causes: (1) The repeated military failures of China made the work of a diplomat difficult. A diplomatic failure usually led to punishment of the negotiators, and wise mandarins avoided posts which gave contact with foreign relations. (2) Appointment of more Chinese would not weaken the control of diplomacy by the Manchus, for there was always at the head of the office a Manchu prince; other members served as a bulwark between him and the urging foreign representatives. But, strangely enough, about the time very important negotiations were carried on, Chinese were generally appointed. Thus, in 1885, during the negotiations with France on the Annam question, seven out of ten new appointees were Chinese; during negotiations with England regarding Burmah, a Chinese was appointed; in 1895 and three years following, only two out of eleven appointees were Manchus. Thus, in every emergency, Chinese were called in; when the storm was over, Manchus were reinstated.

Judging from the personnel and the policies during different periods of the dynasty, it is not too much to say that the Manchus had a reactionary, and the Chinese a liberal, policy in internal as well as foreign affairs. Students of the early diplomatic relation of China used to express their favorable opinion of some Manchu diplomats like Wen Hsiang and Prince Kung. They may have deserved this. But the military defeats that China sustained admitted of nothing else than a conciliatory attitude and a liberal policy. Again, Prince Kung and Wen Hsiang could stand against all pressure of the reactionaries for the period of fifteen years simply because the internal troubles created by the Taiping rebels were then too severe for the Court, so every bit of energy was devoted to its suppression, and the foreign policy for that period was more neglected than liberal. So, when the reactionaries got the upper hand, later in 1900, even Prince Kung, a veteran in diplomacy, a prince of blood and a confidential servant of the old Buddha, could not but yield to the conservatives.

Finally, with all the pomp, prestige and dignity in the Tsung-Li Yamen, the office was under the control of the Council of State; for "whenever cables or telegrams arrive, they shall be speedily translated and sent to the Council of State which, in turn, shall send them to the emperor." [13] This suffices to show that the control of foreign affairs was in the hands of the Councilors of State. Always the majority, if not all of the supervising ministers of the Tsung-Li Yamen, were Grand Councilors; and, sure enough, the

[13] *Ta Tsing Hui Tien*, v. 99.

influential ones had a dominating voice and a directing hand in both formulating and executing foreign policies, even if they were not connected with the office in name. Thus the men behind the Tsung-Li Yamen were the Councilors. Also, on account of several refusals of foreign diplomats to negotiate with Chinese officials who were not ministers of departments, Grand Secretaries, or Councilors, the Government made it a policy to appoint to the foreign office men from the Grand Secretariat, or Council of States: not more than half a dozen of the fifty-two supervising ministers appointed to the Yamen held offices lower than a minister at the time of appointment. Finally, the prevalence of concurrent positions made this practice quite a convenient affair.

Looking through the list of treaties and their signers, one cannot help being convinced that the Manchus held tenaciously to the management of foreign affairs. Up to 1861 all treaties were signed by Manchus, both those signed with England and France in the South and those with Russia in the North. The first treaty bearing the signature of a Chinese was the treaty with France to revise the tariff rates concluded shortly after the signing of the Treaty of Tientsin in 1861. Yet in this a traditional policy of keeping a Manchu majority was upheld.[14] Li Hung Chang indeed signed a number of treaties for China, particularly in relations with France, Russia and Japan in the last part of the 19th century. He succeeded in so doing because he was persona grata on account of advanced age. Li's prestige in the court came from his being a henchman of the head eunuch, Li Lien Ying, and hence on good terms with the Empress Dowager.

In all the diplomatic negotiations in which the Chinese participated, a watchful Manchu eye was always on them; for instance, in the beginning of the Opium War, when Lin was made the plenipotentiary, Ilipu was sent to Chekiang nominally to review the troops but practically to spy on him. Incidentally, it may be mentioned, Ilipu himself was one of the negotiators of the treaty after the war.

[14] Three Manchus and two Chinese signed that treaty.

THE FOREIGN OFFICE 251

Coming back to the problem of personnel viewed from a racial standpoint, the gradual increase of Chinese in the participation of foreign affairs might be explained by another reason besides those already mentioned, namely, the misfortunes of the diplomats. At first the Government looked upon diplomacy as a sort of dealing with vassal states; it judged the success or failure of a diplomatic mission from the gain or loss in the negotiation, in other words, results regardless of the circumstances. The great majority of officials who handled the futile negotiations after military defeats were punished; even the ministers who received the English envoys in 1816 were dismissed on account of the refusal of the latter to kotow in the audience, although this, of course, was no fault of the receiving ministers. This kind of misfortune is well illustrated by an edict of Tao Kuang issued in 1841 to dismiss Chi Shan after he failed to drive the English out.

The edict of Emperor Tao Kuang issued in 1841 says:—

Since the arrival of Chi Shan at Canton, he has been repeatedly instructed and warned with emphasis; but this produced no results. Styling himself Special Commissioner for Barbarian Affairs, he completely ignored A-Tsing-A and Yi-Liang (his associates appointed by the emperor) in all preparations for defense and military operation, while he himself neglected all necessary preparations on these lines.

Depending on the rumor of the return of Ting Hai, he instantly forwarded to Ilipu the letter of Elliot and Elliot's orders (left for the English commander in Chekiang) by relay communications so that Ilipu, on accepting his advice, became an on-looker of the scene thus causing all kinds of delay in preparation.

The importance of Hongkong was stated in former memorials of Chi Shan himself; but now, he memorializes us on its cession and the opening of Canton for trade and residence. This shows that Chi Shan is inconsistent and unreasonable. Moreover, the said governor ordered the formal cession of Hongkong without our previous approval. Within the bounds of the Empire, every foot of the territory and every one of the subjects belongs to the state. Chi Shan ceded Hongkong and granted (the English) the right to trade without our authorization, dares now to beg us of extra-legal leniency in his punishments.

Moreover, as the result of a threat, he memorializes us on the untenability of Canton against foreign attacks, falsely saying that there are no strategic points for defense, neither effective weapons, nor strong army, nor public sentiment to rely on.

We do not know what kind of heart he has to utter such nonsense. He has disregarded our favors, lost his conscience, and betrayed the Empire. He is hereby dismissed from all offices. Lieutenant-General Ying Lung and a sub-prefect to be appointed by Yi-Liang are to send him to Peking in irons for strict cross-examinations. His property shall be confiscated.[15]

Although, later on, Chi Shan, Lin Tse Shu, Ilipu and others were restored to their former posts and dignity, none of them escaped the punishments immediately after, or during, the negotiations. Lack of knowledge of the foreigners and their countries, made success impossible; inadequate military preparation made defeat a certainty; diplomatic success could scarcely follow military defeat; punishment was the sure reward of a diplomatic failure; thus the position of a diplomat became something to be avoided, Manchus kept away from the appointments, and the Chinese had to come in.

Of popular control in China's diplomacy there was none, except once in a while, an over-enthusiastic scholar might send in a memorial to the emperor or express his opinion to high authorities. However, being aware of the evil consequences and fully knowing its futility, even this humble and fruitless act was seldom practiced. Late in the dynasty, some popular demonstration like the Japanese boycott in the Matsu Maru case appeared. Yet, in spite of this, the government held diplomatic dealings as secret as its inefficiently administered political machinery could; and the people were still regarded as "stupid" notwithstanding their newly acquired ability to express their will by action. The rôle of the envoys was just as negligible. No envoy was ever sent out by China up to the third quarter of the 19th century. When they were sent out in the last quarter, it was merely a matter of formality. The low rank of the ministers (usually 2a) served as a check upon their influence. Their

[15] *Tung Hua Lu, Tao Kuang*, v. 43, p. 5.

ignorance of foreign countries formed another obstacle to their success. Most of the relations between China and European countries and Japan consisted of a scramble for rights and concessions; China was the diplomatic arena; a Chinese representative in foreign countries amounted to very little more than a watcher of the game, if indeed, he took the trouble to watch. Were anything to come up, the minister had merely the power to petition the emperor. A study of the memorials of the diplomatic agents would convince one that a minister was only an errand boy. Luckily enough, all Chinese ministers abroad, during the Tsing Dynasty, were ministers resident, and therefore the term "plenipotentiary" did not have to be abused. For special missions, the word full-power was sometimes attached, for instance, to the instructions to Lin Tse Shu in the Opium War, of Li Hung Chang in the treaty of Shiminoseki, of Prince Ching and Li Hung Chang in the Peking Protocol. Yet the emperor was supposed to possess all powers. He could deprive the diplomatic agent of delegated power or recall him at his own sweet will. Lin was dismissed before he completed his mission. Li, instructed by the example of Lin, cabled to Peking for advice upon everything. Even Prince Ching and Li Hung Chang during the negotiations for the Peking Protocol when the Empress Dowager and the emperor were on their "hunting trip" in Si-An-Fu, could do nothing without first obtaining the consent of the throne, as the volumes of memorials and petitions sent in by the plenipotentiaries show. Thus, the term "plenipotentiary" was a decoration for a Chinese diplomat, not a word to denote his share in the game. The nearest approach to a plenipotentiary was the case of Prince Kung, as head of the mission to make treaties with England and France in 1860. Part of the edict conferring full power upon him reads as follows:—[16]

..... Although treaties have been exchanged between us and England and France, their forces withdrawn, yet Prince Kung and

[16] *Tung Hua Lu, Hsien Feng*, v. 96, p. 46.

others shall proceed to make definite arrangements with them so that no further dispute shall ever arise hereafter. Heng Chi and Chung Huo (both Manchus) shall be attachés to Prince Kung and assist him in pacifying the barbarians. Unimportant affairs like commercial treaties they shall handle. But any important arrangement must be approved by Prince Kung first. He shall be responsible to memorialize us. Heng Chi and others shall have no right to do so . . . . .

In this juncture, it may be mentioned that Prince Kung was the first one who was not punished on account of diplomatic dealings. This was largely because of his family connections with the emperor.

Like the European sovereigns of old, the Chinese emperor controlled the foreign affairs of the country. Emperor Kang Hsi claimed to have drawn up the Treaty of Nirchinsk; Emperor Chien Lung's message to the King of England shows clearly his absolute control in diplomacy. Commissioner Lin reported everything to the throne, although he was nominally given full power. The Treaty of Nanking received the mark of the vermilion pen before a final conclusion could be said to have been reached. All treaties after being duly signed had to be submitted to the emperor who made them laws of the land by promulgating them in formal edicts. The reactionary Empress Dowager directed the negotiations in Si-An-Fu during the conferences preceding the Peking Protocol. Thus the control of the emperor in foreign affairs was as complete as his domestic control. And, as in domestic affairs, the large volume of business made it a matter of physical impossibility to play a lone hand. In this sphere of activity the Emperor-in-Council-of-State, with the head supervising minister of the Foreign Office had effective control. The head supervising minister was always a Manchu prince; the Council of State usually had a Manchu majority; hence, racially speaking, foreign relations of China were always in the hands of the Manchus. Their gross ignorance of foreign conditions is undisputed. Whatever policy there was, was thrust upon them and poorly executed.

CHAPTER X

OTHER SERVICES IN THE CENTRAL GOVERNMENT

The foregoing chapters have left two of the six regular departments untouched; namely, the Departments of War and Works, which will be dealt with here, and the Department of Territories, which will be dealt with in Chapter XII. The Manchu Dynasty gained the throne by military conquest. Despite popular prejudice against the enterprise of war and the occupation of a warrior, and despite the weakness of its army, the Manchu Government had a separate department of war. From the *Ta Tsing Hui Tien,* we find the duties of this department stated in these terms:—"In order to assist His Majesty to defend his peoples, this department shall execute military policies, control army officers, attend to appointments, dismissals, rank and titles of military officers, relay communications, training of troops and the census of the Imperial Army."[1] Besides, it had other duties, such as to present military officers to the court, to conduct examinations for military service on approximately the same competitive basis as the Department of Rites in the civil service, and to conduct all military ceremonies. Also it controlled the old navy. Being purely administrative in character, the formulation of military policies was not even mentioned. Whenever uprisings occurred, the Council of State directed the campaign, raised the funds and assumed the responsibility of a general staff. It is clear then this department was strictly administrative in nature. In its administrative work, quite contrary to the general practice of the government as to mixing state business with the emperor's private affairs, this department had in its jurisdiction, purely affairs of the state. The different units of the Imperial Bodyguard, either on account of the jealousy

[1] *Ta Tsing Hui Tien,* v. 43.

of the emperor to keep them under his own control or for the sake of elevating the position of those who were near him, did not come under the jurisdiction of this department. These units, which were in the personal service of the emperor, had 8,646 officers of different ranks,[2] amounting to more than one-third of the army of both Banner soldiers and "Green Battalions," and had nothing whatsoever, as to financing, administration or control, to do with the department.

Four bureaus performed the divers functions of the department: the Bureau of Military Selection (Wu Shuan Sse) for appointments, dismissals, ranks, titles, and organization of army corps; the Bureau of Statistics (Chih Fang Sse) for rewards, punishments, investigation of men already in service, defense, policing, issuance of passports to service men going outside of the country, and enforcement of prohibitive regulations; the Bureau of Communications (Chu Chia Sse) for the raising and supply of horses[3] and relay communications; and the Commissariat Bureau for keeping records of the service men, recruitment of officers from competitive examinations, and the supply of uniforms and ammunitions. The division of the functions here, as elsewhere, is by no means scientific. The enormous size of the bureaus made the administration of a department which had under its control three-quarter million of soldiers and spent seventy-three per cent of the government expenditures, difficult as well as unsatisfactory.

Before further discussion of its organization, one kind of function, strictly administrative, deserves our attention. This department did for the military officers what the Department of Civil Service did for the civil servants. For, to the appointment of military officers, laws of the Department of Civil Service could not apply. So, within the department, a special set of regulations existed. Take appointment for

[2] Figures from *Ta Tsing Hui Tien.*

[3] Training and breeding were performed by the Imperial Stud, which will be dealt with separately in this chapter.

OTHER SERVICES IN CENTRAL GOVERNMENT 257

instance. Lieutenant-generals or higher, in both Manchu and Chinese forces, were specially appointed by the emperor. A second class, one corresponding to brigadiers, was nominated by the department and appointed by the emperor. A third class, equivalent to the field officers, could not be nominated without a record; these appointments were usually made as a promotion, upon recommendation of superior officers and technically for merit. Unlike the civil service system where promotion consisted of one-half rank, a promotion here was one full rank. The posts were divided, like the civil service system, into classes on the basis of bannermen and Green Battalions, say the first position for expectants of the banner forces and the second for the Green Battalion forces, etc. The final appointment, here, as in the foregoing two classes, was made by the emperor. The lowest kind of officers, corresponding to the company officers, were always promoted from the rank and file of the privates. The department made all appointments of the company officers.

A division of posts, based on the nature of the work, imbued with some racial tinge, separated one kind from another. First, there were the "Bannermen's posts," to be occupied only by Manchurian, Mongolian and Chinese bannermen. Secondly, the "Battalion posts," posts in both provincial land and sea forces, which were occupied mostly by Chinese though a few Manchus did invade the field. Thirdly, the "Guard posts," for the safeguarding of canals and rivers, which were occupied entirely by Chinese. Finally, the "Gate posts," for safeguarding the city gates were entirely occupied by Chinese bannermen. As in the civil service system, here again, division could not guarantee intrusion; a qualifying clause sanctioning the occupation of Chinese posts by Manchus, Mongols and Chinese bannermen almost nullified the classification.

Viewing from another angle, the appointments were classified into another four classes. "Concurrent appointment" filled all the high positions in the Imperial Bodyguards and many in the provincial forces: the only office not admitting any concurrent position was the Tartar Generalship. The "extra appointments" gave the field and company officers of the guards and some Manchu forces positions without work. The Green Battalions were not affected by this kind of appointments. The bulk of the officers were chosen by what was called "Regular appointments." The "Trial Appointments" were initial appointments for hereditary title holders or officers newly qualified from competitive examinations.

Here, as in the Department of Civil Service, a "monthly selection" existed. All appointments below a colonelcy (3a) came under this process of selection. Expectants for ranks lower than captaincy were further divided into classes. In all these selections, the seniority rule was strictly held in theory; but the system was just as much, if not more, poisoned by nepotism and commercialism as the civil service system.

Two kinds of command, the direct command and the indirect control, existed in the provincial forces. Take the Province of Kuangtung for example. All the forces of the province were "indirectly controlled" by the viceroy. The viceroy himself had direct command over a few thousand troops in the city of Canton; the governor of the province had another few thousand; the general commander of the province had also a few thousand. So, in the city of Canton, there were three men each commanding a few thousand troops, to a certain extent practically independent of the other, though nominally both the general commander and the governor were under the command of the viceroy, and the governor could command the general commander. Again, the general commander of the province was theoretically the supreme military officer of the province. But the military commissioners of different circuits did not have to take his orders, because he merely "indirectly controlled" them. As none of their superior officers had any direct command over them, as each of them had a few thousand troops at their own command, this served the central government as a perfect check against any ambitious desires of the provincial authorities, but it also hindered the efficiency of provincial authorities. Uniformity of training, supply, and so forth became impossible under the circumstances. Resistance to foreign invasion, even against local rebellion, was made very ineffective through the division of the forces into small posts. This accounts for the mournful truth that history tells, nay, repeats, why disastrous defeats of the army of the border provinces by rebellious barbarian vassal states were suppressed only by expensive expeditions from the central government headed by plenipotentiary generals: it is the full reason why local bandit organizations could increase to the dimensions of anti-dynastic rebellions, testing the validity of the "mandate of heaven" which the emperor so cherished; and quite a few of them in the Chinese history succeeded rather because of the weakness of the government than because of their own strength. The present chaos arising out of the insubordination of local and provincial military commander is, to a limited degree at least, the result of the division of command with which the Manchu emperors checked their "servants" and "slaves." [4] But, in the monarchical period, the division of forces did not break up the Empire; for the Department of War always had perfect control over all provincial troops, and, if its authority failed, the emperor was back of it, so that only in times when the dynasty was falling down, was the control of the central government over provincial forces ineffective.

Besides, two other institutions helped to make easy the control of the central government. First, military officers, higher ones especially, had audiences with the emperor at the beginning and end of their terms of office, thus affording the emperor a splendid opportunity to find out about their fellow officers on the one hand and producing on the officer

[4] The Chinese officials used the term "Your Majesty's servant" for first person when addressing the emperor; the Manchus used the word "slave" instead of "servant" upon the same occasion.

himself the same effect of loyalty to the emperor as a pilgrimage would produce on a pilgrim in religious fidelity on the other. In the provinces, each of the high officials had the right to address the emperor directly, disclosing to his own advantage and for his own advancement and reward whatever ambitious scheme others had and whatever illegitimate desires others harbored. Military officers were recruited from holders of hereditary titles, holders of hereditary ranks, transferees from the civil service, those promoted from the rank and file and successful candidates in the military examinations. Scholar and gentleman in China occupied the same social position as officer and gentleman in Europe. But governments in general and the Manchu government in particular, acted very much against popular desire in this respect: in the award of hereditary titles, the military men shared much better. It was the tradition of the dynasty not to give any title higher than viscount to the civil servants of the state. Then, too, holders of hereditary titles were usually encouraged to enter the military instead of the civil service. The encouragement of the government, the easy requirements for entrance into the service, and the ease with which one could handle a military office combined to swell the number of titular nobles in the expectant list. On account of this about one out of ten appointments was specially reserved for recruits of this kind.

The system of hereditary ranks given to sons of high military officers was exactly the same as the civil; that is, four ranks below the benefactor.[5] But a military rank was not worth as much as a civil; for, in the civil service system, promotion consisted of only one-half rank, while in the military, one full rank was the practice. A civil servant of third rank was privileged to address the emperor directly, but, no military officer below the second rank could do so. Finally, a viceroy or governor of a province, both officials

[5] If the father had first rank, his son, the beneficiary, would have the fifth; if the father had the second, he would have the sixth, and so on.

of second rank, had command over the general commander of the province whose rank was that of the first.

Military officers could gain ranks by transferring from the military to the civil service if they had enough brains for it. The third kind of recruits, transferees from civil service, virtually lost some ranking by the transference. But it was a rare case for one to give up a civil service career for the army except during troublous times. In those cases imperial favors would overrule regulations, a promotion was always the result, and no loss was thus sustained by the transferees.

Aside from bad laws, corrupt administration, ineffective control, inadequate training and what not, the Chinese army was very much undermined by officers promoted from the rank and file. Social prejudice against war extended its prejudice to those who made war their vocation. The flower of the nation, in spite of the glory of victory, the opportunity of service and promotion, were never attracted to the army. "Good boys don't become soldiers." The rank and file were composed of rogues, knaves, desperados, surrendered bandits, and, once in a long while, a few adventurers. When promoted to be officers, it is needless to say that disastrous results were realized. The inefficiency of the Chinese army shown in the different foreign wars during the last fifty years and the unsuccessful attempts to suppress rebellions from the beginning of the 18th century to the end of the Taiping Rebellion can be largely attributed to the ignorance and cowardice of officers, many of whom were promoted from the ranks.

A system of competitive examinations for military service completed the process and means of recruitment of officers. Though run on the same basis as the civil, both the government and the public attached much less importance to them than to the former. Competition was much less keen, because, starting from entrance examinations into the district college, the number of candidates was very small, so small that the government found it necessary not to fix a number of qualified studentships for fear that every applicant would be qualified. The proportion of qualified students and applicants fixed was one to five or six, whereas in the civil examinations, some times one out of a hundred was qualified. Once every three years, after the Educational Commissioner had finished his duties in the civil service examination tours in the districts, he came to give the military examinations. A brigadier-general or colonel would be appointed by the provincial authorities to assist him. The number of military students, both on account of the small number of entrants in the examination and the small number of scholarship provided as a result of its unpopularity, amounted to about one-third of the number of literary students in the districts. In the provincial examinations, the government did not even take the trouble to appoint Examiners; the governor of the province (in case there was no governor, the viceroy) acted as Chief Examiner with the general commander of the province and another high military officer as his assistants. The number of graduates provided in the provincial examinations was 1,034, a little more than one-half of the literary graduates. In the Metropolitan examinations and the Palace examinations, the number of degrees conferred approximately equaled one-half of the civil. All the military examinations were of two sessions, one indoors and one outdoors. Unlike the civil examinations which produced most of the able and faithful servants for the state, the military examinations by no means brought the most brave and capable generals to the front. Recruitment of officers by this method, though better than recruitment from hereditary ranks and titles, or promotion from the rank and file, did not give the satisfactory results expected. Most of the famous generals were transferred from civil service only at the time of war. After all, popular disapproval of war contributed largely to the debasement of the army.

In addition to examinations for recruitment, examination of those already in service took place once every five years, and was conducted on the same basis as for those in the

OTHER SERVICES IN CENTRAL GOVERNMENT 263

Department of Civil Service, only much more as a matter of formality. A system of rewards and punishments, principally after the model of the civil service system, provided the examiner with authority.

In keeping up means of communications, principally for military purposes, the government placed the management and control of the relays in the hands of the Department of War. As it has been pointed out in the beginning of the chapter, the Bureau of Communications had charge of this activity. But the importance of this service requires at least a brief description. As the government owned and operated these means, and as they were not operated on a revenue producing basis, its use was limited to state business and private affairs of high officials.

As far as administration was concerned, the establishment and maintenance of the relay stations occupied most of the attention and took most of the money of the bureau. Five kinds of stations were kept in different parts of the country:—

1. The Interior Stations (Yih) were situated in the provinces of China Proper under the immediate care of the prefects and magistrates and supervised by the Judicial Commissioners of the provinces; also some in Fengtien under the direct control of men specially appointed by the department.

2. The Military stations (Tsan) were purely for military use, managed by lieutenants and sergeants of the Imperial army specially appointed by the department, and supplied with food and other necessities by magistrates. Stations in Kirin and Heilungkiang were also designated by this name. Some of them were under the care of clerks specially appointed by the Tartar-generals of the places. Stations connecting China and Mongolia, cared for by clerks appointed by the Department of Territories, also came under this class. Nearly all stations outside of China Proper were supplied by the Viceroy of Chihli and the Governor of Shansi, but

were managed by clerks appointed by and from the Department of Territories.

3. The quasi-military Stations (Tang) were situated in parts of Kansu, Sinkiang, for military purposes chiefly, under military officers but supplied by civil officials.

4. The Frontier Stations (Tai) in the far Northwest of the country were managed by secretaries of the Department of Territories, supervised by native nobles and under the jurisdiction of the Imperial Residents of Urga. These also were principally for military purpose.

5. The Civil Stations (Pu) were situated in the interior for communications between the different political subdivisions and between them and Peking. The Department of Revenue financed them.

The stations in Altai were managed by officials, who had been exiled, usually for public offenses. On each of the exiled officials, a fine of between thirty-three and forty taels of silver per month was imposed for the upkeep of the stations, during their full term of exile, nominally three years, but frequently recalled to service much earlier. Failure to pay the fine would doom those exiled to life-long hard labor on the frontiers. To require offenders to pay fines for the maintenance of stations was indeed a peculiar arrangement considering that the fine did not come from the labor of the offenders but from their pocket. It is more peculiar when we recollect the low salaries of the officials. Comparing the figures, it required two months' salary of an official of the first rank to pay the minimum fine of an exile. Had the unfortunate punished official not accumulated a little nest egg, his life would be doomed to frontier exile. But were it not for illegitimate incomes where could he get the money to pay the fine? So, even in the execution of justice, an impetus to graft was present.

To even the privileged, only a limited use of the relay teams was allowed. The government regulated this by distributing a number of credentials to each of the high civil and military authorities (those who had the privilege to address the emperor directly) for each year. Two kinds of credentials were used; one when an officer rode and another when a private took the journey. A credential entitled the rider to the supply of food, horses, and bodyguards, if necessary, on land; and boats and sailors on sea. A limited date for the receipt of the document was set.[6] The importance of the document was measured by the speed of the relays in terms of Chinese *li* per day; for instance, 600 *li* was the most important, then 500, then 400, and 300 being the slowest. Delay was a very grave offense. Only a few officials on a few very important occasions, had the permission to use the top speed, the 600-*li*-day.

Under the control of the Department of War were some localities inhabited by aborigines in the provinces of Kansu, Szechuan, Kuangsi, Yunnan, Kueichow, and in Si-Ning and Tibet. Organized in military style, military officers governed these places. In between the Department of War and the local authorities of these places the viceroy or governor in the first five places and the imperial residents in the last two loosely supervised them and were held responsible to the department. Two hundred and eighty-four military officers, mostly aborigines themselves, received appointments from the department for the government of their compatriots. Here, even in the militarily organized regions, the Manchu Government did not forget their excellent principle of "Let them govern themselves," the principle which kept the Chinese under Manchu rule for two hundred and sixty-five years.

Duplicating the service of the Bureau of Communications, the Imperial Stud (Tai Pu Sse), a separate organization with officials directly appointed by, and responsible to, the emperor, attended to the breeding and raising of horses. The Stud performed two kinds of functions—office and field.

[6] From Peking, to Chihli Viceroy's office, 4 days; to Shantung Governor's, 9 days; to Nanking Viceroy's, 23 days; and to Canton Viceroy's 56 days, etc.

Two directors, two assistant directors and a number of minor officials staffed the Stud. Aside from one director and one assistant director, the whole staff consisted of Manchus. The stipulations concerning this office did not conflict with the duties of the Bureau of Communications in the Department of War; for the latter functioned in training and supply while the former in breeding and raising. The Department of War had a rather loose control over it. However clearly the duties of these two organizations might have been divided, the existence of this Stud was an appendix to the political structure. There could not be sufficient reason for separating breeding and raising from training to make the existence of such an organization necessary. But it shows one of the policies of the government, namely, to have as many organizations as possible so that all ambitious and supposedly able persons could have employment. As a result of this policy, they found the almost non-functioning government not having enough things for the divers offices: hence the device of placing one and the same duty in several services at the same time came in handily as a supporter of the policy. So, when Emperor Kuang Hsu came to the administrative reform of the government in 1898, he abolished all the organizations which duplicated functions of others; and the Imperial Stud was one of those abolished. It was re-established by the reactionary Empress Dowager Tzu Hsi after the triumph of the Manchu Party, only to be abolished once more and for all in 1906.

The Department of Works (Kung Pu)

Viewed from the standpoint of rank and honors, the Department of Works was the lowest of the old administrative sextet. Not infrequently was a transference from one position of the department to another of the same rank considered a promotion. But a review of its duties and organizations justified its independent existence though many of its duties were unscientifically assigned. With the supreme duty of helping the emperor to comfort the myriads, this branch of the government presented officials of its own to the court, constructed and repaired all public buildings, controlled transportation, supplied materials for construction, furnished arms and ammunitions to the army, and ships to the navy, purchased and sold for the government, regulated prices in the government sales, determined weights and measurements, managed property, rented houses and collected rents for the government, regulated ships and seafaring, cared for the streets and ditches of the capital, regulated styles of residence of titular nobles and officials, and coined money.

Along the line of constructions and repairs, the department conducted, once every year, an investigation of the imperial tombs, city walls, palaces, temples, offices, government warehouses, barracks, residences of nobles and officials, rivers and canals, and all public real property in the country. Greatest of all the repair work was the repair to river and canal dams and dikes. Every year the Yellow River flooded some part of the country, though millions were spent on the reconstruction of dikes. The expenses were supposed to be collected from the unfortunate people whose homes the flood visited and destroyed. Yet the immediate demand of repair together with the difficulty of collecting big sums of money for the purpose compelled the government to invent some means that could meet the emergency. One of the three following quick methods was usually applied:—

1. The government defrayed all expenses; when the repairs were all over, the people settled down again, collection of the expenses would be made and the government treasury refunded.

2. The government defrayed part of the expenses out of the treasury and the rest out of the provincial officials' allowance. Collections would then be made and both be refunded.

3. The officials defrayed all the expenses and would collect them from the people after the completion of the work.

In all three cases the people were the final payers; whether defrayment was made by the government or the officials or both, the debt had to be paid. But the practical difference lay in the fact that when the government advanced all the expenses, either as a means of courting the people's favor or as showing the government's kindness, most of the debts would be renounced unless the government was in a state of financial stringency. Were a financial partnership formed between the government and the officials, the government would control the policy and method of collection; the strong desire of the officials might be overruled by the generosity of the government. When the officials were the sole creditors, harsh measures for quick collection could reasonably be expected unless the chief official were a lover of the people, an exception to his class.

A few of the numerous points of the government's policy regarding construction and repair, both in the raising of funds and the employment of labor, deserve our attention. For the repairment of city walls, Emperor Kang Hsi awarded quite a number of merits and promotions to military officers for money contributed by them to this cause. In 1684, an edict [7] was issued to call for monetary contributions from the military officers who could secure one official merit for repairing 2,000 Chinese feet [8] of city wall at one's own expense, or the promotion of one grade (one-third of a rank) for 8,000 feet, with proportional increase of reward for proportional increases of length. In the next year, an officer contributing 600 taels of silver for repairment of city walls, was decreed to be entitled to the grant of one "transferable" grade, and for 300 taels a "non-transferable" one. This simple barter continued until 1716 when the originator abolished the project. Private soldiers often were assigned to repair city walls or deepen ditches. Employment of the unfortunate sufferers of a flood or famine to repair city walls was a regular policy of the government which

[7] *Ta Tsing Hui Tien Shih Li*, v. 867.
[8] One Chinese foot equals about 14 inches.

did not want to keep the people idle, nor to give them the aid gratuitously.

In all constructions the particular official from the department, not the department itself, nor all the officials in the department collectively, was responsible for the guarantee. Damages within the guaranteed period had to be made good by the official in charge, sometimes with the help of his superiors or inferiors; and if the death of the official in charge occurred, the law of mutual responsibility applied to members of his family, they being obliged to perform the service.

The organization of this department did not differ from the other five. Each of its four bureaus performed approximately the same amount of duties:—

1. The Bureau of Construction (Ying Shan Ssu) attended to building of city walls, palaces, temples, offices, warehouses, barracks, and residences; supervision of construction; keeping and auditing of accounts; sale of confiscated real property; purchase of materials for constructions; direction of transportation of materials; preparation of machines and tools for building.

2. The Bureau of Weights and Measures (Yu Heng Ssu) determined the standard of weights and measurements; supplied all needs of the officials in an official capacity; furnished arms and ammunitions to the army; and classified pearls which were tributes from Manchuria.

3. The Bureau of Rivers and Canals (Tu Shui Ssu) had charge of all inland water communications between Peking and other parts of China. The rivers and canals, for repairing purposes, were under four viceroyalties, one of the North Rivers, one of the Eastern Rivers, one of the South Rivers, and one of the Grand Canal. Although independent offices at the beginning of the dynasty, they, except the Viceroyalty of Canals, came later to be concurrently held, the first by the Viceroy of Chihli, the second by the Governor of Shantung, and the third by the Viceroy of the Canals, who was

the lowest in rank of all viceroys. Under them were intendents specially appointed to watch over floods and keep the river banks and dikes in good condition. Again, like the sub-divisions of the administrative areas, the intendents had under them a host of military officers and local officials who did the real watching. The viceroys had the right to secure money from the government to carry out the repair work. Requests of this kind scarcely ever met rejection, in fact, river and canal repairs formed a fixed charge in the budget, although the sum could not be fixed as no one could know what damages the rivers would do in a particular year. Construction and supply of naval ships, life boats, ferries and bridges also came under this bureau. Receipts from a few of the customs, gates, and the taxation of the ships went into the treasury of this branch of the department. Cleaning of streets, deepening and watering of ditches, storage and distribution of ice to offices, manufacturing of sacrificial and ceremonial articles such as ancestral tablets, etc., and storage of silk and other wearing apparels completed the list of its duties.

4. The Bureau of Imperial Tombs, Fuels, and Appointments (Tuan Tien Ssu) had charge of repairing of the Imperial Tombs; supply of fuels to all offices; liveries to the emperor, titular nobles, and officials; supervision of all laborers working under the auspices of the department; and appointment of Chinese officials in the department.

Several services performing very important duties, such as the "Precious Source" Mint which nearly matched the mint of the Department of Revenue; the government arsenal that supplied the Imperial army and navy with ammunitions; the Imperial Carpenter Factory, and the Peking Municipal Bureau were attached to this department.

While all the other five departments, true to their title as a department of the government, attended only to state business, this department acted both as the agent of the government in a public capacity and as stewards of the

OTHER SERVICES IN CENTRAL GOVERNMENT 271

emperor and agent of the nobles and high officials. This combination of public and private duties certainly degraded, to some extent, the dignity of the organization. The functions of this department were probably the most varied, most numerous, and, with the exception of rivers and canals work, repair of city walls, and supply of the army, the least important. Its work ranged from the building of a city wall to the manufacturing of an ancestral tablet of the emperor, from the equipment of troops to classification of pearls, from reconstruction of dams during a flood to the spreading of yellow dust before the imperial carriage when the empreor went out of the palace precincts. This variety certainly serves as an example of the indistinct and poor distribution of functions among the different branches of the Manchu government.

The Office of Transmission (Tung Cheng Ssu)

For the simple, undignified task of transmitting petitions from the officials to the emperor, an office with two directors, two assistant directors, two councilors and a host of members of different ranks was specially maintained. The rank, honor and privileges of these officials fully matched those of the Grand Court of Revision, one of the highest judicial trio. But, true to the practice of the Manchu Government, other duties than that of merely transmitting routine memoranda from provincial authorities to the Grand Secretariat, contributed to justify its existence. The office checked the form and date of the petitions with the purpose of finding out and correcting mistakes in writing, elevation of characters to show respect, phraseology, and all other requirements of a formal Chinese document. The office also checked up whether the relay teams had been tardy upon their trips to Peking from the provinces. It also made three copies of each memorial; sent the original to the Grand Secretariat, one copy to the department within its sphere of duties from which the subject of the memorandum arose, a second to the Court of Censors for their reference, and kept the third in the archives of the office. It had the right to impeach any petitioner for delay or mistakes in form.

As far as the keeping of records went, the service was a real one, since its copies provided the departments and censors with documents exhibiting the views of the provincial officials in regard to affairs of the organizations. But it was paying too much for this service. It took the office days to have the petitions copied. It created one more barrier between the ultimate recipient of the petition and its author. The emphasis made in the form of the memorials placed form far above the substance; the duty of the office was not to make any critical or analytical study of the petitions, for the examination had no reference to subject matter. All the office knew and did was to retain the petitions with mistakes and impeach their authors regardless of the merit of the contents of the petitions. Many of the memorials never reached the Grand Secretaries, not to say the emperor. Indeed, Empress Dowager Tsu Hsi employed the finding of mistakes in form and caligraphy as an excuse to "throw back" the memoranda of censors, and sometimes to punish them if the petitions displeased Her Majesty either in an attempt to reveal the unworthiness of the regency, or the corruption of her henchmen.

It may be argued that this office, by reading over the petitions first and eliminating the useless, saved a good deal of the time of the busy emperor and Grand Secretaries. The plausibility of this argument, however, is slight. As it has been pointed out, the petitions with exceedingly valuable plans and information might contain unimportant mistakes in form, while the perfectly polished documents might be nothing more than a combination of phrases meaninglessly put together for the whims and fancy of the emperor and his courtiers. Form is certainly a poor standard of measurement, especially when it is the only standard. Furthermore, only provincial officials of the third rank or above, had the right to address the emperor directly. In both the civil and military services in the provinces, not more than 400 offi-

OTHER SERVICES IN CENTRAL GOVERNMENT 273

cials had that enviable right; from all of them, no more than
an average of some fifty memorials a day could be addressed
to his august majesty for perusal. Dividing them equally
among the Grand Secretaries, one would have less than ten
a day. The Grand Secretariat should have been the office
to consider the provincial petitions as soon as they reached
Peking.

Directors of this office participated in conferences of the
"nine ministers" and those of "six departments and nine
ministers." They also transmitted complaints of the subjects to the emperor. A drum was placed in front of the
office. Complainants could beat the drum to obtain a hearing. After the hearing in the office, the director decided
whether the case merited further trial; if so, the complainants would be sent to the emperor who would appoint some
high official to try the case for him; if not, the complainants would be sent to the Department of Law for punishment. All its duties, except that of keeping records, could
hardly justify its maintenance were it not the policy of the
government to have as many offices, and to separate them
from the emperor and his close associates as far as possible.

The Chancery of Memorials (Tsou Shih Chu)

Like the Office of Transmission, this chancery transmitted
memorials. Headed by a Minister of the Presence, assisted
by an officer of the Imperial Bodyguards and six secretaries
(four from the Imperial Household and two from the six
departments), it received the memorials early in the dawn
of the day when the Councilors of State were not in presence of the emperor. This early hour of the day was the
only hour in which an official in the metropolitan service,
except the specially privileged and the closely associated
ones, could send petitions. But relay communications from
the provinces could be transmitted at any time. Whatever
the memorial was, before it was sent in, an examination for
the purpose of finding out the right of the author to petition

first took place as only the following were given the right directly to address the emperor:—

1. In the Central Government: princes and dukes, a vice-minister or above in the civil service; a Tartar-Lieutenant-General or above in the military service; members of the Hanlin Academy or Supervisorate of Instructions with a concurrent post of Recorder, and censors.

2. In the provinces: Viceroys, governors, Commissioners of Finance, Justice, and Education; Generals or Lieutenant-Generals of the Provincial army; Colonels of the Manchu Garrisons; Imperial Residents of Sinkiang or Commanders of Frontier Troops, Circuit Intendents could send only memoranda of thanks for the appointment or dismissal, or applications for absence of leave.

3. Those specially sent out to provinces for the investigation of special cases.

Were an audience of the emperor demanded by an official, the demand would also be transmitted. Again, only those privileged to memorialize had the right to demand an audience. Presents and tributes were also sent through this Chancery.

It might seem that the function of this chancery was but a duplication of the errand part of the Office of Transmission. A closer examination, however, reveals the difference. Firstly, only one kind of documents from the provinces, technically called "Pen" in Chinese, containing routine duties of the provincial government and regular reports, went through the Office of Transmission, while all other memorials passed through the Chancery, regardless of the nature of their contents. Secondly, when a document reached the Office, it examined its form and made copies; but when one came to the Chancery, it examined only the right of the author to memorialize. As soon as this requirement was fulfilled, the Chancery sealed the document and sent it up to the Council of State. The duty of the Office was to copy, analyse, and criticize; that of the Chancery to guard and transmit. Were any dispute of function or the scope of work to arise between the two, the Chancery, with a wider field assigned to it and with a Minister of Presence at its head, could easily make the Office yield. At any rate, both these organizations hindered direct communication between the emperor and the officials. This barrier bred many misunderstandings and delays and led to general administrative inefficiency. Judging from the standard of the old monarchy, its usefulness was in holding the officials at arm's length from the emperor and upholding his dignity as a supreme human being.

The Academy of Letters (Hanlin Yuan)

By a popular misconception an appointment to this academy has been regarded as the winning of the highest literary degree resulting from the competitive examinations; technically, however, a compilership in this academy was just as much as an appointment to office as any other. The reasons for mistaking this office for a degree have been: (1) the metropolitan graduates coming out highest in examinations and only these graduates were appointed to this office; (2) the functions of this office were of a purely literary nature; (3) after a term of three years, good appointments and rapid promotions could be expected. For these reasons, failure to win an appointment to this academy came to be considered failure to get the highest degree.

To do the examination system and the office justice, it should be pointed out that members of this honorable institution were only successful candidates of examinations in the "eight-legged" essays, by no means the flowers of Chinese scholarship, nor even the pick of Chinese literature. It is merely on account of its importance in the government that a brief description of it is here required. Back in the beginning of the Manchu Dynasty, when the Manchus had little knowledge of Chinese, and very few learned Chinese gave them their service, the academy and the Grand Secretariat were one and the same thing. During the reorganization of the Grand Secretariat in 1659, these two were separated and the academy became an independent organization.[9] Then it went through one more process of combination and separation until, in 1670, Emperor Kang Hsi placed it more or less upon its final basis.

At the eve of the revolution the highest official in the academy was the director concurrently appointed from Grand Secretaries, ministers or vice-ministers charged with the duty of gathering all metropolitan graduates for Palace examinations, sending the third class graduates to the Department of Study (Shu Chang Kuan) giving them an examination at the end of the three years of study, classifying them according to merit, and appointing the first and second class graduates to compilerships of the academy and the third class to magistracies. The compilership in the academy was the very thing which was mistaken for a degree. When it was combined with the Grand Secretariat, promotion of the compilers took place step by step within the service itself; after it became a separate organization, the extraordinarily great number of compilers made promotion very slow, with the result that a position in the academy became much less attractive, and its prestige waned. However, the ban was soon removed. In the last two hundred years if any of the second or third class compilers were suitable for provincial positions, they could be appointed prefects. The director engaged and recommended lecturers on classics to the emperor. He drew up edicts and prepared manuscripts for the Imperial lectures, officiated at sacrificial ceremonies in honor of Confucius, and distributed presents after the sacrifice.

Five assistant directors, five sub-directors, five first class readers, five second class readers and a number of first and second class compilers and correctors (all new graduates) assisted the director in attendance at audiences when the emperor sat in the outer palace or took trips, drafted sacrificial eulogies, speeches conferring titles and ranks and mem-

[9] *Ta Tsing Hui Tien Shih Li*, v. 1044.

oranda for tablets, besides editing all the "Imperially edited" books.[10] In each and every one of the "Imperially edited" books, a list of the editors is found. This list was usually headed by Grand Secretaries or Ministers, but the actual workers were always the members of the academy recommended or appointed by the director.

Being literary advisers to the emperor, the members of the academy periodically gave him lectures on the classics from the second to the fourth and from the eighth to the eleventh month, for about five months in the year. During this period, a daily lecture given by one of the eight lecturers to the emperor took place in the palace. As time wore on, the system became corrupted. Nearly all lectures carried a tone of praise for the emperor. Passages of the classics bearing a warning tone were omitted or only lightly touched upon. The loss of spirit made the lectures formalities or ceremonials that the "son of heaven" had to attend to as a matter of state obligation; the original serious purpose of study was cast overboard.

One aspect of the Academy resembled almost exactly the competitive examination. The appointees to the academy were usually distributed in such a way that every province had some representation in it. Efforts were constantly made to readjust the proportional representation if literary genius or luck was too favorable to some locality and too antagonistic to others. One of the imperial edicts witnesses this point:—

In the seven examinations between 1706 and 1721, every province was represented in appointments to the Academy of Letters. But in 1723, neither the Chinese Banners, nor Szechuan, nor Honan was represented; in 1724, no appointee was from Mongolia, Shansi, Honan, Shensi, Szechuan, Kuangtung, Hunan, Kuangsi, Yunnan and

---

[10] In the Tsing Dynasty, up to 1885, 163 books in government, law, classics, history, geography, encyclopedia, dictionary, etc., were "edited by the emperors;" four during Shun Chi, 39 during Kang Hsi, 9 during Yung Cheng, 74 during Chien Lung, 22 during Chia Cheng, 5 during Tao Kuang, 2 during Hsien Feng, 3 during Tung Chi and 5 during the first ten years of Kuang Hsu.

Kueichow. Li Chung O petitioned that more be selected so that every province would be represented . . . . . Let his proposition be accepted. . . . . .[11]

Since all appointees came from the ranks of metropolitan graduates and the number of metropolitan graduates was proportional to the literary development of the province—but no matter how undeveloped a province might be, some competitors would succeed for political reasons—the tendency was very favorable for geographic distribution.

The tenure of office for compilers or correctors in the Academy of Letters was, as usual, three years, after which period they could be appointed as censors in the capital or as circuit intendents or prefects in the provinces. Senior compilers had the opportunity of a censor's appointment first; while financial enumeration and opportunity for work in a provincial position certainly matched the honor and power of the censors. For students of the Academy (Ssu Chi Sse) only a sub-prefectureship or a magistracy was open.

On the one hand, the Academy served as a storehouse of political talent and a training school for expectants; on the other hand, it formed the refuge of high officials, who formerly belonged to the academy, and were now punished for light official offenses. Viceroys, governors, grand secretaries, and ministers were often appointed as second or third class compilers in the academy as a demotion; but, demotions like this were short lived. The punished official could recover his former rank and honor in the course of a few months. This demoting appointment merely served to intercept the raging of political storms against the unfortunate ones.

Attached to the academy we find a library containing a duplicate of all books in the Imperial Library in Wen Yuin Ko and a great stock of memoranda and other kinds of documents. The librarian was concurrently the administra-

---

[11] Edict of 1725 *Ta Tsing Hui Tien Shih Li*, v. 1045.

tive head of the Imperial Library and overseer of the under-clerks of the academy. The Department of Study (Ssu Chang Kuan), besides giving instructions to the student, had two proctors who acted as supply officers and paymasters of the academy.

The Recording Office (Chi Chu Chu Kuan) had twenty-two recorders who recorded every word or act of the emperor in audiences, in imperial lectures, military, agricultural and sacrificial ceremonies, or visits to imperial tombs, or any other event that the emperor participated in. It even recorded petitions and memoranda addressed to him. This recording formerly formed a part of the functions of the censors; but, after its assignment to this office, the functions of recording and criticising came to be performed by two separate offices. The recorders did merely clerical work, while the critics, not having the necessary information, could not criticize, and the sovereign thus became unimpeachable.

A bureau of Dynastic History drafted all manuscripts for biographies of emperors, members of the imperial family, nobles, officials, scholars, filial sons and daughters, loyal wives, and so on, for the history of the existing dynasty. It also acted as collecting agent of materials for the writing of the history, which, however, was never written during the life of the dynasty.

Looking at the list of its duties and considering the large size of its membership, the Academy of Letters appears flooded with superfluous men. Aside from literary work, its other functions were insignificant. Yet, as an institution, it had many other unofficial functions not written in the *Ta Tsing Hui Tien*. In the first place, it acted as a temporary haven for new graduates. To make the competitive examination appear important before the eyes of the myriads, the government had to provide something for every new graduate; but both provincial and metropolitan positions might be all filled and yet the examinations had to take place at their regular times, and at all coronations and important anniversary celebrations, appointments had to be made. An easy way to do so was to conduct the examinations and put their successful candidates in the academy, there to wait for a vacancy. Secondly, it was a training school for officialdom. New graduates might not be well educated in formal official ceremonies. Older members and higher officials of the academy could teach the "new nobles" all "the tricks of the trade" before they received substantial appointments. The students of the academy (Ssu Chi Sse), nominally appointed to study in the academy under the supervision of the professors, actually drew their meagre salaries and loafed; and while they loafed, they were "mandarinized."

The Supervisorate of Instructions of the Heir Apparent—(Tsin Shih Fu)

In this office, the two supervisors, with two assistant supervisors and fourteen assistants of different ranks, had, as their principal duties, the attendance at audiences, participation in the Palace and Autumn trials, and cooperation with the members of the Academy of Letters in literary work. "During former dynasties, the supervisors participated in the political conferences of the nine ministers, ranking next to the Directors of the Court of Transmission and the Grand Court of Revision." [12] But the Manchus removed the Supervisorate from politics, and this organization came only to supervise the instruction of the heir apparent. But the disappointment of Emperor Kang Hsi at the quarrel of his sons for the position of crown prince doomed that institution. The virtue of following the acts of one's ancestors after his reign caused the appointment of a crown prince to be regarded as a violation of the dynastic house-law. Without a crown prince, the original purpose of this office became naught. Yet its existence continued. The reason for

[12] Wang Yuan Ting, *Accidental Talks of Chi Pei, or Chi Pei Ou Tan*, v. 3, p. 6.

its survival appeared in Emperor Chien Lung's edict.[13] It reads:—

> The Office for editing the *Ta Tsing Hui Tien* presented us the old, unmodified laws and regulations concerning the Supervisorate of Instruction of the Heir Apparent in spite of the change of conditions. The Supervisorate was originally an advisory body to the Crown Prince. But the absence of such institution in our Dynasty does not require the service of this organization. We retain it as a stepping stone for the promotion of the members of the Academy of Letters. (Han-Lin Yuan.)
>
> The ancients looked at the appointment of a crown prince as a fundamentally important measure of the government. We, having the present condition in view, know it impossible to make such appointment; therefore, Our Imperial Father profited by examples of History [probably referring to his father's quarrels with his uncles during Kang Hsi's reign], did not make such choice, and instead he sent old, learned and reputed high officials into the Palaces to instruct the princes. Since we succeeded to the throne, we have been carefully and respectfully abiding by the family tradition [not to appoint a crown prince] . . . . . What the *Hui Tien* says about the seasonal lectures in Spring and Autumn is purely superficial: it shall be corrected and presented to us for approval after correction. Hereafter, the officials in the Supervisorate of Instructions shall have no duty of instruction; the office shall be for the promotion of the members of the Academy of Letters.

This edict, it may be added, shows the policy of the Manchu Government in the establishment of offices: it is to have as many as possible so that both the Manchu and Chinese place-seekers might be placed.[14]

THE COURT OF SACRIFICIAL WORSHIP (TAI CHANG SSU)

Aside from the Department of Rites, an office with purely ceremonial functions was maintained partly for the sake of its antiquity, partly for the sake of showing the government's emphasis on ceremonies, but largely for the sake of employing ninety officials. The Supervising Director of the court was held concurrently by the Manchu Minister of the

---

[13] Issued in 1752, see *Ta Tsing Hui Tien*, v. 70.
[14] For further discussion of this policy, see Chapter 14.

Department of Rites with two directors, two assistant directors, and eighty-seven assistants of different ranks. Of the ninety-two officials, only two were Chinese, all the rest being specially reserved for Manchus.[15] It supplied the materials for sacrificial functions, it supervised the masters of ceremonies, and directed the sacrificial band. Apparently, it duplicated the functions, particularly sacrificial functions, of the Department of Rites; actually, however, their duties could be differentiated. The department had more of the discretionary duties, while this court had everything ministerial. The court performed the private or family sacrifices of the emperor, and the department had the state functions. Even with these differences, the justification for the existence of such a separate organization was very inadequate.

The Court of State Ceremonials (Hung Lu Ssu)

This court controlled ceremonials for the living, just as the Court of Sacrificial Worships had jurisdiction over ceremonials for the dead. Its personnel exactly corresponded to that of the Tai Chang Ssu. This court controlled ceremonies in the audiences, both regular and extraordinary, palace examinations, presentation of new graduates, imperial lecturers, etc. It also announced the appearance and retirement of the emperor, regulated the position of nobles and officials in court and supervised the performance of the ceremonies. Like its twin, the Court of Sacrificial Worships, it had little justification for existence separated from the Department of Rites; so, in 1906, both were amalgamated into the Department of Rites.

The Imperial College (Kuo Tzu Chien)

The only organization with some resemblance of an educational institution as regards the giving of instructions was the Imperial College. At its head was the Chancellor,

---

[15] See *Ta Tsing Hui Tien*, v. 71 and 72.

concurrently appointed from the grand secretaries, ministers or vice-ministers; but the two Libationers (Chi Chiu) actually led the administration of this organization. Below them were the three Tutors (Ssu Yeh) and a host of minor officials. Its academic designation, however, did not rid it of all other functions, particularly the ceremonial; for, in the visits of the emperor, the call of new metropolitan graduates, sacrifices to Confucius, the imperial lectures, etc., more attention was paid to formality than to real study, thus reducing this organization, to some extent, to a decorative rather than to an educational institution. Upon the educational side of this organization, instruction was given to various kinds of students, from provincial graduates down to unqualified students. A nominal schedule kept the students for a period of study, ranging from six months to three years. Being run by the government, the natural tendency was to make it a preparatory school for men in civil service, hence, upon graduation, its students were sent to the departments as secretaries and clerks, or to the provinces as prefectural or magistrate professors. In more than the way just mentioned was this college a part and parcel of the civil service system. A student in the college had first of all the right to compete in the provincial examinations; in fact, many rich or influential students took advantage of the opportunity by purchasing a scholarship in the college as graduation from it would entitle him to participate in the provincial examinations in the capital, thus avoiding the tedious and perilous examination ordeal and risking a shameful failure in one's own district. Then, too, the provincial examinations in the capital were generally easier than those in the provinces, especially in provinces like Kiangsu, Chekiang, Anhui, Kiangsi and Fukien. The degrees in the provincial examination in the capital were geographically distributed. The distant provinces, say Kuangtung, on account of the distance, naturally had fewer contestants and less keen competition, and the holder of the purchased scholarship had the benefit. To the public, a provincial degree from the capital was of less value; to the government, its qualification had the same effect upon the graduate's climb up the service ladder. A full recognition of the government gave to the financially strong, though intellectually weak, individual the advantageous opportunity that the poor but talented could not obtain.

The Banqueting Court (Kuang Lu Ssu)

This was the last of a series of unimportant services having duplicate duties and yet high rank for its officials. Like other courts the supervising ministership was concurrently held by one of the Manchu ministers. The two directors and two assistant directors handled the preparation and arrangement of banquets, distribution of victuals, auditing of accounts, supervision of butchery before a grand sacrifice (sacrifices were considered more important than banquets), and acted as general supply office for all imperial entertainments. The general duty of supply was taken up by four bureaus: the Meat Bureau for meats, vegetables, tables, table linen, and keeping of accounts; the Games Bureau for poultry and cereals; the Wine Bureau for wine, milk, cream and other drinks; and the Salt Bureau for salt, fruit, and other table accessories. One point should not escape our attention: the court managed all banquets and entertainments outside of the Imperial Household. Although many, or nearly all the occasions were personally connected with the emperor or some members of the Imperial Household, the functions were State functions.

The Imperial Household (Nai Wu Fu)

To the Imperial Household, the emperor specially appointed a number of comptrollers. Usually high in rank and power and favored by the emperor, they had a little government to themselves within the Forbidden City. As military officers, they commanded the Upper Three Banners for the emperor. When the emperor performed a sacrifice within the Forbidden City, one of them would officiate at the ceremonies. They acted as stewards of married princes and princesses, arranged all banquets within the Seraglio, and acted as gentlemen-in-waiting to the emperor. Finally, together with the associated grand secretaries, they oversaw the affixing of Imperial and state seals on all important documents. They had all the employees of the household under their control, just as the Departments of Civil Service and War had all public servants. A set of service laws slightly different from those of the departments to suit the condition of the "Grand Interior" [16] with the fundamental principles like the monthly selection, the seniority rule, the triennial examinations, etc., practically the same, was provided for the employees in the emperor's domestic service.

The Treasury of the Household was under one of the comptrollers. Being a "fat job," the comptrollers took it by turns, each for one year. This job was further fattened by the regulation that the accounts were to be audited only once every five years. The treasury consisted of the silver treasury, the fur storage, the porcelain storage, the silk storage, the clothing storage, and a museum of pictures of the famous emperors, statesmen, generals, scholars of the preceding dynasties. The principal functions of this treasury were to supply the emperor and members of his household with money and wearing apparel, and to conduct all celebrations.

The Bureau of Stewards formed a second branch of the household. Most of the domestics in the Imperial Household held military ranks, while those working at the headquarters of the household had civil ranks, thus mixing the domestic with the state military and civil service system. It appointed, paid, examined and kept records of all domestics; and supplied the needs of the bodyguards when the emperor or members of his household left the palace precincts. It should be pointed out that the different units of the Imperial Guards did not come under the command of the

[16] A literary designation of the palaces within the Forbidden City.

Imperial Household; they were units independent of the Department of War and independent of one another, but directly under the personal command of the emperor. It certainly reduced greatly the possibility of having the guards influenced by some one to the disadvantage of the emperor. Being separate units, they checked the Imperial Household, and *vice versa*. The system of checks and balances was carried out everywhere in the government. It also supplied game, fish, honey, and other food stuffs from the wilds.

The Bureau of Ceremonies performed the same duties within the palaces for the private functions of the emperor, as the Department of Rites did for state occasions, besides directing all eunuchs, furnishing fruits, and managing the orchards.

The Audit Bureau took charge of all real property of the Upper Three Banners,[17] collected all rents and put all their income into the Treasury of the household. It selected maids for the court,[18] and eunuchs;[19] repaired the palace precincts; policed the residents inside the Forbidden City, and supplied fuel.

The Pasturage Bureau bred and raised animals for palace use.

The Bureau of Justice exercised jurisdiction over the Upper Three Banners, eunuchs, and all in the employ of the Imperial Household. It could make final decisions on cases requiring punishment lighter than exile: cases for punishment between exile and death were sent to the Department of Law, while those for death punishment were sent to the "Three Supreme Benches."

[17] These three banners had 906 villas, 3,370,965 *mao* of lands and miscellaneous rent collections amounting to 94,565 taels of silver, besides lots of property not listed in the *Ta Tsing Hui Tien*.

[18] Who entered at thirteen and stayed until twenty-five years of age.

[19] Who stayed in the Forbidden City until incapacitated.

In addition to the bureaus, a number of auxiliary services were attached to the Household:—

1. The Palace Stud for care and training of horses. The relation between this stud and the Household was exactly like that between the Imperial Stud and the government.

2. The Palace Armory for supply of arms and ammunition and liveries to all guards not belonging to any independent unit.

3. The Imperial Buttery for duties which its name signifies.

4. The Imperial Library for the collection, classification and preservation of books. It is generally recognized that this library had the largest and most valuable collection of Chinese books. The catalogue of this library has become the standard classification of Chinese books in the old method of cataloguing.

5. The Imperial Printing Office for editing and publishing Government editions.

Many other supplementary offices were either too unimportant or too much of a domestic character to be included in a description of the National Government. Those already enumerated can hardly fail to impress one with the fact that too much attention was paid to the Imperial Household. The prudence of the early emperors made it a dynasty house-law to prohibit the eunuchs from entangling themselves with politics; but, as the house gradually decayed, this tradition went with it. Chang Teh Hai and Li Lien Ying during the Tsu Hsi Regime and Chang Yuan Fu during the Regency of Prince Chun had more influence over their imperial mistresses in politics and received more enrichment from the spoil system than any of their contemporary politicians. Yet, their usurpation of power did not elevate the position of the Imperial Household. As an office, the Nai Wu Fu stayed very well within its bounds in the two hundred and sixty-six years of the Manchu Dynasty, as compared with other periods.

Appendix I
OFFICES AND MEN OF THE CHINESE ARMY (1885)
(Including part of the old Navy)

Rank	Those Under the Department of War			Manchu Forces not under the Department	Total
	The Eight Banners (Manchu)	The Green Battalions (Chinese)	Total		
1st	17	35	52	38	142
2nd	37	246	283	56	622
3rd	249	631	880	718	2,478
4th	1,252	500	1,752	1,922	5,431
5th	1,120	990	2,110	1,213	5,433
6th	1,561	2,125	3,686	4,247	11,619
7th	1	3,625	3,626	117	7,369
8th	0	0	0	0	0
9th	0	8,886	8,886	205	17,977
Not fixed	99	0	99	130	328
Total Officers	4,336	17,038	21,374	8,646	51,494
Total Privates	153,243	460,159	613,402	18,843	1,245,647

Includes aborigines. These figures are taken from *Ta Tsing Hui Tien*.

CHAPTER XI

Provincial Government

Into provinces which worked much more like the states of the American Union under the articles of Confederation than the departments of France, the apparently centralized China was divided.[1] As Manchuria did not become three of the regular provinces until 1907 and the province of Sinkiang was admitted to provincehood on account of frontier troubles, the administration of the eighteen provinces in China Proper will form the principal field of our discussion with only occasional references to the other four. For these eighteen provinces were provided eight viceroys,[2] eighteen governors,[3] nineteen Finance Commissioners,[4] eighteen Judicial Commissioners,[5] ninety-two circuit intendents, one hundred and eighty-five prefects (Chi Fu), forty-one first

---

[1] The eighteen provinces in China Proper are Chihli, Kiangsu, Anhui, Kiangsi, Shantung, Shansi, Honan, Shensi, Kansu, Fukien, Chekiang, Hupeh, Hunan, Szechuan, Kuangtung, Kuangsi, Yunnan, and Kueichow. To these were added Sinkiang in 1884, Fengtien, Kirin, and Heilungkiang in 1907, making twenty-two provinces altogether.

[2] Chihli, Kiangsu-Anhui-Kiangsi, Fukien-Chekiang, Hupeh-Hunan, Shensi-Kansu, Szechuan, Kuangtung-Kuangsi, and Yunnan-Kueichow.

[3] One for each of the provinces of Shantung, Shansi, Honan, Kiangsu, Anhui, Kiangsi, Fukien, Taiwan, Chekiang, Hupeh, Hunan, Shensi, Kansu, Sinkiang, Kuangtung, Kuangsi, Yunnan, Kueichow. The Viceroys of Chihli and Szechuan, had only one province under the jurisdiction of each and concurrently performed the duties of governors of the respective provinces.

[4] Kiangsu had two, one called Kiangning Finance Commissioner residing at Nanking and the other called Kiangsu Finance Commissioner residing at Soochow.

[5] The post of Judicial Commissioner of Sinkiang was concurrently held by the Circuit Intendent of Tsitsihar.

class independent sub-prefects (Chih Li Ting Tung Chi), seventy-two second class independent sub-prefects (Chih Li Chou Chi Chou), and 1,554 district magistrates.[6] These two thousand officials were designated "Principal" officers or Cheng Yin, in order to distinguish them from "accessory" officials or Tso Erh. "Accessory" officials were those appointed by the Government to assist the "Principals,"—for instance, the assistant prefect or assistant magistrate. They could do most of the duties for their principals except the hearing of a case, for only the "Principal" official had the authority to receive the complaint of a litigant. There were 3,138 "accessory" officials in the provinces.

Viceroys, governors, finance commissioners and judicial commissioners received their appointments directly from the emperor; circuit intendents, prefects, and sub-prefects were either recommended to the emperor, sent by the Department of Civil Service to the provinces for appointments, or appointed directly by the provincial authorities; magistrates were sent by the Department of Civil Service and appointed by the provincial authorities. In certain cases viceroys and governors might act for each other, or the finance commissioner or the judicial commissioner might act for them, the acting official was assigned by the emperor directly. The finance commissioner and the judicial commissioner acted for each other or a circuit intendent might act for either of the commissioners. The acting official could be assigned by the emperor or nominated by the viceroy or governor. The acting circuit intendent or prefect was always nominated by the viceroys or governors. The acting sub-prefect or magistrates was assigned directly by the provincial authorities.

Of all the provincial officials, the most important were the viceroys and governors. True to the Chinese official

[6] There were three kinds of districts in China, called Ting, Chou and Hsien. As there was very little material difference between them, for the sake of convenience, we will call all of them districts. Of the three classes, the *Ta Tsing Hui Tien* shows that there were 85 Tings, 152 Chous and 1,317 Hsiens.

tradition, every one of them held a number of concurrent ranks and offices. A viceroy was ex-officio minister of war and junior censor-general; a governor was vice-minister of war and junior associate censor-general. The governors of Shantung, Honan, Kiangsi, Anhui and Shansi,[7] had also the position of general commander of the provincial forces. The governors of Yunnan and Kueichow had the extra title of controller of the military forces of the province. Some viceroys were grand secretaries. An appointment to the Grand Secretariat would not remove a viceroy from his position unless specified. All viceroys and eleven governors [8] had the title of associate controller-general of the salt gabelle. Quite a few of them carried the title of supervisor of waterways. The viceroys of Chihli and Liangkiang were trade commissioners of the North and South Seas respectively. All viceroys and governors were members of the Tsung Li Yamen.

It looks queer to find one official bearing so many titles and holding so many positions, and at the same time the holder of a position exercising as many kinds of powers and functions as the government could delegate. The explanation is that the Chinese had one official perform several kinds of duties in order to increase his responsibility and consolidate the work of a locality in one person, and therefore to give its provincial authorities more titles, ranks and positions. The advancement of the viceroys and governors consisted of an increase in the number of their ranks and titles. Strictly speaking, the duties of a viceroy were to rule over all subjects, control all civil servants, and command all military officers; in short, to be a general manager in the realm to which he was appointed. The duty of a governor was to investigate the work of all commissioners, intendents, prefects, magistrates and other civil officials, report all cases of negligence of duties, oversee provincial

---

[7] This governor always had the Peacock Feather Decoration.

[8] Those of the provinces of Kirin, Heilungkiang, Kiangsu, Anhui, Kiangsi, Honan, Hunan, Kuangsi, Kueichow, Shensi and Sinkiang.

examinations, and act as army commissary in time of war.[9] Each additional rank or post made that part of a viceroy's or governor's duty so much more definite. Theoretically, all memoranda submitted by provincial authorities to the throne had to go through the departments: but, with the concurrent rank of a minister or vice-minister, they could send in their memoranda directly without departmental interference. The choice of the Department of War for the concurrent position can be explained by the fact that the army was centralized, a viceroy or governor commanding all the forces of the provinces. When he made changes or acted as commander of the army, he did so more as minister or vice-minister of the Department of War than as the chief administrator of the region.[10]

Both the viceroy and a governor had the right to impeach any official in the province. In exercising this function, they acted more as a censor than as a governor. Again, very frequently a viceroy or governor memorialized the throne on subjects which came under neither the jurisdiction of his province nor his position. This they could not do without the position of a censor. As a means of checking the governors, the central government sent out to the important cities Tartar generals with the Manchu Garrisons, and to every province a Finance Commissioner, a Judicial Commissioner, an educational commissioner, a commissioner or an intendent for salt, and another for grains, all these came directly from Peking and over none of them had the viceroy or governor any control. A disagreement between them

[9] *Huang Chao Wen Hsien Tung Kao.*

[10] It was decided in a conference participated by Prince Chishu and others in 1669 that since the division of duties between the civil and military officials had taken place, governors should not control the army. But if a province not under the jurisdiction of a viceroy happened to be in a situation requiring drastic measures or quick action, the provincial commanding officer and the generals were to exercise a dual jurisdiction over the forces: All officers from the colonel down were to be under the control of the governor. *Tung Hua Lu,* Kang Hsi, v. 9, p. 21.

could be settled only by submitting it to the throne. Here again, the viceroy or governor could make very effective use of his concurrent position as a censor.

As associate controller-general of the salt gabelle, the supervisor of grains, they could make the salt commissioner or intendent and the grain intendent directly answerable to them in matters of salt and grain within their provinces. Finally, their membership in the Tsung Li Yamen made them somewhat like commissioners of foreign affairs in the province.

In rank, a viceroy was half a grade higher;[11] in theory, a governor was under the viceroy as a finance commissioner was under the governor; but, in practice, in places where a viceroy and a governor resided together, there was an eternal struggle between them, which often resulted in the withdrawal of the less powerful, less clever, or less favored one from the province. Of the eighteen provinces, five were blessed with single authority,[12] nine of them [13] tolerated dual authority residing at different cities; but four [14] suffered a a great deal from the dual administration. When both the viceroy and the governor resided in the same city, they had to memorialize the throne or make announcements to the people under joint signatures. If both names did not appear upon the same document, one would not fail to find the additional statement "His excellency, the viceroy (or the governor) will memorialize (or announce) the same subject presently." This shows the full sway of the check and balance of dual authority; and as a result of the check and balance, neither of them had enough authority to do what one of them could and should have done. The idea of checks and balances could hardly be sustained; for as pointed out

[11] 2a for viceroy and 2b for governor.

[12] Chihli and Szechuan had viceroys, but no governor; Shantung, Shansi and Honan were directly under their governors, independent of viceroys.

[13] Kiangsu, Anhui, Kiangsi, Shensi, Kansu, Chekiang, Hunan, Kuangsi and Kueichow.

[14] Fukien, Hupeh, Kuangtung and Yunnan.

by Hsieh Fu Cheng,[15] if both were bad, they would conceal each other's corruption; if one were good and the other bad, the good one would always suffer in the struggle for power; if both were good, the check would be of no purpose. Unhappy examples of this duality permeated the history of the Manchu dynasty.[16] But, for the Manchus, the checks and balances were of two kinds, political as well as racial. In cities where both viceroy and governor resided, most likely a Manchu was appointed to one and a Chinese to the other office. Whatever advantages this device of check and balance might have had and whatever advantage it might have been to the Manchus in the government of a race far superior to them in civilization, experience showed its glaring defects. So, towards the end of the dynasty, the governorships of Fukien, Hupeh, Kuangtung and Yunnan were one by one abolished, and the viceroys of Fukien-Chekiang, Hupeh-Hunan, Kuangtung-Kuangsi, and Yunnan-Kueichou appointed concurrently governors of the provinces where the viceroyalties resided.

The vastness of the country, the lack of efficient means of communications, and the inactivity of the government necessitated great powers in the hands of the provincial authorities. The different concurrent titles and posts, in a technical way, guaranteed the legitimate exercise of these necessary powers. But history shows that strong provincial officials were often detrimental to central authority and

---

[15] *Reprints of Arts and Politics, Wan Kuo Cheng Chi Yi Hsueh Chuan Shu*, v. 82, p. 3.

[16] During the Taiping Rebellion, Viceroy Wu Wan Yung of Hunan and Hupeh was tricked by Governor Chung Lun of Hupeh to leave the city and fight the rebels while the latter were at their height. He was insufficiently supplied with both food and ammunitions. He died and the city of Wu Chang fell. Governor Kuo Sung Tao of Kuangtung impeached viceroy Jui Lun for the latter's corruption and sale of office; the governor was dismissed. Chang Chi Tung, as viceroy of Liang Kuang, never got along well with any governor; finally the emperor had to appoint him acting governor of Kuangtung.

dangerous to the dynastic life. The early Manchu emperors, torn between the dilemma of meeting the needs of the people and fortifying the position of the throne, instituted this check and balance system first by the establishment of the Tartar garrisons at the strategic points of the country, then, by the appointment of officials like the finance commissioner and the judicial commissioner, who were directly appointed from Peking, responsible to the emperor and independent of the viceregal control; and, finally, by the establishment of the dual governorship making each a spy on the other, both working for the good of their imperial master. The jealousy of viceregal powers felt by the throne can be proved by the fact that "in the first two hundred years of the dynasty, disturbances in the provinces were put down by commissioners specially appointed from Peking. Many of them were princes of royal blood or very influential ministers. So, when they launched their campaign, the Department of Civil Service would help them in the selection of personnel, the Department of Revenue in appropriating money. The viceroy or governor of the province became subordinates." [17]

But the needs of the provinces soon overcame all these crafty devices and institutions. The tide turned at the time of the Taiping Rebellion. At the beginning of the uprising, Emperor Hsien Feng first sent men from Peking to suppress the rebels. Most of these imperial commissioners totally failed. Then he employed the provincial governors and despatched commissioners for the work. A couple of years' experience proved that most of the successful ones were governors.[18] For they had the provinces back of them for

[17] Hsieh Fu Cheng, Essay on the Development of Viceregal Power, *Reprints of Arts and Politics, Wan Kuo Cheng Yi Hsueh Chuan Shu*, v. 82, p. 13.

[18] Tseng Kuo Fan did not accomplish much towards the suppression of the rebellion when he was commissioner with vice-ministerial rank; all his victories over the rebels were won after he was appointed Viceroy of Liang Kiang. Other meritorious officials as Tso Chung Tang, Li Hung Chang, Hu Lin Yi, Shen Pao Cheng, achieved their suppression as viceroys or governors.

the supply of man-power and finance. It was impossible to secure enough financial support from the Department of Revenue at a time when most of the provinces were not sending the customary tax to Peking. The viceroys, on account of the insufficient financial support from the central government, got control of the provincial taxes and appropriated the money for the training and maintenance of the army. The control of the purse string naturally led to the widening of other administrative powers. A score of years or so after the suppression of the rebellion, with the advantage of strong governors fresh in memory, the throne forgot the danger of powerful viceroys and for a time, viceregal dignity and influence easily matched those of feudal princes. When the wounds of the rebellion were healed, the powers of the governors waned a little; but the foundation of it had become firm. So, down to 1900, when the Boxer Uprising broke out, viceroys of the Southern Provinces had both the authority and courage to declare their neutrality in the war between the empress-fostered Boxers and the legations, amounting, practically to a declaration of independence of the Empress Tzu Hsi, who was herself the government.

Towards the end of the monarchical regime, amidst preparations for constitutional and administrative reforms, the governors employed a different method for securing new powers: this time, by the establishment of new administrations, directorates and bureaus. The finance commissioners and judicial commissioners, grain intendents, salt controllers, customs intendents, and a number of other officials appointed directly from Peking were not under control of the governors. Under the cloak of reform, they tried to create different organizations performing the duties of the other officials, and put these new organizations directly under their own control, thus indirectly reducing the power of the other officials and the supervision of the central government. The short period of reform, however, did not yield much power to the viceroys. Yet, without the new acquisition, they were powerful enough to do whatever they pleased within their assigned territories, subject only to instant removal at the pleasure of the emperor and a traditional transference from province to province after a tenure of three years. With all these powers, small wonder it was that foreign observers were generally of the opinion that the provinces in China were more like states of the American Union under the Articles of Confederation than provinces of a centralized government.

Foreign students of Chinese government usually cite the appointment of Chinese to four-fifths of the viceroyalties and governorships as an indication of the management of the Manchu Government by the Chinese. It is true that towards the end of the dynasty, about three-fourths of these important positions were occupied by Chinese. But the tendency to appoint Chinese was much stronger in the later, than in the earlier, part of the dynasty. Roughly speaking, the proportion was about sixty Chinese to forty Manchus in the first hundred years of the dynasty, about two to one in the second hundred and about three to one in the last sixty years. But, at all times, the Chinese got most of the posts. The increase was gradual. The increase during the Taiping Rebellion was imposed on the government. After the suppression, the proportion was kept up by the degeneration of the Manchus. In proportion to their number and ability, the Manchus got more than their share.

Important and numerous as were the duties of a governor, the government, though providing a staff for each of the commissioners,[19] left the viceroy or governor to take care of all his own work. A system of private secretaries or advisers developed. Four advisers, one for judicial affairs, one for finance and supply, one for education, and one for military affairs, made up the advisory staff. All were employed by the governor; each worked in his own field. As all these men being technical experts,[20] the governor to a very great

[19] For the staff of the finance, salt and judicial commissioner, see below.

[20] In the sense that they knew very well laws relating to their own subjects.

extent depended upon them. After the establishment of the Tsung Li Yamen and the appointment of all viceroys and governors to the membership of the new office, an adviser on foreign affairs was added to the list. Finally, with very few exceptions, all governors had a literary adviser, for the drafting of documents. Except the adviser on foreign affairs, the five advisers were included in the staff of prefects, circuit intendents and magistrates. Incapable and ignorant governors left the whole administration to them. Wicked ones used them as instruments of corruption. In general the advisers had personal contact with the governor, and the governor's confidence on them, and their knowledge of official affairs made them more powerful than an ordinary private secretary and more influential than an ordinary adviser.

Aside from the concurrent ministership or vice-ministership of War, a viceroy or governor was a military officer included in the list of the Department of War. But of the two kinds of troops in the provinces the chief administrator had command over only the "Green Battalions," the Banner Garrison was under a Tartar general, higher in rank and usually more favored by the court. And of all the troops in the provinces, a viceroy directly commanded his vice-regal brigades, and a governor, his governor's brigades, each amounting to a few thousand men, though indirectly he controlled the whole army of the province, and nominally he was the supreme military commander of the realm. The 447,876 men in the "Green Battalions" were divided into 127 groups, each under direct command of an officer, with an average of a little over 3,500 per unit.[21] Invariably the Manchu garrison was bigger in number than the biggest Chinese unit in the city. These Chinese troops could easily match the Manchu garrisons in corruption and uselessness, though

---

[21] The figures shown in *Ta Tsing Hui Tien* are: less than 1,000, 6 units; 1,000-2,000, 29 units; 2,000-3,000, 25 units; 3,000-4,000, 20 units; 5,000-6,000, 6 units; 6,000-7,000, 6 units; 7,000-8,000, 4 units; 8,000-9,000, 1 unit; 9,000-10,000, 4 units; over 10,000, 1 unit.

not in favor. Chang Chi Tung, viceroy of Hupeh-Hunan, pointed out in his memorial to the throne [22] their several defects. First, he said, the troops had neither training nor discipline. Secondly, they consisted of the bad elements of the population. Thirdly, as a measure of fattening the officers' pocket, the units usually did not have as many men as the required number. When the review came, all sorts of beggars and laborers were put in to fill the gap. Fourthly, corrupt officers pocketed part of their men's pay. Fifthly, the troops could not keep pace with the advancement of military science. Finally, the officers were very ignorant and luxurious; they went in without the least idea of service and largely with a money-making object.

These criticisms were indeed just. Since the Taiping Rebellion, these troops' functions had been taken over by the militia, and the troops were viewed as parasites on the country. So, even if there were no minute distribution of the command of the troops, a viceroy or governor could not become powerful with the support of such impotent armies. The powerful viceroys, indeed, derived their power from the militia trained by themselves.

Next to the governor in rank and power was the finance commissioner.[23] Being the second (or third, if a viceroy resided in the same city) official of the province, he was appointed directly by the emperor, responsible to the Department of Revenue in financial matters, supervising the collection and remittance of taxes within the province. He took censuses of the provincial population. In some cases, he exercised the power of appointing the magistrates. He performed all the duties of a treasurer of the province. In the absence of the governor or viceroy, he usually acted for the absentee.

[22] *Tung Hua Lu*, Kuang Hsi, v. 131, p. 3.
[23] Some call him lieutenant-governor. His duties were very much like those of a deputy of the chief provincial executive. The designation here is given for the reason that his chief duties were in taxation and finance.

A staff was provided for him by the government. It consisted of a commissary of records (Cheng Li), a law secretary (Li Wan), a corresponding secretary (Chao Mo), a treasury keeper (Ku Ta Ssu), a granary keeper (Chang Ta Ssu). But, except in very busy provinces, his staff generally consisted of three of the five officials. The finance commissioner of Fukien had an assistant secretary. The financial importance of the province decided as to what combination its commissioner should have as these officials were graded according to rank, the more highly ranked officials going to the busier offices.

The judicial commissioner was the third or fourth of the province. As his title indicates, he exercised appellate jurisdiction over all cases arising inside the province, where he was the supreme judge. As the prefects and magistrates were partly civil and partly judicial officials, so, in the triannual examinations of the officials, this commissioner, together with the governor, gave the final verdict on the examined, the governor on the civil, and the commissioner on the judicial side. Appointed directly by the emperor from Peking, he was responsible to the Department of Law. Like the finance commissioner he had a government staff provided for him, only his subordinates were of lower rank and smaller in number.[24] The provision of a government staff by no means enabled them to carry on his work without the help of private secretaries or advisers; for they, as much as the viceroys and governors, had a number of them, and they, in most cases, would find their own secretaries more useful than the government employees.

These two commissioners formed one category of provincial officials, often put together and called "Fan Nieh Liang Ssu." Their independence from the governor certainly checked the latter's freedom of action to some extent, for they too had the right to memorialize the throne. At the end of their term (three years), they paid a duty visit to

[24] His staff consisted of a corresponding secretary (Cheng Li) and Jail Warden (Ssu Yu) and sometimes an archivist (Chao Mo).

Peking. Part of the imperial audience at the time of this visit was devoted to finding out about the other high officials. The Manchu Government was always careful not to appoint Chinese to all three, or four, high positions in the same province.

The salt monopoly was administered in the provinces by salt controllers or intendents. Five of the provinces had the former and the other fourteen had the latter.[25] The controllers at Chihli and Shantung, being controllers of salt areas instead of administrative areas, had the concurrent titles of salt intendents of the provinces of Chihli and Shantung respectively. The Controller of Kiangsu had the concurrent title of Intendent of Military Defense. A commissioner belonged to the category of the finance and judicial commissioner as he was appointed directly from Peking, independent of the governor, responsible to the central government, and invested with the right to memorialize the emperor directly. A salt intendent would be without all the right and privileges and belonged to the next category. Whether he was a commissioner or an intendent, he had a staff of his own, consisting of an assistant controller,[26] receivers, examiners, registrars, superintendents and watchers of different ranks.

Grain intendentship was an irregular institution in the provincial government. To eighteen provinces, only seven intendents were appointed. Kiangsu, the richest, had two; Shantung, Chekiang, Hupeh, Hunan, and Kuangtung had one each. In the provinces of Kiangsi, Fukien, Shensi, Yunnan and Kueichow, it was taken up concurrently by one of the circuit intendents. In Shansi, Kansu, Szechuan and Kuangsi, the finance commissioner bore this title and performed this duty. In case a special official was appointed,

[25] Chihli had a controller called Chang Lu Salt Controller residing in Tientsin. Shantung had one residing at Tsi-nan-fu, Kiangsu had one residing at Yangchou-fu, Chekiang had one residing at Hangchow and Kuangtung had one residing at Canton.

[26] Only in provinces with a commissioner.

his low rank would not deprive him of the privilege of directly memorializing the throne, a privilege his rank did not give. Although appointed from Peking, he was under the governor or viceroy. He acted between the prefects, magistrates and the governor, having nothing to do with the central government.

Other kinds of intendents were for waterways, military affairs, education and the circuits which were the chief administrative subdivisions of the provinces. The number was indefinite, specially in cases of the circuit intendents. All these intendents dealt with special duties, but the circuit intendent was an intermediary official between the governors and the prefects and magistrates. Some of them controlled the whole province while others supervised two or three prefectures. In very important places he had only one prefecture (Tientsin) or one district (Shanghai). Being in the fourth rank, he had no right to memorialize the emperor directly. But Emperor Yung Cheng broke this tradition and gave them this coveted right. His son, Chien Lung, withdrew the right, reserving it for only those who acted as finance commissioners or judicial commissioners and for the Intendent of Tai-wan (Formosa). Emperor Chia Ching later conferred upon them the privilege of submitting "secret memorials," consisting of impeachments of their fellow officials, rather than accounts of the weal and woe of the people.

The viceroy, governor, finance commissioner, judicial commissioner, salt commissioner, and the intendents formed the high authority of the province, called together in Chinese, "Tu Fu Ssu Tao."

After the circuit intendent came the prefect who ruled over a prefecture (Fu). The term Fu was originally applied only to national capitals. At the beginning of the Tang Dynasty there were only two subdivisions called Fu; namely, Cheng Chao and Ho Nan. Later in the dynasty, either to show imperial favor to peoples from certain subdivisions or on account of the fact that an emperor had his residence in that subdivision, administrative areas originally called Chow, subprefecture, were gradually changed to Fu. Most of the prefectures now have the word Chow before the word Fu.[27] The term prefect, Chi Fu, literally translated, means administrator of a prefecture, originally signifying an official from outside of the area to rule over it temporarily. In the Tsing Dynasty, prefects of the Metropolitan Prefecture of China and the Metropolitan Prefecture of Manchuria were called Fu Yun, or Governors of the prefecture, while the prefects of other areas were called Chi Fu, or administrator of a prefecture: this still shows the original difference between a metropolitan prefecture and an ordinary prefecture. In the administrative sense, the term Fu signifies a completely organized administrative area composed of sub-prefectures (Tings, and Chows) and districts. One, two, three or more of them made up a circuit; and they, in turn, were made up of smaller units. Except in the newly created prefectures in the frontier provinces and in Manchuria, where a prefecture was in fact a district, a prefect never directly managed the affairs within his territory, but supervised the different subdivisions under his own jurisdiction.

Next to the prefect were the senior assistant prefects (Tung Chi) and the junior assistant prefects (Tung Pen). Their number in each prefecture was indefinite. Each of them was designated by a title according to either his function or the area he had in control; for instance, assistant prefect charged with a certain class of offenders, say pirates, bandits, salt smugglers, etc., with military jurisdiction, military supplies, naval construction, water communications, coastal defense, or aborigines. When the designation was of a geographical nature, the assistant prefect was a kind of assistant general manager of the area, while those designated with special duties were assistants in the

[27] For detailed and chronological order of the changes, see Works of Kuo Ting Lin, *Yi Chi Lu*, v. 8, p. 5.

particular duties. A prefect had also seventeen other kinds of assistants, all appointed by the provincial authority.[28]

Two classes of sub-prefectures came next to the prefectures in the division of administrative areas; namely, the Tings and Chows which, for lack of better terms, are called here first and second class sub-prefectures. The Chows, we can readily see, were areas formerly upon a par with the prefectures, Fu; but, either not having the fortune of being the home district of a emperor or a favorite prince or having only a small area or population, they were not changed into the new, dignified term, Fu; gradually, they were put under a prefect and became part of a prefecture. The Tings, before the term Fu became a general term of political subdivision, were parts of Chows where an assistant prefect ruled. The office of this assistant prefect was called Ting Shih, meaning an office; later, the word Shih was dropped for convenience, the office came to be called Ting, and the area under that office came to be known as a Ting. Even in the Tsing Dynasty, the official title of a governor of a Ting was exactly the same as the senior assistant prefect, Tung Chi.

As the nation grew, some of the Tings and Chows became too big to be under the supervision of a prefect, but too small to be prefecture itself. A compromise was reached by making the Tings and Chows into "Independent" Tings and Chows. By so doing, an independent sub-prefect came directly under the finance and judicial commissioners without being a prefect. The organization of the government of an independent Ting or Chow approached more nearly to that of a prefecture than that of a district; while the government of an ordinary Ting or Chow was like that of a district, although, in some cases, a Ting or Chow might consist of a number of districts; in those cases, the district magistrate,

[28] They were secretaries, archivists, treasury keepers, granary keepers, jail wardens, prefectural directors of schools, receivers of duties and taxes, examiners of tax, salt and tea examiners, customs examiners, river police inspectors, postmasters, sluice-keepers, and what-not.

though directly under a sub-prefect in name, did not have to take orders from his direct superior. The only time that a magistrate had to see his superior was when he first assumed his duties, and paid the sub-prefect a formal call to report for duty.

Sub-prefects of Tings and Chows, either independent or otherwise, had staffs of their own; the independent ones resembled that of a prefecture and the ordinary ones that of a district.

In spite of all definitions, differences, and technicalities, the districts were the real administrative areas. It was the smallest political subdivision of the empire. Yet, out of the fifteen hundred districts, quite a few had populations of over a million. As far as the size of the population was concerned, the responsibility of some magistrates was as heavy as that of some governors of American States. Three of the very few important functions of the old government, the collection of taxes, the settlement of litigations, and the maintenance of peace and order, were performed by the magistrates. The magistracy formed the boundary line between the government and the people. The magistracy was the place where the people and the government met. A good magistrate would remedy all the mistakes of his superior officials; and a bad one would upset all the benevolence of the government. The magistrate, Chi Hsien, literally meaning administrator of the district, was the real parent-official of the locality. The ancient term for a magistrate in Chinese was Hsien Ling, meaning district official. During the epoch of the Five Dynasties, (904 to 960 A. D.) the very worst elements of officialdom were made magistrates, chaos reigned in all districts, the term magistracy became a by-word of corruption and inefficiency, a magistrate became a favorite subject of stage jokes, and decent officials and respectable scholars all declined appointment as magistrates. At the founding of the Sung Dynasty, Emperor Tai Tso sought to remedy this unsatisfactory situation. Instead of appointing Hsien Lings, Magistrates, to the districts, he appointed officials to manage the affairs of the districts, Chi Hsien Shih. This term thus accidentally came into existence and survived, though the corruption and the inefficiency were not entirely done away with.

Magistrates had staffs of their own consisting of assistant magistrate, registrars, jail wardens, district superintendents of schools, treasury keepers, granary keepers, etc. Besides this government-provided staff, owing to the volume of business and the wide scope of his duty, especially in big districts, the magistrate had to maintain an advisory staff like that of the governor and at his own expenses.

Analyzing the position of a magistrate and the institution of magistracy, we find that; first, the rank of the magistrate was too low (7a) and his salary too small.[29] Then, he was under too many higher officials: above him were the prefect or sub-prefect, the circuit intendent, the commissioners, the governor, and the viceroy. Were a petition submitted by a magistrate, were the magistrate fortunate enough to enlist the sympathy and support of his superiors, it would not reach the ultimate authority, the emperor, before passing through eight or nine hands. Because the rank was low, the appointees, at the best, were fresh graduates from the examinations. Unfortunate districts might have magistrates who bought their positions. Furthermore, the check and balance system was carried down to the district government: all assistants of the magistrate, except his advisers, were appointed by the government with neither his consent, nor his knowledge. Having no right to remove his assistants, and, worse still, in many cases his assistants being men of his superior officials, a magistrate sometimes spent more time in dealing with them than they saved him by their work. The law of avoidance prevented a native, nay, even a man of the province, from being magistrate. He must come from another province. Necessarily, he must be

---

[29] None of them got over 1,000 taels a year from salary, salary by grace and allowance; this sum, in fact, might not be enough for the payment of the salary of one of his secretaries or advisers.

more or less ignorant of the conditions of the place. He would be there only for a term of three years with little possibility of reappointment. The short term gave him no incentive to obtain a thorough knowledge of the local conditions without which no official could make his term a success. If he were energetic and efficient, if he learned the conditions, he would be sent away shortly after he acquired his knowledge, and all his efforts would be in vain. The ignorance of the magistrate himself and the lack of cooperation from his government-appointed assistants naturally made him fall back upon the advisers; but the law of avoidance applied to advisers as well as to their employers, and the utmost they could do to help him was with regard to technical legal points. As far as the actual operation of the affairs of the district required a combination of the knowledge of legal technicalities and of local conditions, the real power and management lay in the hands of the corrupt and parasitic under-clerks.

Civil service laws applicable to the central government also applied in the provinces. The appointing power of a viceroy or governor was slightly greater than that of a minister or vice-minister, for the former could appoint men to fill temporarily the vacancies left by a commissioner or an intendent, though usually even a temporary vacancy of these high offices was filled by an imperial decree. A governor could also fill the vacancy of prefectship or independent sub-prefectship. From the sub-prefects down, the viceroy, governor, or sometimes the finance commissioner made appointments from the ranks of expectants waiting for positions in the province.

New graduates or purchasers of positions, if for provincial service, first cast lots in Peking in the Department of Civil Service to decide as to which province the expectant would go. Then the department sent him to the province that the lot decided. He reported to the viceroy or governor upon arrival at the province. The governor kept a list of positions divided, according to the size of its business and the chance for squeeze, into four classes aptly called "troublesome jobs" (Fan chueh), "important jobs" (Yiao chueh), "poor jobs" (Ko chueh) and "fat jobs" (Yiu chueh).[30] The classification appears to have had for its purpose the equal distribution of the spoils; for outside of these four classes, there was an extra one called "malarious districts."

On the fifth day of the month after his arrival, the expectant would cast lot in the governor's office to decide on his ranking in the waiting list. Once his ranking was determined, his fate was sealed; he had to take whatever position might come up.

An expectant merely gambled in the official market. He first gambled for the place of his service; then gambled for the particular prefecture or district. After these two lots the expectants would be divided into classes according to qualification, whether by graduation, purchase, or promotion, etc. Were luck against one, he got a "poor job," but at the end of his service, he would be put into the list of expectant for "fat jobs." The whole business consisted of a gambling chance for the expectant as well as for the people, and the appointment seems to have been made for the benefit of the official, not for the good of the people.

By sending all expectants to the provinces from Peking, the central government seemed to have succeeded in checking the influence of the viceroy and the governor even in his own province. But, giving the final selecting power to the governor, this check did not work well; for the governor still had the opportunity to choose whomever agreeable to him and let the rest remain expectants for their lifetime. The central government, on the other hand, succeeded in impressing every applicant for a government position with the grandeur of Peking, the favor of the emperor. To casual

[30] This method of division was instituted in the Manchu regime; for even down to the Ming Dynasty, the districts were divided into three classes according to the amount of tax collected in each; the different classes of districts were then ruled by officials of different ranks. The idea of poor or fat jobs never presented itself.

observers, this might seem a matter of formality, having no important influence upon the system of the government, but the moral effect of this trip to Peking was actually as great as that of the pilgrimage of a religious devotee. Thus, without keeping in its hands the final appointing authority, the central government had direct influence over all the provincial officials.

A small district would be too much for a magistrate had there not been further subdivisions, but these subdivisions had nothing to do with the government except that they were organized according to its plan. The organization worked up in a decimal system from the family with the household as the unit. Thus ten households made a *Pei*, ten *Pei* made a *Chia*, and ten *Chia* made a *Pao*. The *Pao*, therefore, was the next important unit after the Hsien. At the head of the *Pao* was the *Pao Chang*, or the elder who was elected by the people independently of the government help or influence. In fact, the government issued orders to the magistrates not to interfere with these elections. The *Pao Chang* was obligated to report to the magistrate all cases of robbery, religious heresy, gambling, runaways, kidnapping, counterfeiting, sale and transportation of contraband goods, swindling, organization of secret societies, unknown and suspicious characters. In the census report, he had to give data in four respects, namely: population of the last census, the new population consisting of males over sixteen, a "dismissed population" consisting of people over sixty, and the actual increase or decrease.[31] He kept a record of transient residents in his own *Pao*, checked up, and reported all suspicious characters. He had to assist the police or troops from neighboring provinces or districts to get an outlaw who happened to be in his own *Pao*. He organized part of the militia in his own district to be under the command of

[31] The increase or decrease of the population formed one factor in determining the merit or demerit of the officials from viceroy down to magistrates. The Banner population was included in the provincial population beginning from 1813.

the magistrate for the purpose of guarding the granaries and treasuries and detecting and dispersing bandits. He had the right to bail a citizen of his own *Pao* in case of a wrongful arrest. The collection of taxes was largely done with his help. So also, in some cases, was the capture of an offender. Standing between the governmental agents and the people, his duties were semiofficial and his position the cornerstone of local government in China.

As an educationally centralized country, the government appointed for each province a commissioner of education.[32] Being sent from Peking, he was independent of the governor, even much more so than the finance and judicial commissioners; for the latter formed part of the provincial administrative machinery while the former had students, graduates and educational affairs in charge. His independence of the administrative officials can be proved by the fact that as soon as a student qualified for a district or prefectural college, he came into the jurisdiction of the commissioner of education and simultaneously out of the jurisdiction of the district magistrate and immune from bodily punishment by an administrative official.[33] Nominally supervising the education of the province, as a matter of fact, his chief duty was to make two tours a year in the districts, to examine the students and qualify them for the district colleges; for the degeneration of government schools left the whole educational system nothing more than a system of competitive examinations. The commissioner represented all the qualified students. In case of any complaint against them, the administrative official had the power to try them, but had no power to impose punishments on them until they were deprived of their degree or scholarship. The commissioner was the only one having authority to make a graduate a plain citizen again.

[32] There were two commissioners for Kiangsu. In Mukden and Formosa, the highest civil authority always acted as commissioner.

[33] For privileges of the district students and graduates, see Chapter VI.

Under the commissioners were 190 prefectural professors. Most of the provinces had from 9 to 11 with the largest number, 17, in Yunnan, and the smallest, 1, in Sinkiang; 210 sub-prefectural professors very unevenly distributed among the provinces. For instance, Yunnan had 30 and Sinkiang had none. There were 1,105 district professors, also unevenly distributed, the number varying from 100 to 3; and 1,512 assistants, varying from 1 in Sinkiang to 121 in Szechuan.[34] These professors gave occasional lectures, corrected essays for the students, helped the commissioner in district examinations, led the students in ceremonies in the different festivals and sacrifices to Confucius. They were appointed from the rank and file of provincial graduates, or senior licentiates (Kung Sheng), never from metropolitan graduates unless they made request to be appointed such, which was an extremely rare case; for these were poor in position, low in rank, powerless, small in pecuniary incomes and incapable of useful service. A professorship was an object of mockery. The traditional respect for education and learning would have been a farce were it not for the fact that they were neither educators nor learned men, but ex-candidates who had failed to get administrative positions. It is hard to tell whether incompetent professors made the professorship a degenerated institution or the unattractiveness of the position draw inefficient men to its service; anyway, both were degenerate and the whole governmental system of education was undermined, or practically destroyed by them.

The military students were also under the commissioner of education and the professors. It seems strange to have these literary men, absolutely ignorant of military tactics and the old art of fighting, giving instructions to warriors to whom physical strength and skill in using spears and swords were essential qualities. This neglect of military

[34] For further details regarding the number of professors and educational officers, see *Ta Tsing Hui Tien.*

education weakened the resistance of the government against both internal rebellions and external aggression.

Finally, the ranks of provincial officials, including the waterway officials, coastal defense officials, miscellaneous officials and the aboriginal officials, ran to nearly nine thousand for the eighteen provinces and Sinkiang. The *Ta Tsing Hui Tien* gives the following figures for the provinces:—

"Principal" officials or Cheng Yin Kuan	1,727
"Accessory" officials or Tso Erh	3,138
Educational officials	3,036
Grain officials	14
Salt officials	183
Coast and River Defense officials	19
Miscellaneous	254
Aboriginals	93
Total	8,718

This list did not include military officers, private secretaries and officials provided by the provinces themselves, nor did it include temporary officials or temporary staff member of any officials. Putting all of these together, the total easily reached 25,000.

Under such conditions were the provinces governed down to the beginning of the twentieth century. As the efficiency of the central government depended on the emperor, the efficiency of a provincial government depended entirely on the viceroy or governor, and of a district, on the magistrate. Unfortunately, however, good governors were as rare as good emperors, and good magistrates were proportionally much smaller in number. So, throughout the whole regime, the government proved a burden instead of a help to the people. Interference occurred more often than did protection. So long as the officials committed no oppressive acts and did not sell decisions to the higher bidding party to litigations, a magistrate would have been respectable. But history tells repeated tales of rebellions arising from the officials' oppression. Yet, were it not for the fact that the

Manchus found it necessary to institute reforms in order to put the government on a level with Western countries, the property and life of the people would still have been trusted to the "parent-officials" picked out for them by the casting of lots; an occasional honest and efficient magistrate would still have been a God-sent saviour of the people; non-interference and non-oppression would still have been acts of government benevolence.

When Manchuria was made into the Three Eastern Provinces, the proposed reform of provincial government was tried out. The program consisted of an attempt to separate powers by instituting a provincial assembly, making the judicial commissioner head of the judicial system, and reorganizing the governor's office, confining him only to the executive field.

Briefly stated, the powers of the provincial assemblies were meagre as they were confined to the expressing of public opinion, advising the executives, and planning the local peace and order. Being a creature of the government, the veto power was reserved to the governor, not to be overruled even by a unanimous vote. Then, too, the governor had the power to dismiss an assemblyman from the assembly and to suspend or to dissolve it at pleasure. Practically, not even the right to enact laws legally and technically belonged to this impotent organization, to say nothing of its constant subjection to crafty governors or oppressive viceroys. The attitude of the government was not at all favorable to it. An imperial edict issued on the inauguration day of the assemblies shows it fully:—

The assemblies of the provinces established by the late Emperor Kuang Hsu for the expression of public opinions. Since my coronation, I have ordered them to be inaugurated so that the glory of our late Emperor would survive. As all preliminary processes of preparation have come to completion, I hereby order them to be inaugurated on the first day of the ninth month. I hereby, upon this day, instruct the assemblymen to work for the good of the province. As I have before mentioned that they shall not let selfish advantage interfere with public good, let temper violate the regulations, take the work too easily, or deliver irresponsible speeches. They shall know their power and stay within their limits. The viceroy and governor shall adopt their measures and execute them with discretion . . . . . After the convention of the assemblies, the governors shall supervise the assemblies according to the Imperial regulations so that assemblymen will strictly stay within their limits . . . . .[35]

This edict says "I have ordered them (the assemblies) to be inaugurated so that the glory of our late Emperor would survive." It is, then, for the glory of the late Emperor, not for the happiness of the living millions. Another purpose was to train up assemblymen for the national assembly to be convened in 1916. With these purposes in view, with very little powers provided by the imperial regulations, with its meagre power robbed by viceregal oppression, stolen by the governor's craft, or misappropriated by factions of the assembly for selfish ends, no wonder the assemblies worked out no satisfactory results. At its best, they could only have acted as boards of advisers to the governor.

On the judicial side, plans were made for judicial independence. First, the judicial commissioner, formerly a sort of chief criminal judge of the province, was changed into a commissioner of justice. This does not show much difference in English, but, in Chinese, the former term "An Chia" was substituted by the new term "Te Fa" and the commissioner's former independence of the governor was further provided for. A set of long regulations providing for three grades of courts was promulgated. Civil cases were given entirely to the commissioner of justice. All the citizens, including the students and provincial graduates were placed under the jurisdiction of the courts. Instead of the assistants in the old way, the commissioner of justice was provided with a regular staff divided into three divisions; namely, the divisions of general, criminal, and prison affairs. Each division to be managed by a division chief, a number of members with technical knowledge and a few clerks; in other words, a functional division was introduced.

[35] *Official Gazette*, Hsuan Tung 1, 30th day, 8th month.

It is on the executive side, however, that the greatest changes were mapped out. By this time, all provinces having both viceroys and governors, residing at the same provincial capital, had had the governorships abolished. Then the viceroy or governor was made the chief executive and deprived of his former almighty capacity. A chancery was provided to assist the governor in the performance of his executive duties. A chief secretary headed the chancery. He attended to the more or less important and confidential affairs and correspondence. Next came the ten divisions in the chancery, namely: foreign affairs, personnel, or civil service, civil affairs, finance, ceremonies, education, military affairs, judicial affairs, agriculture, industry and commerce, and posts and communications.[36] A secretary presided over each section with the assistance of an indefinite number of assistant secretaries, clerks and writers. This represented the substitution of government established committees for the privately employed secretaries.

A council was organized with periodical meetings for the most important questions of government. It consisted of a number of provincial officials nominated by the governor who also could call the people's representatives into the council if he saw fit. By controlling the number of nominated officials and non-officials, the governor would have no trouble in handling this council, much more so as no definite power was vested in it, and its advice could be taken or rejected at the chief executive's will. Then, on the recommendation of Governor Chen Chao Chang of Kirin, an Administrative Council was established in that province. The commissioners and intendents of the province formed the regular members and citizens experienced in administrative and judicial affairs could be called in by the governor to act as associate members. These two councils [37] took the

[36] In Szechuan, there was a section of Tibetan frontier affairs; at Mukden, one for banner affairs and one for frontier affairs; at Tsitsihar, one for banner and Mongolian affairs and one for frontier affairs.

[37] One in all provinces except Kirin.

place of the advisory system of the old regime. Nominally, it looked much better, for they resembled modern organizations, but practically, they were just as much advisory boards as the former advisers, indeed, hardly any members of the new councils could enjoy as much respect and confidence of the chief administrator as the old advisers, for the former were his subordinates while the latter were his guests; again, the council and advice of the former were thrust upon the governor while those of the latter he sought and paid for.

The office of the finance commissioner remained practically the same.

Along the same new line was the reorganized office of the commissioner of education. Popular enthusiasm for new education and the government's emphasis upon it led to the establishment of numerous schools on a modern basis. The government sought to monopolize educational activity by first incorporating the new schools into the examination system, and later by entirely replacing the old competition with the graduation and conferment of degrees by the government. The old attitude towards education, as a stepping-stone to government service, was not changed, but the field of activity of the commissioner of education was widened. For the performance of his numerous new duties, the commissioner had a council with a chairman appointed from the Department of Education (a new department) upon the recommendation of the viceroy or governor, and four members nominated by the commissioner from among the local gentry. His office was divided into six sections: (1) general affairs, (2) common schools, (3) technical schools, (4) industrial schools, (5) textbooks and manuals, and (6) accounts. A section chief headed each section with a number of assistant chiefs, secretaries, and clerks.

Under the commissioner were six inspectors of education who made tours in the province to see that the old schools were changed into new ones. Each district had a district inspector who directed public lectures under the auspices of the government and controlled the lecture courses given by government agents. Several kinds of educational organizations, like the Association for Fostering of Education (Chuan Hsueh So), or Public Education Society (Chiao Yu Hui), sprang up at provincial, prefectural and district centers partly supported by the government and largely staffed by government appointees.

Among the new offices, the most important was the commissioner of foreign affairs. The first one appeared in Fengtien and Kirin in 1907; Yunnan followed in 1909; all other provinces had one before the outbreak of the revolution in 1911.

This officer took the place of the secretary of foreign affairs in the old governor's yamen and deprived the governor of membership in the foreign office.

The intendent of industries was another new official. Being appointed from Peking, he was responsible to both the governor and the ministry. He controlled posts and communications which previously had been illogically vested in the judicial commissioner. His office was worked by sections on approximately the same basis as those of the commissioners. He had representatives called industrial deputies in prefectures and districts to supervise and foster industries.

The third member of the new triumvirate was the police intendent. He had the rank of the intendent of industries, was appointed in the same way, and was responsible to both governor and ministry. His office was worked in the same manner as those of other commissioners and intendents.

New regulations for district self-government, local councils, etc., sprang up like mushrooms. But, in every case, the real power of government remained with the government-appointed officials, as every set of these regulations was given by the emperor and most of them based on Prussian or Japanese models. As a result, the conservatives looked at them as nuisances, the radicals knew them to be a camouflage, the officials masquerading themselves with new ideas and new schemes to make their old positions secure; consequently, nothing worth while was done.

Some attempts of the government, which unfortunately remained attempts to the end of the dynasty, were quite worthy of adoption. The government tried to put the heads of the different commissions together with the governor to work in the same office, and to place all of them beneath him, thus doing away with the former checks and balances which had been a hindrance to efficiency. Then a system of committees and councils was introduced in place of the former advisory system. The division of sections according to functions would, if carried out, have helped a great deal in making the government an efficient concern. But, with the exception of the Manchurian provinces which were newly organized into regular provinces, and had nothing in their way to prevent them from adopting any system whatever, none of the provinces succeeded in accomplishing even one of the intended results. Where some new institutions worked, the old ones, the nominally abolished ones, worked with them side by side, as, for instance, the committees and the private advisers. Many of the old roots remained intact. The under-clerks, the foundation of the old corruption, were changed into clerks and continued their profitable semi-official careers. No attempts at all was made to do away with such sources of inefficiency as the law of avoidance and the impotence of the magistrates; in short, the reforms were in form only and without substance. Regarding the provincial government of the Tsing Dynasty, Wang Tao says:—[38]

. . . . . Generally speaking the defects of this system are four. First, the divisions are too big for effective government. . . . . The size of a province nearly matches that of a state in Europe, (in fact some provinces are bigger than many states in Europe), the means of communications are inadequate, and most of the places are out of the reach of the government. The number of people in a province is large, so that only a small portion of them came directly

[38] *Historical Development of the Provincial System, Chung Kuo Ti Fang Tu Yuan Ke Shih*, p. 121 ff.

under the influence of the government ..... No wonder the places are undeveloped, the people uneducated, and that bandits abound.

Secondly, there is too much decentralization ..... The viceroys, governors, and finance commissioners are responsible directly to the emperor, and exercise all the governing powers without having to receive orders from the departments. Take the provincial armies for instance. Every province raises and trains its own troops without the central government's knowledge. The minister of War knows only the number of "Green Battalions" directly under the central government, not the troops raised by the provinces; even if he knows, he cannot command them. During the Chino-Japanese War, edicts were repeatedly issued to raise troops from the provinces; after months' urgent call, the viceroys and governors reluctantly sent to Peking a handful of untrained beggars ..... Again, during Emperor Kuang Hsu's reign, on account of local uprisings, the authorities of Kuangsi failed to get troops from Hunan and ammunitions from Kuangtung until edicts of the central government so commanded; even then, only weak soldiers and old ammunitions were sent ..... Take finance and taxation for instance. The provincial authorities levied taxes at will; the Department of Revenue dared not intervene. The provincial officials made loans at pleasure; the central government could not control. When money was needed for the reforms, the department could not supply the necessary funds, the provinces refused to do their part: though loans loomed up, reforms were not carried out ..... In the salt monopoly, the central government might have good plans; province A might execute those plans well, but province B would leave the plans to take care of themselves. In education, Peking issued all the regulations, some provinces might live up to them while others dragged behind. The central government might issue strict orders for the adoption or abolition of measures closely related to the weal and woe of the people, the provincial officials could always lay them aside with an excuse. All these are detrimental results of decentralization.

Thirdly, there are too many grades of administrative areas. The Tsing government provided four grades, the most numerous in history. This led to three kinds of difficulties: (1) difficulty in creating public good; (2) difficulty in feeling public opinion; and (3) difficulty in executing government orders. When something was to be done in a place, the approval of the governor or viceroy was necessary and the petition might be filed or an order to execute it might follow. But the inadequate means of communication might mean several days to reach a district magistracy, and weeks to reach the prefect, the circuit intendent and then the viceroy's office. When it got to the provincial capital, it had to go through the commissioner's office, and thence to the governor. By the time it reaches the governor, immeasurable amount of time and money is already wasted. Only the very rich can afford the journey and the very risky dare to take the chance . . . . . Then, during the monarchical period, officials usually looked at the plain subjects as negligibles . . . . . When they were illtreated by the officials, they dared not attempt to have their grievances redressed. If they dared, they had to spend months of time and big sums of money . . . . . Finally, when the government wanted reforms, it issued an order to the viceroys and governors who, in turn, issued one to the commissioners, then from the commissioners to the circuit intendents, from the intendents to the prefect, and from the prefects to the magistrates. Each step took some time. The order could not reach some remote parts of the province until months passed . . . .

The organization is inadequate. Governors in all preceding dynasties had staffs provided by the government . . . . . but the Tsing governor had only advisers and under-clerks. These under-clerks had neither regular education nor experience. The utmost they could do was to render some assistance in bookkeeping, criminal laws, and tax collection. Other administrative affairs were either to be done by the viceroy or governor alone or not to be done at all. Unfortunately, most of the viceroys and governors at the end of the Tsing Dynasty got their appointment by nepotism or money, what wonder could there be to find all administrative work in a mess? Yet, if other officials were able and energetic, something might have been done; but, again, unfortunately, with the exception of the prefects and magistrates, the officials were appointed for the officials, not for the people . . . . . The government, for fear of the disloyalty of the magistrates, appointed a prefect over them; then an intendent over the prefects, then the commissioners over the intendents, then the governor over the commissioners, and the viceroy over the governors, so that each was checked by others and the real work of provincial government left undone: all they did in a place was to desire the absence of uprising, not to work for the development of the place . . . . .

Undoubtedly, these criticisms are just and to the point. It would not have been too severe had this author laid the blame of the chaos of the present time on the provincial government of the Manchus.

CHAPTER XII

Territorial [1] Government

Organizations like the six departments, five courts, the provincial administration described in the preceding chapters, related only to the eighteen provinces in China Proper, the Province of Sinkiang, (after 1884) the Eastern Three Provinces, (after 1907) and Formosa, (before its cession to Japan in 1895) but had nothing to do with the governments of Mongolia, Tibet, and Chinese Turkestan, although these

[1] Political sub-divisions like Mongolia, Tibet and Chinese Turkestan are usually called "dependencies" or "colonies." Neither of these terms is a very appropriate translation of the Chinese term "Fan" which means frontiers. Of the different kinds of political sub-divisions, these places most resemble the "Territories" of the United States. The Chinese government always ruled over them with an aim of making them regular provinces. The tendency was especially strong during the latter part of the dynasty. Part of the former Chinese Turkestan became the Province of Sinkiang in 1884. The provinces of Kirin and Heilungkiang had the government and status of a territory until 1907. Other places were either designed to become provinces or to be more governed as time went on. The central government did make part of the territories prefectures or districts of some provinces by putting the authority of the territorial government under the supervision of a governor or viceroy; to wit, "The three eastern leagues of Inner Mongolia have already been almost subordinated to the provincial administration of Chihli, (the Chosotu League, part of the Chao Uda League, to the prefectures of Cheng Te Fu, and Chao Yang Fu) and Feng Tien (the Cherim League, part of the Chao Uda League to the prefecture of Tao Nan Fu, entirely, and the Western part of the prefectures of Chang Chun Fu, Chang Tu Fu and Hsin Min Fu)" (Brunnert and Hagelstrom, *Present Day Political Organization of China*, p. 458).

Secondly, they were much more governed than other dependencies and protectorates; in fact, some of them were more governed than the provinces. The chief reason for giving it a special form of government was because of tradition and environment.

For these two reasons, the term territory is used here.

places occupy more space on the map than China Proper. Being different from the smaller yet more civilized part of the country in tradition, environment, and customs, they required a government different from the provinces; furthermore, special conditions in particular territories demanded special forms of control. Consequently, each territory had its special government.

This difference in the form or method of government, however, did not prevent them from being under the same department of the central government. The Department of Territories, the only important service in Peking not yet discussed, had charge of all the territories. In rank, it came right after the six regular departments, and before the Court of Censors or Censorate. In organization, it corresponded exactly to the departments. The divisions of this department were:

1. Bureau of Inner Mongolia (Chi Chieh Ssu) which attended to boundaries, titles of nobility, birth registration, official appointments, league conference, military and nomadic communications, and organization of the banner units in Inner Mongolia.

2. Bureau of Receiving Princes of Inner Mongolia (Wang Hui Ssu) which attended to payment of allowances to Mongolian nobles and officials, granting of audiences to visiting princes, entertaining them and determining the kind of imperial largess for them.

3. Bureau of Outer Mongolia (Tien Hsu Ssu) which attended to relay communications, trade in Mongolia between Chinese and Mongols, the nomadic tribes and the Tibetan lamas.

4. Bureau of Receiving Princes of Outer Mongolia and lamas (Yiu Yuan Ssu).

5. Bureau of Eastern Turkestan (Lai Yuan Ssu) which attended to the affairs of Mohammedan tribes in Homi, Turfan, and other districts of Eastern Turkestan.

6. Bureau of Justice (Li Hsing Ssu) which attended to civil and criminal cases in Inner and Outer Mongolia.

Taking the whole department into consideration, the principal duties were to keep complete records of the territories, including the nobles and inhabitants, to appoint officials to the territories, to give aids and charitable gifts, to command the territorial troops, to control the means of communications, to train the territorial princes, nobles, and officials for the performance of the court ceremonies, to regulate trade between the territories and the provinces, and to decide boundary disputes between the territories.

Unlike other departments where the racial distribution of offices was between the Chinese and the Manchus, here the Manchus and the Mongols divided the spoils. This was the only office where no Chinese was allowed in any branch of the service. In the department positions were provided for 65 Manchus, 90 Mongolians and 7 Chinese bannermen. Numerically the Mongols had the better of their conquerors. But, practically, the Manchus held all the key positions, as, for instance, the supervising ministership, the ministership, and the two vice-ministerships, the two directorships of the translation office, and all seven positions in the treasury. Only one of the vice-ministerships, called "extra vice-minister,"[2] was provided for Mongols.

Being a bait for the Mongolian submission, this office aimed more to please than to give power to the Mongols. Even if the Mongolian "extra vice-minister" had an amount of power and influence equal to that of a regular vice-minister, the other two Manchu vice-ministers would have easily outweighed him. Again, this vice-ministership partook more of the nature of a technical expert on Mongolian affairs than of a policy-formulating office. The old system made the vice-ministers something like the under secretaries of the British Government, dealing largely with the depart-

[2] Other departments had two vice-ministers, but this had three; the third one designated as "extra vice-minister."

ment itself and acting as head of the civil service in that organization. So, if an extraordinary Mongol occupied that position, his influence outweighed the other two vice-ministers, but the supervising minister and the minister would still be above him. To have him, or the Mongols, control the department was out of the question. Chinese bannermen performed duties of a clerical and translating character; positions of, or lower than, clerks were assigned to them. The Bureau of Eastern Turkestan came under the complete control of the Mongols.

From the above data it can be seen that the Manchus had a policy of appointing Mongols to minor offices to keep them satisfied. Taking full advantage of the traditional influence of the Mongolian princes and nobles, most of the Mongols appointed to the service of the department were former noblemen; the office of "extra vice-minister" could be held only by princes.

In the administrative reforms of the last few years of the dynasty little noticeable change was brought about in this department. The framework of the department survived. The six bureaus remained intact. Names of the officials in the bureaus were changed, but the number of officials, their relative ranks, importance, functions and position in the department were unaltered. Racial qualifications for appointment in the department were nominally cast overboard, but practically preserved. The establishment of two new bureaus formed the only substantial innovation. They were:—

1. The Bureau of Territorial Development (Chi Tsan Ssu) which took charge of the inhabitants of Mongolia, conservation of forests, improvement of cattle breeding, wild animal preservation, fur curing, and railway construction.

2. Bureau of Frontier Defense (Pien Wei Ssu) which took charge of the training of Mongolian and Tibetan troops, education and trade expansion.

Judging from the organization of the department and the provision of offices for Mongols in the department and the special emphasis laid on Mongolian affairs, Mongolia, on account of its large size and population, had the leading position among all the territories. Both administratively and geographically, Mongolia was divided into Inner and Outer Mongolia. Inner Mongolia was further divided into six leagues. Each league was composed of one to eight tribes; each tribe had one to seven military units called banners. The number of banners in a league ran from five to eleven, having forty-eight banners altogether. Outer Mongolia was further divided into four regions. Each region had one to five leagues; each league, one to two tribes; each tribe, one to twenty-two banners; having twelve leagues, sixteen tribes and one hundred and seventeen banners altogether.[3] Outer Mongolia had one more step of division; namely, the regions. The reason was that Inner Mongolia was treated more or less like the interior of China so far as administrative supervision went: it was under much stricter control by the Peking Government. Outer Mongolia, on the other hand, because of greater geographic separation and the insidious Russian influence during the Czarist regime, was much less controlled by the Peking Government; hence it was cut into four regions to reduce the difficulty of the Chinese officials in the administration of large territories.

But the leagues and the banners were the real administrative units. A banner here meant a group of fifty or more arms-bearing adult males of the same tribe living in the same community or travelling or hunting in the same group in case of nomads, and under the same commander who had the combined duties of a captain in the army, a magistrate in the district, and a feudal lord in the feudal age. The league took the place of the former Aimak of Outer Mongolia. The term Aimak meant a princely appendage of a number of banners related ethnologically, historically, and living in the common dominion of a chieftain who had the rank of a prince. The substitution took place after the

[3] For details of this division and sub-division, see Appendix I of the chapter.

conquest of Mongolia by the Manchus for the purpose of establishing the Manchu supremacy by reducing the power of the Aimak princes and breaking up their traditional mode of government. The banners that formerly made up an Aimak formed a league; the Aimak prince was replaced by a league Captain-general. The composition and administration of the individual banners remained unaltered; but the real change took place in the replacement of a hereditary Aimak prince by a Captain-general, elected among themselves with the approval of the emperor. The league Captain-generals in Inner Mongolia were appointed by, and removable at the pleasure of, the emperor. In Outer Mongolia, a league consisted of at most two tribes; while in Inner Mongolia the policy of the government to break up their tribal organization and tradition worked so vigorously that a number of tribes, sometimes as many as eight, were thrown together to form a league.

It has been said that Inner Mongolia was closely governed by Peking. The central government further controlled its government by reserving the power of calling league conferences, and deciding for the leagues the kind of measures to be discussed. The central government also appointed several Chinese secretaries to the league conferences who reported on everything that took place there. This close supervision and gradual assimilation of the Chinese civilization by the Inner Mongolians will ultimately make Inner Mongolia into one or two regular Chinese provinces. Already, as it has been said, part of four of the six leagues in Inner Mongolia have come under the jurisdiction of authorities of the provinces of Chihli and Fengtien. At places where Chinese influence predominated, assistant prefects ruled. They administered justice, collected taxes, and supervised the transaction of business in the offices of the banner chieftains. To them, even Mongol princes submitted. Places of this kind were, as a matter of fact, governed more like Chinese districts than as Mongolian leagues.

Outer Mongolia had its first Chinese official appointed from Peking, designated as Military Governor of Uliasutai

(Wu Li A Su Tai Chang Chun) in the 18th century during the rebellion of the Dzumgars. Intended to be purely a military command, it was transformed into a mixed office with both military and civil duties after the suppression of the rebellion when local conditions required the maintenance of this office and the extension of its jurisdiction. With the assistance of an Imperial Councilor (Tsan Tsan Ta Chen), usually a civilian, he administered all civil and military affairs of the four Aimaks until the Imperial Resident at Urga (Ku Lun Pan Shih Ta Chan) and his deputy were appointed. The government meant to have them assist the military governor of Uliasutai on the civil side; but, being privileged to address the emperor directly, and being a civilian official, he soon extended his influence and secured imperial sanction for the exercise of his power over two of the four Aimaks, (the Tushet-Khanate and the Tsetsen-Khanate) leaving only two khanates tribes (the Sainnoin and the Dzassacktu-Khanate) to the military governor.

When one of the two deputy military governors was ordered to quarter at Kobdo, he became more or less independent of the governor. In 1834, he received imperial orders to reside there permanently. The Mongols and the Oelot tribes living near Kobdo gradually came under his influence and jurisdiction; then he became quite independent of the governor. Later, the title of Imperial Resident at Kobdo was conferred on the office, his relationship with, or subordination to, the military governor of Uliasutai came to an end. For all the time most of the appointees of the so-called Chinese offices were Manchus.

Chinese officials in Inner Mongolia were:—

1. The Tartar-general of Jehol (Je Ho Tu Tung) who resided in Jehol, and attended to the nomads. But, gradually, the assimilation of Chinese civilization rid the Mongols of their nomad habits, and they settled down for agricultural work. The southern part of Jehol was made Cheng Te Fu, a prefecture under the Viceroy of Chihli. This Tartar-general, though nominally independent of all other mili-

tary and civil officials, exercised only co-jurisdiction over civil and administrative affairs within his district with the Viceroy of Chihli. In memorials to the emperor, both signed.

2. The Tartar-general of Chihar (Cha Ha Erh Tu Tung) who resided in Kalgan. His jurisdiction extended from the Great Wall to the Gobi Desert, to Khalkha Region in the North and to all the nomadic tribes. But all this meant only nominal jurisdiction, as Kalgan, the general's headquarters, was under the jurisdiction of the Viceroy of Chihli; Hsuan Hua Fu, a place near Kalgan, under the Circuit Intendent of Kuo Pei; deputy prefects were appointed to Kalgan, Tu Shih Kuo and Tu Lin No, taking up all duties in relation to tax collection and judicial matters; and Chinese residing in the region came under the Viceroy of Chihli: his status, was at its best, equivalent to that of the Tartar-general of Jehol.

3. The Tartar-general of Sui Yuan Cheng (Sui Yuan Cheng Chang Chun) resided in Sui Yuan Cheng, Province of Shansi. He had charge of all people of the Tumet Tribe residing in the interior. But in civil affairs relating to Chinese, he had only co-jurisdiction with the Governor of Shansi.

All these Chinese officials, like those of other parts of China, attended to duties thrust upon them by the central government or by the natives. Their inactivity, hence the looseness of the government, left a great deal to the natives. "As regards local government, this is carried on by the Mongols themselves with almost no interference from the Chinese higher authorities."[4] The banner was the local unit. A Dzassack headed the whole banner. Most of the Dzassacks held their office for life; the majority of them inherited their positions. All of them held the position with the approval of the emperor. In this respect, they corresponded more to

[4] Brunnert and Hagelstrom: *Present Day Political Organization in China*, p. 443.

vassal lords than to officials. The Dzassack had a staff consisting of an assistant administrator (Hsieh Li Tai Chi), an adjutant (Kuan Chi Chang Cheng) and a number of colonels, captains and lieutenants. The assistants of the Dzassack were appointed by the emperor upon the recommendation of the Dzassack. When a vacancy occurred, the Dzassack made the nomination and the emperor made the appointment. As far as the processes of recommendation and appointment went, they seemed like formalities. But the recommending power of the Dzassack was very much restricted by civil service laws; thus, only nobles and colonels could be recommended for assistant administrator and adjutant, only captains for colonels, and only lieutenants for captains, etc.

The activities of the Dzassacks were not confined to administrative work, for they were granted the power to levy a limited commodity tax upon the people who lived under their banners. The annual rates were about five per cent of the property, for instance, one sheep on owners of five cows or twenty sheep, two sheep on owners of forty sheep, etc. It was a heavy tax in comparison with the rates applied in China Proper. A small appropriation from the public funds or a small levy was allowed when the princes or Dzassacks made their tribute to the emperor, had a wedding, or started on a hunting trip. About ten per cent of the tax collected by the central government was appropriated for grants to the nobles; the other parts of the tax were spent on the maintenance of the territorial government.

A separate code of laws applied to Mongolia, nominally only to the Mongols, practically for disputes arising between the Chinese and the Mongols. As a matter of fact, most of the disputes between the Mongols themselves were settled either by themselves or by their native officials. In principle, a Chinese violating laws in Mongolia was to be punished by Mongolian laws; a Mongol violating laws in China by Chinese laws; but when Mongolian laws were silent, Chinese laws were applied. In case an act violated both Chinese and Mongolian laws, the heavier punishment applied. The essence of the whole Mongolian code was to provide detail regulations for punishment of law violating acts likely to occur often in Mongolia, as stealing of cattle; easy enforcement of punishments as whipping and confiscation of cattle; and simple and easy interpretation by the native nobles who presided over benches of banners. Appellate jurisdiction and important cases came under the Imperial Resident and a judicial commissioner.

Being organized on a military basis, conscription formed a part of the government policy. Two out of three adult males in a family had to render military service. The heaviest punishment befell evaders of conscription; the degree of punishment was proportional to their legal status in the tribe, as, for example, punishment of 100 horses for a first or second-class prince, 75 horses for a fifth or sixth class prince or duke, and 50 horses for a titular noble. Not only evasion, but tardy report for duty was severely punished.

Undoubtedly Mongolia was a source of material for the Manchu armies; the military characteristic of the organization were no less prominent than the banner forces. After getting them into service, the government placed all of them under the training and command of the Tartar-general or the resident governor, who, we must recollect, was nearly always a Manchu. Training was more or less nominal. The real control came in the form of annual reviews; every year, all the men in service had to be reviewed by the Manchu officials residing in the territories, and once in every few years by one appointed directly from Peking. By these reviews, the Manchus sought to keep the Mongols under their control and to freshen their obligation to the emperor. The obedience of the Mongols throughout the dynasty, with possible exception of the very last part, proved the wisdom of these measures.

Tibet, like Mongolia, had two kinds of political authority; namely, the native, and the so-called Chinese. Up to 1694, the Peking government only loosely controlled Tibet, its temporal head then being a Ti Pa. Later, the struggle between the secular and temporal power for political influence showed a strong tendency to end Chinese control. The central government gained impetus to re-enforce their governmental authority. It suppressed the struggle, vested the spiritual powers in the Dalai Lama, and gave all the temporal powers to the Imperial resident. At that time the troops of the central government in Tibet were under command of two officers one in "Front" Tibet and another in "Rear" Tibet. In 1720, Prince Kang Chi Hai, commander of the "Front" Tibetan garrisons was assassinated by native officials. Daidji [5] Pu-lo-hai captured the assassin before the arrival of troops from Peking. As a reward for this service the government gave the troops in the "Front" Tibet to him; he became the sole administrator of the Tibetan affairs. But when the central government wanted further to strengthen its foothold in Tibet, two imperial residents of equal rank and power, one for "Front" Tibet and another for "Rear" Tibet were appointed. In name, they attended to temporal affairs; in fact, their powers far exceeded those of the Dalai Lama; for they had absolute control of all things temporal and spiritual, and the appointment of a lama had to be by the imperial resident's consent. The principal duties of these officials were to command the Chinese and Tibetan troops in both Tibets, to act as a medium of communication between the Chinese government and the Napal court, to control the means of communications and regulate trades, to control Ta Mu Meng Ko,[6] to transfer officials appointed by the Dalai Lama to Peking for approval, to appoint official to the local units, to guard the frontiers, to issue passports to Tibetans going into China and to audit the accounts of the lama hierarchy. Appointed usually from influential Manchus, he had the right of memorializing the throne directly, and the rank equivalent to viceroys and governors of neighboring provinces.

[5] A title of nobility in Mongolia.
[6] A strip of territory lying between Kokonor and Tibet inhabited by eight banners of people largely Mongols.

His staff consisted of:—

1. Four Kalons (Councilors of state) nominated by the imperial resident and appointed by the emperor from the ranks of superior military officers in the Tibetan army. Being under the immediate supervision of the resident, they helped him in the general management of state affairs.

2. Three Tsai-Pengs (Councilors of the Treasury) appointed in the same manner and under the control of one of the Kalons.

3. Two Shang Chodbas (second class Councilors of Treasury) to assist the Tsai-Pengs.

4. Two Yertsangbas (Controllers of the revenue).

5. Two Langtsahias (Controller of streets and roads).

6. Two Hierbangs (Commissioners of justice).

7. Two Shedibas (Superintendents of Police).

8. Two Tapengs (Controller of the Stud).

9. Five Chung Yis (Secretaries of the council) two of them had the title "Ta," meaning senior and three of them had the title "Hsiao," meaning junior.

10. Three Chonirs (second class secretaries of the council).

Ying, meaning battalion, was the local unit of Tibet. There were one hundred and sixty-five Ying in all, each under the command of a commander appointed by the imperial resident from the lay natives. The official rank of the commander varied from the third to the seventh according to the size of the Ying and the qualification of the commander at the time of appointment. The tenure of the commander was three years.

On the ecclesiastical side, the Dalai and the Panshen Erdeni Lama and a host of minor lamas nominally shared the temporal administrative powers and functions of the imperial resident; practically, however, they were subjected entirely to the domination of the Chinese official, as far as government went. When a weak imperial resident presided over the Tibetan capital, the Buddhist priest might have some voice in government, but with a strong man at the helm, the chances were that they had to submit. The last and most effective measure in unarming the lamas in the political arena was the transference of the taxing power from the priests to the resident. Prior to 1792, the Dalai Lama took charge of all tax collections. The total sum amounted to approximately 120,000 taels per year. This sum was spent on the allowances of the lamas and the pay of the troops. That sum should have sufficed for the two mentioned items with the central government defraying all expenses of the imperial residency. But the Dalai Lama for a long time appointed one of his relatives to head the treasury, corruption abounded, and income fell far short of expenditures. So, in that year, Emperor Chien Lung issued an edict appointing the imperial resident joint treasurer and sole auditor of the accounts. With the financial control gone, the temporal powers of the Dalai Lama virtually ended, and the control of the Chinese government over Tibet became complete and absolute until English ambition in the territory stirred up the insubordination of the Dalai Lama.

Ching-Hai (Kokonor) was inhabited by five tribes, namely: the Khoshoit, the Khalkha, the Choros, the Khoit and the Tourgouths. Like Mongolia, these tribes were further divided into banners: the Khoshoit had 21, the Khalkha had 1, the Choros had 2, the Khoits had 1 and the Tourgouths had 4, making 29 altogether. Each of these banners was under a Dzassack; but, unlike the Mongolian banners, they did not combine to make leagues or to elect one of their generic chieftains as Captain-general of the league. Whenever inter-banner relationship developed, the Imperial Resident in Si Ning (Si Ning Pan Shih Ta Chen) called together the generic chieftains. He acted as the Captain-general. This resident was an appointee of the central government residing at the City of Si Ning, Kansu. He also commanded the troops of Ching Hai.

Some inhabitants of Kokonor did not belong to any Dzassack, but to some lama. These lamas recognized the supremacy of the Dalai Lama in Lassa. When they had a following of their own, they usually received the title of Dzassack-Lama from the central government, enjoyed the rights and privileges of the Dzassack and were treated as such by both the central government and the imperial resident. Before 1884, the year the province of Sinkiang was made out of a former territory which used to be called Huei Chiang (Mohammedan Dominion), the government of that territory had a special organization. Two types of local government had existed there previously: the Mohammedan type and the Mongolian type. In Hami [7] and Turfan [8] Mongols, the dominating inhabitants, had a form of government like the local units in Mongolia; namely banners ruled by Dzassacks. But the Mohammedans occupied by far the larger part of this territory. In the Mohammedan communities, the local officials were called Beg, meaning chieftain. When the expeditionary forces despatched by Emperor Chien Lung suppressed the Mohammedan rebellion in 1759, he allowed the old government to remain unchanged. So, at the eve of its transformation into a province, one found many kinds of Begs, as the Akim Beg, (Local governor) the Ishhan Beg, (Assistant local governor) the Shang Beg, (Collector of Revenue) the Katsonatchi Beg, (Collector of Revenue) the Hatze Beg, (Judge) the Mirabu Beg (Superintendent of agriculture) etc. All the Begs were local officials appointed by the emperor upon the recommendation of the imperial resident or by the imperial resident directly. They had ranks varying from three to seven. None of them was inheritable. The Hubi Chiang Chi Li records about thirty kinds of Beg, each for one specialized kind of duty; for instance, a particular Beg attended only to settlement of disputes, another to religious matters, another to legal consultation and advice, another to the market, and still another to the transference of real estate. Their specialization corresponded to modern government. Another feature in the

[7] In Chinese it is called Ha Mi Ting.
[8] In Chinese it is Kuang An Cheng.

civil service of Huei Chiang was that by the edict of 1776, Emperor Chien Lung ordered meritorious civil servants of the territory to be given a raise of official rank and an increase of salary instead of promotion to a higher office which was the practice in the Chinese civil service system. Strangely enough, that rule was never applied to any other place or service.

In 1762 Emperor Chien Lung appointed the first officials to Ili with the title of Tartar General of Ili. He commanded troops on the two slopes of Tien Shan, the garrison, the troops for frontier defense, and two Mongolian leagues. Two Tsan Tsan Ta Chen (Councilors) one residing in the same city (Hui Yuan Cheng) as the Tartar General and one residing in another portion of the territory, assisted him in civil affairs. Each of them had a staff for himself. Five commanders of the military colonists (Ling Tui Ta Chen) were appointed to Ili and Tarbargatai. On the military side, the Tartar General was aided by two Brigadier-generals (Fu Tu Tung) residing at Kuldja and Chukuchak.

Communications between Peking and the territories were kept up by relay stations; hence, one of the most important duties of the department and of the Chinese officials was to keep up the means of communication. A number of relay stations were maintained in each relay area.[9] All the stations belonged to the Department of Territories, managed some by local officials, others by the military governor, and still others directly by appointees of the department. Like the highways of the Roman Empire, all these led to the national capital and performed the important function of keeping Peking in touch with the territories.

The administrative reforms of 1906 and the years following did not affect the territories so far as organization of government was concerned except that the assistant mili-

[9] In the Kalgan area, there were 45 stations leading from Kalgan straight to the Gobi desert; in the Hsi Feng Kuo area, 4; in the Ku Pei Kuo area, 16; in the Tu Shih Kuo area, 7; and in the Sha Hu Kuo area, 12; altogether 84.

tary governor, (called Hebei-Amban) in Mongolia, and the imperial residents in different territories, represented the central government in a stricter governing sense; that is, exercised more of the governing powers than they used to by taking more matters of importance into their own hands. In Outer Mongolia a more definite division between Chinese and Mongolian affairs took place with the appointment of two officials subordinated to the Hebei-Amban, one attending to Chinese and the other to Mongolian affairs.

Throughout the whole period nearly all the imperial appointees, whether military governors or imperial residents, were Manchus. Many appointees, particularly those assigned to the military post-roads of Altai and other frontier regions, received their appointments as a result of poor records in service or some special errors. Many people were sent there as exiles. This treatment of the territories resembled the early treatment of Australia by Great Britain. No doubt it was a poor policy. It largely accounted for the lack of development of these places under the Manchu Government. Emperor Tao Kuang inaugurated a policy of military settlement.[10] He proposed to give the settlers pieces of land and to hold them responsible for military service when the government demanded. But the continued policies of sending exiles to the place made this offer so unattractive that this plan was a complete failure. Very few other serious attempts at reform were made after this; virtually the territories were left to take care of themselves.

Toward the provinces the attitude of the government was patriarchal; but toward the territories it was paternalistic. Its paternalism was manifested in measures of two kinds; namely, humoring the influential natives and forbidding communications with the Chinese. After the conquest of a place, the Manchus always made it a cardinal point to leave the original form of government untouched: to the territories they gave local autonomy. With the exception of the

[10] See His edict of 20th of 9th month, 1831 in *Huei Chiang Chi Lo.*

control of the army and finance, the vanquished were allowed to do whatever they pleased. Their powers of local autonomy were sometimes reduced after the suppression of a rebellion. But they had sense enough not to persecute the poor people, as every one of these rebellions came from ambitious rulers, not from the people.

With the preservation of the local form of government the nobles and the privileged classes always received recognition and support. The Manchus disarmed the Aimaks of Outer Mongolia by introducing a system of election of the league Captain-generals; they degraded the natives by creating another kind of title or rank higher than the original: never in any case had one class of nobles the misfortune of being swept away by the abolition of the class. Then, to remind them of the supremacy of the central government, tributes in the form of native products [11] had to be sent at regular periods [12] by a very high noble or official of the territory. The required quantity was almost negligible, for it was not a matter of gain by the central government, but, as it was said, to keep them in touch with the central government, since every time tribute was made, imperial largess to the ruler and officials of the tribute-paying country equaled, if they did not exceed, the tribute in quantity or value.

Also the nobles had to pay personal visits to the emperor at fixed times. In 1654 Emperor Shun Chi divided the nobles of Mongolia into two groups, each of which was alternately to send a representative to Peking at the end of the year to visit the emperor and to stay in the capital for the new year festival. In 1726 Emperor Yung Cheng redivided them into three groups. Redivision took place in the reigns of different emperors. Each changed the number of groups as if to inform the Mongol nobles that a new emperor had come to the throne, and to show them his authority by

[11] Animals, animal products, minerals, fruits, jewelry, curios, fur, etc.
[12] Annual, bi-annual, triennial, etc.

this simple and unimportant act. At any rate, the practice had no interruption except during the reign of Hsien Feng when the Taipings were testing the right and might of the government. They were then excused from paying the traditional visit, as a recognition of their military service. The visit was also required of the Tibetan, Mohammedan and other nobles though the frequency and times were different. To further strengthen the bond between Peking and Urga, a number of young Mongol Princes were appointed, or rather given the title of Imperial Attendant in the Chien Ching Palace (Chien Ching Kung Hsing Tsou) or Attaché to the Emperor's Suite (Yu Chien Hsing Tsou). These appointments were highly valued by the Mongol princes; the central government used the empty titles very effectively in cementing the relationship of the territories.

Another method of cementing the nobles of Mongolia to the Manchus was the marriage of Manchu princesses and ladies to Mongol nobles. The government encouraged this practice by two regulations: (1) after the marriage of a princess or lady to a Mongol living in Mongolia, her allowance was continued or increased; (2) after marriage of a princess or lady to a person other than a territorial noble, or to a Mongol not living in the territories, her allowance was stopped and her maiden title forfeited. But matrimonial relations of the Mongols with the Manchus worked only one way; for Manchu princes seldom married Mongol ladies. In no case was a Mongol made empress or imperial concubine.

All nobles in the territories received allowances from the central government. The sum was always less than what a Manchu or Chinese of equal rank in Peking would receive. In most cases when the noble paid their required visits to the emperor, special allowance was given. The purchase of official rank was open to territorial subjects; titles of nobility were also purchasable by them. In purchase of a title, the allowance received after the purchase corresponded to the interest of the investment. Free lands were given to the nomads. Government relief work was done in the territories.

All these facts show the bright side of Manchu paternalism. Restrictions more than counteracting the beneficial effects of these provisions existed.

So far as the methods and processes of enticement went, the Manchus showed up very well. But the darker side of their territorial administration lay in the selfishness of the Manchus. The first step they took was to cut off the means of communications between the territories and China Proper and between the territories themselves. At the beginning of the dynasty, Emperor Kang Hsi foresaw the influence of Chinese civilization on the Manchus, the Mongols, the Tibetans and the Mohammedans: he also foresaw that the assimilation of Chinese civilization by these people would be dangerous to the Manchu supremacy. So he tried to introduce Western civilization to check the influence of the Chinese on the one hand, and enacted laws to prohibit migration of the Chinese to the territories and intermarriage between the Chinese and the other peoples, on the other hand. Emperor Chien Lung discontinued his grandfather's policy of introducing Western civilization, but continued his policy of separating the Chinese and other races.

A law forbidding intermarriage of Chinese and Mongols was enacted at the beginning of the dynasty, repealed in 1787, and re-enacted in 1801. Cohabitation of Chinese and Mongols was forbidden by law in 1748; Chinese immigration into Mongolia was forbidden by edicts of 1800, 1808, 1823, 1824, and 1826. Mortgage of Mongol land to Chinese and transportation of arms into Mongolia were prohibited by the law of 1761. Mongols were not allowed to go into China; if specially permitted, they had to come through one of the six gates [13] and have their passports and belongings very strictly examined. Besides the required visits, a

---

[13] Shanhaikuan, Shih Feng Kuo, Ku Pei Kuo, Chang Chia Kuo, Tu Shih Kuo, Hu Sha Kuo.

noble's trip to Peking must be first approved by the Department of Territories; no visit could exceed a term of six months. A Manchu princess married to a Mongol could not stay in Peking on an approved trip for longer than twelve months. They were not allowed to indulge in Chinese theatricals, to have names similar to Chinese, to employ Chinese teachers, to study Chinese, or to use the Chinese language in official documents.

All these prohibitive laws remained until almost the end of the dynasty when Russian ambitions threatened the continuation of the Manchu supremacy. But the long separation had created misunderstanding and mutual distrust between the Chinese and the Mongols; so, with the Manchus fallen, the authority of the Chinese not yet established, and the insiduous Russian influence working full time, the Mongols tried to have complete independence of the Chinese authority.

For Tibet, no direct correspondence between the local officials and the different departments in Peking was allowed; all had to go through the imperial resident. Tibetans were forbidden to cross the borders and to have commercial transactions with the bordering Chinese or to intermarry with the Chinese.

It is evident enough that the Manchus wanted to keep the peoples of the different territories from coming together with one another in general, and to keep them from coming together with Chinese in particular. On the other hand, they attempted to draw each and every one of them towards the Manchus, making themselves supreme over all the rest and living on the dissentions of others. So long as the geographic separation of China was maintained, that policy seemed quite wise for the Manchus, though detrimental to the Chinese and the natives of the territories. But, when the door opened, and England stepped into Tibet, Russia pushed at the gates of Mongolia, and Japan marched into the Manchurian bean fields and forests, the Manchus began to realize the folly of their time-honored policy. They began, when it was almost too late, to encourage Chinese immigration into the regions of the great north and to repeal the intermarriage prohibition laws. Had these suicidal territorial policies been changed earlier, China's frontier troubles would have been reduced and her frontier development much more advanced.

APPENDIX I
TABLE SHOWING ADMINISTRATIVE AREAS OF MONGOLIA

Part of Mongolia	Region	League	Tribes	No. of Banners in Tribe	No. of Banners in League
Inner		A. Cherim	1. Khorchin	6	
			2. Djalait	1	
			3. Durbet	1	
			4. Ghorlos	3	11
		B. Chosotu	1. Kharachin	3	
			2. Tumet	2	5
		C. Chao Uda	1. Ao Khan	1	
			2. Naiman	1	
			3. Barin	2	
			4. Djarud	2	
			5. Aru-Khorchin	2	
			6. Ongniod	1	
			7. Keshihteng	1	
			8. Khalkha (left)	1	11
		D. Slinghol	1. Uchumuchin	2	
			2. Khaochit	2	
			3. Sunit	2	
			4. Abaga	1	
			5. Abaganar	1	8
		E. Ulan Chap	1. Durban-Keuket	1	
			2. Mao Mingau	1	
			3. Urat	3	
			4. Khalkha (right)	1	6
		F. Ikh Ch'ao	1. Ordos	7	7
Outer	I. Khalkha	A. Har-Ulin	1. Tushetu-Khanate	20	20
		B. Tsetserlikh	1. Sain Noin	22	
			2. Oelut	2	24
		C. Kerulen-bars-hoto	1. Tsetsen-Khanate	23	23
		D. Purduriya-Nov	1. Dzassacktu-Khanate	18	
			2. Khoits	1	19
	II. Durbet	A. Sain Tsayagatu (left wing)	1. Durbet	10	
			2. Khoits	1	11
		B. Sain Tsayagatu (right wing)	1. Durbet	3	
			2. Khoits	1	4
	III. Tourgouths	A. South Urianghai	1. Tourgouths	4	4
		B. North Urianghai	1. Tourgouths	4	4
		C. East Urianghai	1. Tourgouths	2	2
		D. West Urianghai	1. Tourgouths	1	1
		E. Ching Setkhiltu	1. Tourgouths	2	2
	IV. Khoshoit	A. Patu-Setkhiltu	1. Khoshoit	3	3

CHAPTER XIII

Changes After 1898

A form of government designed 3,000 years ago to meet the needs of an agricultural community [1] was found, at the end of the nineteenth century, inadequate to satisfy a people who, in their attitude towards government, had grown from a stage of passive recognition to one of desire for active participation. With weaklings and minors on the throne, petticoat tyrants pulling the wires behind, adventurous eunuchs helping the pulling, ignorant and unscrupulous men in the offices, the civil service laws defunct, and the civil service examinations prostituted, the Tsing Dynasty tottered through the second half of the 19th and the first decade of the 20th century. But internal rot was not the only disease that the Manchu Dynasty had contracted. Outside of Peking and the provincial offices, the thinking portion of the people, taught either by the traditional Chinese philosophy of the superiority of the Chinese and the ultimate expulsion of the Manchus or by European ideas of nationalism, liberty and freedom, secretly and yet insistently worked for the termination of the Tartar regime. Outside of China, the powerful states of Europe and Japan, having their territorial ambitions aroused by the weakness, and their economic desire stimulated by the richness, of China, had the desire to partition the old Empire, as partition seemed the best means of attaining their political and economic ends. Both from within and without, then, the life of the Manchu Dynasty seemed unsustainable unless changes were made.

[1] The fundamental features of this government and its principal organizations can be found in *Chou Li*, or Institutions of the Chou Dynasty. The kings of the Chou Dynasty reigned from 1122 to 255 B. C.

Awakened by defeats in war and commerce, threatened by the danger of partition, without means of resistance to Western aggression, aroused by the reformers' enthusiasm and frightened by the revolutionists' activities, the Manchu Government, at the dawn of the twentieth century, was torn between the desire of maintaining the old condition of things under which the extraordinary power, privilege, and honor of the rulers exacted envy of the greatest European monarchs, and the fear of being overthrown by revolution or external invasion, the crafty Empress Dowager Tsu Hsi and her supporters adopted a policy, expressed in a program of reforms, to give away as little of the emperor's special rights as she had to and to delay the act of giving as long as possible. Throughout the period of the so-called reforms, one finds very little action, though many preparations and a superabundance of writings and noise.

Besides the Tsung Li Yamen, the government had nothing, in 1898, as an addition to the old structure. Aside from the Hundred-day Reform, the program was never a consequence of honest conviction or promoted with sincerity. Even the Hundred-day Reform was looked at rather as a means of building military strength than as a measure for the improvement of the people's welfare, or a sign of the government's surrender of the governing power. The most talked-of measures of reform in the last three years of the nineteenth century was the training of a good army corps. The purification and systematization of finance had a place in the memorials and edicts only because money was a necessity in building up a new army. Strangely enough, no action was taken, or designed to be taken, towards the disbandment of the old troops. Side by side with the modern drilled troops, the government kept and fed, though not trained, the old "Green Battalions" and the "Eight Banners." While the new army demanded additional expenditures, seventy-three per cent of the old budget continued to go into the officers' pockets and the old soldiers' stomachs.

Amidst ambitious schemes and loud clamours for reforms, within that short period of one hundred days, four very important steps were taken. The first took shape in the abolition of superfluous offices which duplicated functions of other yamens or had no function at all. Some of the abolished offices in the central government were: (1) The Supervisorate of Instructions of the Crown Prince, (Tsin Shih Fu) an office with no functions; (2) The Office of Transmission (Tung Tseng Ssu) an office not only unnecessary, but serving as a barrier between the emperor and his ministers; (3) The Court of Banquets (Kuang Lu Ssu) duplicating functions of the Imperial Household and some of the functions of the Department of Rite; (4) The Court of State Ceremonials (Hung Lu Ssu) duplicating functions of the Department of Rite; (5) The Imperial Stud (Tai Pu Ssu) duplicating functions of the Department of War; (6) The Grand Court of Revision (Tai Li Ssu) duplicating functions of the Department of Law. The provincial offices abolished in the same reform were: (1) the governorships of Hupeh, Kuangtung and Yunnan which duplicated functions of the Viceroys of Hukuang, Liangkuang and Yun-Kuei; (2) the Viceroyalties of the Eastern Rivers and the Canals, duties of the former could be performed by the governor of Hunan and those of the latter by clerks in the provincial governor's office; (3) a number of offices in the salt monoply which were established for the protégés of high officials to meet the demands of the office purchasers.

Financial administration was one of the weakest points in the government; relation between central and local finance was a sensitive nerve of that weak spot. Kuang Hsu ordered the provinces to make an annual report on the provincial treasuries with the aim of securing data hitherto never obtained. A greater novelty, he ordered these reports to be printed and distributed to the people.

An attempt was made, too, to change the civil service system from the bottom up by changing the civil service examinations. The imperial decree of 1898 [2] says:—

[2] *Tung Hua Lu*, Kuang Hsu, v. 142, p. 24.

> Beginning from 1900 all the provincial examinations, from 1901 all the metropolitan examinations in military service shall consist of artillery and marksmanship instead of archery. The examination in writing ancient tactics from memory shall be abolished . . . . .

This change meant encouragement of the people to enter the new military schools. Along military lines, memorials regarding examinations brought many new schemes but the brevity of time did not allow their execution.

With the abolition of the Office of Transmission, the reformers removed one barrier between the emperor and the ministers; but practice required that only certain kinds of memoranda could be sent to the emperor on certain days no matter whether the business in the memorandum demanded immediate attention or not. Therefore, the emperor ordered all memoranda sent in the day they reached the Council of State.

But the tide soon turned. A *coup d' état* restored all the useless and abolished offices. Low officials were again forbidden to address the throne. Edicts to stop the issuance of a government newspaper, to protect Buddhist and Taoist temples from being turned into schools, to restore the "eight-legged" essays for literary examinations, to suppress private newspapers and political organizations, and in short, to end the reforms followed one another in rapid succession. The work of Emperor Kuang Hsu and his enthusiastic supporters went for naught. In a little more than two years, China was again governed by the old government with the reactionaries at the helm nursing the "stupid" people's prejudice against everything foreign until the failure of the Boxers demonstrated that either the government must introduce reforms or the whole government would be overthrown.

From 1901 to 1906 the government staggered on with few changes or additions except the establishment of the Department of Commerce on the 15th of the 7th month, the 29th year of Kuang Hsu (1903) and the alterations in the civil service examination in 1902. The organization of the new department heralded, or served as an example for, the organization of other departments in 1906. It did away with the racial representation in departments where there were one Manchu and one Chinese minister, two Manchu and two Chinese vice-ministers each. The dual headship of other departments was discarded; only one minister and two vice-ministers made up the upper stratum of the department. But, taking full advantage of the lack of racial representation, the Empress Dowager appointed Prince Tsai Chen, an imperial clansman, to the ministership and two Chinese to the vice-ministerships, thus deliberately maintaining the principle of equal racial representation with the Manchus above the Chinese and the imperial clansmen taking the place of the Manchus.

Throughout the early years of the reform movement up to 1906, for lack of organizations specially devoted to the purpose of planning reforms and executing them, the Tsung Li Yamen and the Department of Foreign Affairs served as the headquarters of reform measures and all things foreign. From this, we can safely infer that the government did not regard the reform measures as serious projects with which to save the government and the country. In the administrative reform of 1906, the government had a more sincere attitude and a more ambitious program: a number of committees was created, and the foreign office ceased to be the sole source of innovations.

The Committee of Ministers (Hui Yi Tseng Wu Chu) organized in 1901 and reorganized in 1905 for the purpose of examining reports concerning reform measures, assumed a considerable part of the extra duties of the Department of Foreign Affairs. It was composed of grand secretaries, councilors of state and ministers of state. By the time it was organized, it had eighteen members, six imperial clansmen, six Manchus and six Chinese. At the hour when the talk of doing away with racial distinction sounded the loudest, the number of representatives from each race in such an important organization was exactly equal for both races with a third equal number assigned to a new class, the imperial clansmen.

The Committee for Drawing up Regulations for Constitutional Government (Hsien Tseng Pien Cha Kuan) which came into existence at 1905 was originally known as Office for Investigation of Politics and Government (Kou Cha Tseng Tse Kuan). Its duty was to supervise everything connected with introduction of constitutional government, to draft a constitution, and to discuss the most important of state affairs. It had two councilors of state as regular committeemen and a large staff to do the work.

At the request of the Committee for Drawing up Regulations for Constitutional Government, a Codification Committee (Hsiu Ting Fa Li Kuan) was organized in 1907 for the purpose of studying codes of foreign countries, customs and conditions of China, and then drawing up regulations from the comparative study and presenting them to the emperor for adoption. Three officials with vice-ministerial or lower rank sat in this committee.

Other bodies for administrative reform, like the Commission for the Reorganization of the Navy (Chiu Pan Hai Chun Shih Wu Chu), the Commission for the Revision of the Banner Organizations (Pien Tung Chi Tsi Chu), the General Staff of the Army (Chun Tsu Fu) etc. sprang up like mushrooms, either for the serious purpose of reform or for the childish idea of putting up a new office so that the people and the foreign countries would be deceived and believe in the Manchu camouflage. Nevertheless, everyone of these organizations took away from the foreign office some of the work so that in 1906 one found the foreign office no longer overburdened with reform activities.

The reorganization of the executive and administrative organs constituted the greatest change in 1906. In this eventful year, the age-long traditional administrative sextet was turned into a body of ten ministries corresponding to the cabinets of European countries. The new ministries were:—

(1) The Ministry of Foreign Affairs (Wei Wu Pu), the same in organization and function as it was in 1901 when it first came into existence as a result of the Peking Protocol.

(2) The Ministry of Civil Affairs (Min Tseng Pu). This succeeded to the Department of Police established in 1905 and took up a new field of activity like sanitation, police, and other civil affairs formerly neglected by the government.

(3) The Ministry of Finance (Tu Chi Pu). This took up the duties of the Department of Revenue. The Boards of Customs Control (Shui Wu Chu) and the Finance Committee were subordinated to it.

(4) The Ministry of War (Lu Chun Pu) succeeded to the Department of War. The Imperial Stud, the Commission of Army Reorganizations organized in 1903, and the Navy Bureau were subordinated to this ministry.

(5) The Ministry of Justice (Fa Pu) succeeded to the Department of Law.

(6) The Ministry of Agriculture, Industry and Commerce (Nung Kung Shang Pu) was a new organization taking up part of the duties formerly performed by the Department of Works.

(7) The Ministry of Territories (Li Fan Pu) succeeded to the Department of Territories with practically no change. Formerly this branch of administration was not one of the regular departments; in this organization, it was incorporated into the ministry.

(8) The Ministry of Rites (Li Pu) succeeded the Department of Rites without much change, but it incorporated the Court of Sacrificial Worships, the Court of State Ceremonials and the Court of Banquets which formerly duplicated some of the functions of the Department of Rites.

(9) The Ministry of Communications (Yiu Chuan Pu) was a new addition to the administration, taking up work on posts and communications formerly done by the Departments of War and Works.

(10) The Ministry of Education (Hsueh Pu) was another new organization taking up work formerly done by the Department of Rites.

Except the Department of Civil Service, all the old departments survived under new names. Within the ministry, however, many changes took place. First the former dual headship of the departments shared by the Manchus and the Chinese together was done away with; single heads consisting of one minister and two vice-ministers were provided, thus reducing by one-half the working force of the old departments. An attempt to break the racial barrier by removing the racial qualifications for ministership and vice-ministerships was made. Nominally it succeeded, but practically the old system remained, for out of the eight ministers appointed on the day of reorganization, we find four Chinese and four Manchus. We also find seven Manchus and eight Chinese out of the fifteen vice-ministers appointed on the same day.[3] Two new ministers, those of Finance and Rites, were imperial clansmen, an innovation resulting probably from the removal of racial qualifications. The old principle of balance of power or equality in appointment was quietly maintained. Of all new appointees, only two vice-ministers belonged to the new school, while the other twenty-one were old scholars. The Ministry of War was entirely staffed by Manchus. It thus appeared as if a new policy of giving the key positions to the Manchus was inaugurated, as a consequence of the removal of the racial qualification.

In addition to the changes described above, alterations in the ministries took shape in the inauguration of a council (Cheng Tseng Ting) and a general secretariat (Tsan Shih Ting); the former had two councilors attending to the general affairs of the ministry while the latter was composed of two secretaries for secretarial work, drawing regulations,

---

[3] Appointments of ministers and vice-ministers to the Ministries of Civil Affairs, Education, and Agriculture, Industry and Commerce were not made on the same day.

compiling records and handling very important correspondence. The essentially new feature of these offices lay in the fact that they stood between the ministers and the civil service staff members of the ministry, having a status similar to the under secretaryship of the British ministry. The organization of the bureaus was also changed; the ministry itself became the principal factor in the determination of the number and work of bureaus. The former basis of division, division by provinces, was retained as a secondary determining factor. The number of bureau chiefs, senior and junior clerks in each bureau was to be decided by the amount of work that the bureau had.

Separation of powers or an attempt at separation, was really the central point of the administrative reorganization. The program included a scheme to delegate the executive power to the cabinet with members of the cabinet responsible to the emperor, individually for affairs in their own ministry and collectively for the executive side of the government as a whole. The judicial power, hitherto a supplementary power of the executive, was to be made independent of the executive with the ministry of Justice representing judicial administration in the government and the Supreme Court (Ta Li Yuan) independent of the executives, as the highest bench of appeal for justice. The emperor's judicial power which he possessed and exercised in the good old days would have ended had the plans for judicial reorganization been carried out. The legislative powers, according to the program, were to be exercised as follows:—

(1) The Advisory Council (Tsu Tseng Yuan), though without the final powers of deciding a measure, had the right of expressing public opinion and the opportunity of getting their decisions heard.

(2) The Censorate (Tu Cha Yuan) which still exercised its old function of "eyes and ears" with the special duty and privilege of supervising and impeaching the executive although the final power of decision belonged, as in the old regime, to the emperor.

(3) The Auditing Bureau (Shen Chi Yuan) which supervised the finances of the ministeries. All these three organizations were independent of the executive.

The reform program left the Ministry of Foreign Affairs untouched; in fact the organization of the Department of Foreign Affairs served as a model for the other newly reorganized ministries. A number of other services and organizations should have been, but were not, abolished. The most important of them were the Grand Secretariat and the Council of State which would conflict with the new ministries if they should demand of the government the full share of the promised powers or the necessary amount of power to carry out their work efficiently. Other decorative agencies like the Imperial Clan Court, the numerous units of the imperial bodyguards (old fashioned) the infantry gendarmerie and the five departments in Manchuria, etc., should have met the same fate as the Court of State Ceremonials, the Court of Sacrificial Worships, and the Court of Banquets.

One of the finest features in the proposed program was the abolition of concurrent positions. But examining carefully the list of the committeemen in the important committees like the Committee for Drawing up Regulations for Constitutional Government, the Committee of Ministers or the Codification Committee, one cannot fail to find that nearly everyone of the members held a number of positions besides those upon the committees. This bad practice, in spite of the clamours against it, survived the Tsing Dynasty and became a fashion of Republican officialdom.

To casual observers, it would seem that, in the last few years of the Manchu Dynasty, rapid strides towards constitutionalism were being made, for, in less than two years after the foregoing administrative reform were effective, steps towards promulgating a constitution were taken. The most conspicuous of these was the submitting of a proposed constitution by Princes Ching and Pu Lun on August 27, 1908 and the approval of it by the Empress Dowager on the same day.[4] Yet a careful study of this document will convince one that it merely confirmed the powers of the emperor, that it gave little power to the people and their representatives, and that it was utilized to decorate the measure of reform, not to set down the fundamental rules of organization and operation of the government.

The proposed constitution was almost a duplicate of the Japanese Constitution. A number of articles of the proposed constitution corresponded exactly to those of the Japanese as shown in the following table:—

Chinese Constitution Articles	Japanese Constitution Articles
1	1
2	3
4	7
5	10
6	11 and 12
7	13
8	14
9	15 and 16
10	57 and part of 9
11	9
12	8
13	66 (Not exactly, the Chinese is more favorable to the government)
15	19
16	29
17	23
18	24
20	27 (Not exactly, the Chinese is more favorable to the government)
21	20 and 21
26	64 (Not exactly, the Chinese is more favorable to the government)

It is to be observed that even the sequence of articles, or the order of the clauses in the constitution was almost the same in both documents. Whenever there was a difference

[4] See Appendix I.

in substance the Chinese constitution gave more power to the government.

Indeed, a number of articles in the Chinese constitution gave powers to the emperor which the Japanese did not give to the Mikado. Article 3 of the Chinese constitution gave the emperor the power to propose laws in parliament while the Japanese constitution [5] states that the Japanese emperor exercises the legislative power only with the consent of the Imperial Diet. Article 4 of the Chinese constitution gave the emperor power to dissolve both houses of parliament; the Japanese constitution [6] gives the Mikado only the power to dissolve the lower house. Article 12 of the Chinese constitution gave the emperor power to raise funds when parliament was not sitting thus depriving the parliament of its control over the purse string of the government; but no provision equal to this appears in the Japanese constitution. It is provided in the Japanese constitution [7] that imperial ordinances issued in place of law when the Imperial Diet is not sitting "are to be laid before the Imperial Diet at its next session, and when the Diet does not approve the said ordinances, the government shall declare them to be invalid in the future;" but the Chinese constitution was silent as to the future validity of the laws issued under such conditions. All it said [8] was that "such imperial ordinances are to be laid before the parliament at the next session." Article 13 of the Chinese constitution gave the power to the emperor to determine the expenditures of the Imperial Household without the interference of parliament: such a provision of absolute decision by the emperor is not found in the Japanese instrument. The climax of absolutism in the Chinese constitution was reached in Article 29 which forbade members of the parliament to petition the emperor, while Article 49 of the Japanese constitution expressly gives this right to members of the Imperial Diet.

[5] Article 5.
[6] Article 7.
[7] Article 8.
[8] Article 12.

Only four chapters of the constitution were drawn up. All fourteen articles of Chapter I affirmatively stated the powers of the emperor. The nine articles of Chapter II provided for private rights and duties of the subjects. Seven of the ten articles in Chapter III either limited the powers of, or provided punishment for, the members of parliament. The government treated the parliament simply like one of the departments or courts with the presiding officer responsible to the emperor and having wide controlling power over the members whom the government wanted to treat as clerks in the civil service.

This proposed constitution represented the mental attitude of the Manchu Government in the last few years of its life, namely, a strong tendency to imitate Japan and Japanese institutions. Secondly, it produces the impression that it was merely a piece of patch work done in a haphazard manner, for it was incomplete as a constitution and yet with some unnecessary provisions incorporated in it. It was done under the direction of the Committee for Drafting the Constitution (Chuan Yi Hsien Fa Ta Chen), a committee of two members, Prince Pu Lun and Duke Tsai Cha, both imperial clansmen, closely related by blood to the emperor. With the primary purpose of affirming the imperial power, the document implied the principle that all powers belong to the emperor, that the cabinet should assist him in the executive, the parliament in the legislative and the judiciary in the judicial powers. The insincere attitude of the government, the undue bias of the constitution for the emperor, and the almost unlimited amount of power it gave to him, made the drafting of this constitution a matter of form, not to be executed; and if executed, unsatisfactory to the people.

About the time the proposed constitution was drafted, a proposed program of preparation for constitutional government was drawn up. The program extended over a period of nine years, from 1908 to 1916. In 1908, the first year of preparation, the government was to prepare for the convening of the provincial assemblies, promulgate regulations for self-government of cities, towns and villages, promulgate regulations for purifying and systematizing the central government finances, provide means of livelihood for the bannermen, wipe out the racial difference of the Manchus and the Chinese, edit elementary and grades school textbooks, and codify criminal, civil and commercial codes, and codes for civil and criminal procedures.

In the second year, 1909, the government was to convene the provincial assemblies, promulgate laws of the Advisory Council (Tsu Tseng Yuan), conduct elections for the members of the council, make preparations for the establishment of organizations for the study of self government in cities, towns and villages, promulgate regulations for self-government in the sub-prefectural and district towns, take a census of the population in terms of persons and households, find out the total incomes and expenditures of the provincial governments, make plans for the reorganization of the Metropolitan Prefecture, draw up regulations for civil service examinations, appointment of civil servants and their salaries, promulgate laws for the organization of the courts of law in provincial capitals and open ports, examine and edit the new criminal code, distribute elementary schools and grades school textbooks, establish schools of reading in the sub-prefectural and district towns, and make out a program for the establishment of police forces in sub-prefectural and district towns.

In the third year of preparation, 1910, the government was to convene the Advisory Council, continue the preparation of the cities, towns and villages for self-government, initiate self-government in sub-prefectural and district towns, take a population census, codify citizenship laws, re-examine the total incomes and expenditures of the provincial governments, edit regulations for local tax, introduce, on a probationary basis, the provincial estimates and budget, draft plans for the reorganization of the provincial governments, promulgate laws for civil service examinations, appointment, and salaries, have the different grades of courts of laws established in the provincial capitals and open ports within one year, promulgate the new criminal code, extend the system of elementary schools for reading in sub-prefectural and district towns, and have the police force organized in sub-prefectural and district towns within one year.

In the fourth year of preparation, 1911, the government was to continue the preparation of the cities, towns and villages for self-government, continue the program of self-government in sub-prefectural and district towns, take another census of population, draft auditing laws, find out the exact incomes and expenditures of both the central and provincial governments, promulgate laws for local taxes, draft regulations for taxation in the whole country, enforce new laws regarding civil service examinations, appointment and salaries, plan organization of the different grades of courts of law in prefectural, sub-prefectural, and district towns and independent townships, establish elementary schools of reading in small towns and villages, plan for the establishment of police forces in small towns and villages and examine, and edit new civil and criminal codes and codes of civil and criminal procedures.

In the fifth year of preparation, 1912, the government was to have plans for local self-government of towns and villages ready for operation within one year, continue preparation for self-government of sub-prefectural and district towns, take a census of population, promulgate citizenship laws, promulgate tax laws, announce the new administrative organization of both the central and the provincial government, have the different grades of courts of law in the prefectural, sub-prefectural and district towns ready for operation within one year, extend the elementary schools of reading in small towns and villages, and extend the police system to small towns and villages.

In the sixth year of preparation, 1913, the government was to enforce the citizenship laws, make estimates for the national budget, establish administrative courts, have different grades of courts of law well established in the prefectural, sub-prefectural and district towns, plan for the establishment of local courts in the small towns and villages, promulgate the new civil and criminal codes and codes of civil and criminal procedures, have the local self-government of small towns and villages in actual operation, have plans for self-government of sub-prefectural and district towns ready for operation within one year, and have plans for police system in small towns and villages ready for operation within one year.

In the seventh year of preparation, 1914, the government was to make up a budget for the central government, promulgate auditing laws, put the new administrative organization on probation, have local self-government in all sub-prefectural and district towns, and have plans for local courts in small towns and villages ready for operation within one year.

In the eighth year of preparation, 1915, the government was to determine the expenses of the Imperial Household, have all necessary provisions for the bannermen done and all racial difference between the Chinese and the Manchus removed, establish the Bureau of Auditing, enforce auditing laws, have local courts established in all small towns and villages, enforce the new civil and criminal and commercial codes and the new codes of civil and criminal procedures, and have police forces organized in all small towns and villages.

In the ninth year of preparation, 1916, the government was to promulgate the constitution, provide for ceremonies for the adoption of the new constitution, promulgate parliamentary laws, promulgate election laws for the members of both houses, conduct an election for members of both houses of parliament, make definite financial estimates for the central government, make a budget for the coming fiscal year, and have it ready to be submitted to the parliament, operate, without exception, laws regarding the organization of the provincial and central government, establish the Privy Council and appoint the Privy Councilors.

What a comprehensive yet logical program! Were drawing up and promulgation of regulations as beneficial to the people as actual reforms, the Chinese would have been a blessed people. Since plans and work are not one and the same thing, we have to find out how much was accomplished. The Revolution which overthrew the Manchu Government in 1911 deprived the Tsing Government of its opportunity to carry out plans made for the last five years of preparation, but an examination of its work for the first four years, from 1908 to 1911, will give a fair estimate of the relation between its schemes and its actual accomplishments.

The program included chiefly two things: drafting of laws and regulations, and actual work. Generally speaking, most of the codes, laws, and regulations came out as scheduled, but little or nothing requiring action ever took place. Taking the program year by year, the first year had everything on paper, hence the whole program was carried out to the letter. The second year began a little program of real work, half of which, the convening of the provincial assemblies and the organizations for the study of local self-government, was carried out, while the other half, consisting of important measures like taking of the population census and the financial reorganization, was left untouched. As usual, all the codes, laws, and regulations scheduled for the year were drafted, edited, or promulgated. The only solid accomplishment in the preparation of constitutional government in 1910 was the convening of the powerless Advisory Council, controlled and utilized by high officials, and serving rather to show the impracticability of the working of a legislative organ under the absolute monarchical regime than to lay the foundation of a really popular national assembly. Other measures like the institution of the new style local self-government in the sub-prefectural and district towns, the taking of a population census, the making of provincial estimates and budgets, the establishment of new courts of law in provincial capitals and open ports, the increase of elementary schools for reading in the sub-prefectural and district towns, and the organization of police forces in sub-prefectural and district towns and independent townships, etc., were left to take care of themselves.

What was left undone in 1910 was not accomplished in the two-thirds of the year 1911 before the Manchu Dynasty fell. With an insincere attitude and a desire to keep back whatever old rights and privileges they had, they seemed to draw up a program to humor the people along on the one hand, and purposely to delay the execution of the program on the other. Without doubt, in the name of constitutional government, they learned from Europe and Japan more of the ways of safeguarding the rights of the government and the throne than to give to the people, or help the people to get, their share in the government. Amidst this failure to execute measures for reorganization, the contraction of new foreign loans, increase of taxes, confiscation of private railways, and what-not, gave the people new grievances and new dissatisfaction without new means to get redress or adjustment.

As for the most popular and novel institution of the Tsing Dynasty, the Advisory Council, one cannot help being convinced of the great jealousy with which the government hoarded its power. The Council consisted of two kinds of members, 100 elected from the provincial assemblies and 100 appointed by the emperor. Of the appointed members, the proportion for different classes was as follows:—

1. Imperial clansmen with title 16
2. Manchu titular nobles 7
3. Chinese titular nobles 5
4. Titular nobles of the territories.................... 14
5. Imperial clansmen and alternatives without title.. 6
6. Representatives of executive offices 32
7. Learned scholars 10
8. Heavy tax payers 10

The government, besides, appointed one president and one vice-president. Numerically, the strength of the provincial representatives equaled that of the imperial appointees, but, in case of a tie, the president or vice-president would cast the deciding vote, and he was a government appointee, appointed to offset the equality of strength. Under ordinary circumstances, the government bloc would be much more solid and unified. With the help of the deciding vote to be cast by the additional appointed member, the provincial representatives had no means of offering an effective opposition to the government even if they could make a solid bloc.

In the preceding discussion we assumed too much that this Council possessed the general power of a legislative organ. First, the emperor had the power to convene, close or dissolve the Council collectively or dismiss the members individually. Very often, the necessity of dissolving a legislature could be easily avoided by simply dismissing one or a few of its powerful members who obstructed, or planned to obstruct, government measures. Also the Council had no final deciding power. Article III, Section 16 of the laws for the regulation of the Advisory Council [9] provided that "after the decision of the Council is reached, the President or Vice-President of the Council shall send the bill over to the cabinet which shall memorialize the throne for decision." So, even if the popular bloc were solid and effective and the emperor gracious enough to let it remain, it could not offer effective opposition.

Nominally, the Council had the power to discuss the financial estimates, the budget, taxes and public loans and the enactment and amendment of all laws except those provided by the constitution. But the records of its life show that it only dealt with a few bills proposed by the government on local education, copyright laws, newspaper censorship laws, transportation laws and some other unimportant measures. Here it looks as if the government wanted to send the members of the Council through a milling process

[9] See Official Gazette, No. 1323, p. 6, July 1911.

by first giving them some unimportant measures for discussion and gradually converting them to its own way as it had mandarinized successful candidates of the old regime by first giving them appointments with little work attached to them.

Nearly all these time-killing measures came from the government, for the government had a free hand to initiate bills, though it required thirty members of the Council to initiate a measure.[10] After a bill had been passed in the Council, it had to be sent to the cabinet which could either memorialize the throne on the bill or send it back to the Council for reconsideration. If conflict arose between the Council and the cabinet, the cabinet and the president of the Council could both memorialize the throne, and the emperor was to settle the dispute by giving an arbitrary and yet final decision. Cabinet members could be present in the sessions and had the right of speech though not of voting; on the other hand, members of cabinet were under the obligation of answering the questions of, and supplying informations to, members of the Council. But the cabinet was by no means responsible to the Council. In answering a request of the Council to make the cabinet responsible to it, the emperor (under the influence of the Regent) issued the following edict:—[11]

> The President of the Advisory Council petitioned that owing to lack of responsibility of the ministers to the Council, it is difficult for the Council to assist them. We know fully what this petition aims at. But the power of organizing service, determining scales of compensation, appointment and dismissal belongs to the government. This is expressly provided in the Constitution promulgated by the late Emperor Kuang Hsu. Whether the Councilors of State and the cabinet shall be responsible to the Advisory Council or not, the government will decide. The President of the Advisory Council has no right to interfere with this . . . . .

As long as the government could decide whether it was to be responsible to the Advisory Council, it would never be

---

[10] Article VII, Section 35.
[11] Official Gazette, No. 1130, p. 2, Dec. 19, 1910.

responsible; for no government wants to subject itself to the legislature unless it cannot help it; and the Manchus knew full well that it was much easier to control ten ministers of the cabinet than two hundred members of the Council.

Finally, this impotent body was denied many of the ordinary rights of a legislature. It did not have the right to petition the emperor. The president and the vice-president of the Council had it, but the government could reject or ignore their petitions. The immunity from arrest and the freedom of speech, universal rights of members of legislative bodies, were not fully possessed by this body. The president of the Council had the power to order any of the members to retire from the session or deprive him of the right of speech on account of misbehavior. The president, being an appointee of the government, could easily abuse this stipulation and make it an effective weapon against the opposition. Then, too, the administrative law of avoidance was applied to this Council: if the bill in discussion related to the members, members of his family, or his office, he had to retire.[12]

Such a legislative body was a farce. Soon after it was convened, dissatisfactions rose and petitions for convening of a real parliament began pouring in. As to these, the government took an unyielding attitude expressed in an edict of Dec. 26, 1910 which read:—[13]

When Shih Liang, Viceroy of Manchuria, submitted a memorial for the gentry and citizens of the Province of Fengtien, petitioning the convention of the National Assembly in the following year, we had then issued an edict to curtail the period of preparation. The date for the convening of the National Assembly was deliberated on in the court Conference, decided, and announced with a decree, therefore, should no longer be a subject of petition. But, Chen Kuei Lung, Viceroy of Chihli, memorialized us by telegram, on behalf of the Provincial Assembly of Chihli and the Metropolitan Prefecture, with a request of the early convening of the National Assem-

[12] Article 7, Section 38.
[13] Official Gazette, No. 1136, p. 2.

bly, we ordered him, by telegram, to sincerely and earnestly explain to the representatives the situation of the government, and to forbid further joint petitions on this subject; if persuasion and instructions fail, and the decree were disobeyed by the masses, he was authorized to conduct an investigation, arrest the ringleaders and punish them severely. Now that the Councilors of State petition us again: this is not right either.

The date for the convention of the National Assembly is submitted to us by the ministers of state after their deliberation. It is decided on by us. When we announced it, we expressly stated that after the announcement no discussion for a change would be tolerated; for the shortening of this period had already put us in difficulty in view of the little time we had and the many steps we had to take. Most of the viceroys and governors of the provinces know it too. Yet the senseless fools, ignorant of the attitude of the government, still make demands on us without restraint. They usually gather together their crowds and intimidate our officials. Now, they petition us again in the name of the Three Eastern Provinces. These repeated annoyances are outrageous. The Ministry of Civil Affairs and the Infantry Gendarmerie are hereby ordered to send these people back to their respective provinces at once. We have time and again pardoned our senseless stupid people who, impressed with the present difficulties, petition us in wrong manners or on wrong subjects. Is it possible that the citizens do not want to abide by our law? We deeply fear that unscrupulous men (meaning the revolutionists) may, on pretense of the lateness of the date, secretly work against the peace and order of the country. It will brew troubles if not suppressed early enough.

Hereafter, the Ministry of Civil Affairs and the Infantry Gendarmerie shall be responsible for the presence of such troublemakers in Peking. In the provinces, if they gather for the forbidden activities, they will no longer be considered good subjects; the viceroy and governor shall make arrests according to the edict of the 3rd, day of the 10th month without leniency so that the people will be pacified and the hidden troubles be prevented from their outbreak.

This edict assures us of one thing, that the government did not want to have any unscheduled change although the scheduled changes were not realized as planned.

With all these changes in appearance the operation of the government remained unaltered. While the competitive literary examinations for provincial and metropolitan graduates were abolished, competitive examinations for senior licentiates (Yiu Kung and Pi Kung) took place as late as 1910. While the organization of almost the entire government was changed, the worst method of assigning work and offices or provinces for the new expectant officials, the casting of lots, still determined the fate of the applicant. Amidst the clamours of judicial reforms, and codification of new laws, the imperial clansmen and alternatives, simply on account of their blood relationship to the emperor, had a special code, one very different from the ordinary, for their exclusive application: the idea of equality before the law, a fundamental idea of constitutionalism, was totally disregarded. No wonder that, as a result of the dissatisfaction on the part of the people of the government's execution of the reform program at the end of the fourth year of preparation, a revolution broke out and wiped out the government itself.

Shortly before this outburst, the program of preparation for constitutional government was shortened and 1913 was chosen as the year for the convening of a National Assembly. No doubt this came about as a result of the government's fear of the activities of the revolutionists which threatened to take the life of the dynasty. As a forerunner of the convention of the National Assembly, the old ministry was made a cabinet. A number of the old offices like the Grand Secretariat, the Council of State, the Committee of Ministers, the Committee for Drawing up Regulations for Constitutional Government, the Auditing Bureau, etc., were abolished in spite of the fact that some of them came into existence as parts of the program of constitutionalism. With the exception of the abolition of the Ministry of Rites and the addition of the Ministry of Navy, the new cabinet was exactly the same as the old ministry organized in 1906.

At the head of the cabinet was a premier and two assistant premiers. The ministers were:—

The Ministry	The Minister	Race
1. Premier	Prince Ching	Manchu (Imperial clansmen)
2. Premier (Assist.)	Na Tung	Manchu
3. Premier (Assist.)	Hsu Shih Chang	Chinese
4. Foreign Affairs (Supervising)	Prince Ching	Manchu (Imperial clansmen)
5. Foreign Affairs	Liang Tun Yen	Chinese
6. Civil Affairs	Shan Chi	Manchu
7. Finance	Duke Tsai Cha	Manchu (Imperial clansmen)
8. War	Yin Chang	Manchu
9. Education	Tang Ching Chung	Chinese
10. Justice	Shao Chang	Manchu
11. Navy	Prince Tsai Shun	Manchu (Imperial clansmen)
12. Agriculture, Industry and Commerce	Prince Pu Lun	Manchu (Imperial clansmen)
13. Territories	Shao Chi	Manchu
14. Communications	Shang Hsuan Huai	Chinese

The appointment of a prince of blood as premier, one Manchu and one Chinese as assistant premiers fairly represented the policy of the government. In the ten ministers, we find the ministerships almost equally divided between the three classes of officials, namely, the imperial clansmen, the Manchus and the Chinese. In the face of a renunciation of the old racial difference and amidst preparations for ways and means to eradicate it, the old racial difference was not only maintained, but intensified. The division changed from a bi-racial into a tri-class-racial division with the imperial clansmen, the new members of the trio getting the biggest share. Not only was there a numerical division of positions, but qualitatively, all positions were carefully weighed before the division of the spoil took place. Two considerations at least entered when the appointments were made: (1) the relative importance of the position in the government; (2) the profits that the position could yield to the minister. All the three positions that the Manchus thought to be very important, the ministerships of finance, navy and war, were held by Manchus with two of them in the hands of the princes. The Ministry of Foreign Affairs certainly belonged to this important group; but the ignorance of the Manchus did not allow the appointment of one of them in spite of the tradition of having a Manchu to head the foreign office; so a Chinese was appointed with Prince Ching as "Controlling" or "Supervising" minister. Speaking from the standpoint of the officials' private gain and chances for illegal earnings, each group had two "fat jobs" [14] and a "lean one." [15]

No new designation or organization could change the actual relationship between the emperor and his assistants. The new cabinet, exactly the same as the old ministry of 1906 and the old administrative sextet of the nineteenth century, was individually and collectively responsible to the "Son of Heaven," appointed by him and removable at his pleasure, exercising merely what powers he liked to delegate to them at whatever time he thought fit. The emperor still possessed and exercised all executive powers. Because the ministry was not responsible to parliament, impeachment was the utmost that parliament could do.

It took simple minded persons to expect such immaterial changes to satisfy the desire of the people and the active revolutionists. To the people these were acts of disappointment, proving the Manchus' inability and unwillingness to reform and urging them to take the matter into their own hands. So, following the outbreak at Wu Chang, province after province turned against the reigning house and an empire of two hundred and sixty-six years fell three months after the day of the uprising.

During the Revolution, a final struggle for existence took place in the dismissal of the imperial clansmen from the

[14] The Imperial clansmen had the Ministries of Finance and Navy; the Manchus had the Ministries of Civil Affairs and War; the Chinese had the Ministries of Foreign Affairs and Communications.

[15] The Imperial clansmen had the Ministry of Agriculture, Industry and Commerce; the Manchu had that of Justice and the Chinese had that of Education.

government, the organization of a Chinese cabinet, the promulgation of the Nineteen Articles, and the promise of an immediate convention of the National Assembly.

These Nineteen Articles [16] embodied the fundamental principles of constitutional monarchism. A comparison between these articles and the proposed constitution of 1908 furnishes a counterpart to a comparison between the English and the Japanese constitutions, the most and the least democratic of constitutional documents.

Contrary to the proposed constitution of 1908, most clauses of which affirm and assure the powers of the emperor and limit the powers of the legislature, seventeen of these new Nineteen Articles expressly give governing powers to the legislature, making it almost as powerful as the British House of Commons. It was too good to be true. The insincerity of the government in its early reforms and its purposed delay of the program made the people very skeptical as to the government's willingness to enforce these articles if the revolutionists should lay down their arms. So, the Manchus' last appeal went for naught.

Yuan Shih Kai, the new premier, went to Peking and a new situation developed. He began at once to fortify his own position by getting the control of the government. He first cut off the communications between the Regent, the Empress Dowager, and other officials. This he accomplished by stopping the audiences of the Regent to the officials except the premier and ministers of state. Then he directed all petitions and memoranda requiring the attention of the Regent, to be sent to the cabinet. He placed the Ministry of Interior above the Imperial Household. This ministry conducted all domestic business between the palace precincts and the outside world. The Minister of Interior transferred to the throne all memoranda regarding the Household and discussed with the Regent all matters concerning it; but he was forbidden to discuss politics. He

[16] For texts of the Articles, see Appendix II.

abolished the Office of Transmission (Tsou Shih Chu) and directed all petitions to be sent to the Cabinet Office.

Secondly he appointed many of his own men to military commands. The Official Gazette shows that from the first month of the year to the appointment of Yuan Shih Kai, during a period of nine months, the Prince Regent made only sixty-two appointments and transfers of military officers of the rank of, or higher than, a brigadier-general with the highest number ten, the lowest two and the average a little more than seven, appointments per month. When Yuan came in, he made twenty-five appointments in the tenth, thirteen in the eleventh, and thirteen in the twelfth, month. Thus, in a period of three months, he made almost as many appointments as the Prince Regent had made in nine months.

Thirdly, with the dismissal of the Prince Regent, Yuan adopted a policy of settling the disputes between the revolutionists and the Peking government peacefully while he clearly saw that without the abdication of the Manchu Emperor, no peace settlement could be affected. Tang Shao Yi, Yuan's delegate to the peace conference in Shanghai, said in a telegram sent to Yuan, ". . . . . The Revolutionary Army aims at the establishment of a republican form of government; if we do not yield this point, further conference cannot be held . . . . . When I left Peking, your order was for peaceful settlement . . . . ." With these Yuan's well planned schemes working at top speed, the Manchu Government had soon to issue the edict of abdication, and made the treaty of peace which ended its own life.

Looking back at the Manchu program and work of reform, one cannot help concluding that the Manchu Government spent its last ten years in cheating the people with talk, documents, and regulations of reform, none of which resulted in any practical good to the people except possibly the system of schools established after the abolition of the examinations. Even in the best phases of its reforms, the results left much to be desired; for, throughout that dynasty, textbooks in primary and high schools were censored by the government. It was only due to the inefficiency of the government that the original plan of having the government publish and distribute all elementary textbooks was not carried out. Then, too, the theory and practice of the monopoly of literary and academic degrees by the government survived the competitive examinations. In each graduation, a petition for the conferment of degrees on the graduates by the emperor was made. Finally, the disposition of the government and also of the majority of the people still looked at education merely as a stepping stone towards officialdom. In some cases people identified graduation from school as appointment to office as under the old regime.

APPENDIX I.

THE PROPOSED CONSTITUTION OF THE TSING DYNASTY CONTAINED IN THE JOINT MEMORIAL SUBMITTED BY PRINCES CHING AND PU LUN ON AUGUST 27, 1908, AND PROMULGATED BY IMPERIAL EDICT ON THE SAME DAY. For original, see *Tung Hua Lu*, Kuang Hsu, v. 219, p. 3.

1. The Emperor of the Ta Tsing Dynasty shall reign and govern the Ta Tsing Empire with His Majesty's unbroken line of succession for ages eternal.

2. The Emperor shall be sacred and inviolable.

3. The Emperor promulgates all laws and may propose laws in Parliament.

> No law which has passed the Parliament shall have effect until promulgated by Imperial Decree.

4. The Emperor convokes Parliament, opens, closes, prologues and dissolves it.

> After dissolution of Parliament, a new election may be ordered. Members of the dissolved Parliament become equals of citizens. Any attempt of the members of the Parliament who obstructs dissolution, shall be punishable by due provisions of law.

5. The Emperor determines the organization of the different branches of the administration, and the salaries of the civil and military officers, and appoints and dismisses the same.

> All powers of appointment and dismissal shall be exercised by the Emperor with the advice and assistance of the ministers: Parliament shall not interfere.

6. The Emperor has the supreme command of the army and navy, and determines the organization of the same.

> The Emperor has the full power to determine the size of the standing army and mobilizes all troops of the country: Parliament shall not interfere with anything relating to the army and navy.

7. The Emperor declares war, makes peace, concludes treaties, appoints and receives diplomatic agents.

> All diplomatic dealings shall be personally handled by the Emperor: they shall not be given to Parliament for decision.

8. The Emperor proclaims a state of siege.

> During periods of emergency, the rights of citizens may be restricted by Imperial Decree.

9. The Emperor confers titles of nobility, grants pardon, commutation of punishment and rehabilitation.

Favors come from the Emperor; the powers of granting favors shall not be shared by Parliament.

10. The judicial powers shall be exercised by the courts of law in the name of the Emperor according to laws promulgated by the Emperor; but no ordinances shall in any way alter the existing laws.

The judicial power belongs to the Emperor. Judges are appointed by the Emperor. In order to avoid confusion, only laws formally promulgated by Imperial Decrees shall apply.

11. The Emperor issues, or causes to be issued, ordinances. But no duly enacted and promulgated laws shall be amended or repealed without the advice of the Parliament and the approval of the Emperor.

12. The Emperor, in consequence of urgent necessity, issues, when Parliament is not sitting, imperial ordinances in the place of laws, and raises necessary funds by ordinances.

Such imperial ordinances are to be laid before Parliament in the next session.

13. The Emperor determines the expenses of the Imperial Household, appropriates and determines sums directly from the National Treasury: Parliament shall not question the sums.

14. Important ceremonials of the Imperial Household shall be performed by the Emperor and imperial clansmen; ministers may be appointed to assist in, and advise on, the ceremonials, but Parliament shall not interfere with them.

Rights and Duties of Subjects

15. Chinese subjects may, according to qualifications determined by law or ordinances, be appointed to civil and military offices, or be elected members of Parliament.

16. Chinese subjects shall, within the limits of law, enjoy the liberty of speech, writing, publication, public meeting and association.

17. No Chinese subject shall be arrested, detained, tried, or punished unless according to law.

18. No Chinese subject shall be deprived of the right of being tried by judges according to law.

19. Chinese subjects shall be tried only by courts of law provided by law.

20. Except in cases provided by law, the property and houses of Chinese subjects shall be inviolable.

21. Chinese subjects are amenable to duties of paying taxes and to serve in the army and navy according to provisions of law.

22. Chinese subjects shall continue to pay taxes according to the prevailing rates until changed by law.

23. Chinese subjects are amenable to the duty of obeying the laws.

The Parliament

24. The Parliament has only legislative, not executive, power: all laws enacted by Parliament must await imperial approval before going into effect.

25. Expenditures determined by the Emperor or provided by law shall not be curtailed or cut by acts of Parliament unless with the advice and consent of the Cabinet.

26. The annual budget shall be made with the advice and assistance of Parliament.

27. The Parliament may impeach the ministers when they violate laws; but the final power of removal shall be exercised by the Government.

28. A law must have passed both Houses before being submitted to the Emperor for promulgation.

29. Members of Parliament have no right to petition the Emperor. Petitions from either House of Parliament shall be sent by, and in the name of, the President or the Speaker.

30. Members of Parliament shall not use irrespectful language in reference to the Court, or indecent language in reference to subjects: violator of this law shall be punished according to the severity of the offense.

31. During the session, the Presiding Officer commands the police and keeps the order of the floor: members violating laws of the House shall be deprived of the right of speech or requested to retire.

32. Members not properly qualified shall at once be dismissed from Parliament by the President or Speaker when sufficient proof of disqualification is found.

33. Organizations for the study of parliamentary procedures established by scholars and gentry in the provinces shall be organized exactly in accordance with laws provided for public meetings and associations. Local administrative officials have power to dissolve such organizations in case these organizations are found detrimental to the peace and order of the locality.

Election Laws

34. The prefects and magistrates shall supervise all elections.
35. The following are disfranchised:—
    (a) Men of bad conduct and demagogues.
    (b) Those who have been punished by imprisonment or heavier penalties.
    (c) Men of illegitimate professions.

(d) Bankrupts.
(e) Opium smokers.
(f) Lunatics.
(g) Members of disreputable families.
(h) Illiterates.

36. During elections, controllers and superintendents shall be appointed to oversee the delivery and the opening of the ballots.

37. Violators of election laws shall be punished by laws specially provided.

38. Elections shall be conducted by ballots. Qualified candidates receiving the plurality votes shall be declared elected.

39. Qualified voters, in order to exercise the right of voting, must reside in their native place at least one year preceding the election.

Appendix II.

THE NINETEEN ARTICLES OF CONSTITUTION PROMULGATED BY THE EMPEROR BEFORE HIS ANCESTRAL TEMPLES, NOV. 4, 1911.

1. The Ta Tsing Empire shall be reigned over and governed by a line of Emperors unbroken for ages eternal.

2. The Emperor is sacred and inviolable.

3. The power of the Emperor shall be what is given him by the Constitution.

4. Succession to the Imperial Throne shall be in accordance with Constitutional provisions.

5. The Constitution shall be drafted by the Advisory Council and promulgated by the Emperor.

6. The power of amending the Constitution belongs to the National Assembly.

7. Members of the Upper House of Parliament shall be elected by popular votes from qualified candidates.

8. The Premier shall be elected by the National Assembly and appointed by the Emperor; other members of the Cabinet shall be nominated by the Premier and appointed by the Emperor.

> No member of the imperial clan shall be appointed Premier, minister of state or principal executive officers of the provinces.

9. If the Premier is impeached by the National Assembly, either the Premier resigns or the National Assembly is dissolved: but one and the same Premier shall not dissolve the National Assembly twice successively on the same issue.

10. The Emperor commands the army and navy. But he shall not use either the army or the navy to settle internal issues without the sanction of the National Assembly.

11. No ordinances issued by the Emperor shall take the place of law: except in cases of emergency which are specially defined, all ordinances shall be issued strictly within legal requirements.

12. No treaty shall be concluded without the approval of the National Assembly. In case peace is made or war declared when the National Assembly is not sitting, the act shall be laid before the National Assembly for approval in the next session.

13. The organization of the administration and administrative laws shall be determined by law.

14. Items of expenditure in the budget of the preceding year shall have no force as a precedent, therefore, shall not be the basis of items in the estimates of the current year if the National Assembly does not approve of such items. Fix items of expenditure shall not be included in the estimates. The Government shall not make extra-budgetary appropriations.

15. The amount of expenditure of the Imperial Household, its increase or decrease, shall be determined by the National Assembly.

16. No ceremonials of the Imperial Household shall be contradictory to the provisions of the Constitution.

17. The Executive and Judicial organizations shall be organized by the Legislature.

18. The Emperor shall promulgate all laws and sign all bills passed by the National Assembly.

19. Articles 8, 9, 12, 13, 14, 15, and 18 shall be applicable to the Advisory Council before the convention of the National Assembly.

CHAPTER XIV

POLICIES OF THE GOVERNMENT: CONCLUSION

By sheer force of arms the Manchus invaded and conquered China; at the point of the bayonet, the vanquished Chinese unwillingly submitted to the newly founded dynasty. Void of ancient and advanced civilization,[1] totally ignorant of the art of politics and the Chinese political institutions, the Manchus, after their hard-fought conquest, found themselves confronted with the task of ruling over a civilized people with 21,068,609 adult males,[2] who might at any moment turn against their new conquerors and drive out the invaders. It was indeed a difficult task, so much more so when force, their instrument of conquest, could not be applied to the delicate art of government. With the early emperors' unqualified admiration of the Chinese civilization, their diligence in quest of its secret, their untiring efforts towards the processes of assimilation, and the help of the Chinese ministers, they soon learned the secret and were converted into Chinese emperors in thought and action as well as in name.

But, unfortunately, the political institutions of China were then at their lowest ebb: the institution of emperor was more corrupted than ever before. Huang Li Chou, one

---

[1] It can be safely said that the Manchus had little or no civilization when they conquered China. The *Tsing Chien I Chi Lu* records that there was no written Manchu language until 1623, Emperor Tai Tsu, grandfather of Shun Chi ordered to have the Mongol system of writing adopted to the Manchu dialect and made a written Manchu language.

[2] The first complete census of the Manchu Dynasty was taken in 1661. These records show that there were 21,068,609 adult males. By adult is meant a male subject between 16 and 60. See *Huang Chao Wen Hsien Tung Kao*, v. 19.

of the three greatest scholars at the beginning of the Tsing Dynasty, in his *Essay on the Emperor* well observed:—

..... Kings of later dynasties thought that all powers belonged to them; they took all the profits and left all the injuries, making all the people to be afraid of any private gain. Cloaking their great selfishness under the veil of working for the salvation of the empire, they took the throne for the greatest personal gain, to be bequeathed to their descendents for an unbroken line of succession for ages eternal . . . . . Nowadays, the king is the master and the empire his slave. It is the king that causes all turmoils and disturbances. When he has not secured the throne, he speculates on securing it at the expenses of poisoning the brains of the nation without realizing the tragic fact that he is merely enslaving himself to acquire property for his descendents. When he has secured it, he satisfies his vulgar instincts by sucking the people's blood and proudly says to the world, "This is the dividend of my investment."

..... Supposing one can inherit this property to an unbroken line of perpetual succession, small wonder there is to see every one struggling towards that goal for oneself. But if the throne be treated as personal property, who would not like to have it? How, then, can one fight against the whole country in the throne struggle, if everyone has the desire?[3]

In his *Essay on Law*, he continued:—

..... Therefore, laws of later dynasties are devised to keep the throne. Its occupant wants to keep all the profit for himself and leave nothing to others. When he appoints a man, he suspects the selfishness of the appointee; so he appoints another man to spy on him. When he does one thing, he fears deception; so he does another thing to counteract it. Everyone knows what is in the pocket and where the pocket is; its owner worries over its loss, so he built a set of laws as a fence around the pocket: out of the fence, disturbances come . . . . .[4]

The Manchus went into China at the moment when the old theory "the throne for the virtuous," had become a mere shiboleth of scholars: it had entirely lost its influence in the government. It was the moment when the ancient revolutions which Confucius hailed as the deliverance of the people almost came to be denounced as rebellions. It was

[3] *Ming I Tai Fang Lu*, p. 2.
[4] *Ibid*, p. 6.

the end of the Ming Dynasty when Mencius almost lost his seat in the Confucian Temple because his theory was not favorable to the monarch. Most of the desirable qualities and elements of the old theory and institutions had died out. A new form of monarchism, built on the patriarchism and the sovereign's great power advocated by Confucius without its accompanying virtues, had taken the place of the old system. On the part of the emperors, the idea of gain had been substituted for the idea of service: the throne had become a coveted prize as a reward to those who could "poison" the people's brain and "suck" their blood.

Under those circumstances and with the desire of upholding the throne to the highest degree, the Manchus adopted a policy, or rather cherished a desire, of keeping the throne as long as possible by monopolizing as much power as they could. This policy shows, too, that as soon as they sat on the throne, they followed implicitly the beaten path of the emperors of the preceding dynasties. But they had a long history from which to reflect their own position and consequently their devices were more wicked. They studied Chinese history very thoroughly and provided themselves at almost every turn with preventives against the fall of their dynasty.

Liang Chi Chao[5] points out ten reasons in addition to rebellions and foreign invasions, for the fall of a dynasty: (1) dictatorship of imperial clansmen, (2) usurpation of power by the empress, (3) struggle for throne between the older and younger sons of the emperor, (4) struggle for throne between factions of different princes for succession at the extinction of the direct male line, (5) usurpation of imperial power by imperial clansmen who have been made lords of some territories, (6) dethronement or regicide by a powerful minister, (7) disobedience of military commanders, (8) usurpation of imperial powers by matrimonial and maternal relatives, (9) dictatorship of disloyal ministers, (10) usurpations of imperial powers by eunuchs and court stew-

[5] *Yin Ping Shih Tsi Yiu Shu*, p. 2.

ards. While learning to be emperors, the Manchus thoroughly studied these causes and carefully prepared themselves against their occurrence.

Taking these causes one by one, we find that, to avoid the first cause, the Manchus had a policy of keeping the imperial clansmen disarmed. The house-law forbade imperial clansmen to interfere with politics which, of course, meant that the powers of the emperor were not shared by them. Except late in the dynasty, they were not appointed to important administrative positions. Emperor Yung Cheng removed the command of the "Five Inferior Banners" from the princes and placed it in the hands of his own appointees, thus entirely separating them from Manchu military commanders and stripping them of their military powers. Later edicts were issued to forbid the princes to have intercourse with important ministers in Peking or high officials in the provinces; hence, to secure help from civil officials became impossible to the princes. Financially the dynasty adopted a policy of keeping them impotent by giving only low pensions, allowances and grants. So, after the struggle of Emperor Yung Cheng with his brothers, the victory of the emperor in the struggle, and the removal of their sources of aid,[6] the Tsing Dynasty had no trouble in handling the imperial clansmen.

For the second cause, the house-law of the Manchu Dynasty provided unwritten but firm clauses against petticoat government. Empress Dowager Tsu Hsi with her senior partner, Empress Dowager Tsu An, was the first and last woman who ever wielded the imperial power. The abolition of the institution of a crown prince practically removed the danger of a struggle for the throne between the sons of the emperor. By removing the command of the "Lower Five Banners" from the princes and alienating them from civil officials in the provinces and the metropolis, the fourth cause, struggle between factions of princes for the throne at

[6] Except only one incident, that of Su Shun during the "hunting trip" of Empress Dowager Tsu Hsi and Emperor Kuang Hsu.

the extinction of the direct male line, could not take shape
in open wars. The fact that the first seven emperors had
direct male descendents entirely removed this cause for the
first two hundred and twenty years. But when Emperors
Tung Chi and Kuang Hsu died childless, this struggle did
not take the shape of even an under-current strong enough
to hinder the smooth sailing of the ship of state. The fifth
cause could not form a source of trouble as the Tsing Government always kept the imperial clansmen in Peking. No
other dynasty had fewer powerful ministers, and treated
the powerful ministers worse, than the Tsing Dynasty. The
sixth cause, dethronement or a regicide by a powerful minister did not worry the Manchus. One opportunity for the
dethronement of the Manchu emperor was shattered by the
bad influence of the Taiping Rebellion. The check and
balance of the military commanders,[7] made them too impotent to test the authority of the central government. The
seventh cause gave them no danger.

As the matrimonial and maternal relatives of the emperor
were rendered more impotent than the imperial clansmen,
they could scarcely become favored enough to produce any
influence on the emperor, not to say powerful enough to
shake the foundations of the dynasty. Here again, the
policy of the government was to give the imperial relative
pensions and keep them out of politics. The ninth cause,
dictatorship of disloyal ministers, was removed by the same
laws and methods as the sixth. When the ministers were
powerless, their disloyalty could not harm the government.
As to eunuchs, the Manchu rulers, except Empress Dowager
Tsu Hsi, treated them as mere domestics. They had absolutely no chance to influence politics.

Thus far, it seems that the Manchu dynasty had removed
all causes of a fall and their fantastic hope and cherished
desire of having the throne of China held by descendents of
Nurachi in an unbroken line of succession for ages eternal
seems realizable. But, outside of the preventive measures

[7] See Chapters X and XI.

already mentioned, a complicated set of laws was promulgated and a great deal of statecraft employed as a premium paid to insure the life of the dynasty.

One of the devices was censorship of the press. This went on in three directions. The burning of books, an act of tyranny for which the Chinese never forgive the first emperor of the Chin Dynasty (Chi Huang Ti), strangely enough, was the act of the Manchus, admirers of Chinese civilization. The *Complete History of the Tsing Dynasty* (Tsing Chao Chuan Shih) gives a very brief and yet accurate account of Emperor Chien Lung's activity with regard to the censorship of press:—

About the same time when the imperial catalogue for the Four Libraries was completed, an edict tabooing the circulation of some books should not escape our notice. The forbidden books were historical accounts of the early Manchu emperors written by scholars living down from the Ming Dynasty. The edict says that this kind of publication is dangerous to the policy of unification, therefore, should not be allowed to circulate. But the fact is that the weak and literary Southerners, after being subdued by the Manchus by physical force, employed writing as the effective political weapon against the Manchus. A great many books of this kind were written. Emperor Chien Lung, then, not only wished to suppress this kind of publications but also to destroy all dynastic histories. What an unjust act! The time-limit for destroying all these works was from 1774 to 1778. Two years' extension for their completion was given in 1778 and another year of grace was granted in 1781. The Department of War reported that twenty-four burnings took place: 538 publications and 13,862 volumes were destroyed.

This was not all. An edict urging destruction of the tabooed books was again issued in 1788, "to be strictly obeyed." Generally speaking, the prohibition was much more effective in the North than in the South . . . . . The reason is that some governors in the Southern provinces took up this work rather half-heartedly. *The Works of Chien Yi Hsien*, which was afterwards preserved in Japan, was also burned at this time.*

Comparing this act with the act of the First Emperor, the difference is only one of degree. Every Chinese dynasty, after the completion of the dynastic history of the preced-

* *Tsing Chao Chuan Shih*, vol. 2, part 1, p. 12.

ing dynasty, burned all records in the archives; but none except the Chin and the Tsing ever deliberately burned any book outside of the source material of the dynastic history. But this was only a very small part of the Manchu activities in the censorship of the press. Imitating the First Emperor in the burying of the scholars alive, the Tsing Emperors executed quite a few of the writers. Wang Yung Pao and Shih Kuo Ying give a pathetic account of a case connected with the censorship:—[10]

> The Emperor (Kang Hsi) respected literary genius and treated the scholars well, but his cruel massacres of the literati far exceeded those of other Manchu emperors and formed unique cases in history . . . . . Take the case of Chuang Ting Lung for instance. Chuang secured the original manuscripts of the family history of the Ming Emperors from a member of the Chu Family. He asked famous scholars of the South to edit it and published it as Court Annals and Memoires of Emperor Chung Tseng. It was sold in the market. For sometime, everything went on smoothly.
>
> Unfortunately, Wu Chi Yung, dismissed magistrate of the Kuei An District, was scheming for reappointment. He accused the editors of treasonable writing. One of the vice-ministers of law was appointed to handle this case. He persecuted the whole Chuang clan, all the editors, many purchasers of the book and many female members in the families of the readers of this book.
>
> The case of Tai Ming Shih is another. Tai wrote the *Nan Shan Chi* quoting some statements from a book called *Tien Chien Chi Wen Chung Yu* by Fang Shiao Piao. Censor Chao Hsin Chao impeached Tai of treason. The Nine Ministers were ordered to try the case. The author, all members of his clan, and more than seventy others were executed.

Other cases of literary persecution and press censorship abounded throughout the dynastic history of the Manchus. Chin Sheng Tan was executed because his criticisms and comments on the novels were found stimulating enough to contradict the government policy of moulding the thoughts of the people and therefore, dangerous to peace and order. Cha Shu Ting and Wang Ching Chi lost their lives because they criticized Emperor Kang Hsi in their diaries: the

---

[10] *Tsing Shih Chang I*, vol. 2, p. 31.

Province of Chekiang could not have provincial examinations for three years because Cha happened to have been born in that province. "Lu Sheng Nan lost his head on account of his authorship of seventeen essays on history. The *Essay on Feudalism* decided his fate. In this he upheld feudalism and attacked centralization. The underlying cause, however, was the struggle of the princes for feudal states while the emperor (Yung Cheng) was spending every bit of his energy in centralizing the government. His other essays on Appointment of the Heir Apparent, on Military System, on the Limitation of the Emperor's Power, all incurred the wrath of the emperor . . . . ."[11] To illustrate the injustice of the literary persecution, let us examine a few lines of the *Essay on Feudalism,* the one thing that cost the life of its author. Part of the essay reads:—

. . . . . The ruler is a public servant. The state is public property, not property of the ruler. The people are the sovereign, the ruler their creature. This is the truth of the situation. This is the original, uncorrupted political conception of the Chinese . . . . .

Such utterances are, in a way, a repetition or interpretation of parts of the Confucian philosophy. They express the general conception on government, people and ruler of the real Confucian scholars. Thousands of Chinese scholars had expressed, though in different language, the same thought thousands of times before this unfortunate scholar put it in his essay. Even imperial edicts sometimes contained words expressing the same train of thought. There was, outside of the struggle of the princes for the throne, the emperor's desire to keep the throne for himself and his wish to show his power as an emperor, absolutely no reason to execute a scholar for the crime of treason just because of such writing. Indeed, in no other country can one find a stricter censorship of the press, and heavier punishments for the violation of the censorship laws.

The censorship policy continued down to the very last days of the Manchu supremacy. So, even after the dawn of

[11] *Tsing Chao Chuan Shih,* vol. 1, part 4, p. 22 ff.

the twentieth century, the persecution of authors, suppression of publications, and issuance of orders to close newspaper offices were almost a regular part of the official duties. When the Advisory Council (Tsu Cheng Yuan) a forerunner of the National Assembly, was convened, one of the first subjects given to the Council for deliberation was a set of newspaper censorship laws. From the amount of attention they devoted to censorship and the pitiless methods with which they treated the accused, the thought of the people would have been moulded as was that of the German people by the Prussian Government were it not for the inefficiency of the government and the half-heartedness of some of the Chinese officials in the execution of these laws.

Yet, in censorship, the Manchu Government was responsible for more than prohibitive laws and ruthless suppressions and persecutions. While they executed those they did not like, they, at the same time, employed those they liked, to edit standard books for the people. More than two hundred large, important works were edited or written by scholars employed by the government in the name of the emperor. In the annotation of classics, they took the most conservative views. In the writing of histories, they concealed, changed, and put in facts to make them look agreeable. It can hardly be doubted that the government reaped more profit from the official publications which taught the people what their government wanted them to know than from the prohibition of private publications which it succeeded only partially in keeping from the people. The loss of true historical facts was, of course, the worst thing resulting from the government's action.

Certainly the dynastic histories served as an effective means of censorship. They were written principally from materials found in the *Court Records* (Shih Lu) which were always censored before being printed. Also the historians were always appointed by the government. After completion of the histories, the emperor or some of his confidential delegates would run over the text; rarely did the histories

POLICIES OF THE GOVERNMENT: CONCLUSION 385

go into print without addition or deletions by the vermilion pencil. All the archives were then destroyed so that there would be no way to check up the truth of the censored version. That is why proportionally, very little outside of the court affairs and the emperor is contained in the official histories. That is why Emperor Tai Chung of the Manchus said, "It seems to me that in the Chinese histories, too much flowery language has been employed. We cannot be benefited even by reading through all of them . . . . ." That is also why Chang Tai Yen said, in a letter to a friend, "The imperially edited books represent the worst form of editing." Finding that censorship could do more to help them keep their throne than the burning of books and the burying alive of scholars could help the Chin Dynasty to inherit the newly centralized empire to the ten thousandth emperor, they devised means other than censorship to keep China subdued.

Next to censorship was the principle of appointing both Manchus and Chinese to the same province or service. It is evident that, in the offices in Peking, a certain number of offices were assigned to each race. In the provincial governments where no definite division of positions took place on a racial basis, the government exercised careful judgment to make whenever possible the number of appointees from each race equal. The same principle was applied to new organizations established near the end of the dynasty when the talk of abolishing racial distinction spread throughout the length and breadth of the empire. The government had confidence in the Manchu and yet depended on the Chinese for real work. By putting both in the same office and locality, a system of mutual spying could be expected. This mutual spying was one of the most effective methods of the check and balance system.

Unlike the central offices, the provincial offices were not assigned on a racial basis, but, as we have seen in Chapter XI, great care was exercised in the appointment of high officials to put officials of both races in the same province and to carry out the unwritten law concerning the division of the offices. In the central government, even appointments to positions of clerks were made on a racial basis. The *Ta Tsing Hui Tien* [12] gives very fair examples. It says, "In the Department of Civil Service, there shall be two ministers, one Manchu and one Chinese; two senior vice-ministers, one Manchu and one Chinese two junior vice-ministers, one Manchu and one Chinese." "In the archive, there shall be two Manchu junior secretaries . . . . . In the Documents Division (in Chinese language) there shall be three junior secretaries, two Manchus and one Chinese bannerman, and twelve clerks." [13] Again, "In the Bureau of Appointments, there shall be seven bureau chiefs, four Manchus, one Mongol and two Chinese; six senior secretaries, three Manchus and three Chinese; and five junior secretaries, two Manchus and three Chinese."

Roughly speaking, the proportion between Chinese and Manchus in the central government was about one to two in favor of the Manchus. As it has been said, the Manchus employed Chinese simply because they could not get along smoothly without them. The day the Prince Regent Jui entered Peking, he issued an edict ordering all officials in the service of the Ming government to remain, thus laying a foundation for the division of positions. But soon after the newly founded dynasty got on its own feet it gradually changed its policy. Before Emperor Shun Chi's death, he issued an edict containing these words:—[14]

> The Ming Dynasty fell on account of the one-sided employment of civilians in government service. I did not profit by their experience as I appointed too many Chinese to important offices in the different departments. This disheartened the Manchus. It was my error . .

Edicts of this kind show that the emperor had forgotten the fact that, without the help of the treacherous Chinese (treacherous from Ming government's point of view) they

---

[12] Vols. 4, 6, and 7.
[13] All clerkships in the departments were held by Manchus.
[14] *Tsing Chien I Chih Lu.*

could never conquer China; and that without the help of the despised civilian, they could never, after all the war and disorder, put the house again in order. But edicts of this kind express the true idea of the employment of Chinese in the government: this edict did create some prejudice among later emperors against putting Chinese in the high offices and trusting Chinese with important tasks. For, seven years afterwards, Emperor Kang Hsi issued an edict providing that the governorship of Shansi could be held only by Manchus. His son, Yung Cheng cancelled the reservation in the first year of his reign.

Two cases very well illustrate the attitude of the government. In 1728, Man-Chu-Shih-Li, an imperial clansman holding the position of Tartar General, petitioned the emperor to appoint some Manchus to provincial military positions ranking from colonelcy to captaincy which used to be held by Chinese alone. In reply, Emperor Yung Cheng said in his edict, "The population of the Manchus is so small that we can appoint them only to key positions in the central as well as to the provincial governments: we cannot find enough Manchus to hold all positions in the army ranking from colonelcy to captaincy."[15] After that Manchus were time and again appointed to positions specially reserved for Chinese. In 1654, Li Cheng Hsiang, director of the Supervisorate of Instructions of the Crown Prince, petitioned to have only Chinese appointed to that office, as the work of the office was principally literary in character. The emperor rejected the petition, dismissed the petitioner, and sent him into exile. What a difference of treatment! Of all organizations in Peking, in only two, the Academy of Letters and the Imperial College, did the number of Chinese exceed that of Manchus. But these were literary institutions that had absolutely no political powers.

Wherever, compelled by circumstances, Chinese were appointed to high offices or given important commissions, say a military campaign for instance, a Manchu was appointed,

[15] *Tung Hua Lu*, Yung Cheng, v. 6.

nominally to assist, practically to spy on him. Even during the Taiping Rebellion when Tseng Kuo Fan virtually held the life of the Manchu Dynasty in his hands, Prince Kokorinchin, a Mongol prince of Khorchin Tribe, was despatched to Tseng's camp as assistant-commander-in-chief. This assistant signed all documents and reports. He could make special or separate reports to the government. Tso Tsung Tang, in the suppression of the Mohammedan Rebellion, had the first opportunity of taking an absolute command unchecked by spies from the court.

Gradually, as the Manchus were getting converted amidst Chinese luxuries, without getting imbued with wisdom from the Chinese knowledge, the government, in order to keep at least an appearance of living up to the Confucian theory of intellectual aristocracy, appointed more and more Chinese in its service. The suppression of the Taiping Rebellion marked the climax of this change; for, immediately after the suppression, nearly all the important offices in the provinces went to the Chinese candidates. Near the end of the dynasty, strong efforts, according to official documents, were made to eliminate racial distinctions from government service. The conventional division did not apply, but, as discussed in the last chapter, the positions were carefully weighed before the appointments were made. A tri-racial class division took the place of the bi-racial division: a class formerly forbidden to meddle with politics obtained one-third of the spoils, and that the fattest third.

But the division could not be maintained without a distinctive separation of the races, and, therefore, intermarriage between Chinese and Manchus was forbidden at the beginning of the dynasty. Emperor Cha Ching repeated the prohibition in 1813. Emperor Kuang Hsu, or Empress Dowager Tsu Hsi rather, repealed these laws in 1901. But separation of these two races had been so complete theretofore that a mere edict, though it removed the legal difference, could not erase all the social prejudice.

The Manchu policy of separating the Chinese from the Mongols, the Tibetans, and the Mohammedans was vigorously executed. It is plain enough that the Manchus wanted to play one race against another, and remain supreme over them all.

Thirdly, with the aim of strengthening their own position, the Manchus tried to tear up social traditions by the root by making the military officers the equal, if not the superior, of the civil officials. It is too well known to be reiterated here that the Chinese worshiped literature and despised fighting and that the scholar was identified with the gentleman, and the soldier was the symbol of a rogue. But the Manchus, knowing their own weakness and the strength of the Chinese, attempted, by elevating the value of their military ability, to elevate themselves. In the government, as Meadows [16] observed, they "substituted physical despotism for morally supported autocracy." They created laws and practices in favor of the military officers. But, by this, the Manchus aimed only secondarily to elevate themselves: their primary purpose was the same as that which they had when they broke up the powerful princely appendages of Outer Mongolia by the institution of an elected Captain-general of the *Aimak*. The compulsory wearing of the queue was for the same purpose.

The queue was merely a matter of dressing the hair, external and unimportant, while the difference of attitude towards the civil and military officers was a mental attitude, expressing social opinion, resulted from their culture, an element of the civilization, and a tradition of the people. Despite the emperor's power and influence, a government policy, when running against the social current in a country like China where passive resistance often defeated vigorous execution of government policies, could not alter a social attitude. Centuries of government efforts could not create, in China, the institution of "officer and gentleman."

History shows numerous other measures adopted by the Manchus to keep the people and the government under their control. The whole set of administrative laws, notably the

---

[16] *The Chinese and Their Rebellions.*

law of avoidance and the law of mutual responsibility, served as a means of controlling the officials. All methods of manipulation used by preceding dynasties, such as the absence of great powerful ministers, the prescribed form of examination essays, the prescribed books for the preparation for examinations, etc., helped the Manchus to perfect their control of the government, if not the country. The appointments of special envoys and special commissioners on special occasions strengthened the central, by reducing the powers of the provincial, government. The triennial visit of high provincial officials to Peking tended to quicken their allegiance to the throne and check the illegitimate desires of the too powerful viceroys. The government attempted to win over the loyal ministers of the Ming Dynasty by appointing sons and relatives of the Ming officials or the officials themselves to positions of trust and influence. It also gave a high title of nobility to the direct descent of the Chu Family.[17] It tried to win over the Chinese by building mausoleums for the last Ming Emperor and Empress. It endeavored to secure the Mongols' good will by matrimonial alliances. On the one hand, it did all it could towards winning over the different peoples and classes; on the other, it devised means to keep in their own hands as much power as possible. Throughout the one hundred volumes of the *Ta Tsing Hui Tien,* one cannot find the word "power" ever used, as these volumes defined the duties of the offices and officials. This word, whenever used, was used in connection with the emperor.

All these laws, methods and crafts contributed to produce the undesirable results which we now come to. The first result of the successful manipulation is what Prof. W. W. Willoughby [18] calls a cause "hindering constitutional development in China," lack of political leadership. The organization of the government offered no opportunity to low officials to commit very grave mistakes; but it took one a long

[17] See Chapter III.
[18] *Constitutional Government in China,* p. 38.

time to climb to the top of the ladder. As soon as one got up, responsibilities began to crowd on him at the same time that they began to bring him occasions for making mistakes. This and other methods dealt death-blows to the training of leadership while the suspicion and consequent execution of the able and powerful ministers screwed in the coffin nails.

Some interesting anecdotes about Tseng Kuo Fan, the conqueror of the Taiping Rebels, may serve to illustrate the imperial suspicion. After the suppression of the rebellion, and, consequently, the disbandment of part of Tseng's troops, this powerful scholar-soldier-politician still had his former subordinates and supporters at the head of different provincial administrations, and, to a certain extent, in the central administration. Not long before his death, he was thrice maliciously impeached by a Mongol censor, Fu-Erh-Kuo-Tsung. Under ordinary circumstances, impeachment of such a high and influential official without solid proofs and the backing of other rival officials would undoubtedly have resulted in the punishment of the censor. According to the law of the "eight criticisms" [19] the censor was guilty of criticizing a learned scholar, a high official, and a very serviceable man to the government. But he was merely deprived of his official title and this was not done until the third impeachment, while another censor was demoted for once impeaching the chief henchman of the Empress Dowager, the chief eunuch Li Lien Ying. The daring yet unsubstantiated charges could show nothing other than the government's suspicion on Tseng. Without the Empress Dowager's or her henchmen's support, no censor would dare do it. Also,

During the reign of Hsien Feng, Tseng Kuo Fan, a vice-minister on "mourning leave" put down the uprising in Hupeh with the militia that he himself trained. When the report of victory reached Peking, the Emperor heartily expressed his joy over the deed and said to the councilors of states in attendance, "What a miracle! Tseng Kuo Fan, a scholar, could achieve such wonderful conquest." Chi Chun

[19] See Chapter VII.

Tsao, a grand councilor, replied, "Tseng, a vice-minister on leave, is nothing more than a private subject. It is not a blessing for the dynasty to have private subjects who could gather together thousands of men at a single call." For a while, the Emperor was silenced with dismay . . . . .[20]

Suspicion of the powerful was not relaxed at the moment when the heavy blows of the rebels shook the very foundations of the dynasty and on the very person who was most serviceable in putting down the rebellion. Yet, Tseng, a learned Confucian philosopher, extremely reserved and modest, very sensitive of the danger awaiting him, shrinking from power and honor at every turn, was the first really serviceable and powerful minister in the dynasty who died a natural death. His diary and his letters show a great deal of his consciousness of the danger: they tell how, during those days of absolute monarchism, a master of the situation had to behave after the government thought that he had outlived his usefulness.

Pursuing the policy of breaking down the traditions of the conquered people and supplanting them with new practices and institutions, almost every emperor after his accession, tried to build up his own body of supporters by removing powerful and favorite ministers of his predecessor. Sir E. Backhouse in his *Annals and Memoirs of the Court of Peking*,[21] well observes:—

> It is interesting at this point, to observe that the whole history of the Manchu Dynasty illustrates the quality that Mill has described as peculiar characteristic of the Orientals, the quality of inveterate jealousy, which successive emperors and their advisers, displayed towards high officials who had attained to influence in the council of their predecessors. Thus in Shun Chi's reign, we have the posthumous deposition of the Regent, Prince Jui; Kang Hsi dismisses his Board of Regents; Cha Ching orders the death of his father's favorite; Tao Kuang dismisses his father's all powerful eunuch; Hsien Feng orders Mu Yang-A into retirement; Tung Chi (under the influence of Tsu Hsi) rids himself of the usurping

[20] *Tsing Shih Kiang Yau*, vol. 12, p. 14.
[21] p. 242.

regent; and finally to come to our own days, the Empress Lung Yu, in the name of His Majesty Hsuan Tung, dismisses Yuan Shih Kai.

But many others were executed without the excuse of building up influence for a new emperor. Outside of the cases mentioned by Sir E. Backhouse, we have cases where the emperors ordered the death of their own protégés simply because the latter had acquired more power than their masters wanted them to have. Nien Keng Yao and Yu Chung Chi, both Chinese military officers of unusual ability who had rendered invaluable service in the suppression of different rebellions lost their heads after they had made their military contributions to the government. These two cases kept many Chinese officials from acquisition of powers: they made Tseng Kuo Fan aware of his own danger.

The net result of this policy was that no official could be very powerful at a young age: when they became powerful, they would be so near to the grave that they would prefer an easy life to a hard struggle; even if ambition did not die with the advance of age, they would not have the energy to fight against the emperor. If, perchance, an official got to high positions at an energetic period of his life, he dared not accumulate power knowing that this would bring him more harm than good. Possible opposition to the emperor was thus quietly and effectively eliminated. So, except for the descendents of Nurachi who sat on the throne by tradition, one can find hardly a man who was leader enough to found a new dynasty. For the emperor and the Tsing Dynasty, this indeed worked very well. But the government and the emperor were two different things; even if that lack of leadership were good for the emperor, it was not necessarily good for the government; and if, finally, the absence of strong, honest public servants was a reason for the Manchu downfall, the Manchu Government reaped what it had sown. But the pity is that the Tsing Dynasty made its successor, the Republic Government, pay very dearly for its selfish device: the present chaotic situation certainly may be partly attributed to the lack of leadership, for it is hard to find strong leaders after two hundred and sixty-six years of suppression.

Side by side with the suppression of political leadership, as a means of fortifying their own position, the Manchus forbade the organization of political parties. One emperor after another issued edicts or wrote essays to warn the ministers against organizing factions. Emperor Chien Lung even prohibited the princes to receive presents from the provincial officials.[22] His father forbade the princes to befriend the ministers; he, in the eighth year of his reign, reenforced that prohibition with an edict which reads:—

> The late emperor issued an edict forbidding the princes and the ministers to befriend one another. He meant to end one of the causes which would give rise to the organization of factions. It is law, therefore, should be obeyed forever.

All the prohibitive measures which succeeded in checking the organization of regular political parties did not wipe out two forms of organizations. When two powerful ministers served at the same time, two factions usually existed, as in the case of Grand Secretaries O Erh Tai and Chang Ting Yu during Chien Lung's reign. Then, the "teacher-pupil" parties, under the veil of literary purposes, were organized for the purposes of making headway in the fight for administrative positions. Sometimes factions of literary men sprang up from differences in methods of study or style of writing which developed into struggles for political powers. Once in a while these kinds of organization became so strong that the emperor thought it necessary to stress again the prohibitive laws. Relationship closer than the usual bonds of official superior or inferior always came out of competitive examinations in which the examiner occupied the position of teacher and the successful candidates that of the pupils. Protectors and protégés also addressed one another as teachers and pupils. To become pupil of so-and-so meant to come under his flag in the scramble for positions. Em-

---

[22] Edict of 1767, see *Ta Tsing Hui Tien Shih Li*.

peror Kang Hsi tried in vain to put an end to this institution.[23]

Neither of these types of organization, however, could rid itself of the personal element: neither fought for any principle. The real parties of a political nature in the Tsing Dynasty, therefore, were the secret societies, the Elders, the Triads, the Little Daggers, etc. These had in view one and only one object, the termination of the Manchu supremacy. Cloaked under the robe of religious and fraternal interests, they secretly worked for the overthrow of the reigning government. But having practically no representatives in the government service, stumbling under the heavy blows of prohibitive laws, weakened by the absence of able leaders and the lack of assistance of the scholars, they soon degenerated into gangs of robbers, thiefs, and desperadoes. However, they consistently retained their original purpose of driving out the Manchus. Their degeneration further estranged from them men of ability and principle, so that, to the end of the dynasty, they remained outlaws despised by the elite. The descendents of Nurachi, as a result of their clever statecraft, sat all the while on the throne without strong rivals.

A third result of the policy of the Manchus was their conservatism. This policy did not show itself until the time of the Taiping Rebellion and the reforms. Far back in Kang Hsi's reign, that illustrious emperor, for fear of being himself denationalized, endeavored to introduce Western civilization to counteract the influence of the Chinese civilization which had begun gradually, surely and successfully to captivate the sturdy Manchu invaders. He clearly saw the irresistibility of the advance of the Chinese civilization on the Manchus; he clearly knew that assimilation of the Chinese civilization by the Manchus would mean ultimate conquest of the Manchus by the Chinese. By bringing in elements of Western civilization, he expected to draw away the Manchu subject from their process of being conquered

[23] See his edict issued 1673, *Ta Tsing Hui Tien Shih Li.*

by Chinese civilization. But his grandson, Emperor Chien Lung altered this course by a new policy of exclusion. First of all, he underestimated the Western countries. He was afraid that some other nations might come into China to replace the Manchus just as they replace the Chinese. Reigning in a "golden age" of the dynasty, he did not want new relations, the old aggressive spirit of the Manchus had waned; he wanted a protracted period of peace wherein he could enjoy his trips and literary pursuit not knowing that the government would rot for lack of fresh energy and that this rot would remain an unhealable wound in the body politic.

The Taiping Rebellion further upheld the Manchu reactionary attitude. The Taipings revolted as much against the Chinese civilization as against the Manchu Government. The Chinese generals, Tseng, Tso, Li, and Hu, learned Confucian scholars one and all, came to the rescue of their own civilization. Incidentally, it should be mentioned that the suppression of the Taipings was a unique case, in 4,000 years of Chinese history, where a nation-wide rebellion was put down by a group of scholars. Tseng at first trained his militia for the protection of his home town, not for Emperor Hsien Feng on the throne. Tso, it is said, at first tried to submit plans to the Taiping chief for the dethronement of the Manchu emperor and the preservation of the Chinese civilization, but Hung Hsiu Chuan rejected his plans and Tso went into the service of the imperial army at Tseng's command. The suppression of the Taipings ended the revolt against the Chinese civilization. By dint of statecraft and legal provisions, they had so ridded China of political leadership, by the process of assimilation they had so imbued the Chinese civilization that, without revolting against the Chinese civilization, it was almost impossible to revolt against the Manchu government. So the Manchus had learned that by upholding the old regime, they could maintain their power and privileges, they objected to changes of any sort, knowing that any change would weaken their line of defense, the old order of things. They undertook a program of reforms near the end of the dynasty, only because they had learned that reforms would change only part of the old order while lack of reforms might wipe out the whole government.

So long as the Chinese saw no necessity to break away from any of their traditions, so long as they wanted to keep every bit of their old civilization intact, Manchu conservatism served to keep them on the throne. The Revolution of 1911 was, in some respects, against Chinese civilization. The difference was that, in the sixties, the Chinese saw no necessity to modify, nay, they thought it their duty to preserve, their civilization; while, in 1911, they had learned something about the Western civilization and come to the conclusion that part of their own old civilization must be modified. With the destruction of the firm belief in the superiority of the Chinese civilization in every way went the superstitious reverence and unqualified loyalty to the emperor. Also, the Western theory of nationalism helped to strengthen their old racial consciousness and turn their hidden racial feelings into angry anti-Manchu outbursts. With part of the Chinese civilization modified, many kinds of old prestige gradually disappeared. The inevitable change had to come; changes were needed. So, when the political change, a part of the civilization, came, the people gladly took it, and the Manchu Dynasty fell.

Coming to the discussion of the administrative machinery of the Manchus, we find an admixture of weak and strong qualities. Since the day the Regent, Prince Jui, ordered the administrative machinery to be retained and the officials to continue their service, we find his nephew, Emperor Shun Chi, and his nephew's descendants faithfully executing this policy throughout the two hundred and sixty-six years of the life of the dynasty. With the exception of changes caused by influence of the Western countries, the original form of government, found at the end of the Ming and adopted by the Tsing, Dynasty, at the founding of the latter, suffered no serious change as far as the suitableness of the institutions to the people was concerned. Local government, the foundation of the central administration, remained practically intact for all the period. Not only for the Chinese, but also, as shown in Chapter XII, for the territories, can one find the faithful pursuance of this policy. We can say, without the least hesitation, that the real political compass to steer their ship of state through strange waters was to let the peoples, whom they conquered by force, be governed by their own methods and institutions. They went even far enough to appoint most of the officials from the natives themselves to govern in their own territories. In the long run this policy served the Manchus very well in keeping their subjects satisfied, though the satisfaction was, as it had always been, expressed in passive recognition rather than active consent.

Strict observance of traditions and faithful following of public opinion in China helped the Manchus a long way towards organizing their government and reigning over the peoples. Yet, sometimes, as pointed out, they purposely tried to break down traditions of the conquered peoples, supplant them with new ones so as to show their authority. But whenever they followed the local traditions and the local form of government, they always controlled the situation by creating some supervisory organs in Peking or by manipulating the powerful local officials. To the Chinese in particular, they usually gave places in the work of governing, made them do their best, and appointed some Manchus to supervise them. Thus, by adopting the native form of government, the Manchus kept them satisfied; by controlling the organs after adopting them, and checking whatever forces might turn against the government, they perfected the control.

Adopting the Chinese government *in toto,* they took into the government all the weaknesses that made the government inefficient. Formality in court, dress, documents, etc., perfected by other dynasties, had a full status here. In fact, the Manchu Government depended on formality to uphold their dignity and to keep the officials down. From the writing of an examination paper to the issuance of an imperial edict, from the duty call of an inferior to an audience with the emperor, prescribed forms ruled supreme. Outward formality, to a great extent, replaced the old propriety (Li).

Numerous disastrous results came from formality. Liu Kun Yi and Chang Chi Tung, in a joint memorial to the emperor said:—

> ..... The third thing to start a new regime is to break all traditional formalities. At the beginning of the dynasty, the channels of communications between the court and the officials were wide open. The difficulties of the people were easily made known and hidden talents easily discovered. Since the middle period, formalities and ceremonies have come in to block all channels of communications and cover up all the hidden talents . . . . .[24]

The result of all the court and official formality was, that the official had on the one hand, to remain inactive to avoid making mistakes, thus maintaining their position; and on the other, to submit enough false memoranda and camouflaged reports about the prosperity of the people that the government might believe that its servants were doing their best. Such conditions, tolerable in the ages of seclusion, could not meet the rushing activities of a modern government.

So, in the preparation of reforms, the abolition of formalities was recognized even by Princes Ching and Pu Lun as one of the three necessities for an efficient government. In the audience, the pretended dignity of the emperor made the officials tremble while they knelt out in the courtyard. They could not, had no chance to, say all they wanted to express. In petitions and memorials, special attention had to be devoted to form and words; a single mistake in calligraphy, elevation of character or what-not would send the document to the wastebasket and might subject the author to severe punishment. The Empress Dowager Tsu Hsi deliberately employed the picking up of wrong words and

[24] *Tung Hua Lu*, Kuang Hsu, v. 169, p. 16.

wrong forms in a memorial as an excuse to chastise the officials when she disliked either the contents or the author. After an unnecessarily great amount of time and energy had been wasted in making the memorials exactly conforming to regular form, a petitioner was always afraid that the contents might invoke the anger of his or her august majesty, thus costing him the loss of favor, an advancement in his official career, a severe punishment or even his life.

What existed in the court existed in the offices of the mandarins. The ceremonies of an audience were, to a less extent, applied in an interview given by a superior to an inferior official. The dignity of an emperor on the throne was mildly enjoyed by an official in his own office. The same degree of incommunicability that blocked the channels of communications between the emperor and his servants hindered the circulation of opinion between the officials and the people. Mandarins looked down on the people, kept out of touch with them, dazzled the people's eyes with their retinues, and frightened them with their lashes and whips. They knew nothing of the people, cared less for them. On the side of the people, absence of officials meant a blessing; for besides exacting from and punishing them, rarely did the officials go to the people: and when they went, they had to be satisfied. Such were the results of seclusion. From it the Manchu emperors and officials, both Manchus and Chinese derived their dignity: for it they paid the high price of being overthrown.

In the organization of the government, a characteristic, a fundamentally bad one, was to appoint one man to several offices, to appoint many men to the same office at the same time, and to provide many offices for the same function. The first practice might have been a result of low salaries. The compensations of the officials were so low that without getting several positions one could hardly live. In the matter of salaries the government showed its conservatism. Knowing the insufficiency it gave compensation under several names as "salaries by grace," "allowances," "special grants," etc., but did not raise the regular salaries. Yet with that little honest and legitimate income of one hundred and eighty taels a years, Ho Shen, a grand councilor of state during Chien Lung's regime, mustered a fortune of eight hundred millions. So, not getting sufficient compensation out of the government, the officials got it outside of the government. With the exception of censors, the only officials of consequence not allowed to hold concurrent positions, all officials of rank and importance held more than one office. The result was that an official could spend a very short period of his working hours in each office, was not at all familiar with the work of the different organizations to which he belonged; and the under-clerks, administrative parasites, performed all the duties that should have been performed by the officials themselves.

When an official was under several superiors, each of the heads shared, but none of them assumed all, the responsibility. This was exactly the case with almost all offices in the central administration. Worse still, each of the officials would naturally try to avoid responsibility of any kind. Having no special responsibility and under no special obligation, the several heads of the office shifted the work from one to another and made the work a sort of "everybody's business." The happiest case possible of occurrence under these circumstances was to have a strong, responsible man dominating all the rest, assuming all the responsibility and bearing all the blame. But the "inveterate jealousy" of absolute monarchism did not allow this, and, as a result, very little was done; if anything was done it was with the utmost inefficiency.

Providing several offices for the same duty might have been due to the government's desire to place all capable men in the service so that it would not have any opposition. Whatever the cause, its effect was great wastefulness in human energy. In the provinces, watchfulness came from the many grades of officials from the viceroy down to the magistrate. Koo Ting Lin, in his *Sixth Essay on Centrali-*

zation,[25] pointed out in a vivid manner the wastefulness of this system. He said:—

> . . . . . Take horses for instance. Hundreds of thousands of horses are annually employed in relay communications, in sending reports to direct superiors and sending off and receiving superiors. From 60 to 70 per cent of these horses employed did not do government work. 70 to 80 per cent of the paper used by the government can be saved by cutting off reports to different grades of superiors, which, in fact, is unnecessary duplicate . . . . . Other corresponding wastes are numerous.

No wonder, in 1906, Prince Ching and others, in a memorial connected with the reforms, said the following:—[26]

> . . . . . The chief difficulty in clearing up all corruptions in the administration is due to lack of responsibility, which, in turn, rises out of three sources:—
>
> (1) There is a lack of separation of powers . . . . .
>
> (2) The officials' lack of knowledge of the working of their own positions. Each department has a number of vice-ministers most of whom are superfluous. Each official goes through many departments the work of none of which he knows much about: specialization is absent . . . . .
>
> (3) The duties of the officials do not correspond to their names. The Department of Civil Service only casts lots, but does not select and appoint the officials. The Department of Revenue merely receives and disburses the government incomes and expenditures, but has nothing to do with the budget and the financial policy . . . . . The Department of War merely attends to the promotion and demotion of officers, but does not command or control the army . . . .

Out of the rules of selection, the monthly appointment, the seniority rule, etc., a "waiting list" came. The sale of offices considerably enlarged this list. Keener competition resulted from its enlargement: all sorts of corruptions, bribery particularly, issued from this keen competition. It was almost an impossibility to get an appointment without something more than real qualifications. The whole set of civil service laws became almost obsolete. Civil service be-

[25] *Works of Kuo Ting Lin*, v. 1, p. 6.
[26] *Tung Hua Lu*, Kuang Hsu, v. 202, p. 12.

came an industry of the quasi-literati: the whole administration was thus disintegrated.

Under a system where men counted more than laws, one could expect the government to be personalized. Yet no where and in no other government was the personal element such an important factor as in the Manchu Government. First, for every promotion or appointment, the promoted or the appointee was required to submit a letter of thanks to the emperor: this corresponded to the taking of an oath of office. But this letter expressed thanks for the emperor's favor, while in the oath, the appointee would declare his acceptance and faithfulness to the state and the office.

Then also the lack of distinction between the government treasury and the emperor's private purse made public property the private possession of the emperor. From this attitude came the practice of appointing men to office as an expression of gratitude towards the appointee's service which might be purely personal in nature. Let an edict of Emperor Kang Hsi illustrate this point:—

My father's nurses served and guarded him well: they were loved and praised by him from his infancy. I want to confer some favor on them. The Department of Rites is hereby ordered to find out where their sons and grandsons are, what they have been doing and how to reward them. Report the findings to me.[27]

Emperor Yung Cheng promoted a private to a colonelcy in 1733 because he returned a lost purse to the emperor. It would not have been so bad were this where the personal element stopped. The evil effect, however, was that the question of personal feelings usually outweighed other considerations. An official had to spend more of his time and energy in the study of his superiors' likes and dislikes and in the application of the art of pleasing them than in the performance of his duties. Flattery, indeed, was a regular institution in the Tsing Government. The unlimited powers of the monarch, the insecurity of the officials' position and

[27] This edict was issued in 1722, *Tung Hua Lu*, Kang Hsi.

life, the jealousy of the colleagues, the malice of unscrupulous censors, all contributed to make the business of pleasing everybody the universal art of officialdom. As time went on, the new laws and institutions all tended to elevate the position of the emperor and to degrade that of the ministers. A study of the history of development of absolutism shows that most of the laws and devices for the elevation of the emperor were work of flattering ministers done with the aim of gaining imperial favor. The *Tung Hua Lu* records a great number of memorials submitted by opportunistic ministers who took any unusual natural phenomenon as a sign of prosperity or as heaven's appreciation of the emperor's virtues although the emperor might be in fact, a person of "active wickedness" or "vicious indolence."

Pleasing the emperor would not have been a crime had it not been for the fact that the tendency to please invariably went together with the fear of incurring wrath. This fear led to the ministers' lack of courage in pointing out mistakes of the emperor, communicating to him the difficulties and sufferings of the people, and exposing the weaknesses of the government. Extending this downward, we find the same attitude in dealings between the ministers and their inferiors. At the end, the people's opportunity of having their grievances redressed and getting their case heard was almost entirely lost. The numerous uprisings which took place during the reign of Chia Ching were the results of this state of affairs: the deprivation of the people's opportunity of getting their grievances redressed left them only one thing to do, to rebel against the government. The flourishing of secret societies in the Tsing Dynasty might be partly attributed to this.

Profiting by the experience of bygone dynasties which fell because of powerful ministers, the Manchus provided for the frequent transference and removal of the high provincial officials, the independence of one of the high officials of another, and other methods of manipulation, without knowing that while this helped them to keep the throne, they made the officials disloyal and the people dissatisfied. When they devised and copied these ways and means to keep the throne, they did not dream that some day, these would cause their descendants' downfall.

Fair-minded Chinese agree that in the matter of improving the government, the Manchus did practically nothing. To say that the Manchus wanted to get as much out of, and do as little for, China as possible is no extravagant statement. Wang Tao [28] says, "In the administration of rivers and canals, only remedial, but no preventive, work was done (by the government). In taxes and excises, the best was to cancel the extra levy, but did not take an accurate census and purify the administration from its root. In the encouragement of industries, all was paper talk." In spite of the fact that the Tsing Dynasty produced some good emperors, the Manchu Government was one of the most, if not the most, corrupt that China ever had.

The Revolution of 1911 was of course due to a mixture of political and racial motives. Intercourse with the West had exercised more influence upon the political than upon the racial side. It is absurd to say that the racial consciousness of the Chinese was a product of the European theory of nationalism and that the revolution was the work of Cantonese Yale graduates; for racial feelings existed in 1644 when the Prince Regent entered Peking. Emperor Chung Tseng (the last Ming emperor) could boast of more loyal, though incapable, ministers who gave up their lives at the downfall of the dynasty than any other emperor in the history of China. Some, like Hung Cheng Chou, entered the service of the Manchus and worked for the restoration of the Chinese by devising suicidal laws for the Manchus such as the laws to prohibit inter-racial marriages, the laws forbidding imperial clansmen, alternatives and bannermen to trade and labor, etc. Others, like Kuo Ting Lin and Huang Li Chou, refused to serve the new dynasty and endeavored, by their writings, to arouse the people.

[28] *Li Chi Shih Lio*, p. 89.

During the reign of Emperor Chien Lung, long before the influence of Western theories reached China, and right in the golden ages of the dynasty, numerous secret societies, masonic in name and politico-racial in character, sprang up in different parts of the country. Only the ability of the emperor kept them from open revolt. So, right after his death, rebels raised their flags one after another until the climax was reached in the Taiping Rebellion. The Manchus were saved from this rebellion because it was as much against Chinese civilization as against the government. The imperial generals, Chinese, and champions of orthodox learning, saw that, without saving the government, their civilization could not be saved; so, in their attempt to save the civilization, they incidentally saved the government. But when the revolution came in 1911, the Chinese had come to realize that their civilization must be modified; hence even the imperial officials made little resistance to the onward march of the revolutionary army.

The Manchus conquered China by force and governed her by statecraft. Against every cause that had ever cost the life of a dynasty, they sought to make ample provisions. Yet new causes developed and Tsing fell. Their idea of perpetuating their reign, seemingly possible with all the well devised safeguards, turned out to be merely an idea. Almost each and every one of the phases of government activity formed a cause of their downfall. Their repeated assertions of their conquest of China by force served to arouse the latent racial consciousness of the Chinese. The "vicious indolence" of Emperors Chia Ching, Tao Kuang, Hsien Feng, and Tung Chi, four in succession, greatly undermined the health of the dynasty. The policy of putting imperial clansmen out of politics weakened the power of the Manchus; the maintenance of the banner garrisons enervated the bannermen and stimulated the hatred of the vanquished. The corruption of the civil service system and the prostitution of the civil service examinations disintegrated the traditional intellectual aristocracy. The mismanagement of finance impoverished the government. The gross abuses of the judicial powers by the civil officials were grievous to the people. Commercial, military, and diplomatic defeats at the hands of the Western countries and Japan strongly exhibited the incapacity of the government. Finally, the lack of sincerity in the reforms and the inability to carry out the reform measures impressed the people with the feeling that the Manchu Dynasty had outlived its usefulness and that nothing short of overthrowing that effete dynasty could save the country.

BIBLIOGRAPHY

BIBLIOGRAPHY

I. BOOKS IN THE CHINESE LANGUAGE

A. *Government Publications*

Chin Ting Ta Tsing Hui Tien: Collected Institutes of the Tsing Dynasty. Five editions, the first in 1694, the second in 1727, the third in 1764, the fourth in 1815 and the fifth in 1885 were issued. The latest official issuance, that of 1885, is used here. 100 *chuan*.[1]

Chin Ting Ta Tsing Hui Tien Shih Li: Amendments to (or Cases on) the Collected Institutes of the Tsing Dynasty. Five editions of this book were issued about the same time the Collected Institutes of the Tsing Dynasty appeared. The fifth edition is here used. 1200 *chuan*.

Chin Ting Ku Tsin Tu Shu Chi Cheng: The Chinese Encyclopedia. For details of this book, see: Lionel Giles, An Alphabetical Index to the Chinese Encyclopedia, published by the British Museum, London, 1911.

Ta Tsing Lü Li Lui Chi Pien Lan: The Penal Code of the Tsing Dynasty. For details of this book, see: Sir George Staunton's translation.

Nei Ko Kung Pao or Cheng Fu Kung Pao: The Official Gazette. A daily publication of the government.

Chin Ting Huang Chao Tung Chi: Tung Chi of the Tsing Dynasty. Published 1767. This contains records of political and economic institutions of the Tsing Dynasty. The style of writing is based on the *Tung Chi* by Cheng Chao. 200 *chuan*.

Chin Ting Huang Chao Tung Tien: Tung Tien of the Tsing Dynasty. Published 1767. It contains records of the political and economic institutions of the dynasty written in the same style as the *Tung Tien* by Tu Yao. 100 *chuan*.

Chin Ting Huang Chao Wen Hsien Tung Kao: Wen Hsien Tung Kao of the Tsing Dynasty. Published 1747. A record of the political and economic institutions of the Tsing Dynasty written in the same style as the *Wen Hsien Tung Kao* by Ma Tuan Lin. 266 *chuan*.

[1] One *chuan* in a Chinese book contains from about 25 to 100 pages. One Chinese page equals two English pages. The word *Chuan* means a roll which was the standard of the size of a book before the invention of printing in China.

Chin Ting Hu Pu Tsi Li: Regulations of the Department of Revenues. Published 1874. 100 *chuan*.

Chin Ting Tsung Shu Tseng Kao: Regulations of the Department of War. Published 1825. 32 *chuan*.

Chin Ting Li Fan Yuan Tsi Li: Regulations of the Department of Territories. Published 1817. 63 *chuan*.

Hsin Tsuan Yueh Tung Sheng Li: Regulations for the Government of the Province of Kuangtung. Written under the direction of Governor Huang Un Tung. Published by the provincial government of Kuangtung, 1846. 8 *chuan*.

Chin Ting Hui Chiang Tsi Li: Regulations for the Government of the Mohammedan Territories. Published 1814. 4 *chuan*.

Chin Ting Ba Chi Tung Chi: Gazetteer of the Banner Forces. Published 1739. 250 *chuan*.

Chin Ting Li Tai Tsi Kuan Piao: History of the Government Offices. It shows the historical development of the different offices and institutions both in description and tables from 2205 B. C. to date of publication, 1784 A. D. 72 *chuan*.

Ta Tsing Tso Ti Chüan Han: Official Directory of the Tsing Government. Two editions, one published in 1836 and another in 1911, of this book have been used in the present study.

Huang Chao Tsou Yi: Petitions and Memorials to the Emperor of the Tsing Dynasty. Published by the Bureau of Dynastic History (Kuo Shih Kuan). No date of publication is shown although the dates of the memorials show that these petitions and memorials were submitted to Emperor Shun Chi (1644 to 1662) in the early years of his reign.

Wai Chiao Pu Yuan Ke Chi Loh: A Brief Sketch of the Development of the Ministry of Foreign Affairs. Written by Wu Cheng Chang, published by the Ministry of Foreign Affairs Press, Peking, 1913. 1 volume.

Kang Yung Chien Tao Shi Chao Tiao Yu: Treaties signed during the reign of Emperors Kang Hsi, Yung Cheng, Chien Lung, and Tao Kuang. Published by the Ministry of Foreign Affairs Press, Peking. 2 volumes.

Hsien Feng Tiao Yu: Treaties signed during the reign of Emperor Hsien Feng. Published by the Ministry of Foreign Affairs Press, Peking, 1916. 4 volumes.

Kuang Hsu Tiao Yu: Treaties signed during the reign of Emperor Kuang Hsu. Published by the Ministry of Foreign Affairs Press, Peking. 6 volumes.

Hsuan Tung Tiao Yu: Treaties signed during the reign of Emperor Hsuan Tung. Published by the Ministry of Foreign Affairs Press, Peking. 2 volumes.

B. *Semi-official Publications*

Tung Hua Lu: Annals and Memoirs of the Court. The first part of the book, from Emperor Tien Ming to Emperor Tung Chi (1616 to 1874) was edited by Wang Hsien Chien, and published by Liu San Chang Shih, Hui Chi District, 1882; the second part, that of Emperor Kuang Hsu, (1875 to 1908) was edited by Chu Shao Peng, and published by Chi Cheng Press, Shanghai, 1909. About 850 *chuan*.

Tsing Chien Yi Chi Lu: Annals and Memoirs of Early Tsing Dynasty. Published in Japanese, edited by Shakukei Murayama and Genkoyu Nagane. Neither date of publication nor name of the press is shown. 16 *chuan*.

Shu Huan Chi Loh: Short Notes on the Council of State. Written under the direction of Prince Kung based on an earlier work of the same nature and name by Liang Chang Chu, which appeared in 1823. This was published in 1878. 28 *chuan*.

Tsung Shu Tien Ku Lui Chi: Notes on the Grand Secretariat and Its Staff. Written by Wang Cheng Kung who was more than twenty years connected with the secretarial staff of the Grand Secretariat. Published by Cha Yi Tang, Wu Hsing District, 1765. 8 *chuan*.

Nei Ko Chi: Notes on the Grand Secretariat. Written by Wu Ao who served in the secretarial staff of the Grand Secretariat more than twenty-five years. 1 *chuan*.

Chung Kuo Fa Tien Pien Tsuan Yuan Ke Shih: History of the Chinese Codes. Written by Torao Asai of Japan and translated into Chinese by Chen Chung Ming. Published under the auspices of the Ministry of Interior, Peking, 1919. 1 volume.

Chung Kuo Ti Fang Tsi Tu Tsi Yuan Ke: Historical Development of the Provincial Administrations in China. Written by Wang Tao, published under the auspices of the Ministry of Interior, 1918. 1 volume.

Li Chi Shih Loh: Brief Sketch of Good Officials. Written by Wang Tao, published under the auspices of the Ministry of Interior.

Hui Chiang Chi Yiu: Principal features of the Government of the Mohammedan Territories. A manuscript. 6 *chuan*.

Tsung Shih Wang Kung Chang Ching Shih Chih Cho Ti Han: A Family Record of the Imperial Clansmen from the Beginning of the dynasty to the reign of Emperor Kuang Hsu, showing the direct lineage of the first emperor of the dynasty, his descendents, and the creation and inheritance of the high titles of nobility. A manuscript. 4 *chuan*.

C. *Private Publications*

Tsing Chao Chuan Shih: Complete History of the Tsing Dynasty. Written by Kunzan Inaba of Japan and translated into Chinese by Tan Tao. Published by the Chung Hua Book Company, Shanghai, 2nd edition, 1915. 2 volumes.

Tsing Shih Kang Yiu: Essence of the History of the Tsing Dynasty. Edited by Wu Tseng Chi and others, Commercial Press, Shanghai, 4th edition, 1921. 14 *chuan*.

Tsing Shih Chang Yi: Lectures on the History of the Tsing Dynasty. Written by Wang Yung Pao and Hsu Kuo Ying, Commercial Press, Shanghai, 4th edition, 1922. 2 volumes.

Chung Kuo Chin Shih Wai Chiao Shih: Modern Diplomatic History of China. Written by Liu Yin, the Pacific Press, Shanghai, 3rd edition, 1921.

Min Kuo Tsai Tseng Shih: Financial History of the Chinese Republic. Written by Cha Shih Yih, Commercial Press, Shanghai, 1917. 2 volumes.

Chung Kuo Tsai Tseng Lun Kang: Essence of Chinese Public Finance. Written by Chow Tang, published by Shuko-Sha, Tokyo, Japan, 2nd edition, 1912.

Yin Fa Tung Chi: The Salt Encyclopedia. Written by Chow Ching Yung, the Wen Ming Press, Shanghai, 1914. 100 *chuan*.

Tsing Tai Hsueh Suh Kai Lun: Development of Philosophy and Literature during the Tsing Dynasty. Written by Liang Chi Chao, Commercial Press, Shanghai, 3rd edition, 1922.

Chung Kuo Chiao Yu Chih Tu Yuan Ke Shih: Historical Development of Educational System in China. Written by P. W. Kuo, Commercial Press, Shanghai, 2nd edition, 1920.

Yih Chi Lu: Notes on Daily Learning. Written by Koo Ting Lin. Published by the Chung Wen Press, Hupeh, 1872. 32 *chuan*.

Ming I Tai Fang Lu: A series of essays on politics and government by Huang Li Chou.

Wu Su Tseng Pien Chi: The Reform of 1898, by Liang Chi Chao.

Yin Ping Shi Tsi Yiao Shu: A series of essays by Liang Chi Chao, Commercial Press, Shanghai, 1916.

Tsung Ming Meng Yu Lu: Short Notes on Government, Public Offices, and Officials of the late Ming and the early Tsing Dynasties. Written by Sun Cheng Cha, published by Shi Fen Yin Kuan, Canton, 1883.

Chi Pei O Tan: Short Notes on Offices and Officials, mostly exceptional cases. Written by Wang Yuan Ting, Wen Sui Tang Press, 1691.

Hsin Shih Chung Han: Reprints of Hsin Shih, a series of stories about the Manchu Government which do not appear in the official publications. Written by Meng Hsin, Commercial Press, Shanghai, 1916. 3 volumes.

Ting Lin Wen Chih: Works of Koo Ting Lin. Published by Wen Jui Low Press, Shanghai. 6 *chuan*.

Tang Tai Ba Cha Wen Chao: Works of Eight Great Contemporary Authors. Published by Chung Kuo Press, 1916. 16 *chuan*.

Wan Kuo Tseng Chi Chuan Shu: Almanac of Politics and Political Organizations. A series of essays and treaties on the organization and operation of the governments of different countries prepared for the use of candidates in the competitive literary examinations during the first few years after the abolition of the "eight legged" style of essay in the examinations. Published by Hung Wen Press, Shanghai, 1901. 180 *chuan*.

Cha Yu: The Academic Narratives. Part of the Works of Confucius edited by Tsi Sei, his grandson and one of his disciples.

Shu Ching: The Canon of History.

Li Chi: The Canon of Rites.

Chou Li: Institutions of the Chou Government.

Han Shu: History of the Han Dynasty.

Hsin Suan Hoo Han Yang Nien Chi: Comparative chronology of Japan, China and Europe. Revised. Edited by Teizan Kawamura, published by Keitaro Tanaka, Tokyo, Japan.

II. Books in English

Backhouse, E. and Bland, J. O. P.: Annals and Memoirs of the Court of Peking.

Bland, J. O. P. and Backhouse, E.: China Under the Empress Dowager.

Brunnert, H. S. and Hagelstrom, V. V.: Present Day Political Organization of China.

Chen, Shao Kwan: The System of Taxation in China under the Tsing Dynasty, 1644-1911.

Chinese Repository, The.

Giles, H. A.: China and the Manchus.

Giles, H. A.: Chinese English Dictionary.

Hart, Sir Robert: These from the Land of Sinim.

Jernegan, T. R.: China in Law and Commerce.

Jernegan, T. R.: China's Business Method and Policy.

Kent, Percy H.: The Passing of the Manchus.

Li, Chuan Shih: Relation of Central and Local Finance in China.

Mayers, William Frederick: The Chinese Government.

Meadows, Thomas Taylor: The Chinese and Their Rebellions.

Morse, H. B.: The Trade and Administration of China.

MacMurray, J. V. M.: Treaties and Agreements with and concerning China.

Wen Ching: The Great Crisis From Within.

Williams, S. W.: Middle Kingdom.

Willoughby, W. W.: Constitutional Government in China.